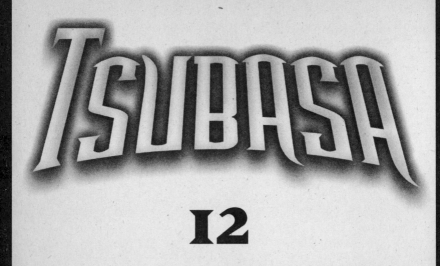

TSUBASA

12

CLAMP

TRANSLATED AND ADAPTED BY
William Flanagan

LETTERED BY
Dana Hayward

DEL
REY

BALLANTINE BOOKS · NEW YORK

Tsubasa, vol. 12 is a work of fiction. Names, characters, places, and incidents are the products of the author's imagination or are used fictitiously. Any resemblance to actual events, locales, or persons, living or dead, is entirely coincidental.

A Del Rey Trade Paperback Original

Published in the United States by Del Rey Books, an imprint of The Random House Publishing Group, a division of Random House, Inc., New York.

Publication rights arranged through Kodansha, Ltd.

First published in Japan in 2005 by Kodansha, Ltd., Tokyo.

ISBN 978-0-345-48532-8

Printed in the United States of America

www.delreymanga.com

9 8 7 6 5 4 3 2 1

Translator and adaptator—William Flanagan

Lettering—Dana Hayward

Contents

Tsubasa crosses over with *xxxHOLiC*. Although it isn't necessary to read *xxxHOLiC* to understand the events in *Tsubasa*, you'll get to see the same events from different perspectives if you read both series!

Honorifics Explained

Throughout the Del Rey Manga books, you will find Japanese honorifics left intact in the translations. For those not familiar with how the Japanese use honorifics and, more important, how they differ from American honorifics, we present this brief overview.

Politeness has always been a critical facet of Japanese culture. Ever since the feudal era, when Japan was a highly stratified society, use of honorifics—which can be defined as polite speech that indicates relationship or status—has played an essential role in the Japanese language. When addressing someone in Japanese, an honorific usually takes the form of a suffix attached to one's name (example: "Asuna-san"), or as a title at the end of one's name or in place of the name itself (example: "Negi-sensei," or simply "Sensei!").

Honorifics can be expressions of respect or endearment. In the context of manga and anime, honorifics give insight into the nature of the relationship between characters. Many English translations leave out these important honorifics, and therefore distort the feel of the original Japanese. Because Japanese honorifics contain nuances that English honorifics lack, it is our policy at Del Rey not to translate them. Here, instead, is a guide to some of the honorifics you may encounter in Del Rey Manga.

-san: This is the most common honorific, and is equivalent to Mr., Miss, Ms., Mrs. It is the all-purpose honorific and can be used in any situation where politeness is required.

-sama: This is one level higher than "-san." It is used to confer great respect.

-dono: This comes from the word "tono," which means "lord." It is an even higher level than "-sama" and confers utmost respect.

-kun: This suffix is used at the end of boys' names to express familiarity or endearment. It is also sometimes used by men amongst friends, or when addressing someone younger or of a lower station.

-chan: This is used to express endearment, mostly toward girls. It is also used for little boys, pets, and even among lovers. It gives a sense of childish cuteness.

Bozu: This is an informal way to refer to a boy, similar to the English term "kid" or "squirt."

Sempai/Senpai: This title suggests that the addressee is one's senior in a group or organization. It is most often used in a school setting, where underclassmen refer to their upperclassmen as "sempai." It can also be used in the workplace, such as when a newer employee addresses an employee who has seniority in the company.

Kohai: This is the opposite of "sempai," and is used toward underclassmen in school or newcomers in the workplace. It connotes that the addressee is of a lower station.

Sensei: Literally meaning "one who has come before," this title is used for teachers, doctors, or masters of any profession or art.

-[blank]: This is usually forgotten in these lists, but it is perhaps the most significant difference between Japanese and English. The lack of honorific means that the speaker has permission to address the person in a very intimate way. Usually, only family, spouses, or very close friends have this kind of permission. Known as *yobisute*, it can be gratifying when someone who has earned the intimacy starts to call one by one's name without an honorific. But when that intimacy hasn't been earned, it can be very insulting.

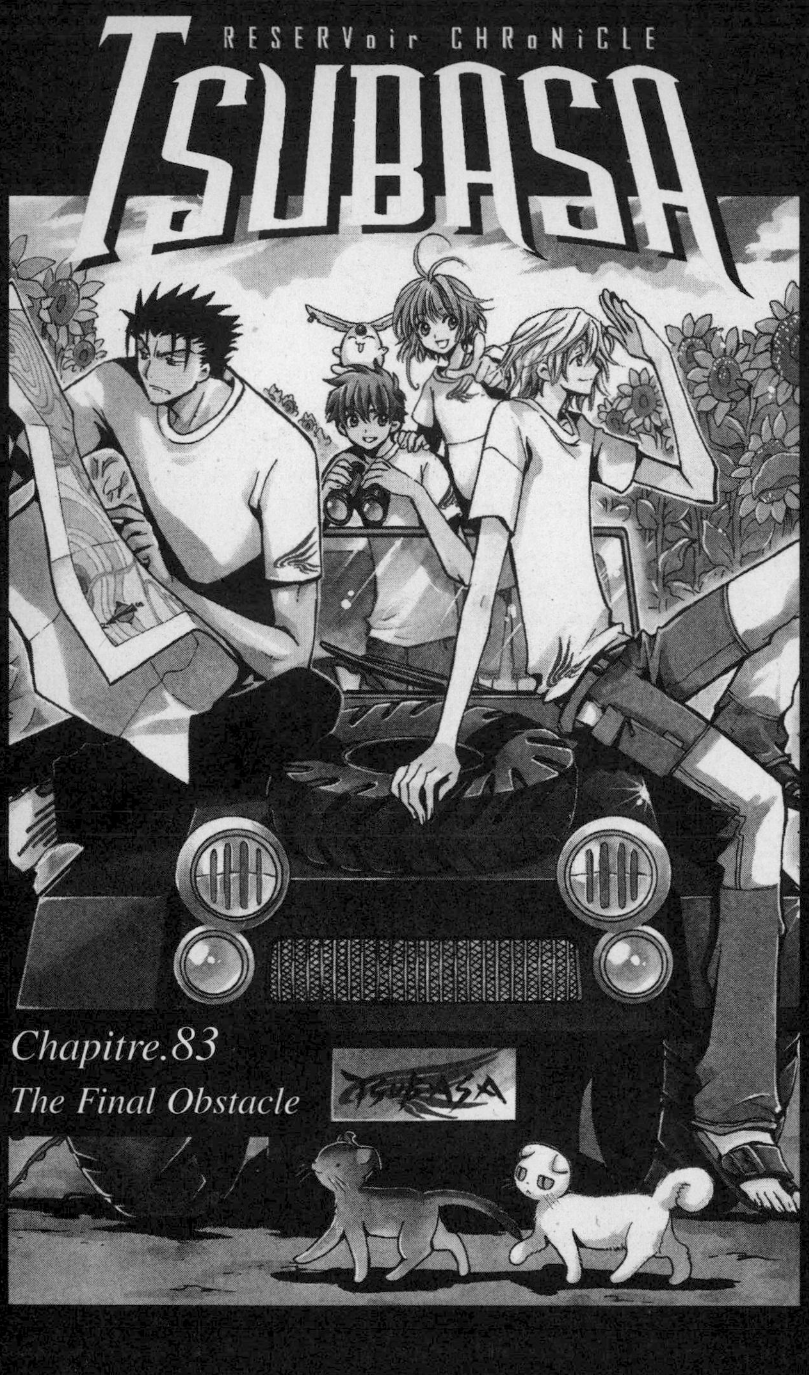
RESERVoir CHRoNiCLE
TSUBASA
Chapitre.83
The Final Obstacle
TSUBASA

ツバサ

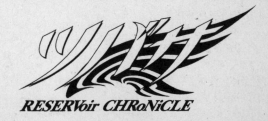

RESERVoir CHRoNiCLE

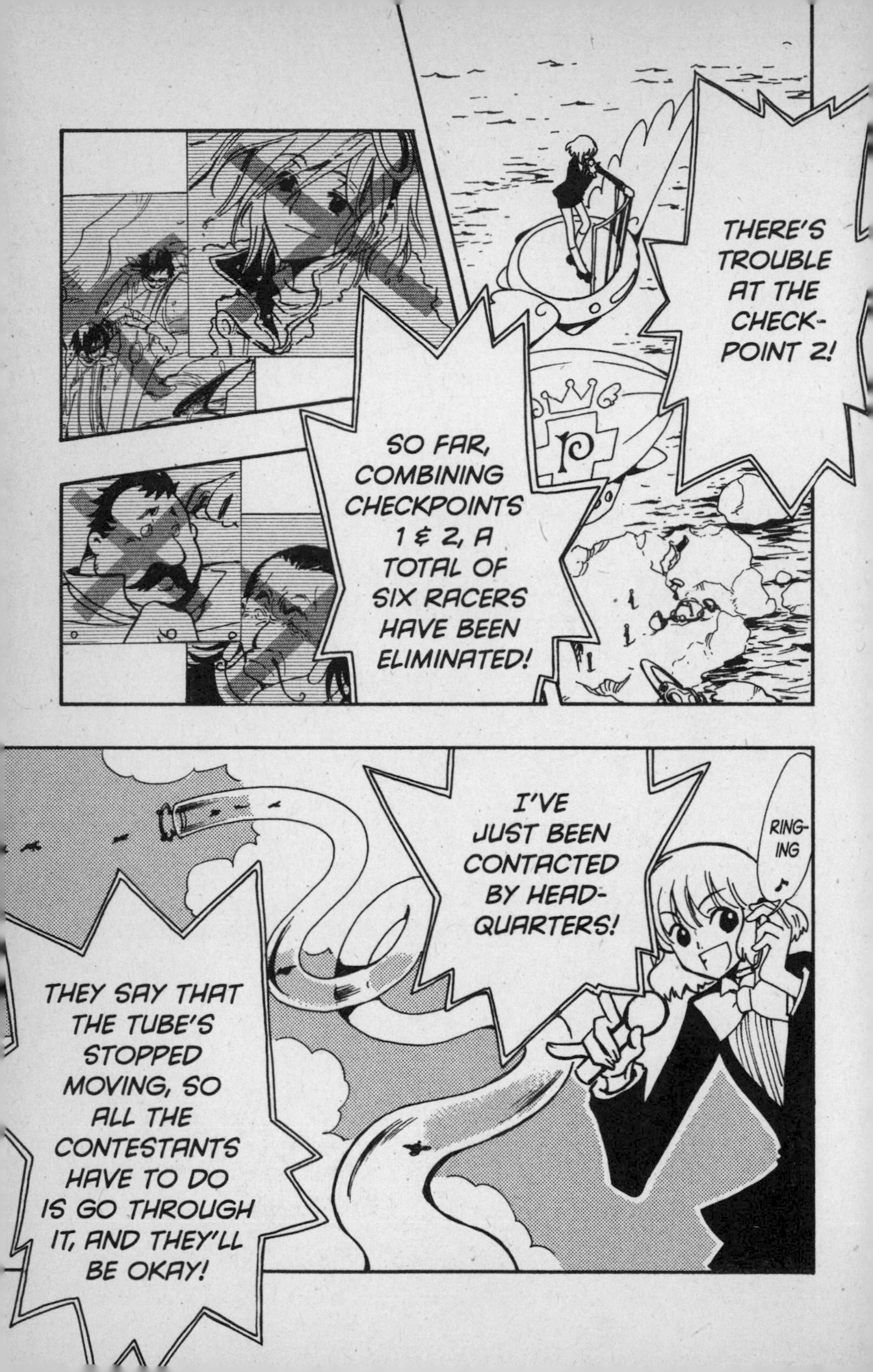
THERE'S TROUBLE AT THE CHECK-POINT 2!
SO FAR, COMBINING CHECKPOINTS 1 & 2, A TOTAL OF SIX RACERS HAVE BEEN ELIMINATED!
RING-ING
I'VE JUST BEEN CONTACTED BY HEAD-QUARTERS!
THEY SAY THAT THE TUBE'S STOPPED MOVING, SO ALL THE CONTESTANTS HAVE TO DO IS GO THROUGH IT, AND THEY'LL BE OKAY!

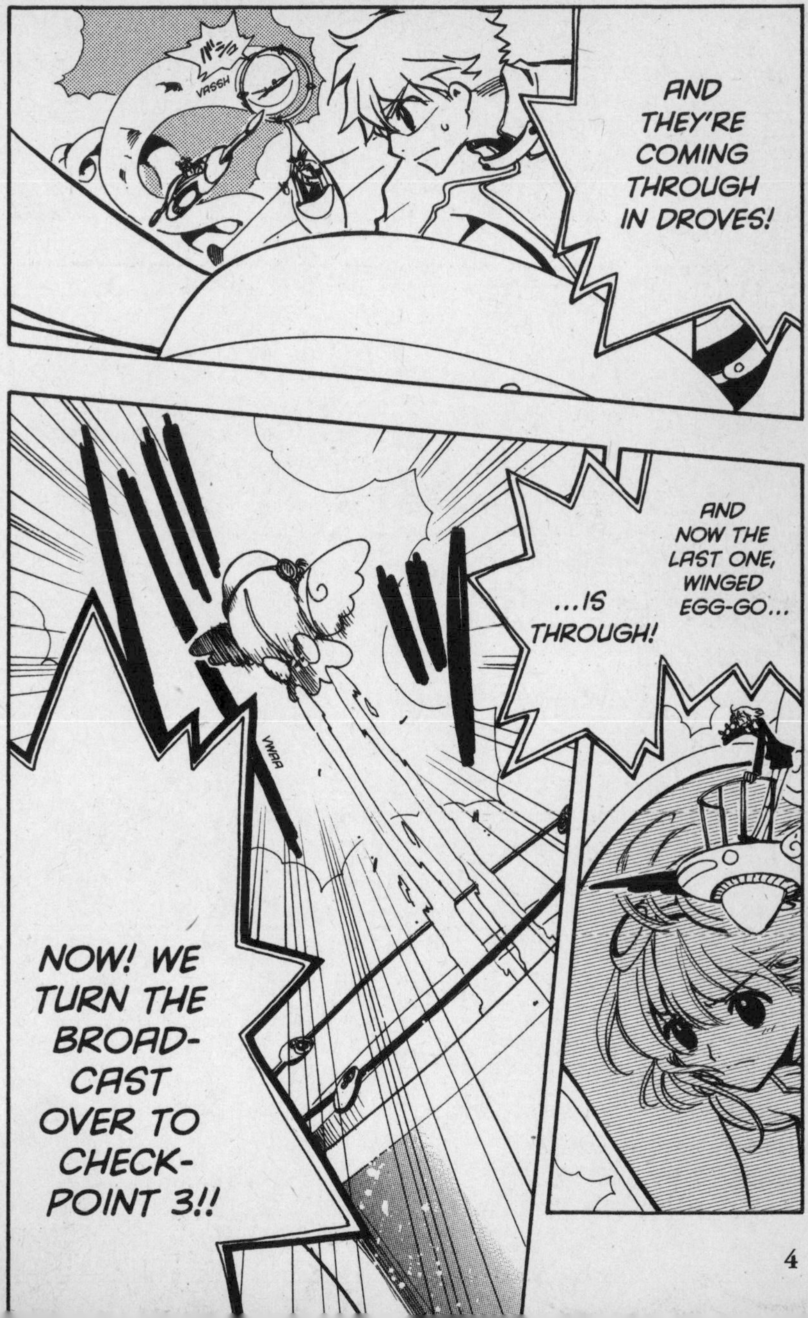
VASSH
AND THEY'RE COMING THROUGH IN DROVES!
AND NOW THE LAST ONE, WINGED EGG-GO...
...IS THROUGH!
VWAA
NOW! WE TURN THE BROAD-CAST OVER TO CHECK-POINT 3!!

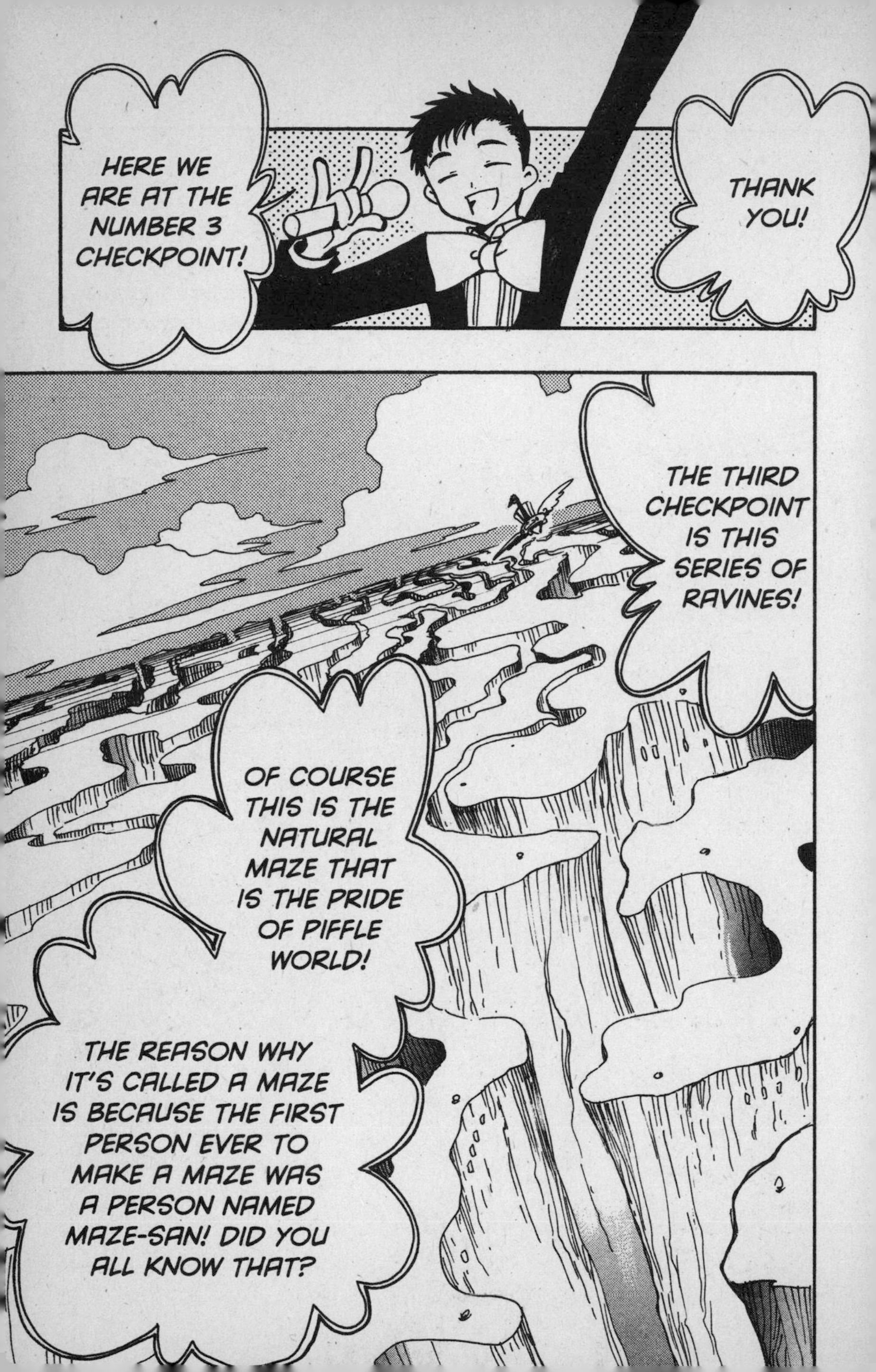
THANK YOU!
HERE WE ARE AT THE NUMBER 3 CHECKPOINT!
THE THIRD CHECKPOINT IS THIS SERIES OF RAVINES!
OF COURSE THIS IS THE NATURAL MAZE THAT IS THE PRIDE OF PIFFLE WORLD!
THE REASON WHY IT'S CALLED A MAZE IS BECAUSE THE FIRST PERSON EVER TO MAKE A MAZE WAS A PERSON NAMED MAZE-SAN! DID YOU ALL KNOW THAT?

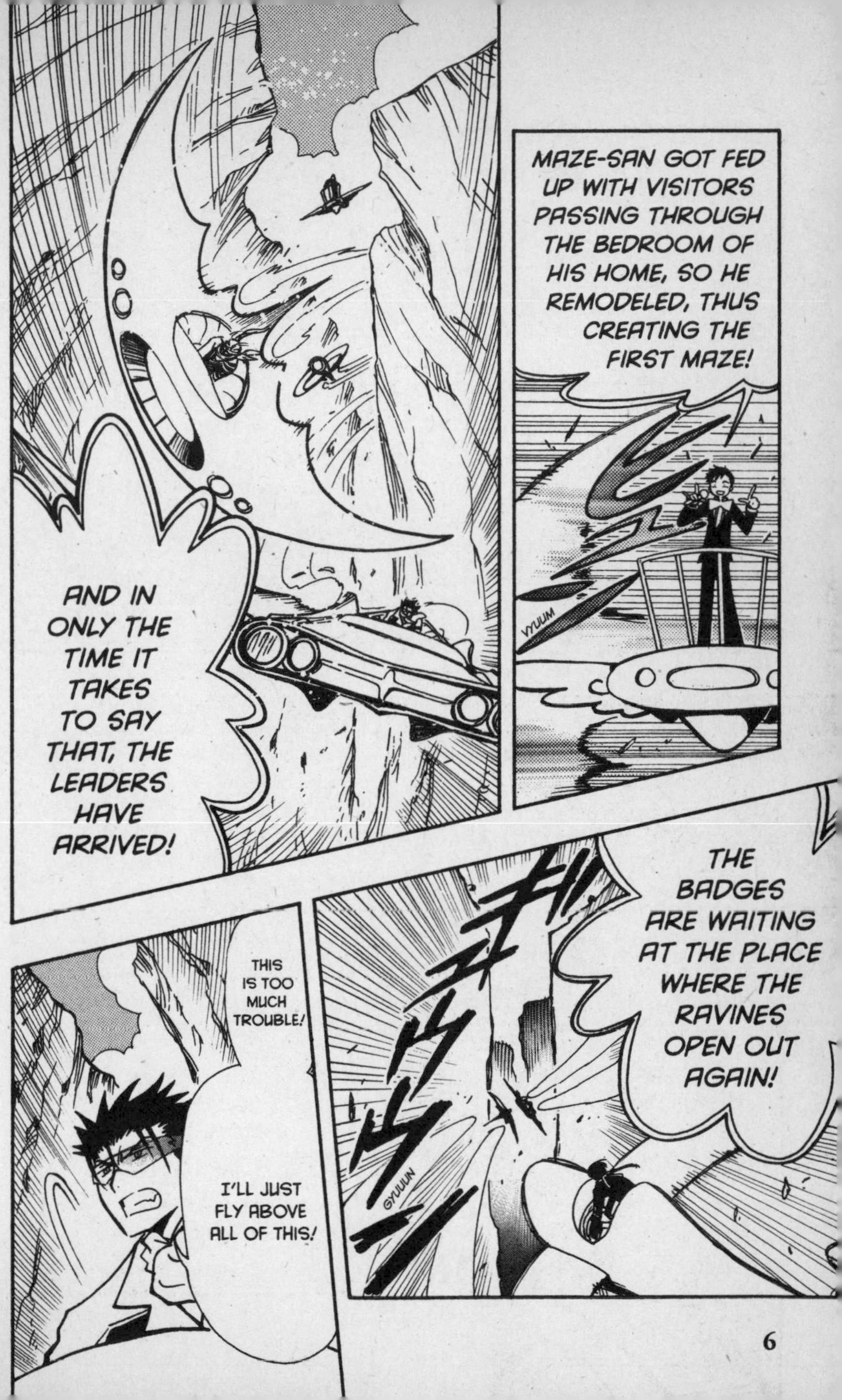
MAZE-SAN GOT FED UP WITH VISITORS PASSING THROUGH THE BEDROOM OF HIS HOME, SO HE REMODELED, THUS CREATING THE FIRST MAZE!
VYUUM
AND IN ONLY THE TIME IT TAKES TO SAY THAT, THE LEADERS HAVE ARRIVED!
THE BADGES ARE WAITING AT THE PLACE WHERE THE RAVINES OPEN OUT AGAIN!
GYUUUN
THIS IS TOO MUCH TROUBLE!
I'LL JUST FLY ABOVE ALL OF THIS!

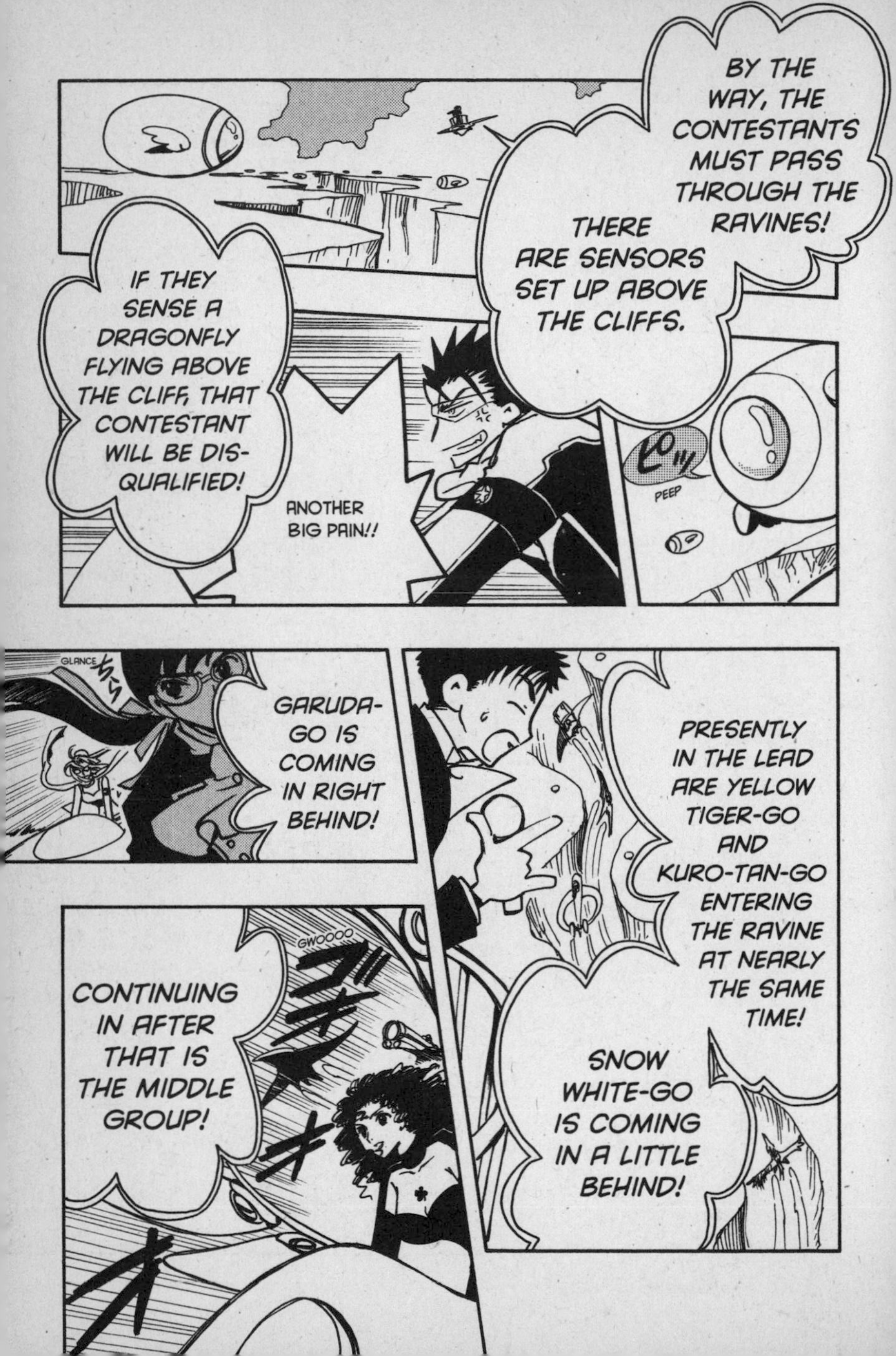
BY THE WAY, THE CONTESTANTS MUST PASS THROUGH THE RAVINES!
THERE ARE SENSORS SET UP ABOVE THE CLIFFS.
IF THEY SENSE A DRAGONFLY FLYING ABOVE THE CLIFF, THAT CONTESTANT WILL BE DIS-QUALIFIED!
PEEP
ANOTHER BIG PAIN!!
PRESENTLY IN THE LEAD ARE YELLOW TIGER-GO AND KURO-TAN-GO ENTERING THE RAVINE AT NEARLY THE SAME TIME!
SNOW WHITE-GO IS COMING IN A LITTLE BEHIND!
GLANCE
GARUDA-GO IS COMING IN RIGHT BEHIND!
GWOOOO
CONTINUING IN AFTER THAT IS THE MIDDLE GROUP!

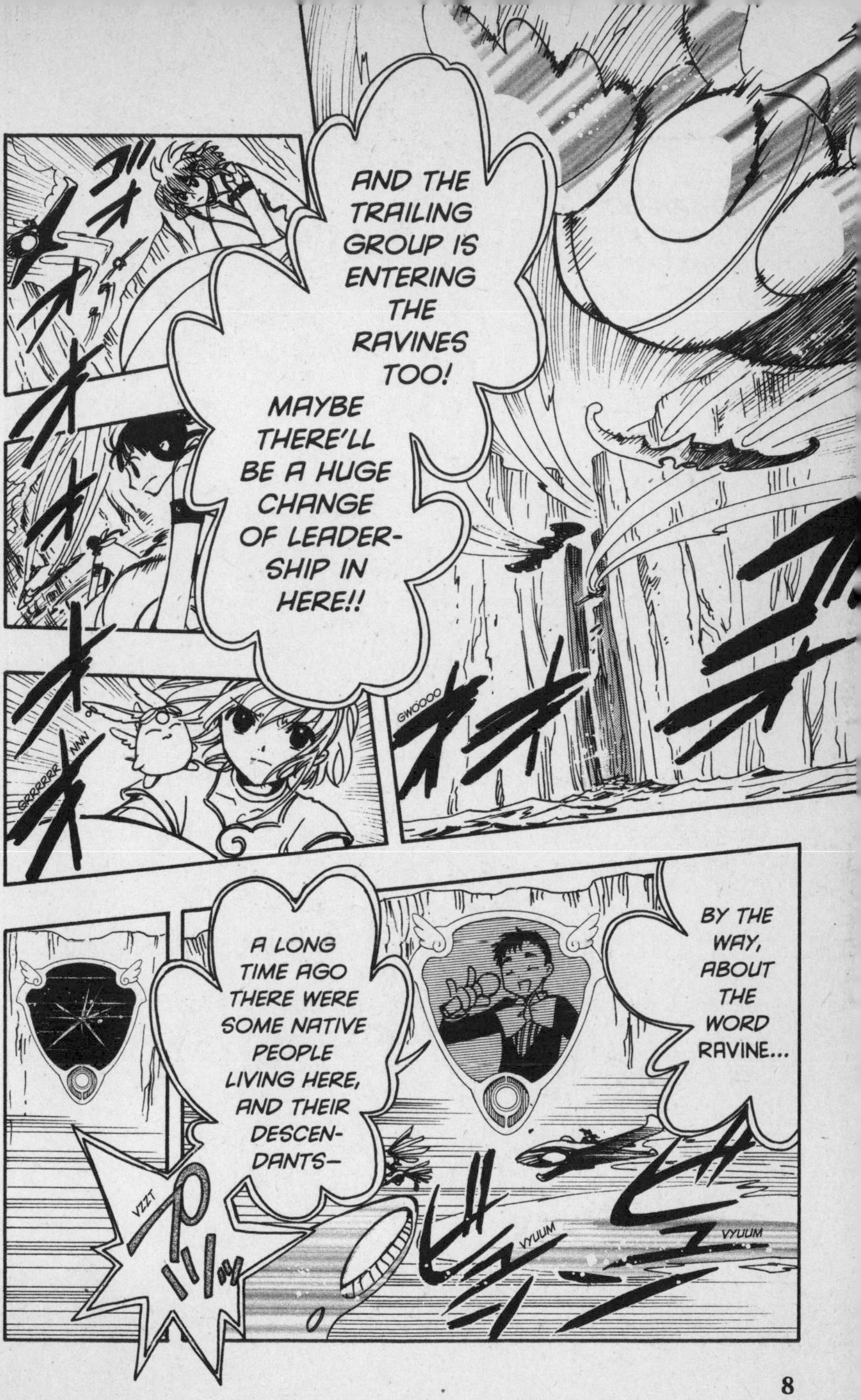
AND THE TRAILING GROUP IS ENTERING THE RAVINES TOO!
MAYBE THERE'LL BE A HUGE CHANGE OF LEADER-SHIP IN HERE!!
GWOOOO
GRRRRRR NNN
BY THE WAY, ABOUT THE WORD RAVINE...
VYUUM
VYUUM
A LONG TIME AGO THERE WERE SOME NATIVE PEOPLE LIVING HERE, AND THEIR DESCEN-DANTS–
VZZT

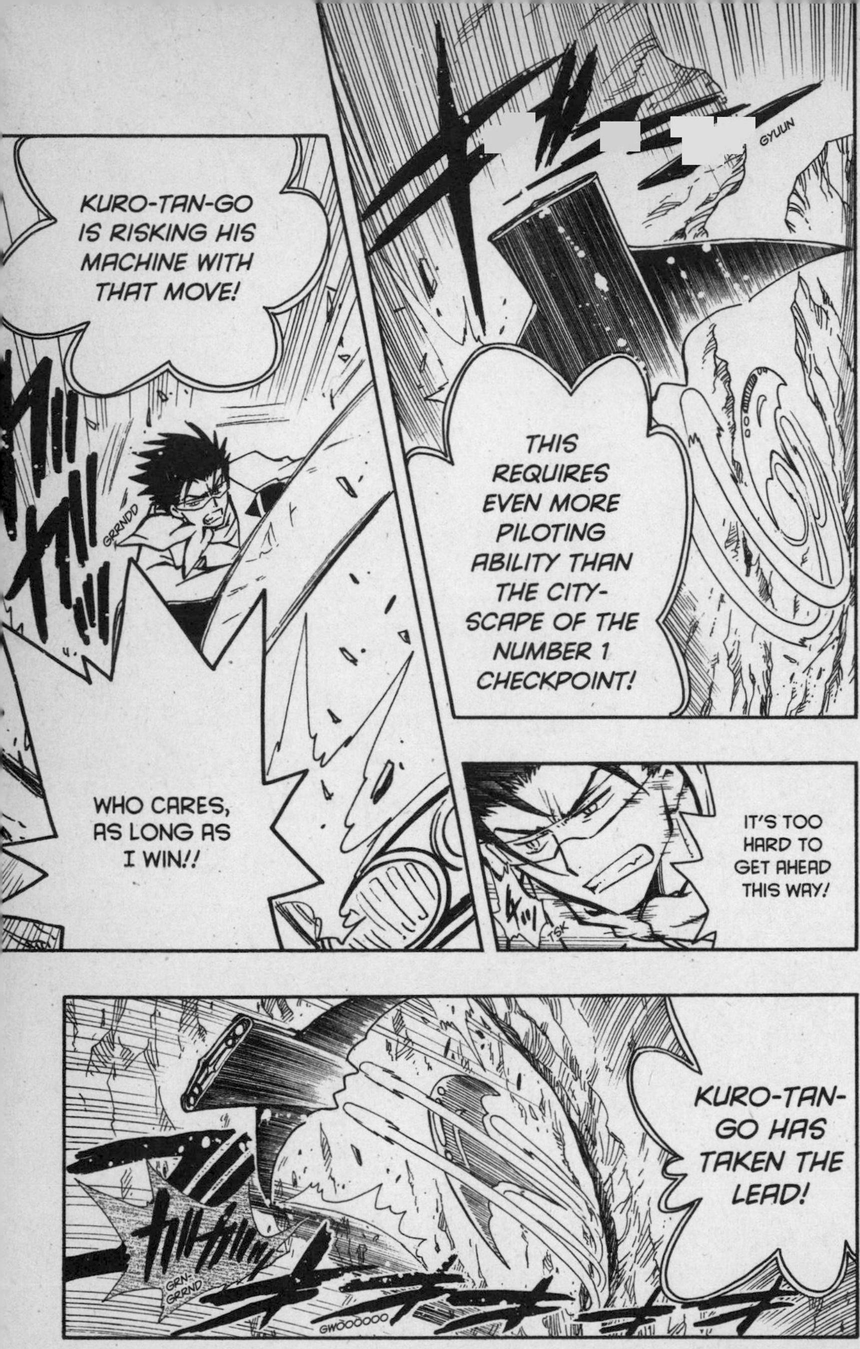
GYUUN
THIS REQUIRES EVEN MORE PILOTING ABILITY THAN THE CITY-SCAPE OF THE NUMBER 1 CHECKPOINT!
IT'S TOO HARD TO GET AHEAD THIS WAY!
TSK
KURO-TAN-GO IS RISKING HIS MACHINE WITH THAT MOVE!
GRRNDD
WHO CARES, AS LONG AS I WIN!!
KURO-TAN-GO HAS TAKEN THE LEAD!
GRN-GRRND
GWOOOOOO

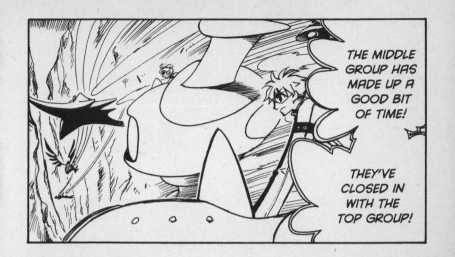

THE MIDDLE GROUP HAS MADE UP A GOOD BIT OF TIME!

THEY'VE CLOSED IN WITH THE TOP GROUP!

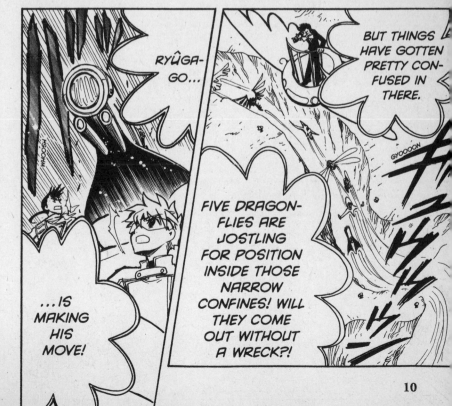

RYÛGA-GO...

BUT THINGS HAVE GOTTEN PRETTY CONFUSED IN THERE.

FIVE DRAGONFLIES ARE JOSTLING FOR POSITION INSIDE THOSE NARROW CONFINES! WILL THEY COME OUT WITHOUT A WRECK?!

...IS MAKING HIS MOVE!

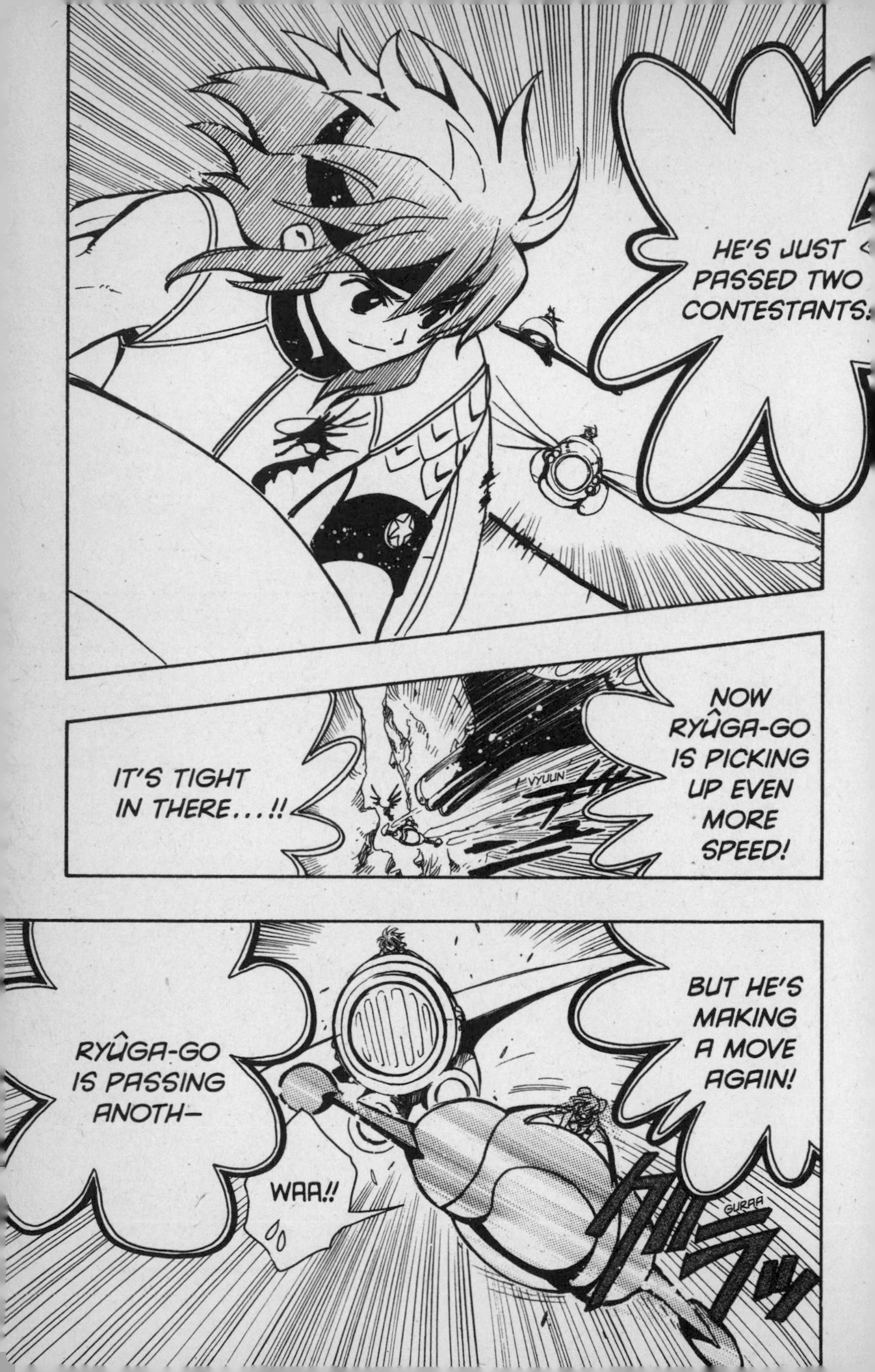
HE'S JUST PASSED TWO CONTESTANTS!
NOW RYÛGA-GO IS PICKING UP EVEN MORE SPEED!
VYUUN
IT'S TIGHT IN THERE...!!
BUT HE'S MAKING A MOVE AGAIN!
RYÛGA-GO IS PASSING ANOTH–
GURAA
WAA!!

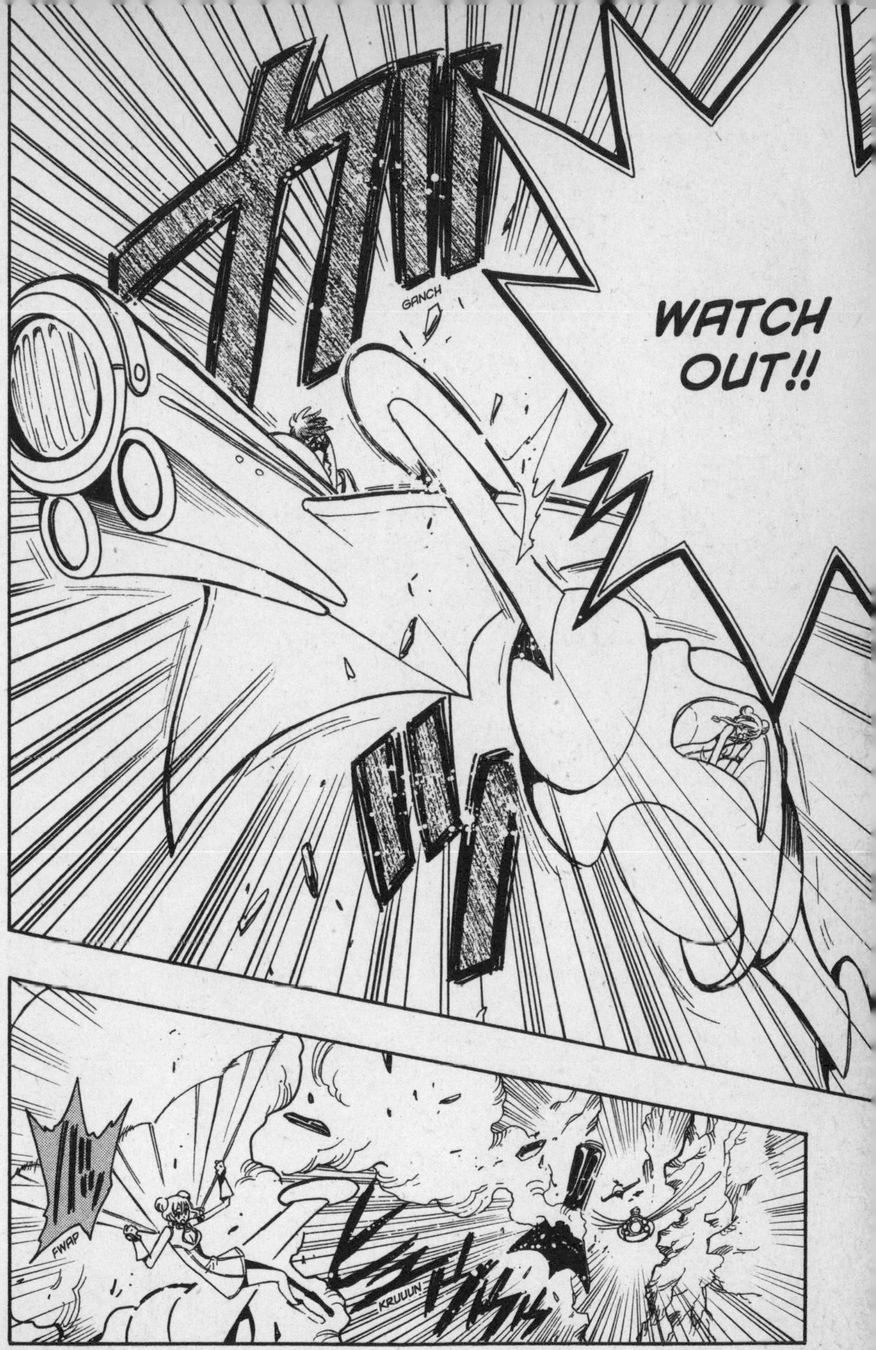
WATCH OUT!!
GANCH
KRUUUN
FWAP

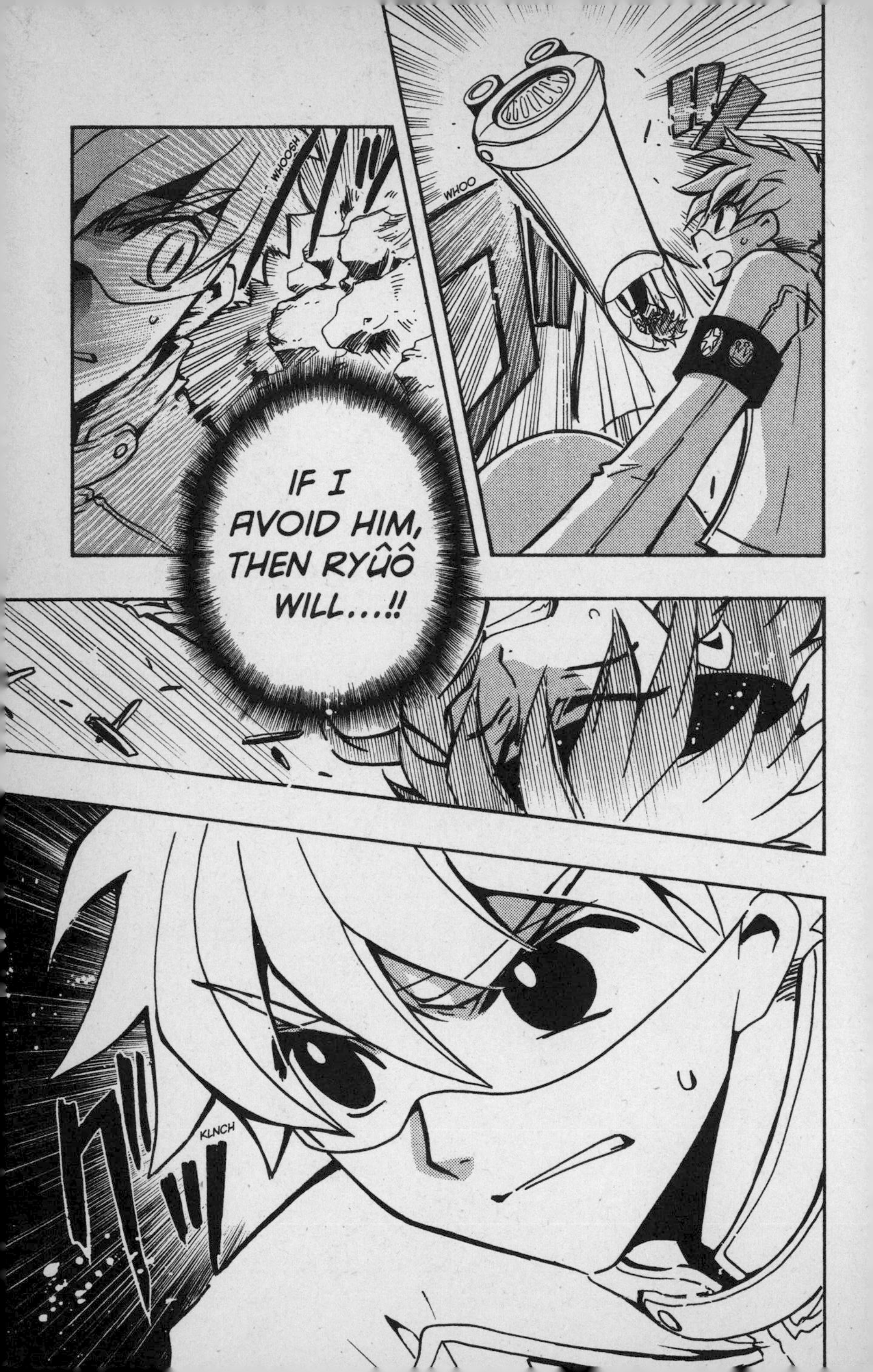
WHOO
WHOOSH
IF I AVOID HIM, THEN RYÛÔ WILL...!!
KLNCH

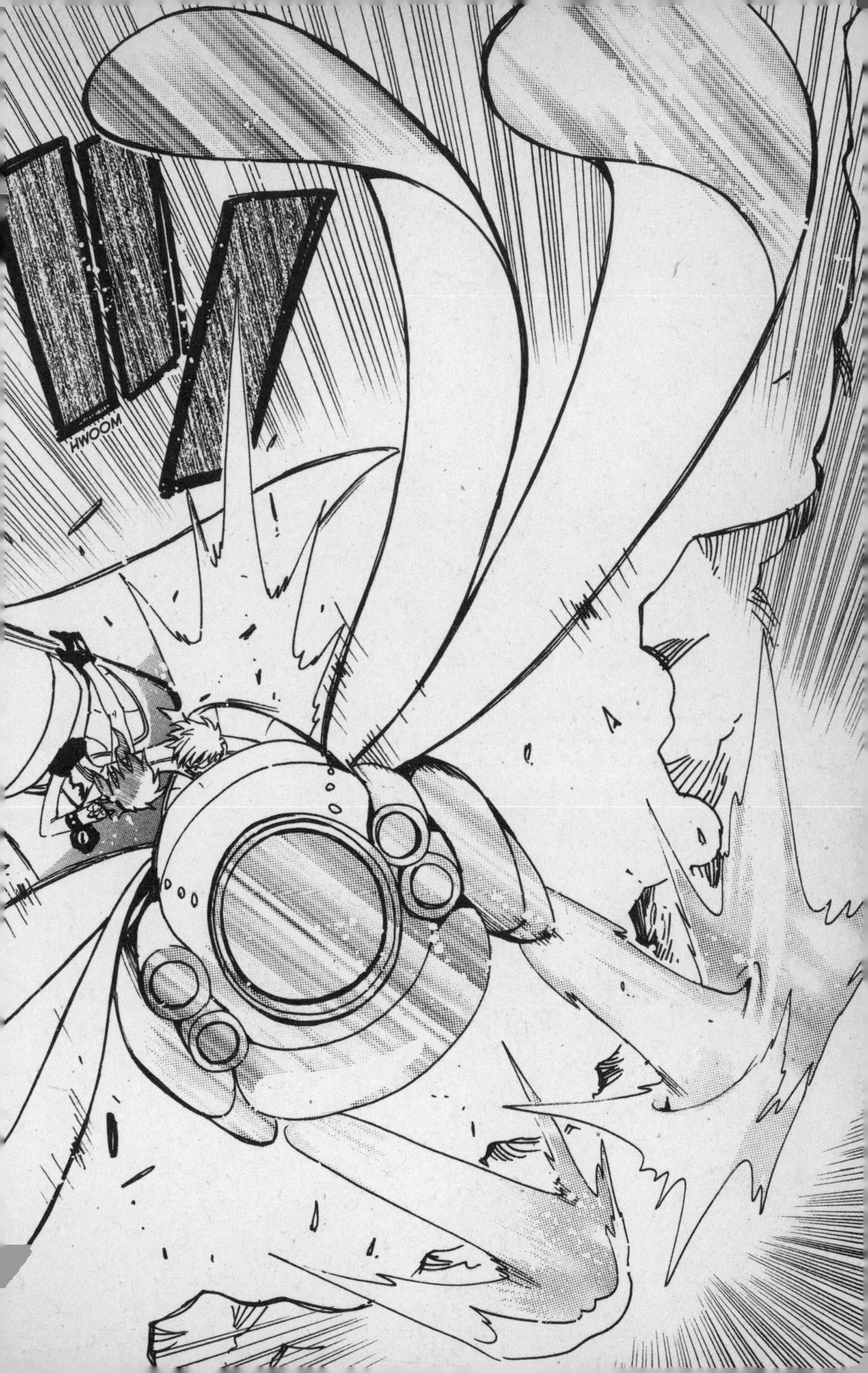
HWOOM

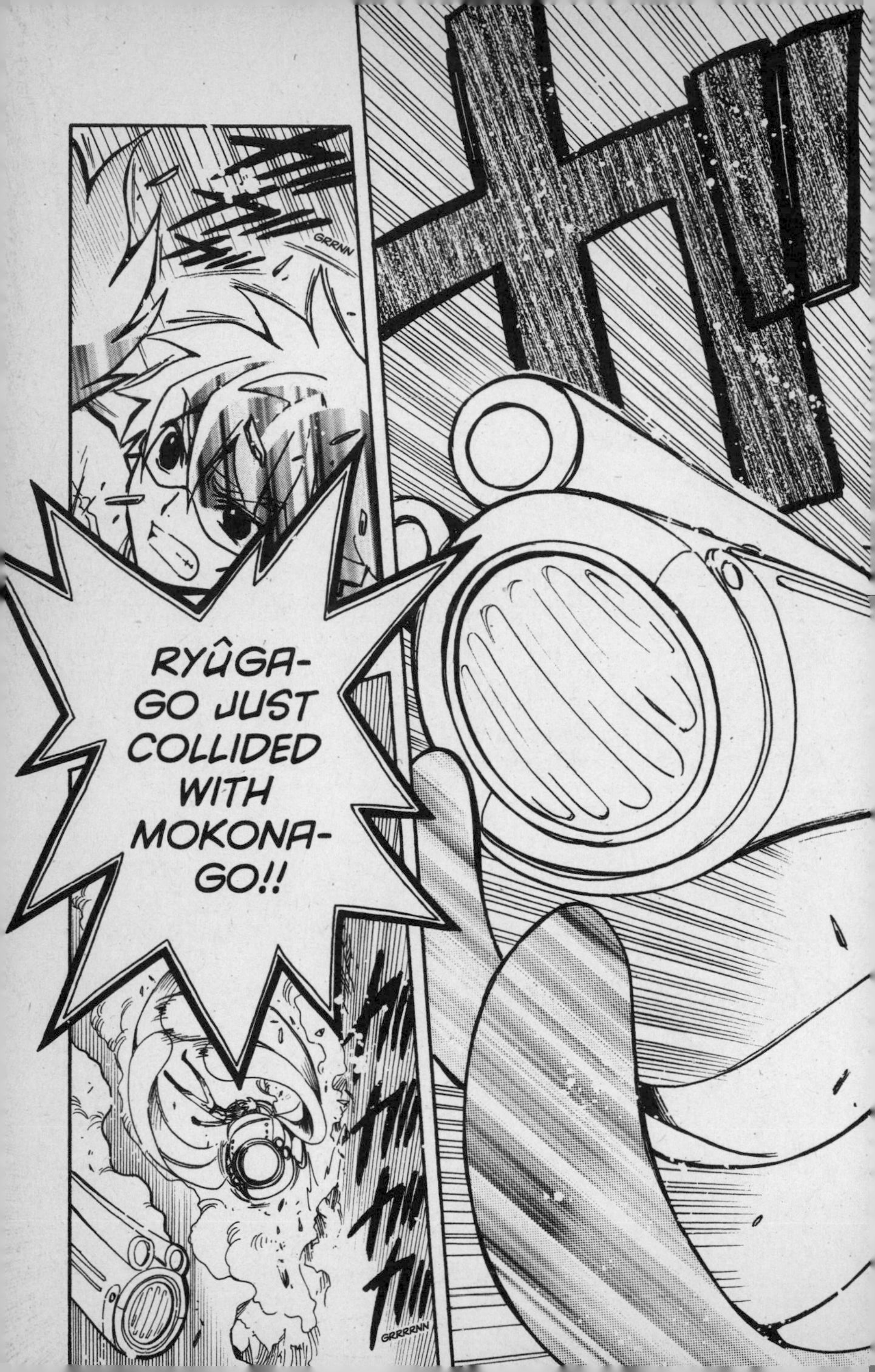
GRRNN
RYÛGA-GO JUST COLLIDED WITH MOKONA-GO!!
GRRRRNN

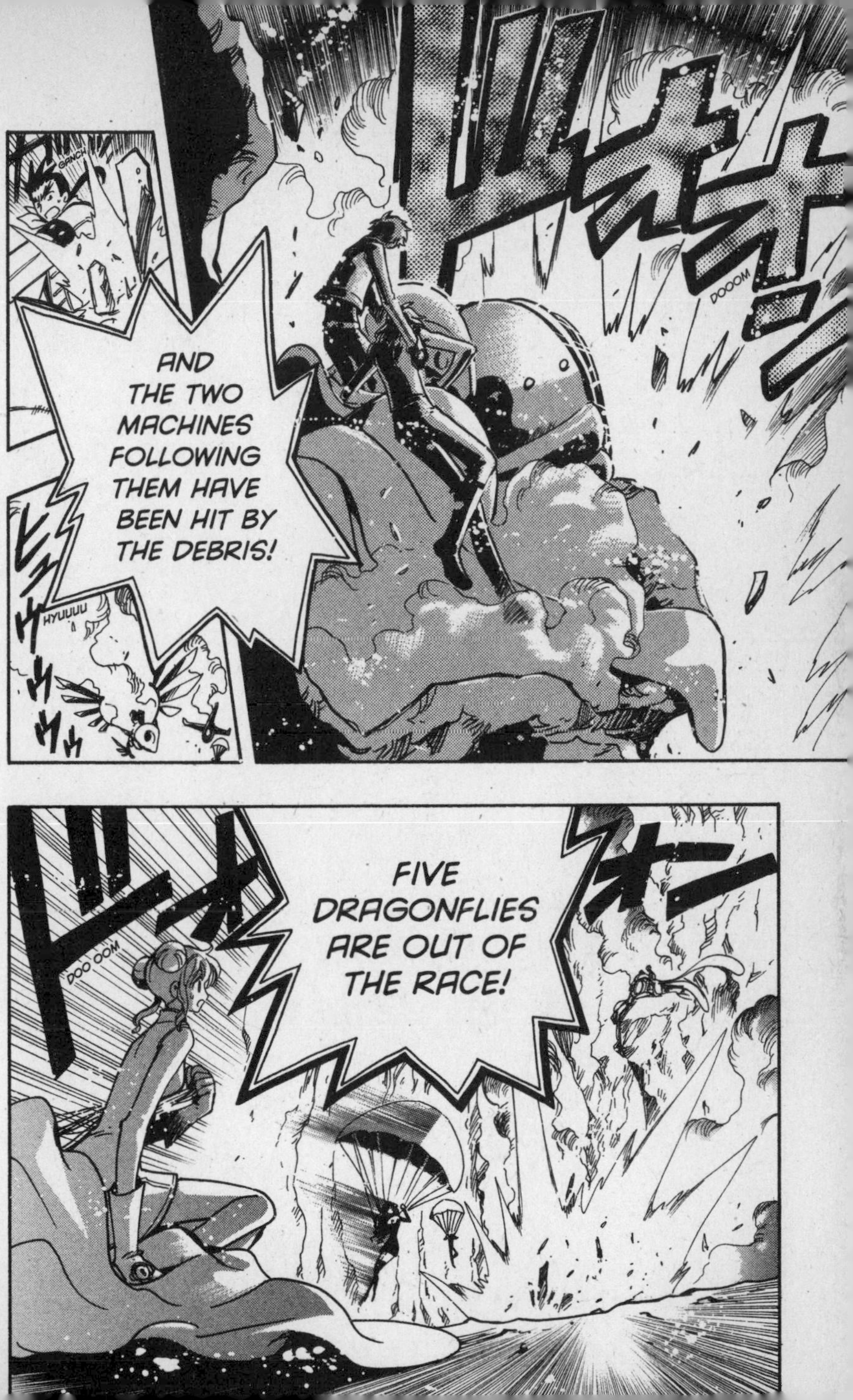
DOOOM
AND THE TWO MACHINES FOLLOWING THEM HAVE BEEN HIT BY THE DEBRIS!
GANCH
HYUUUU
FIVE DRAGONFLIES ARE OUT OF THE RACE!
DOO OOM

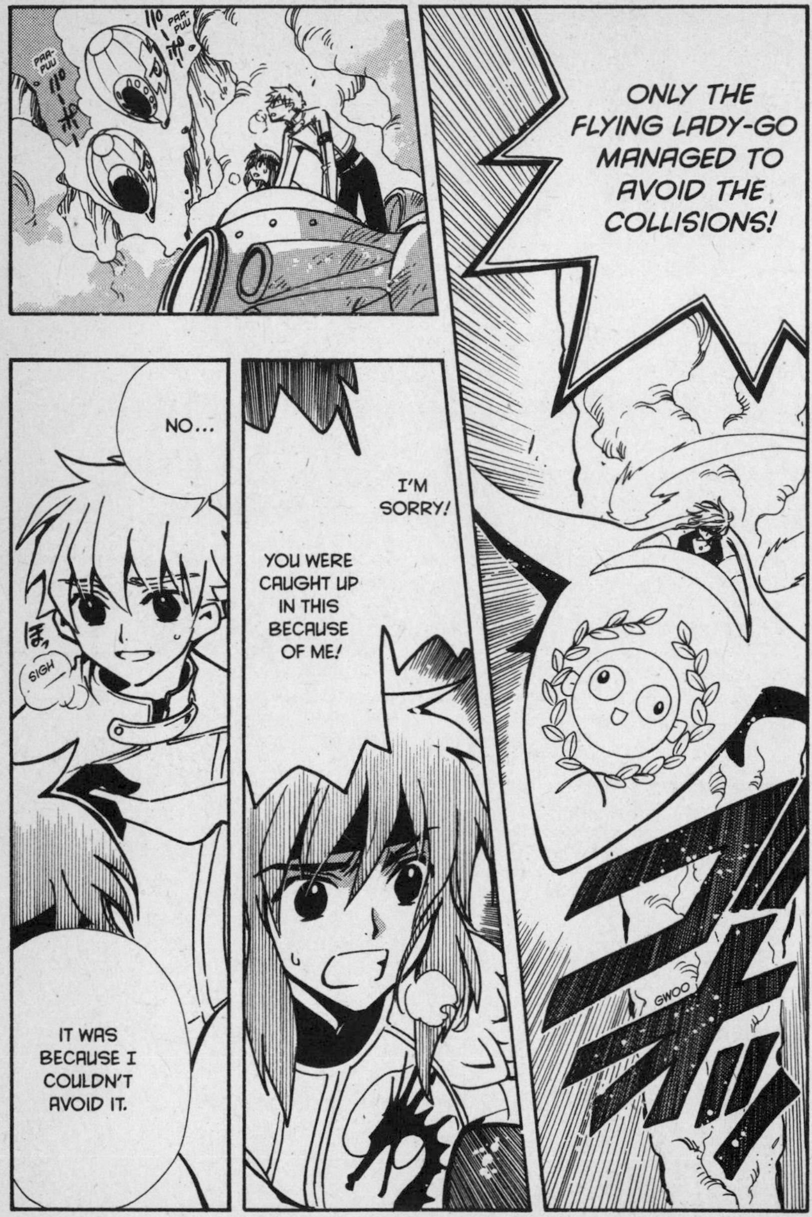
ONLY THE FLYING LADY-GO MANAGED TO AVOID THE COLLISIONS!
GWOO
PAA-PUU
PAA-PUU
I'M SORRY!
YOU WERE CAUGHT UP IN THIS BECAUSE OF ME!
NO...
SIGH
IT WAS BECAUSE I COULDN'T AVOID IT.

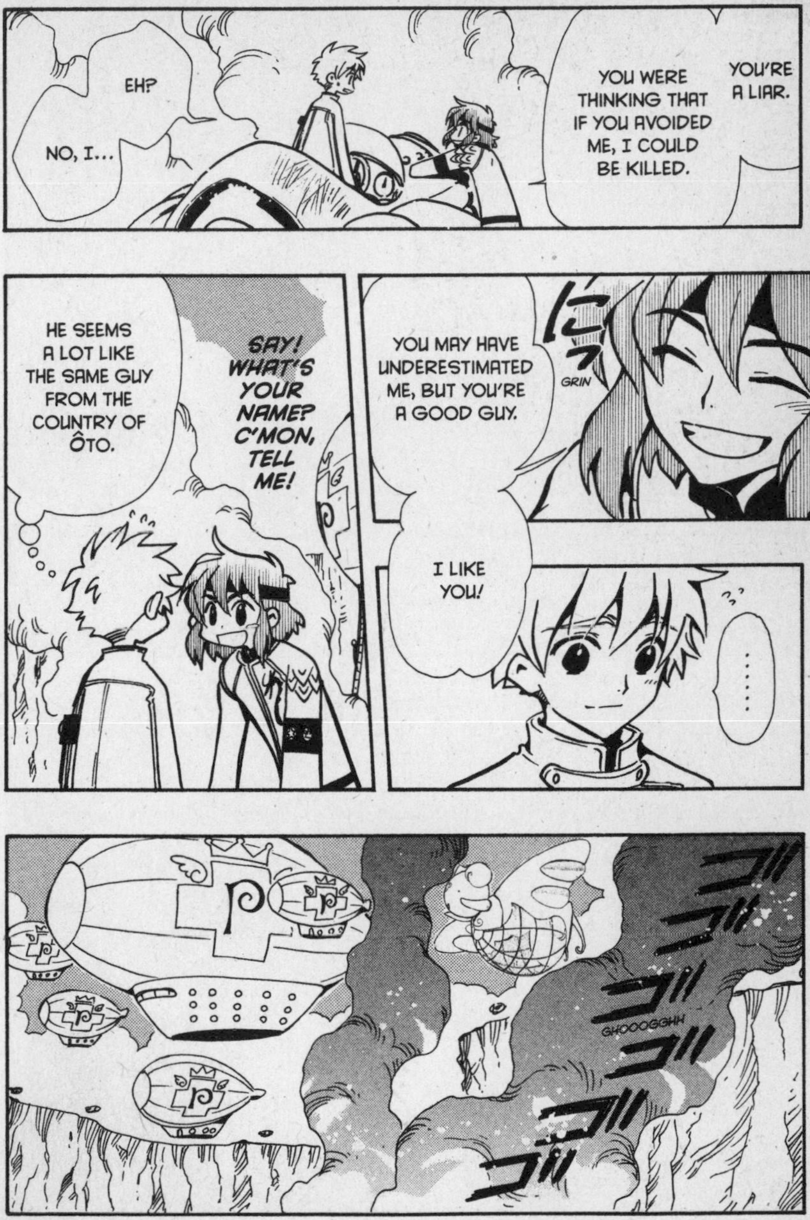
YOU'RE A LIAR.
YOU WERE THINKING THAT IF YOU AVOIDED ME, I COULD BE KILLED.
EH?
NO, I...
YOU MAY HAVE UNDERESTIMATED ME, BUT YOU'RE A GOOD GUY.
にっ
GRIN
I LIKE YOU!
......
SAY! WHAT'S YOUR NAME? C'MON, TELL ME!
HE SEEMS A LOT LIKE THE SAME GUY FROM THE COUNTRY OF ÔTO.
GHOOOGGHH

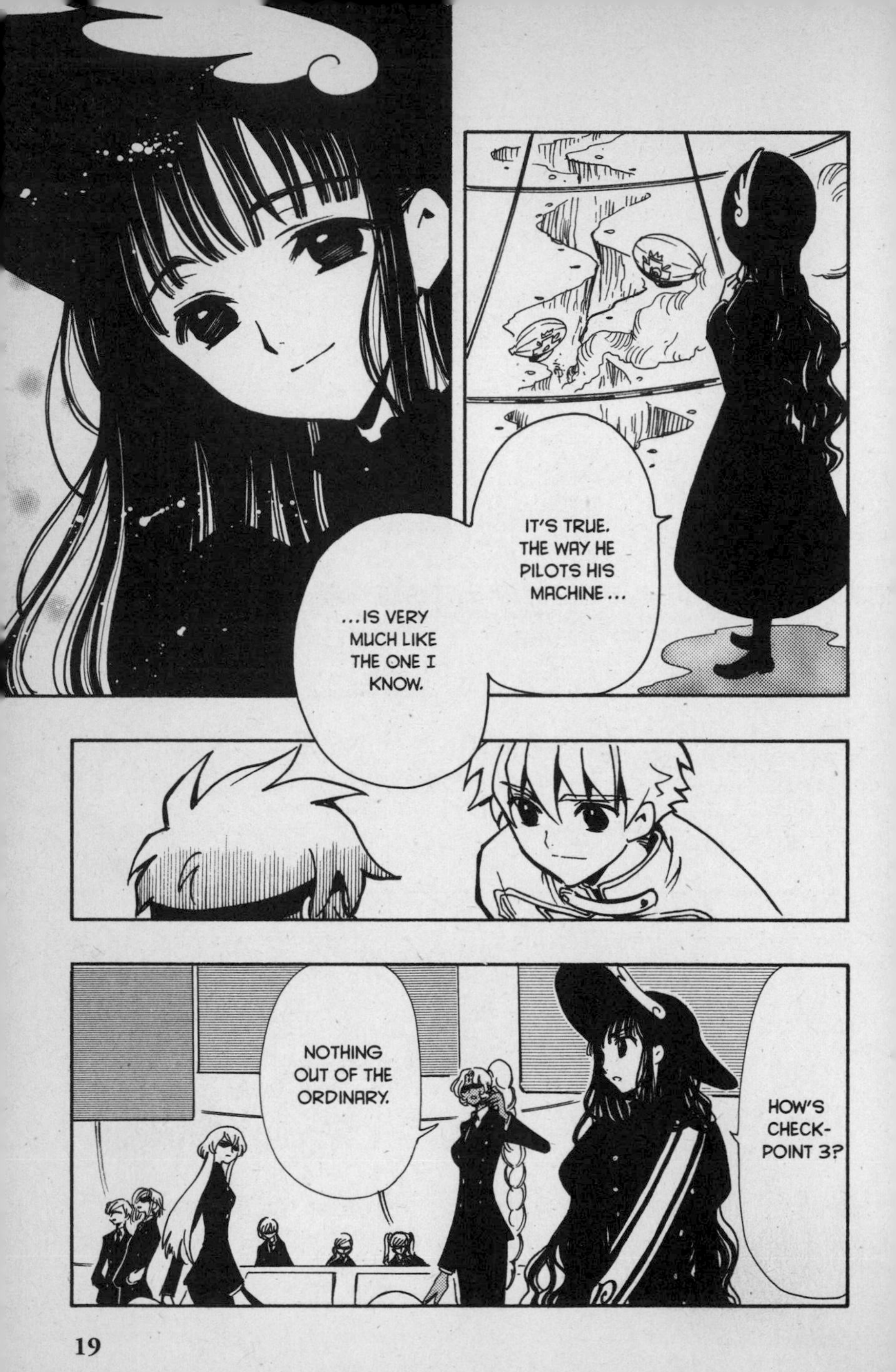
IT'S TRUE. THE WAY HE PILOTS HIS MACHINE...
...IS VERY MUCH LIKE THE ONE I KNOW.
HOW'S CHECK-POINT 3?
NOTHING OUT OF THE ORDINARY.

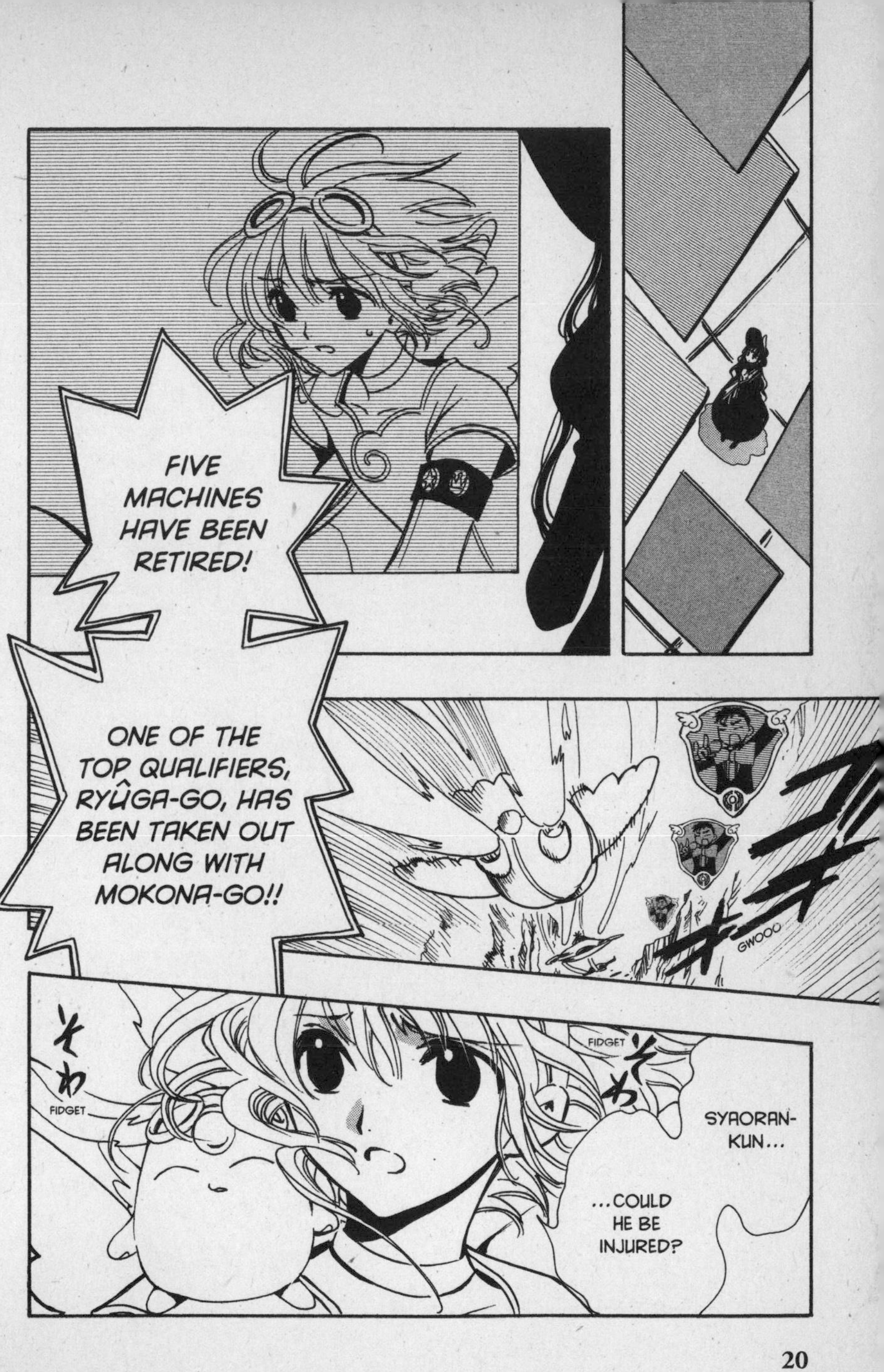
FIVE MACHINES HAVE BEEN RETIRED!
ONE OF THE TOP QUALIFIERS, RYÛGA-GO, HAS BEEN TAKEN OUT ALONG WITH MOKONA-GO!!
GWOOO
そわ
FIDGET
SYAORAN-KUN...
...COULD HE BE INJURED?
そわ
FIDGET

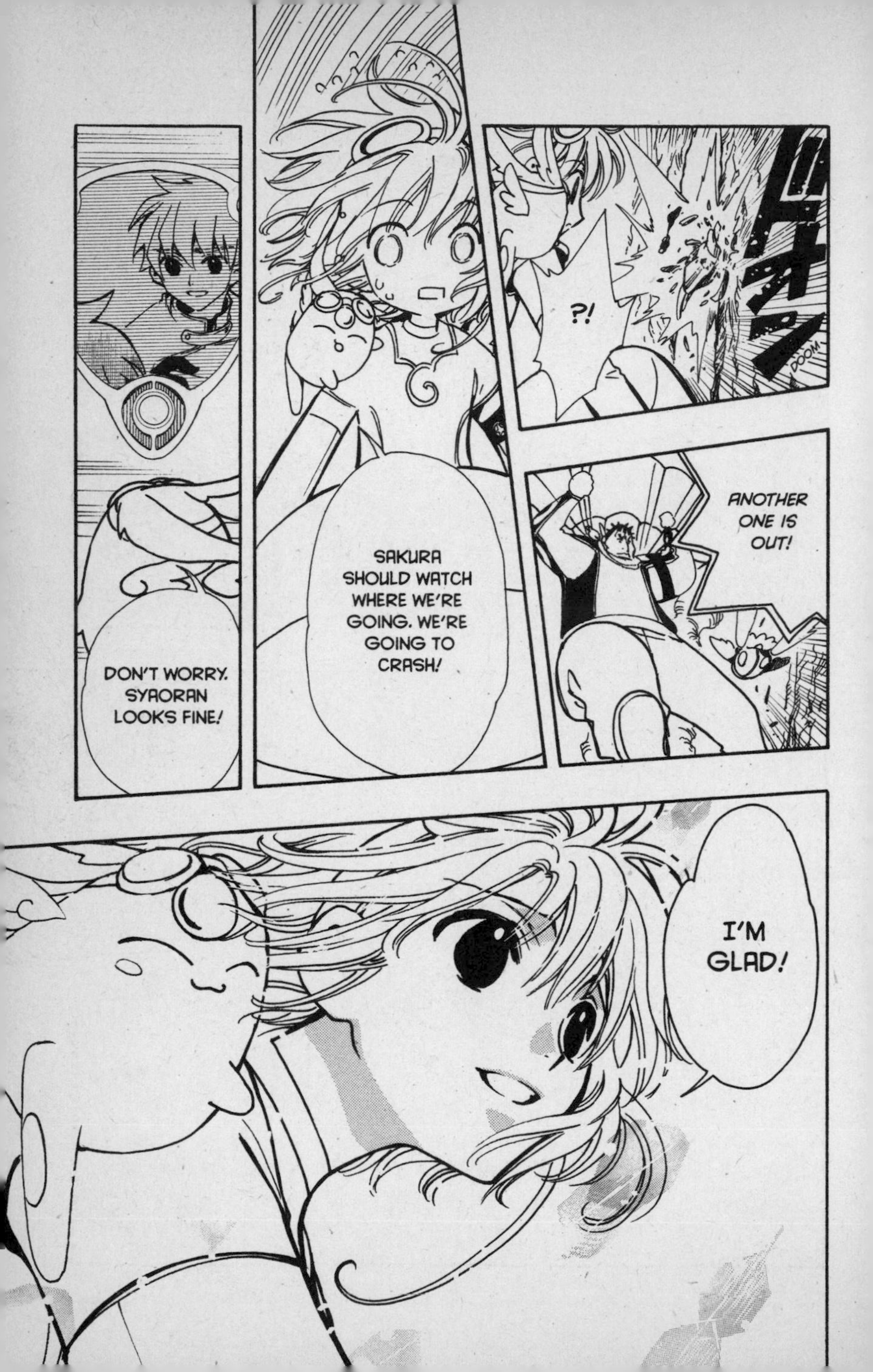

?!
DOOM
ANOTHER ONE IS OUT!
SAKURA SHOULD WATCH WHERE WE'RE GOING. WE'RE GOING TO CRASH!
DON'T WORRY. SYAORAN LOOKS FINE!
I'M GLAD!

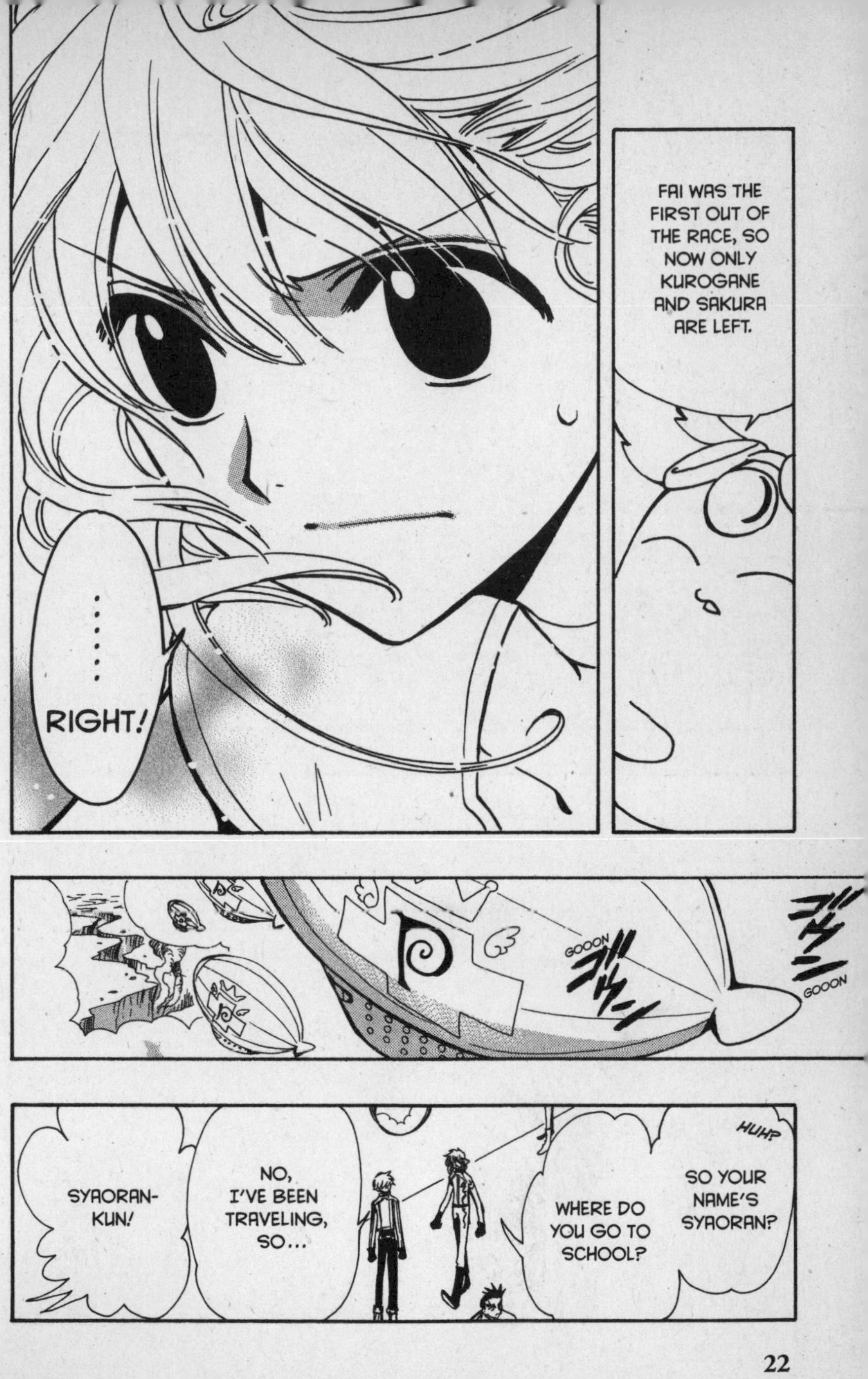
FAI WAS THE FIRST OUT OF THE RACE, SO NOW ONLY KUROGANE AND SAKURA ARE LEFT.
...... RIGHT!
GOOON
GOOON
HUH?
SO YOUR NAME'S SYAORAN?
WHERE DO YOU GO TO SCHOOL?
NO, I'VE BEEN TRAVELING, SO...
SYAORAN-KUN!

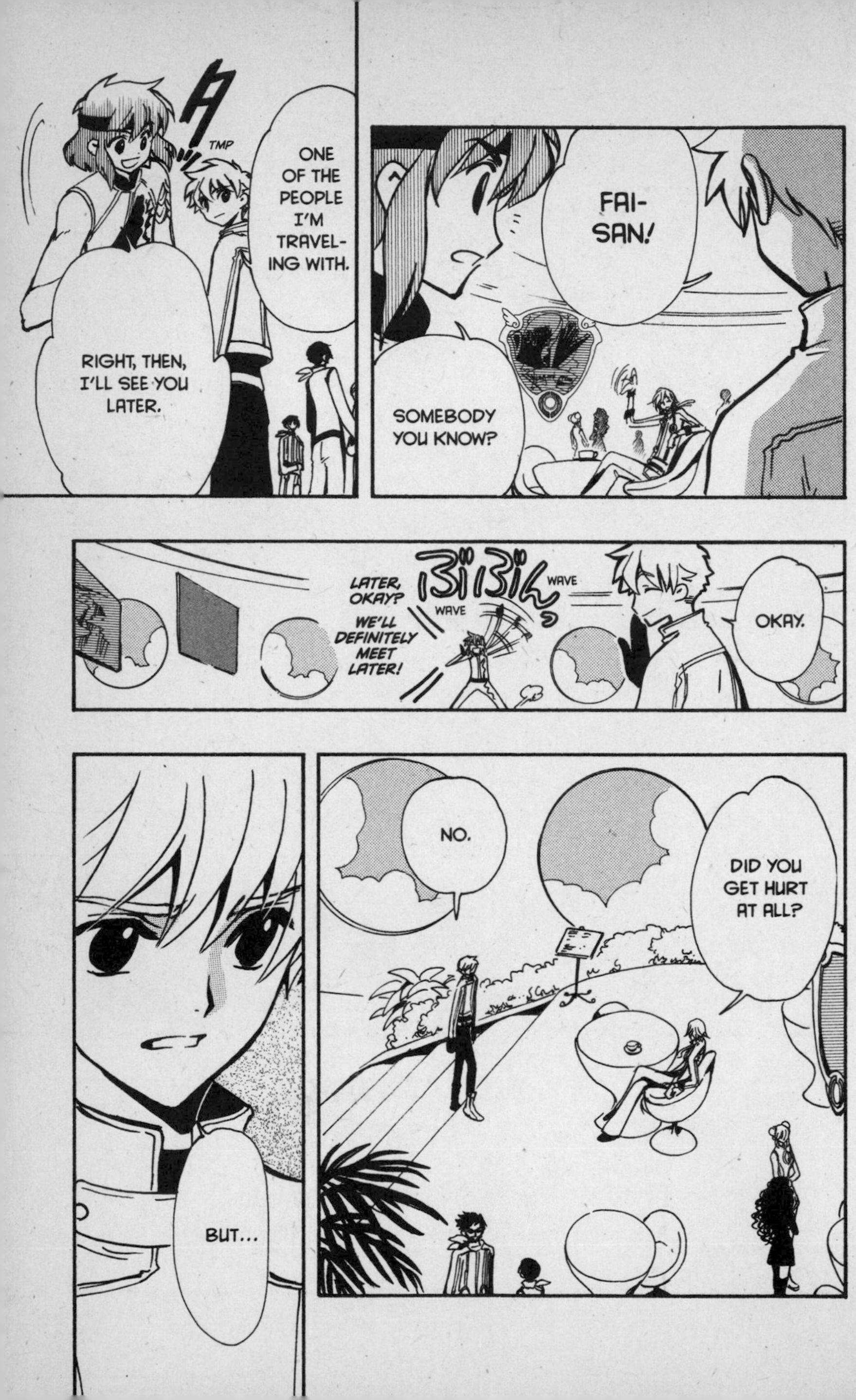
FAI-SAN!
SOMEBODY YOU KNOW?
ONE OF THE PEOPLE I'M TRAVEL-ING WITH.
TMP
RIGHT, THEN, I'LL SEE YOU LATER.
OKAY.
WAVE
WAVE
LATER, OKAY? WE'LL DEFINITELY MEET LATER!
DID YOU GET HURT AT ALL?
NO.
BUT...

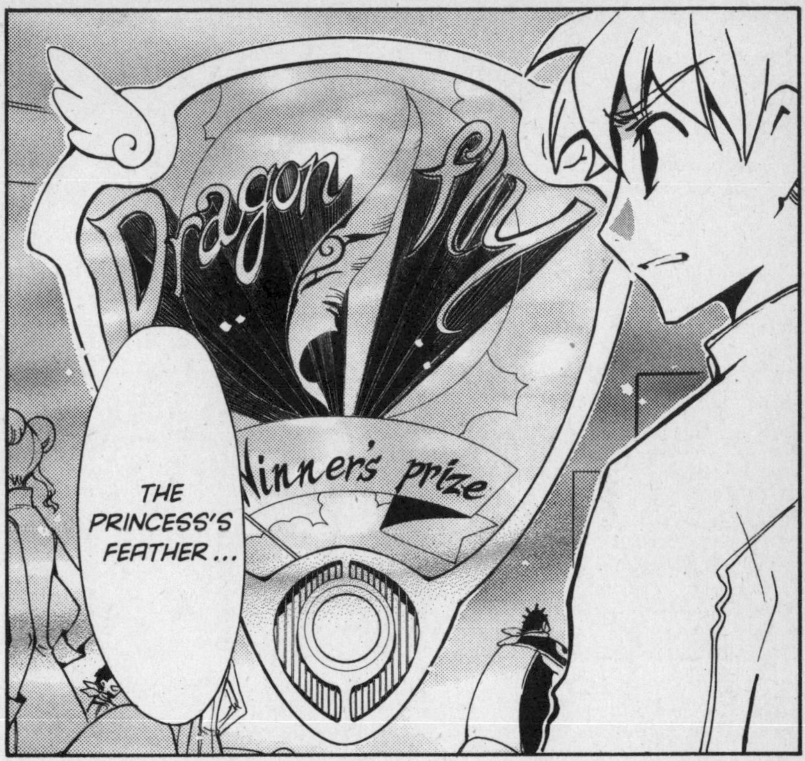
Dragon fly
Winner's prize
THE PRINCESS'S FEATHER ...
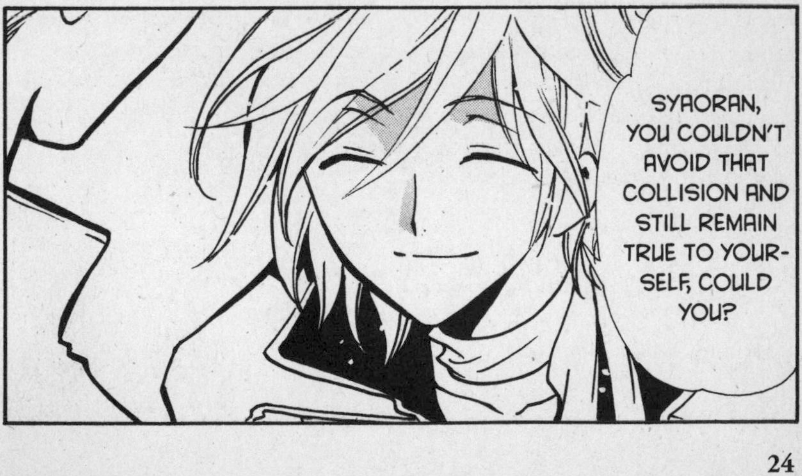
SYAORAN, YOU COULDN'T AVOID THAT COLLISION AND STILL REMAIN TRUE TO YOUR-SELF, COULD YOU?

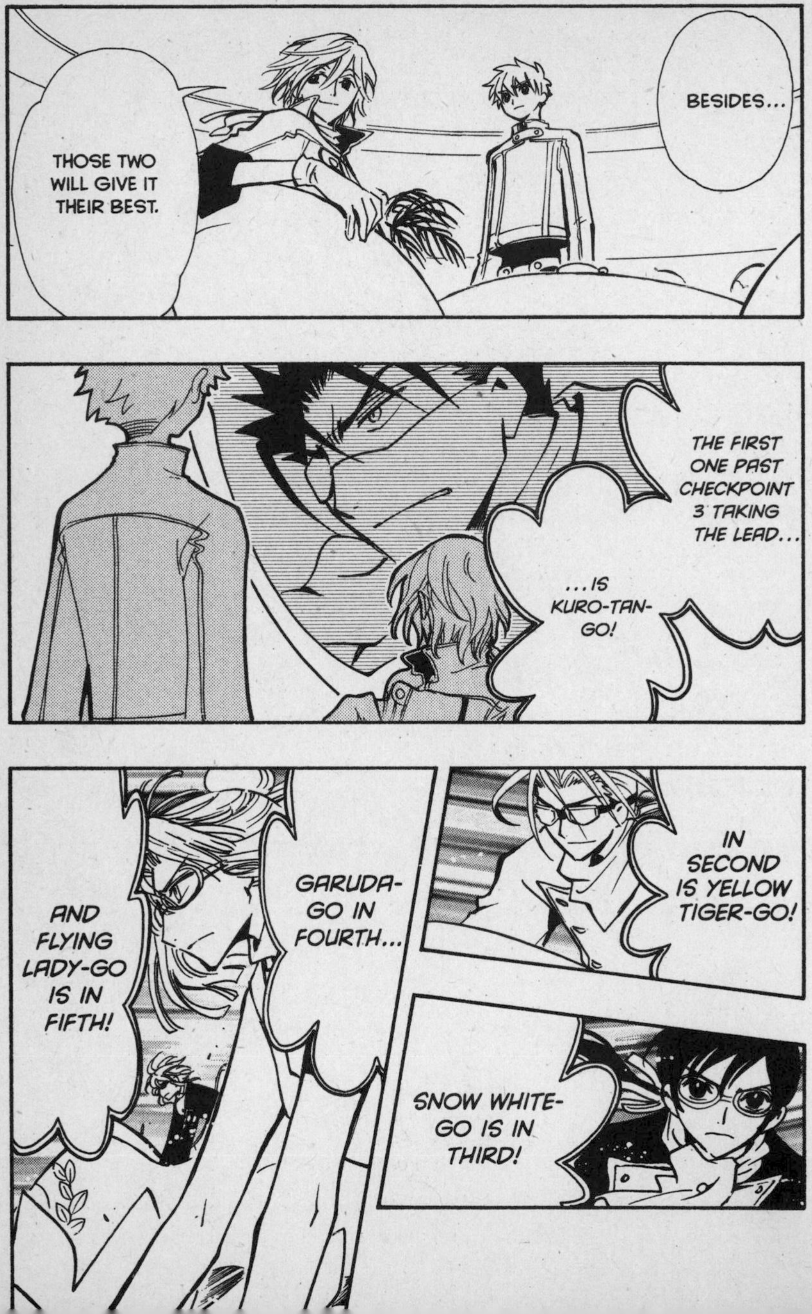
BESIDES...
THOSE TWO WILL GIVE IT THEIR BEST.
THE FIRST ONE PAST CHECKPOINT 3 TAKING THE LEAD...
...IS KURO-TAN-GO!
IN SECOND IS YELLOW TIGER-GO!
SNOW WHITE-GO IS IN THIRD!
GARUDA-GO IN FOURTH...
AND FLYING LADY-GO IS IN FIFTH!

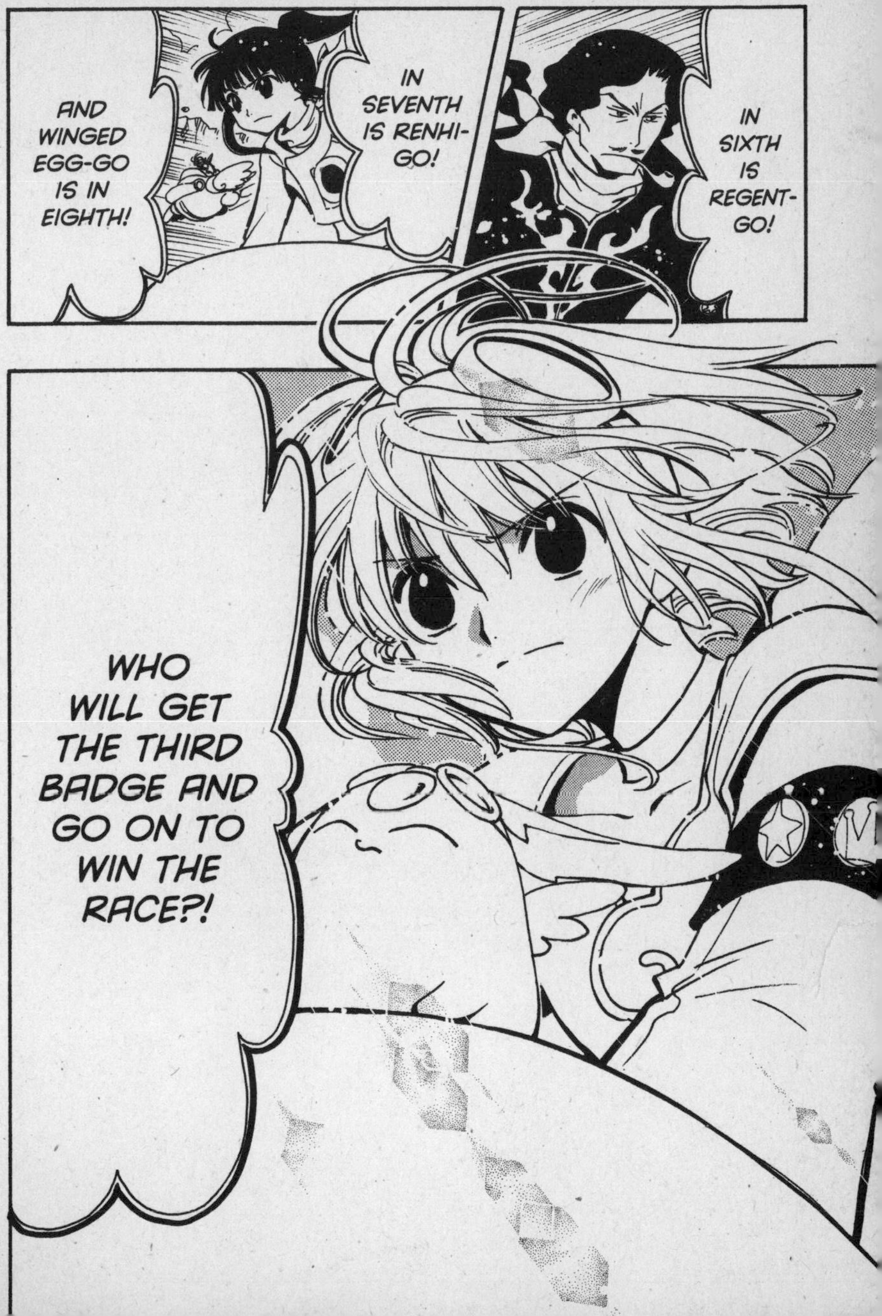
IN SIXTH IS REGENT-GO!
IN SEVENTH IS RENHI-GO!
AND WINGED EGG-GO IS IN EIGHTH!
WHO WILL GET THE THIRD BADGE AND GO ON TO WIN THE RACE?!

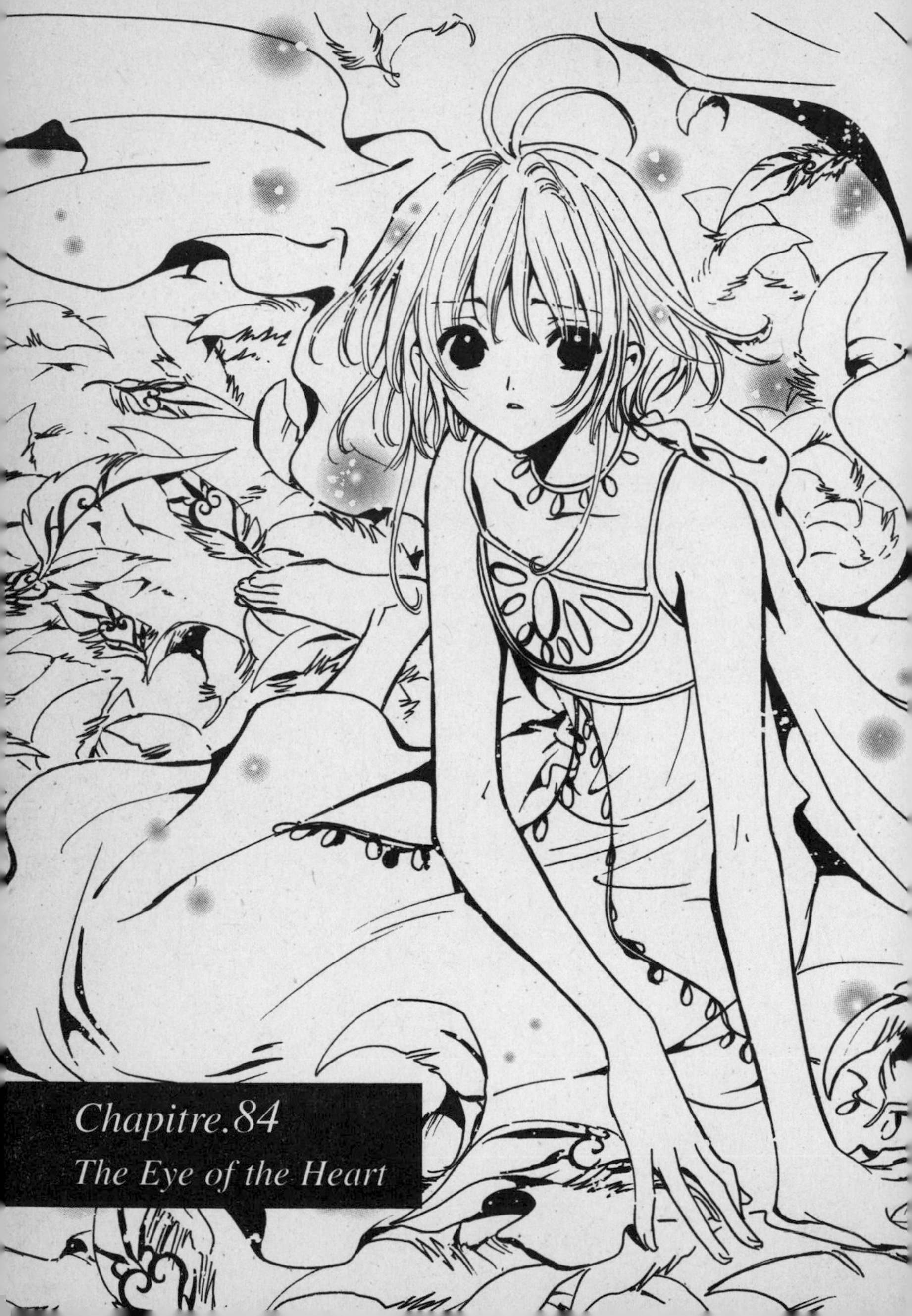
Chapitre.84
The Eye of the Heart

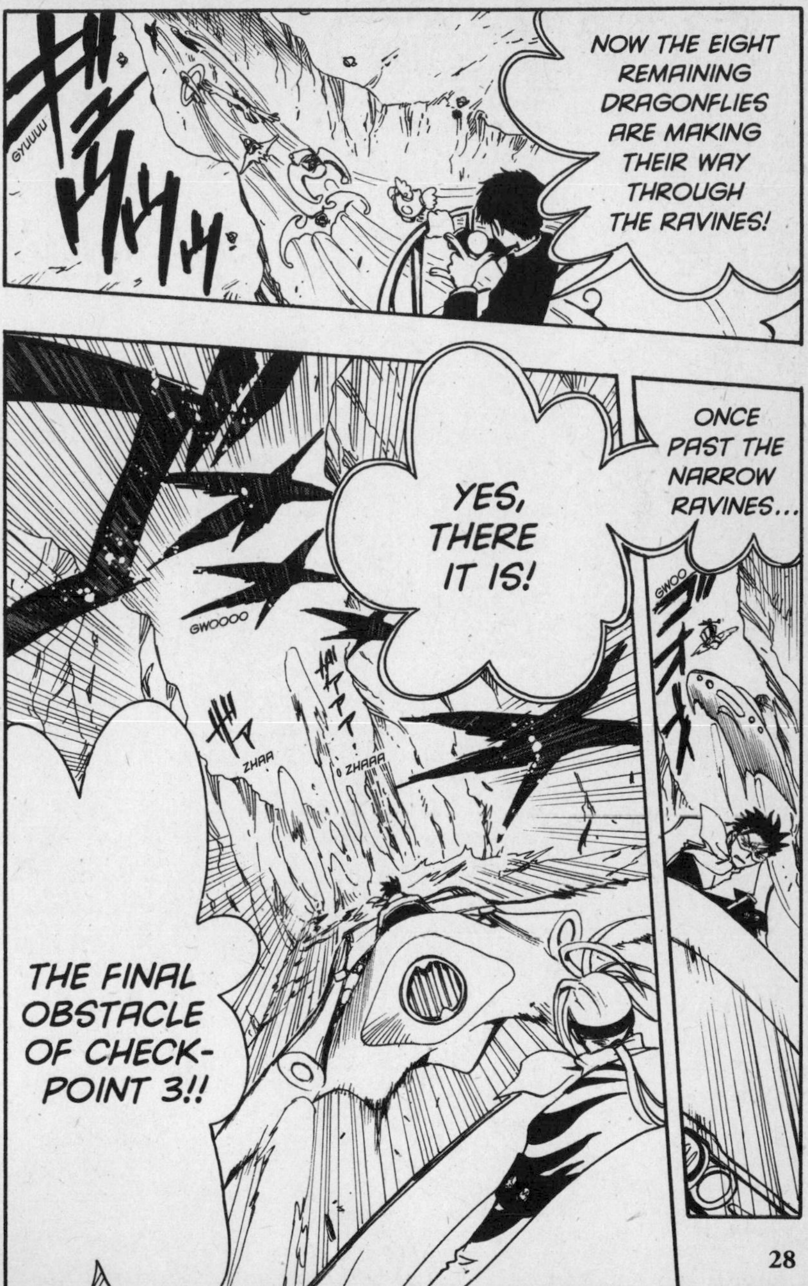
NOW THE EIGHT REMAINING DRAGONFLIES ARE MAKING THEIR WAY THROUGH THE RAVINES!
GYUUUU
ONCE PAST THE NARROW RAVINES...
GWOO
YES, THERE IT IS!
GWOOOO
ZHAAA
ZHAA
THE FINAL OBSTACLE OF CHECK-POINT 3!!

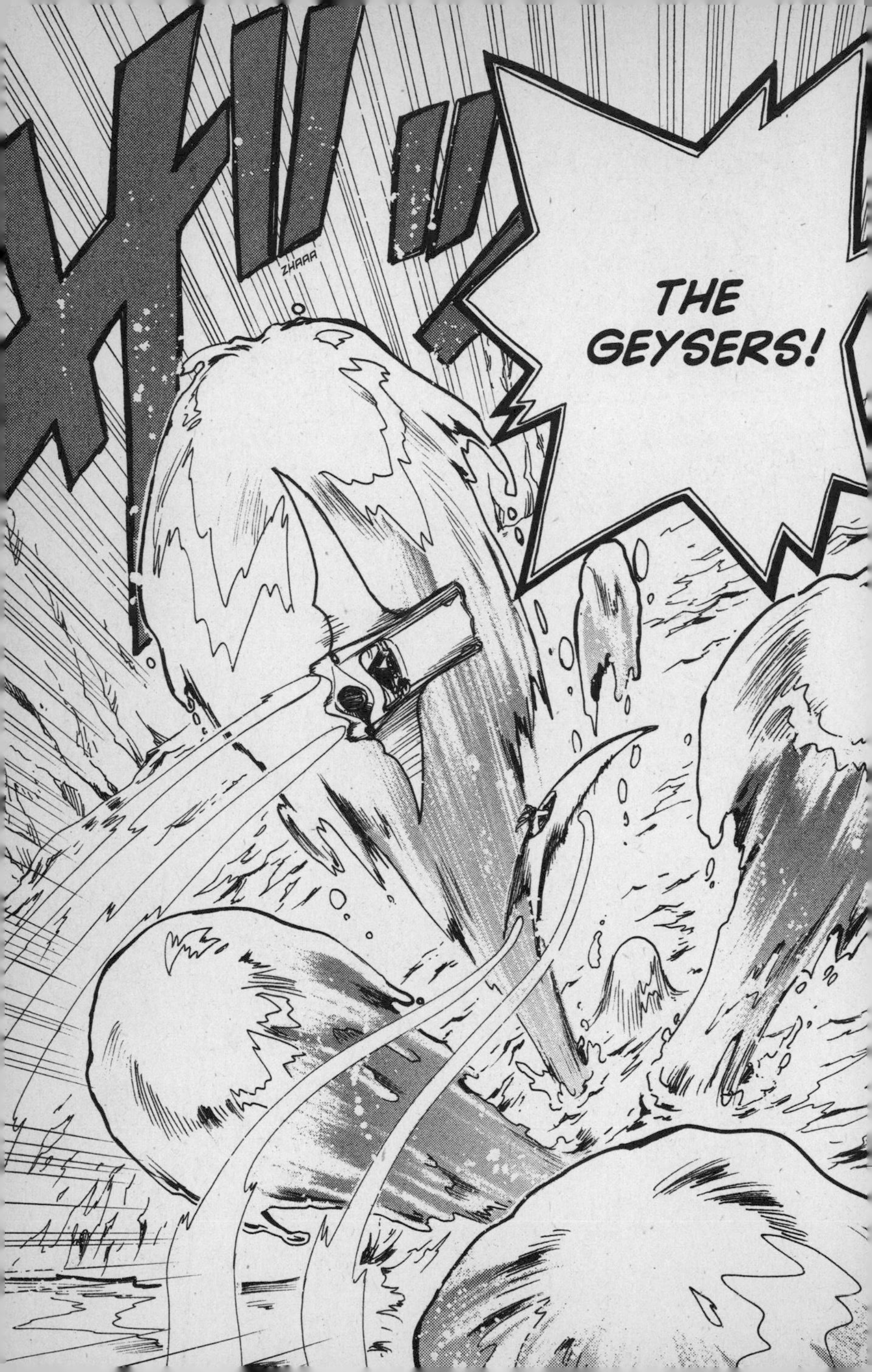
THE GEYSERS!
ZHAAA

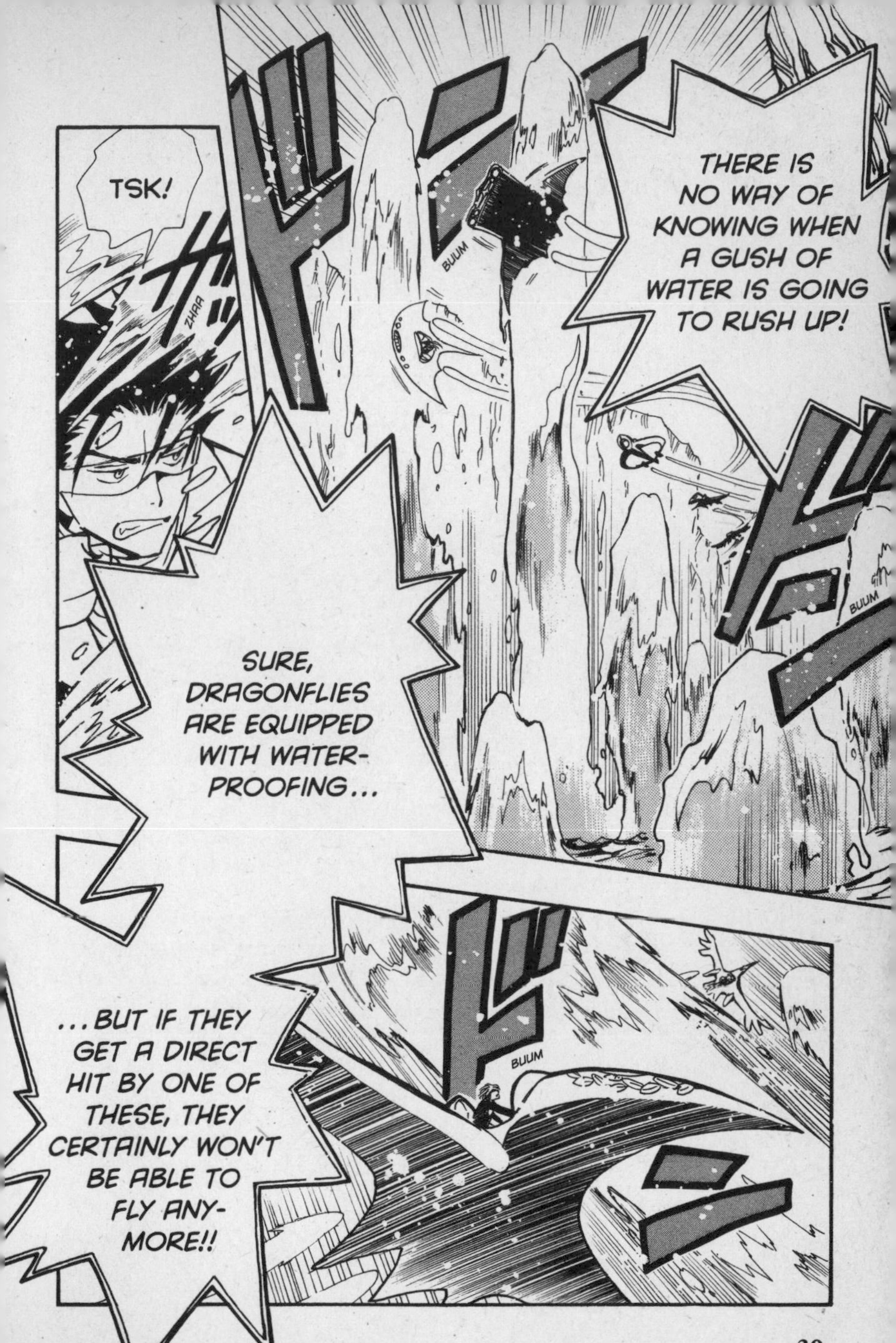
THERE IS NO WAY OF KNOWING WHEN A GUSH OF WATER IS GOING TO RUSH UP!
BUUM
BUUM
TSK!
ZHAA
SURE, DRAGONFLIES ARE EQUIPPED WITH WATER-PROOFING...
BUUM
...BUT IF THEY GET A DIRECT HIT BY ONE OF THESE, THEY CERTAINLY WON'T BE ABLE TO FLY ANY-MORE!!

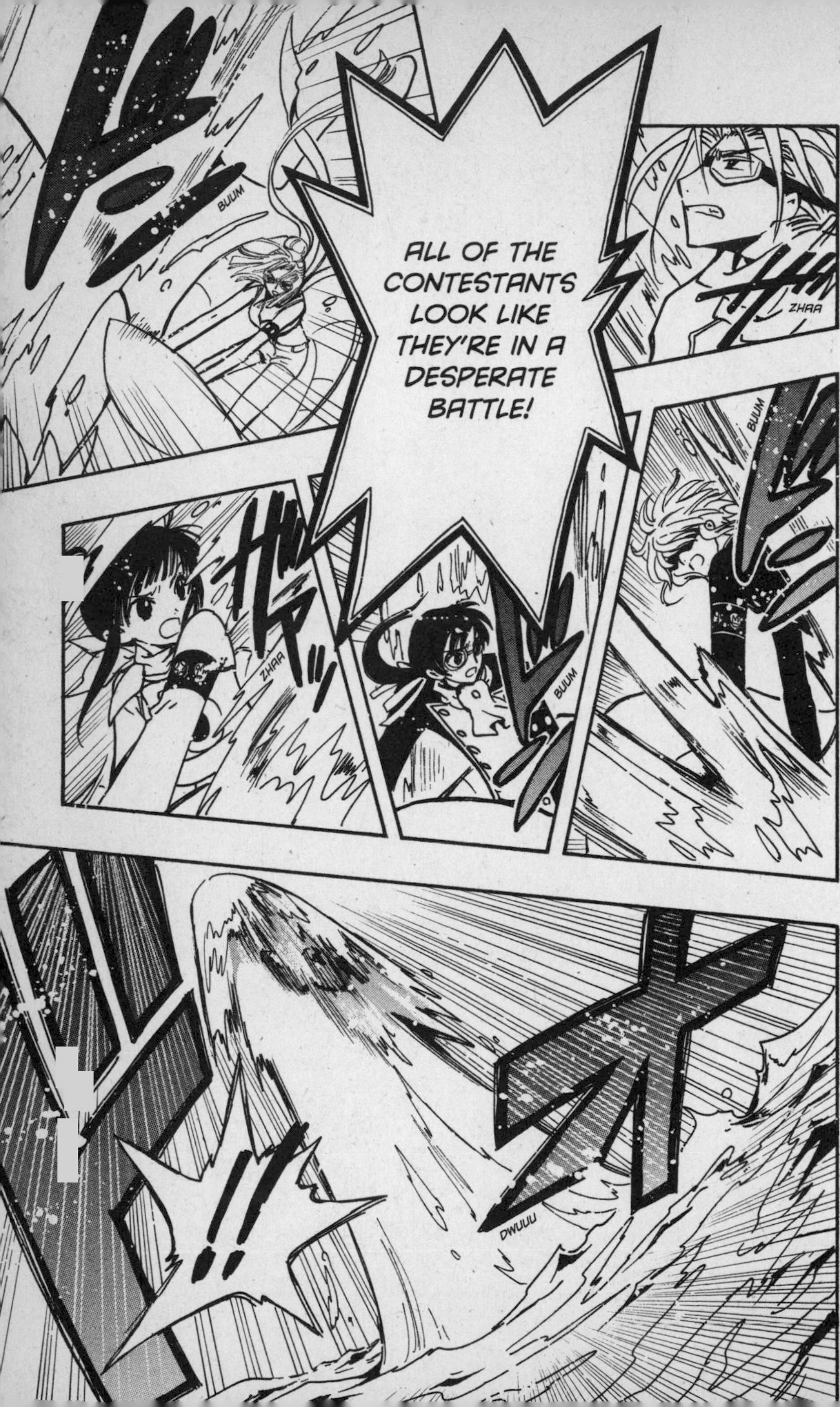
ZHAA
ALL OF THE CONTESTANTS LOOK LIKE THEY'RE IN A DESPERATE BATTLE!
BUUM
BUUM
BUUM
ZHAA
DWUUU
!!

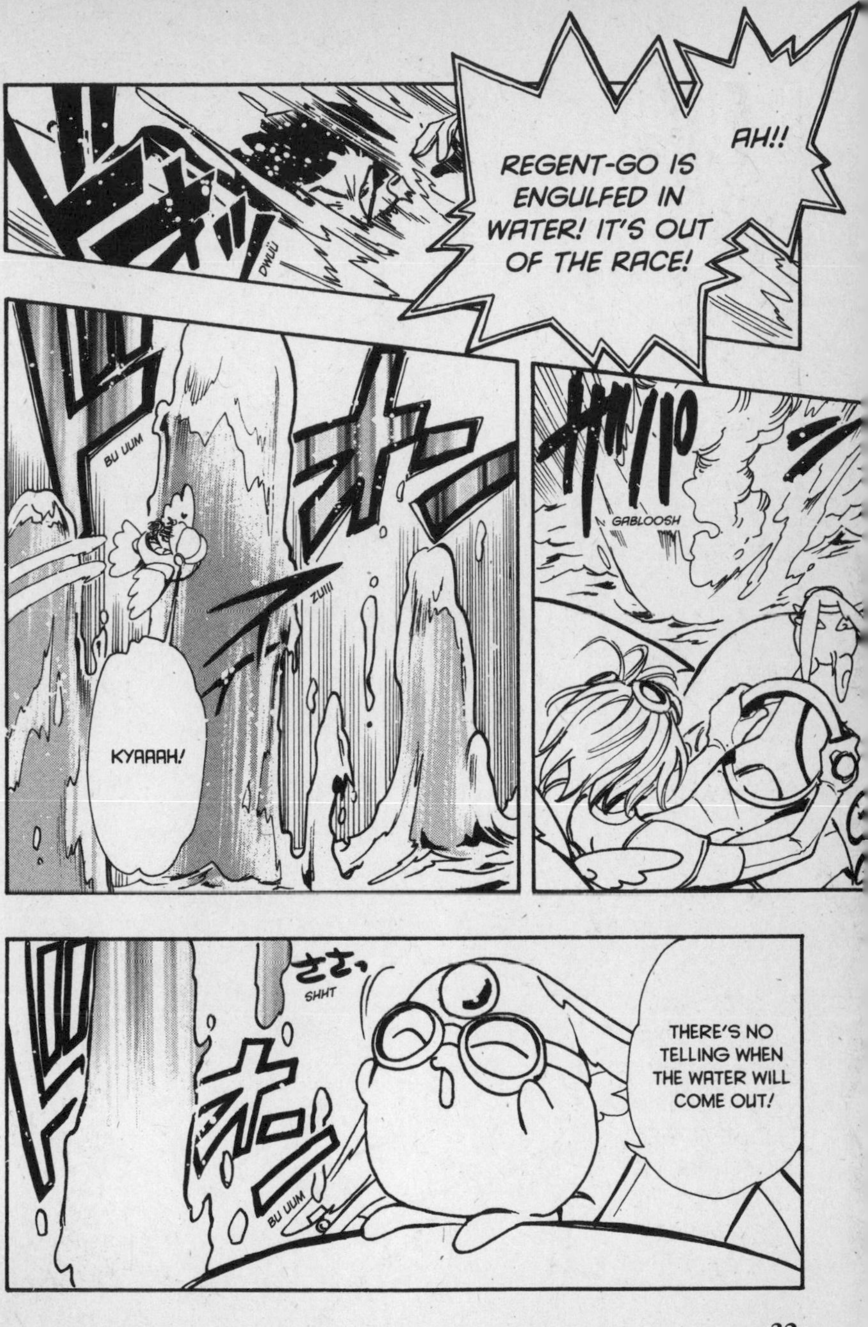
AH!!
REGENT-GO IS ENGULFED IN WATER! IT'S OUT OF THE RACE!
DWUÜ
GABLOOSH
BU UUM
ZUIII
KYAAAH!
SHHT
THERE'S NO TELLING WHEN THE WATER WILL COME OUT!
BU UUM

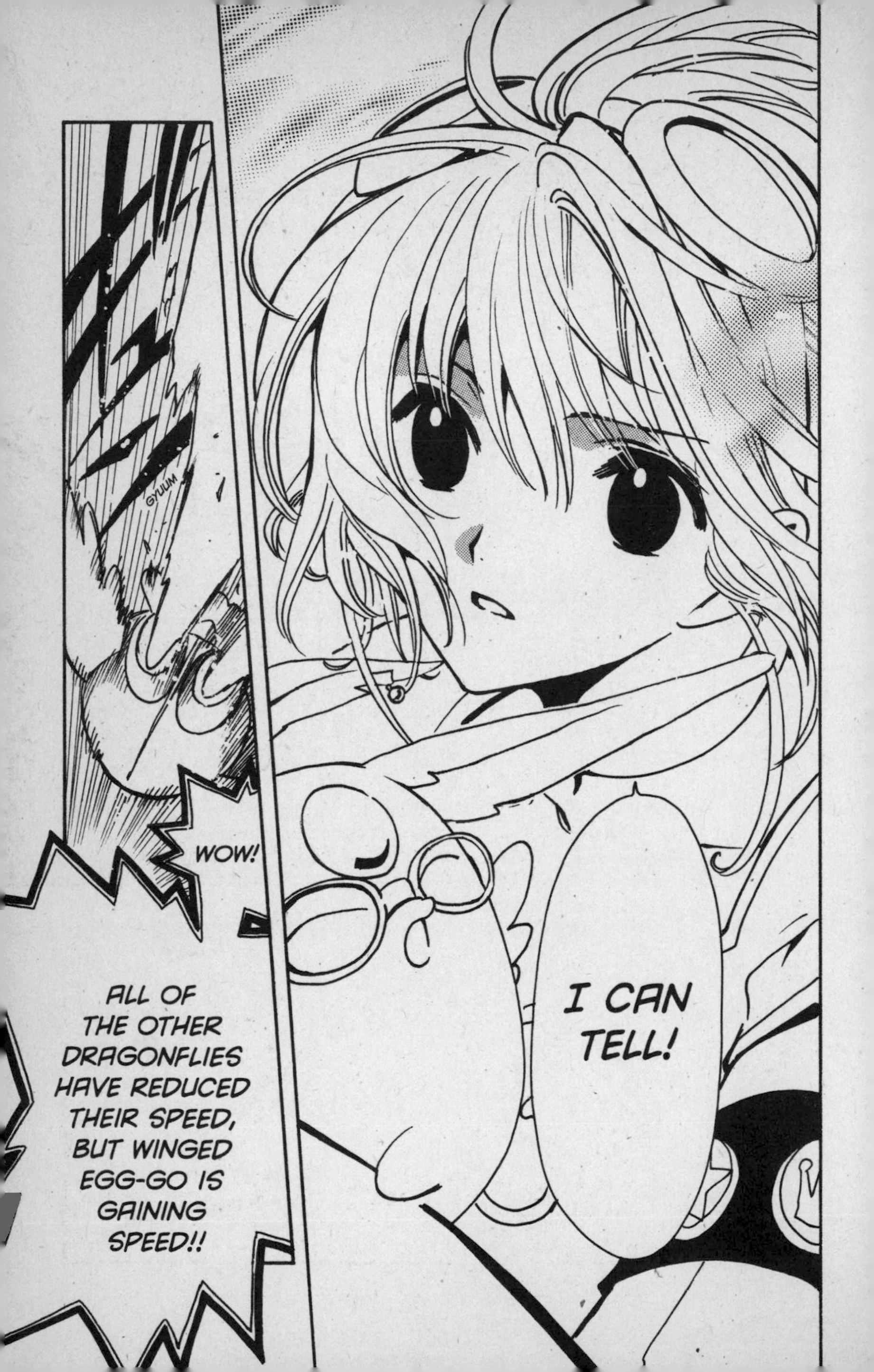
I CAN TELL!
GYUUM
WOW!
ALL OF THE OTHER DRAGONFLIES HAVE REDUCED THEIR SPEED, BUT WINGED EGG-GO IS GAINING SPEED!!

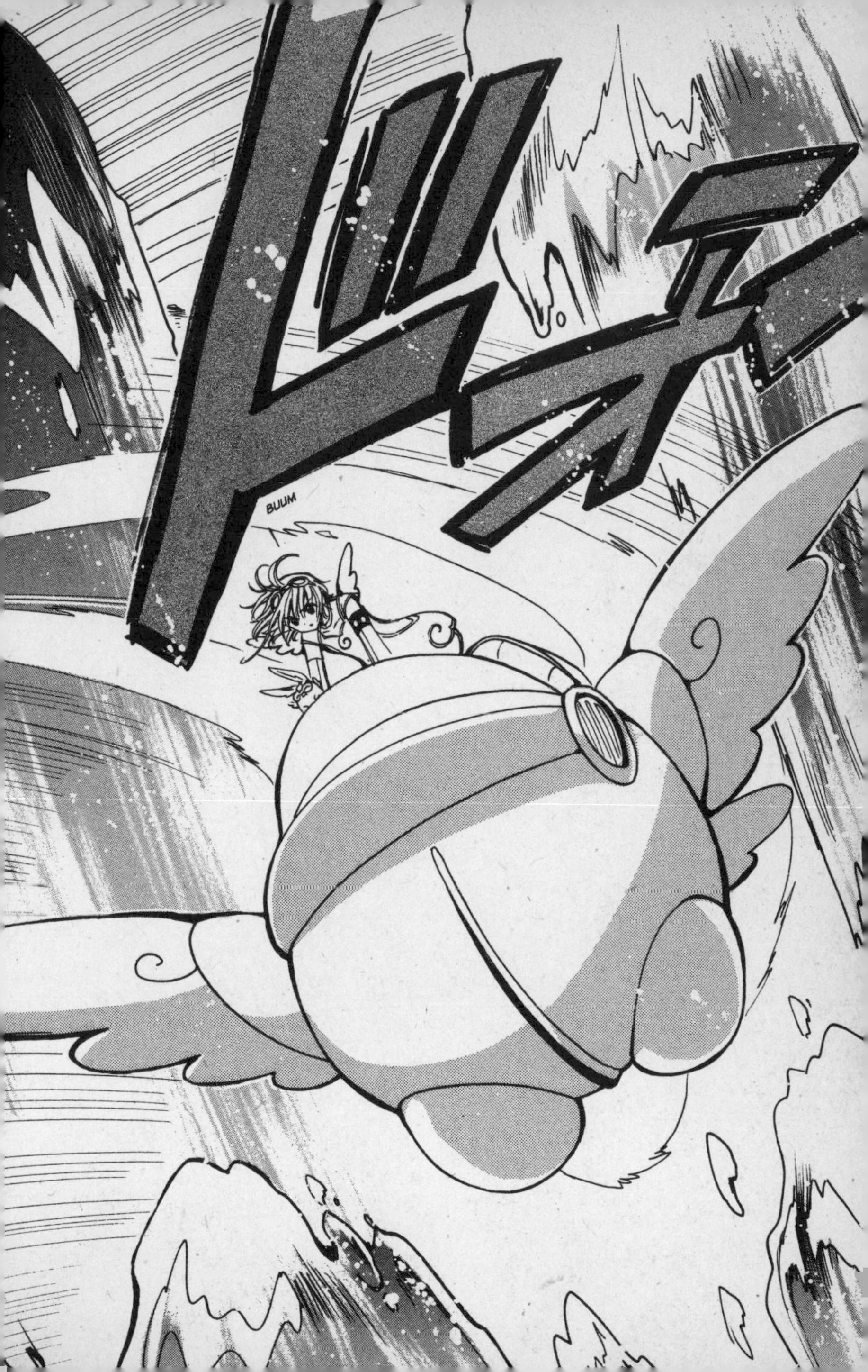
BUUM

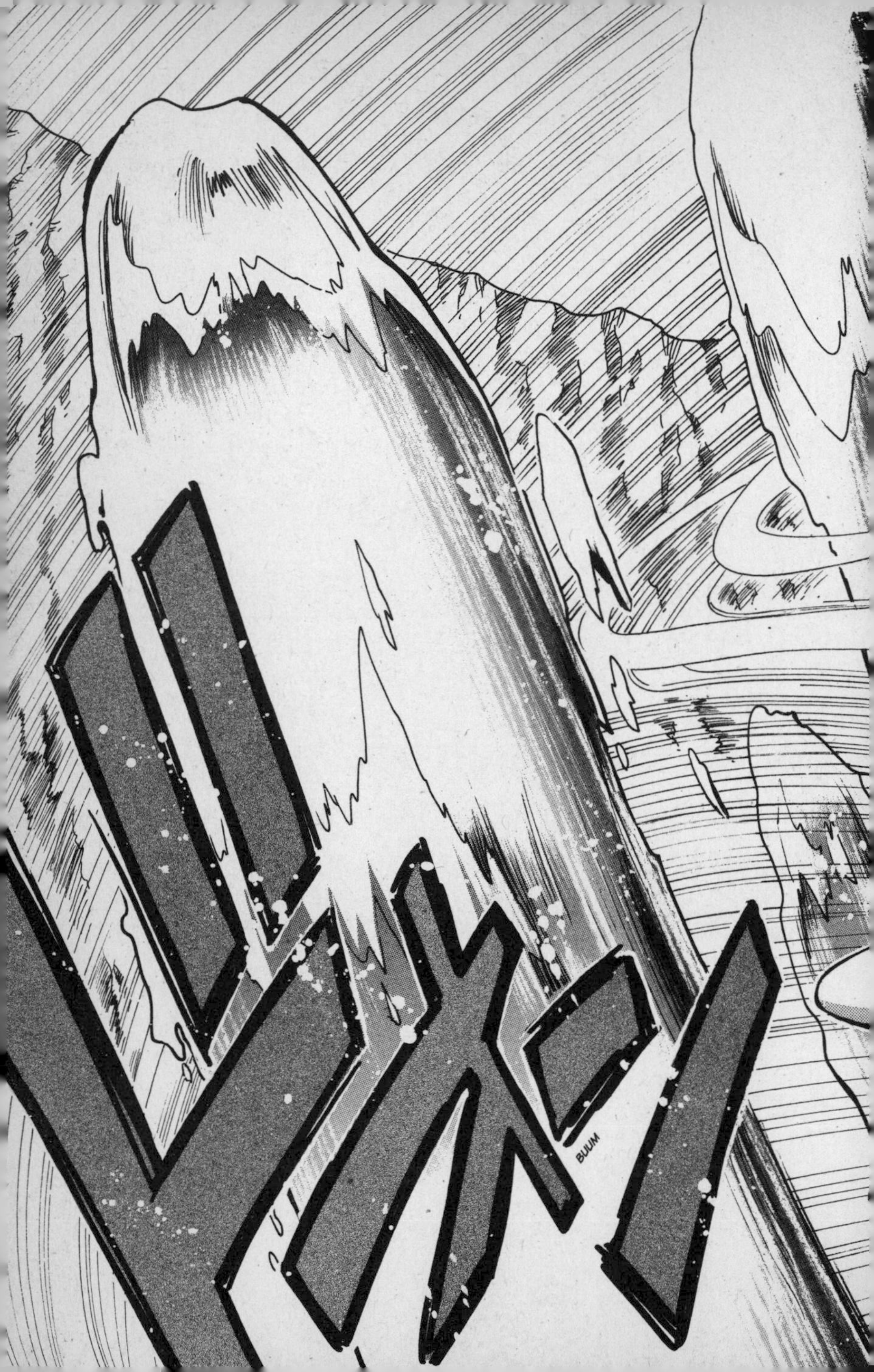
BUUM

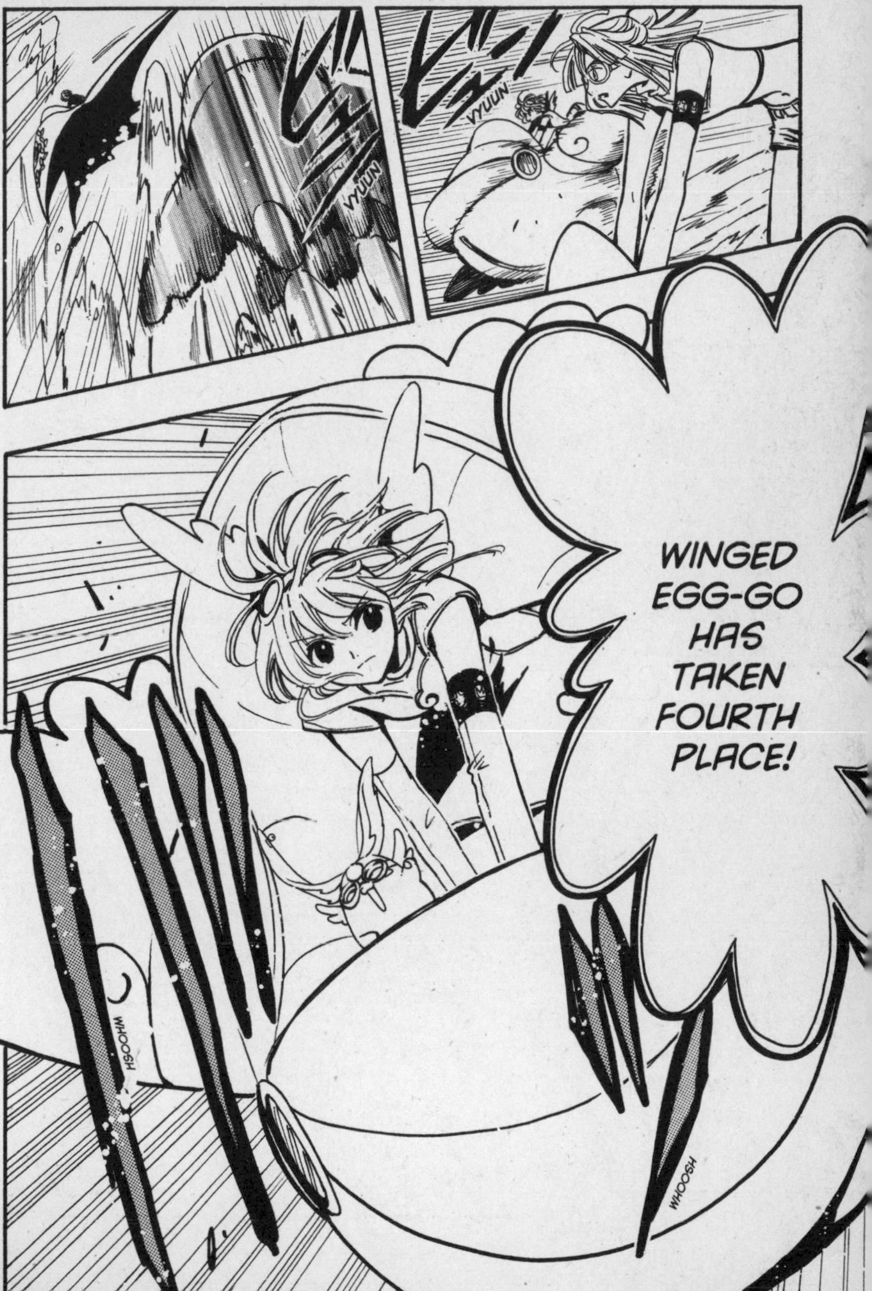
VYUUN
VYUUN
WINGED EGG-GO HAS TAKEN FOURTH PLACE!
WHOOSH
WHOOSH

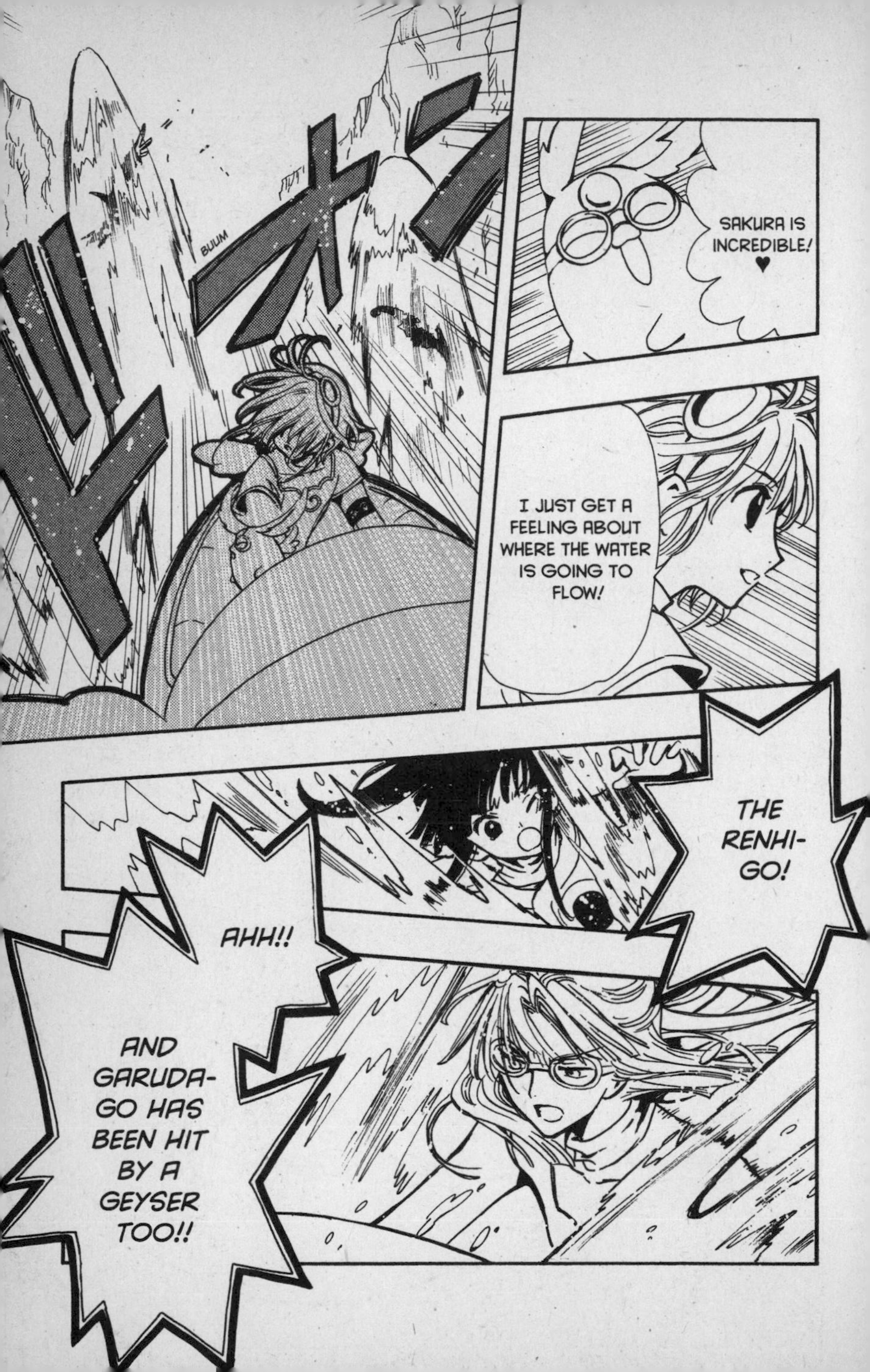
SAKURA IS INCREDIBLE! ♥
I JUST GET A FEELING ABOUT WHERE THE WATER IS GOING TO FLOW!
BUUM
THE RENHI-GO!
AHH!!
AND GARUDA-GO HAS BEEN HIT BY A GEYSER TOO!!

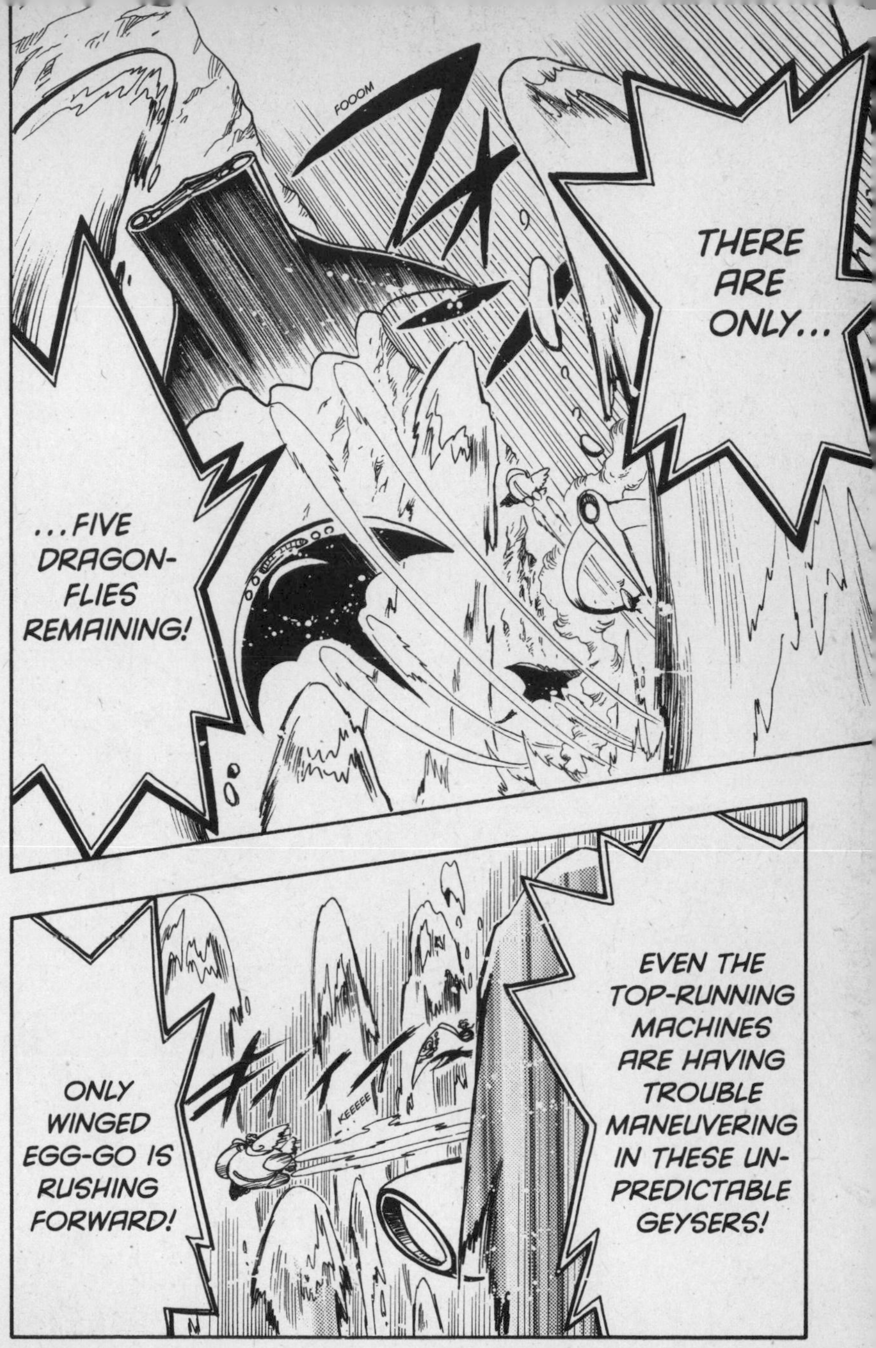
FOOOM
THERE ARE ONLY...
...FIVE DRAGON-FLIES REMAINING!
EVEN THE TOP-RUNNING MACHINES ARE HAVING TROUBLE MANEUVERING IN THESE UN-PREDICTABLE GEYSERS!
KEEEEE
ONLY WINGED EGG-GO IS RUSHING FORWARD!

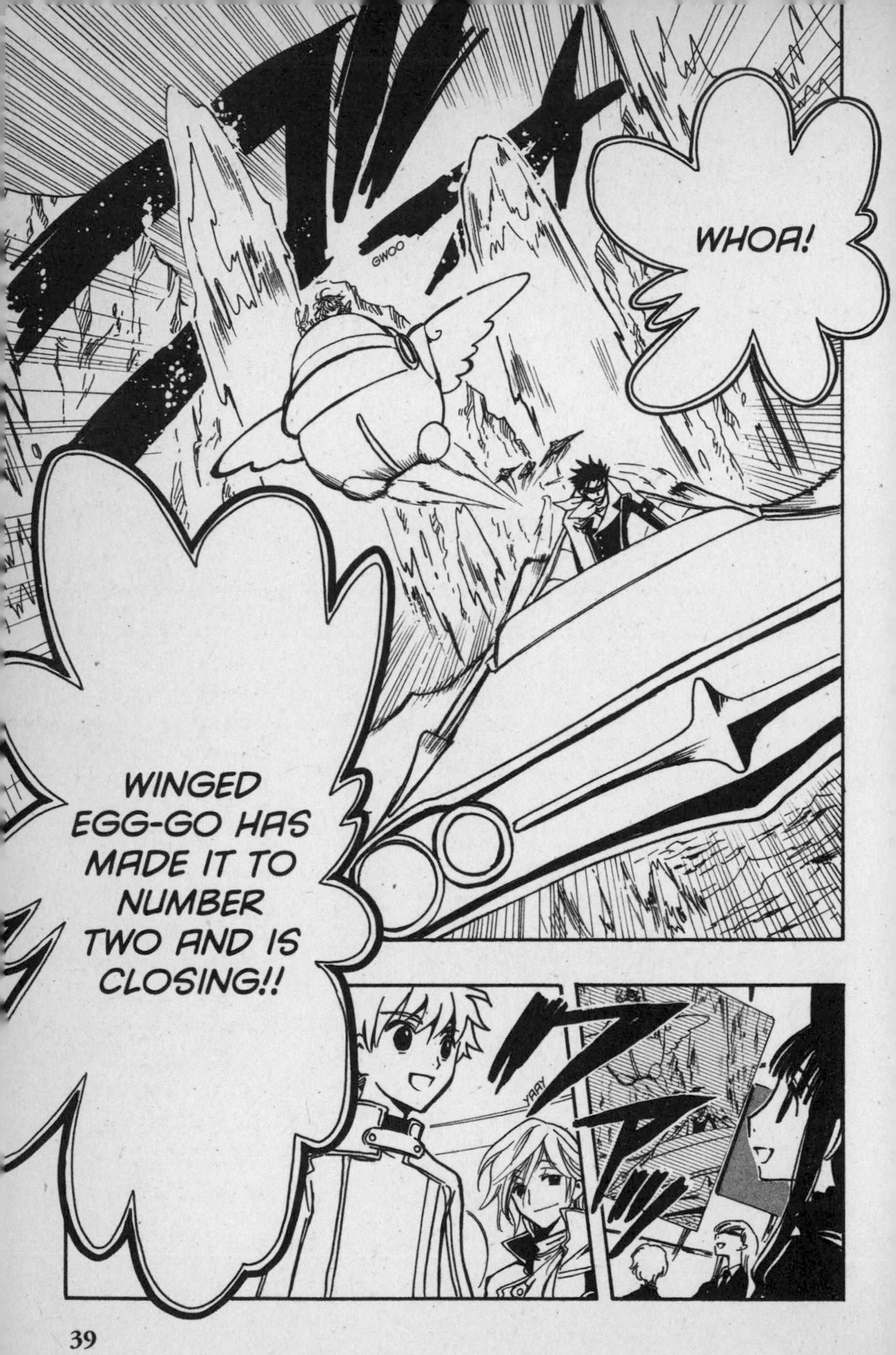
WHOA!
GWOO
WINGED EGG-GO HAS MADE IT TO NUMBER TWO AND IS CLOSING!!
YAAY

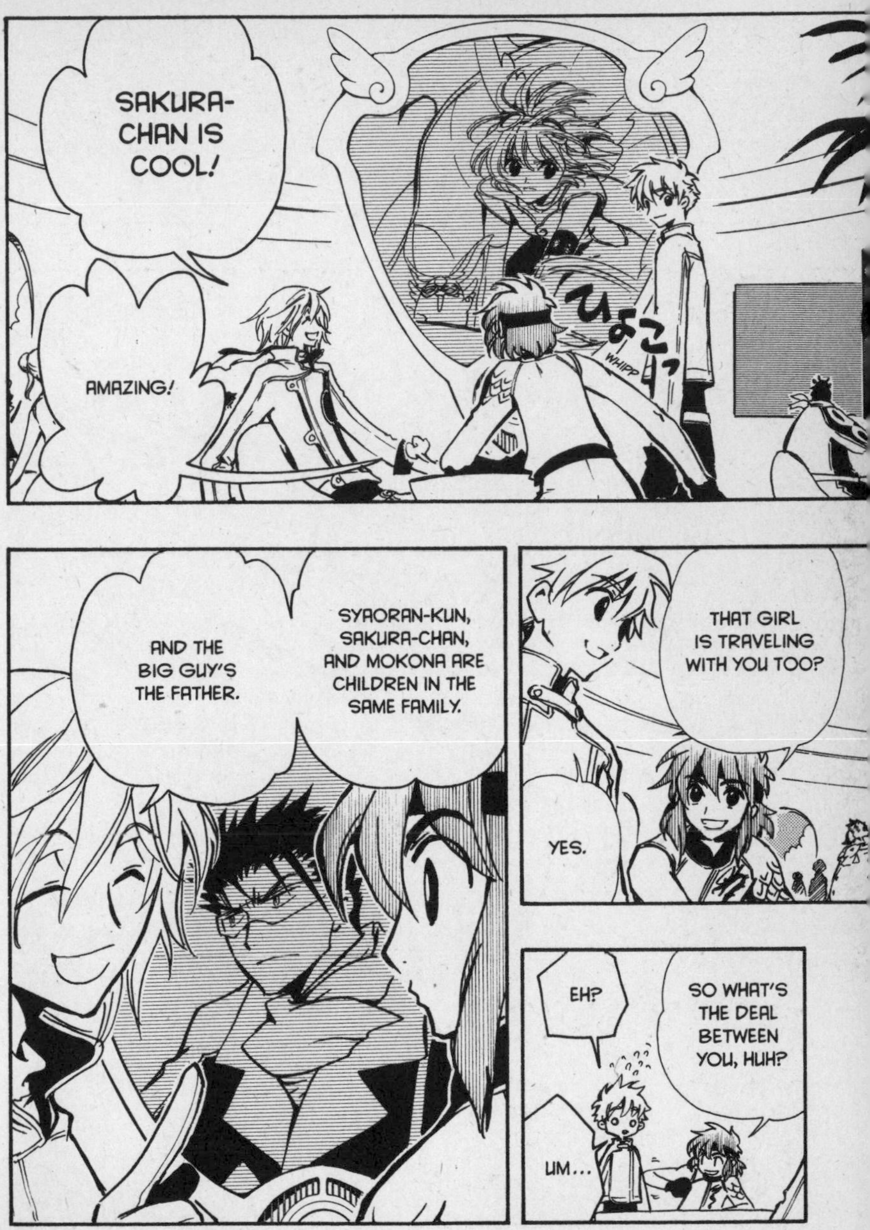
SAKURA-CHAN IS COOL!
AMAZING!
ひょこっ
WHIPP
THAT GIRL IS TRAVELING WITH YOU TOO?
YES.
SO WHAT'S THE DEAL BETWEEN YOU, HUH?
EH?
UM...
SYAORAN-KUN, SAKURA-CHAN, AND MOKONA ARE CHILDREN IN THE SAME FAMILY.
AND THE BIG GUY'S THE FATHER.

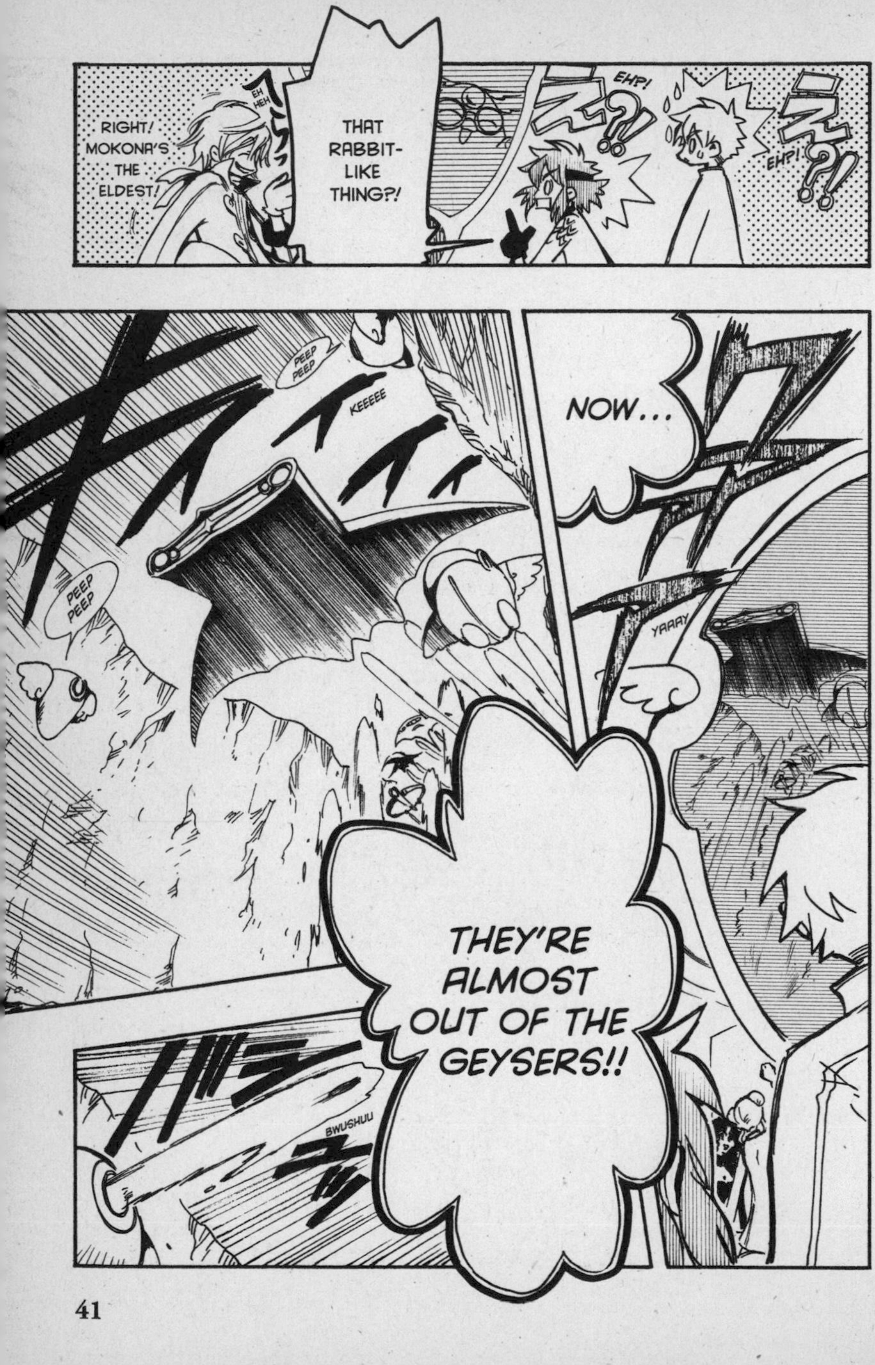
EH?!
EH?!
THAT RABBIT-LIKE THING?!
EH HEH
RIGHT! MOKONA'S THE ELDEST!
NOW...
YAAAY
THEY'RE ALMOST OUT OF THE GEYSERS!!
PEEP PEEP
KEEEEE
PEEP PEEP
BWUSHUU

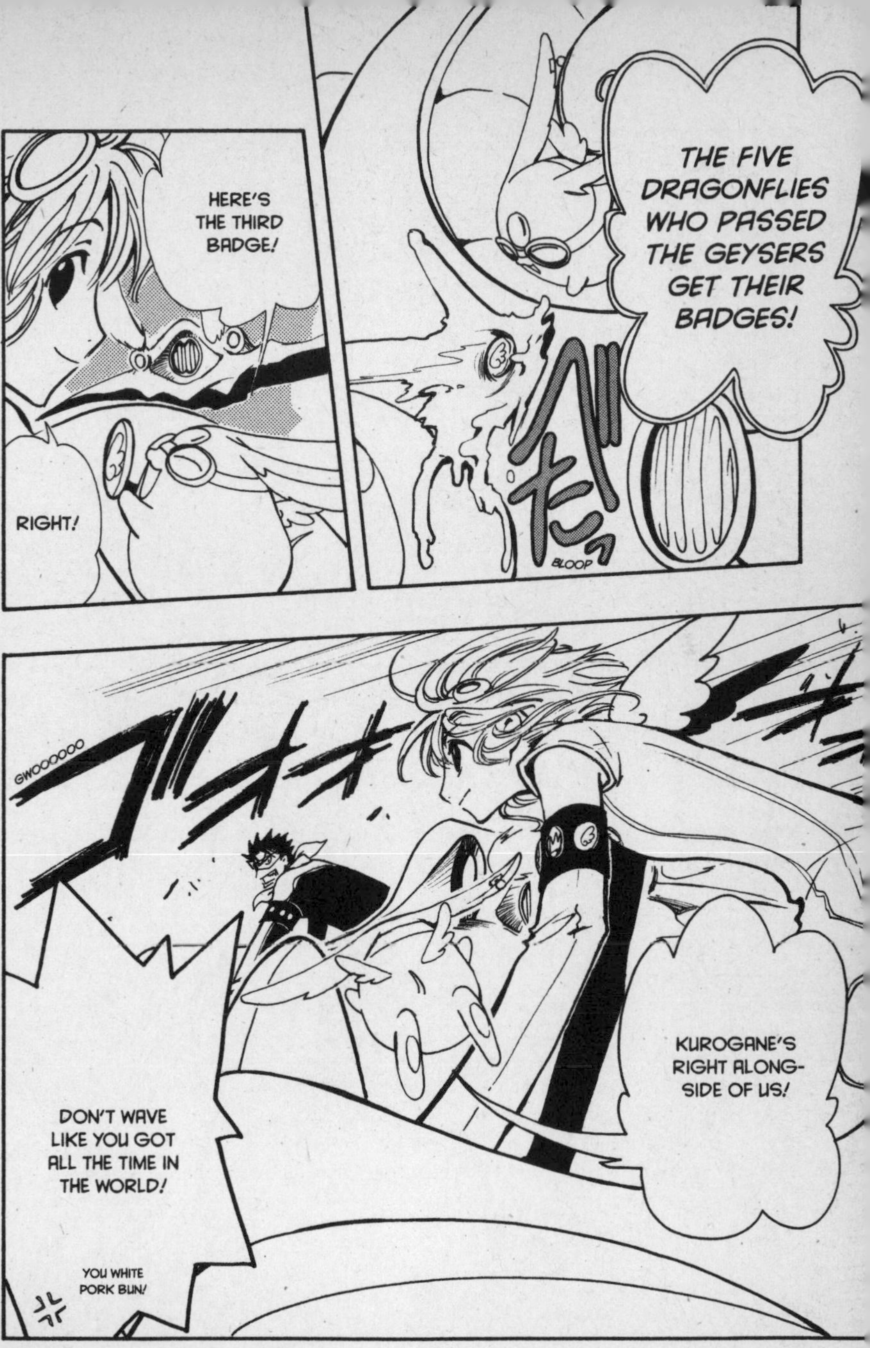
THE FIVE DRAGONFLIES WHO PASSED THE GEYSERS GET THEIR BADGES!
BLOOP
HERE'S THE THIRD BADGE!
RIGHT!
KUROGANE'S RIGHT ALONG-SIDE OF US!
GWOOOOOO
DON'T WAVE LIKE YOU GOT ALL THE TIME IN THE WORLD!
YOU WHITE PORK BUN!

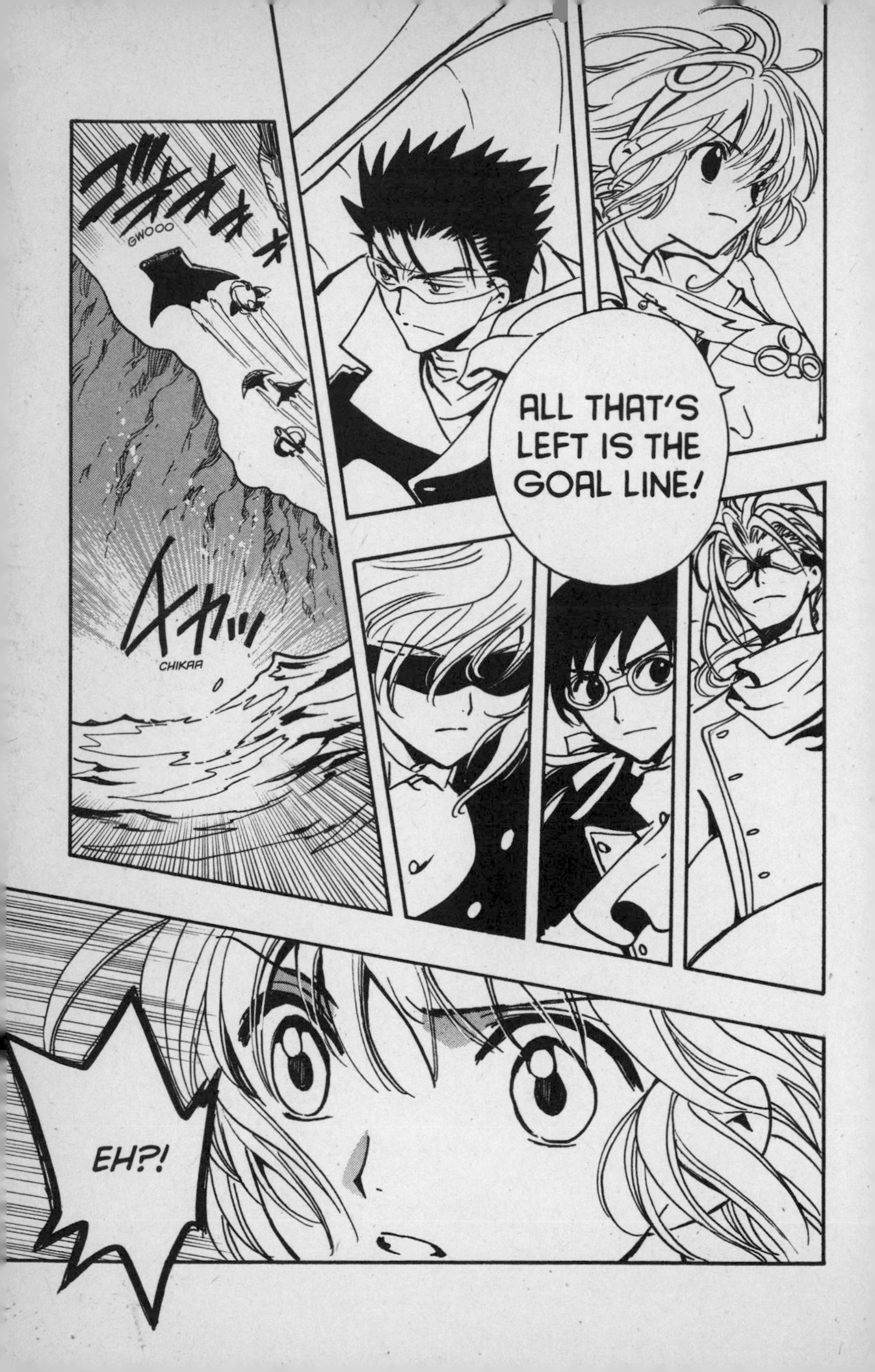
ALL THAT'S LEFT IS THE GOAL LINE!
GWOOO
CHIKAA
EH?!

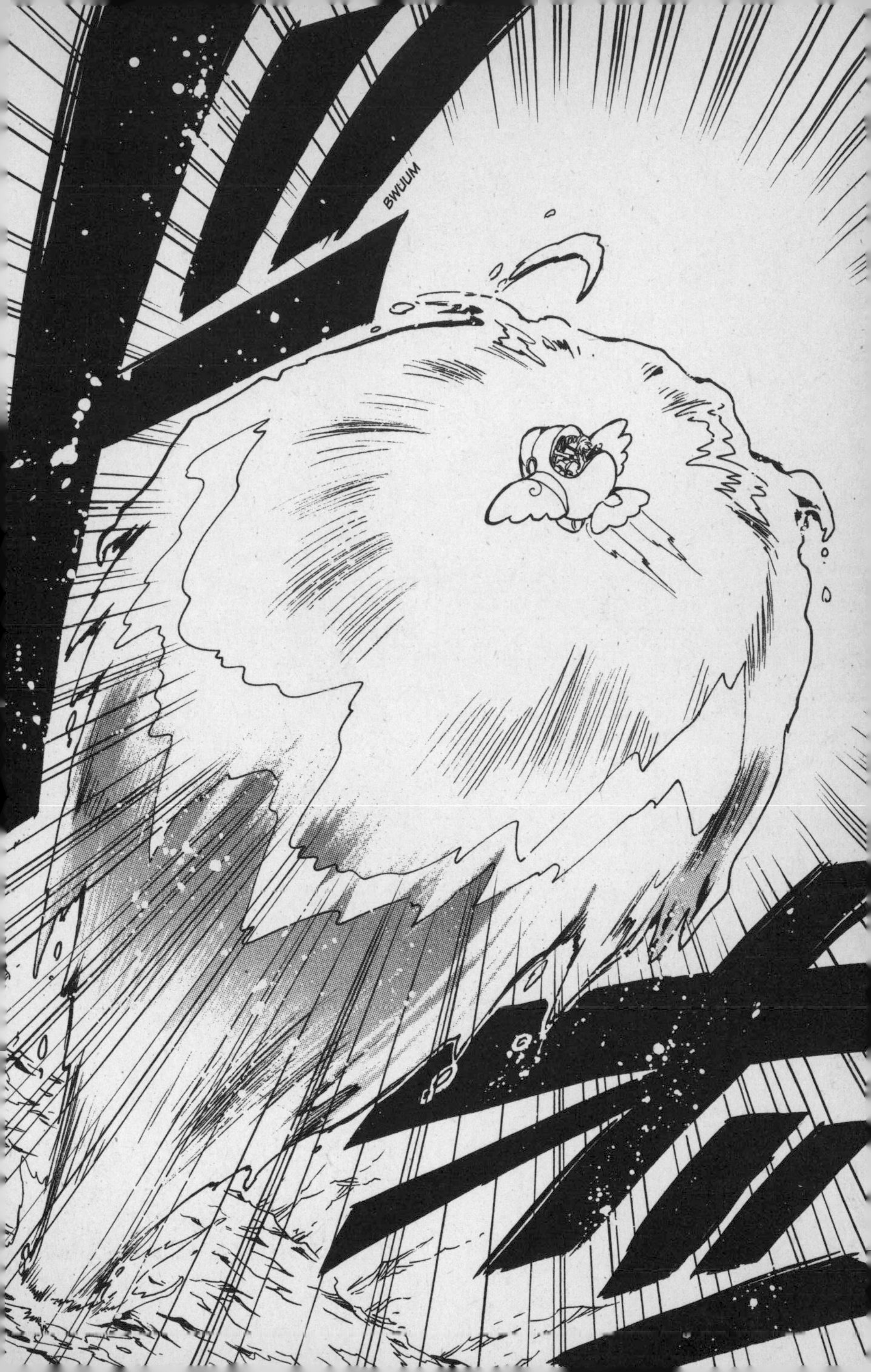
BWUUM

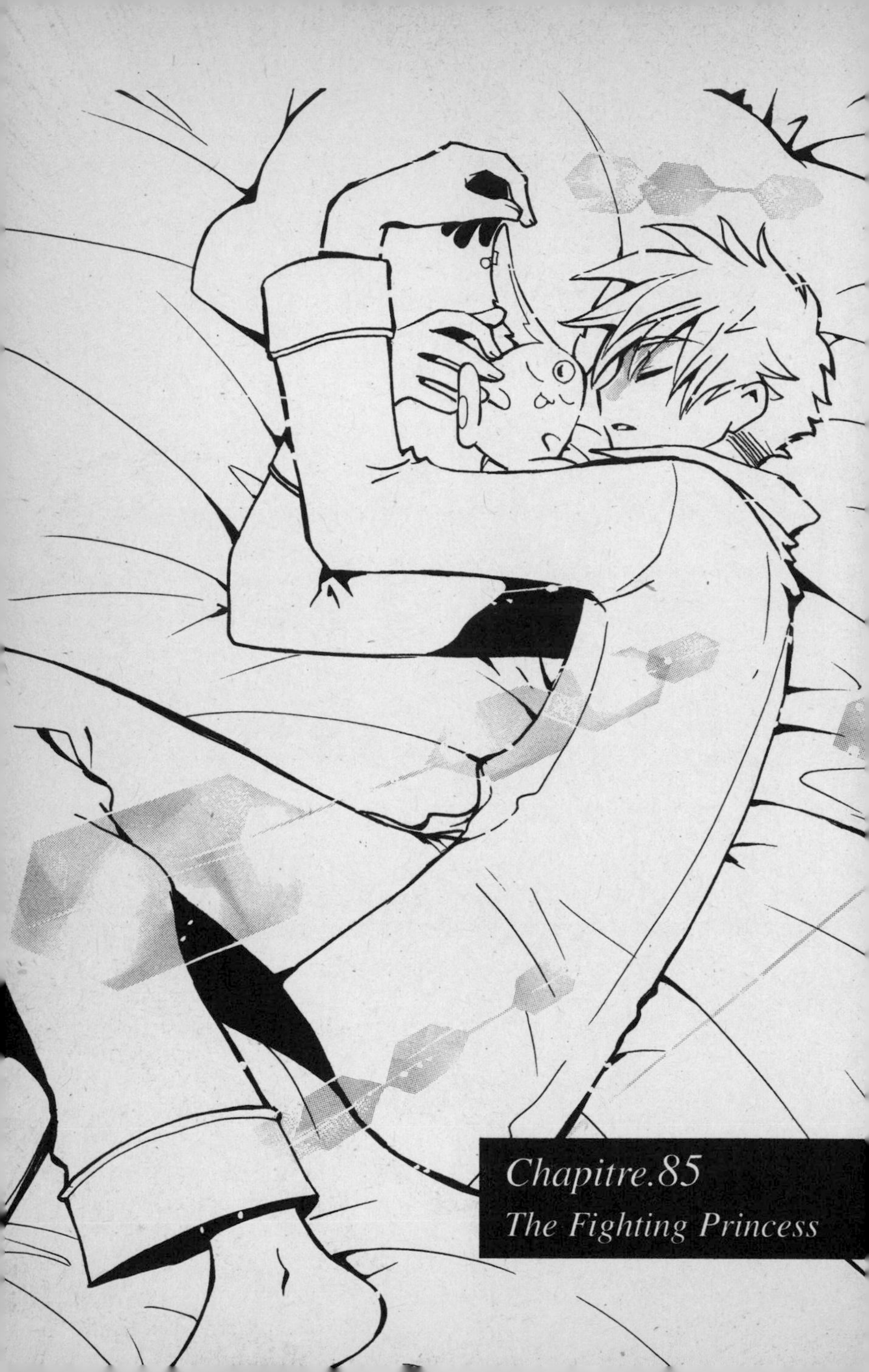

Chapitre.85
The Fighting Princess

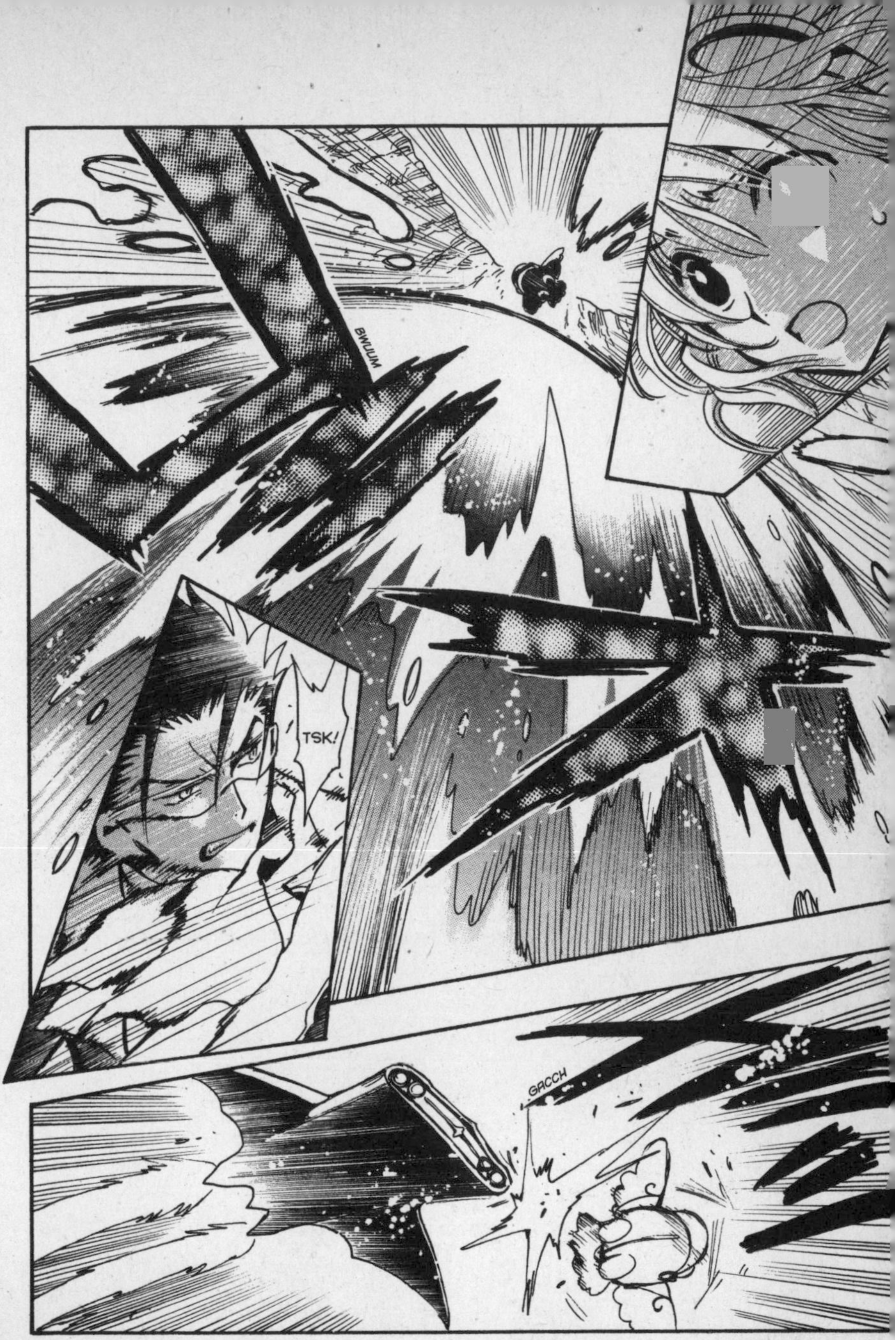
BWUUM
TSK!
GACCH

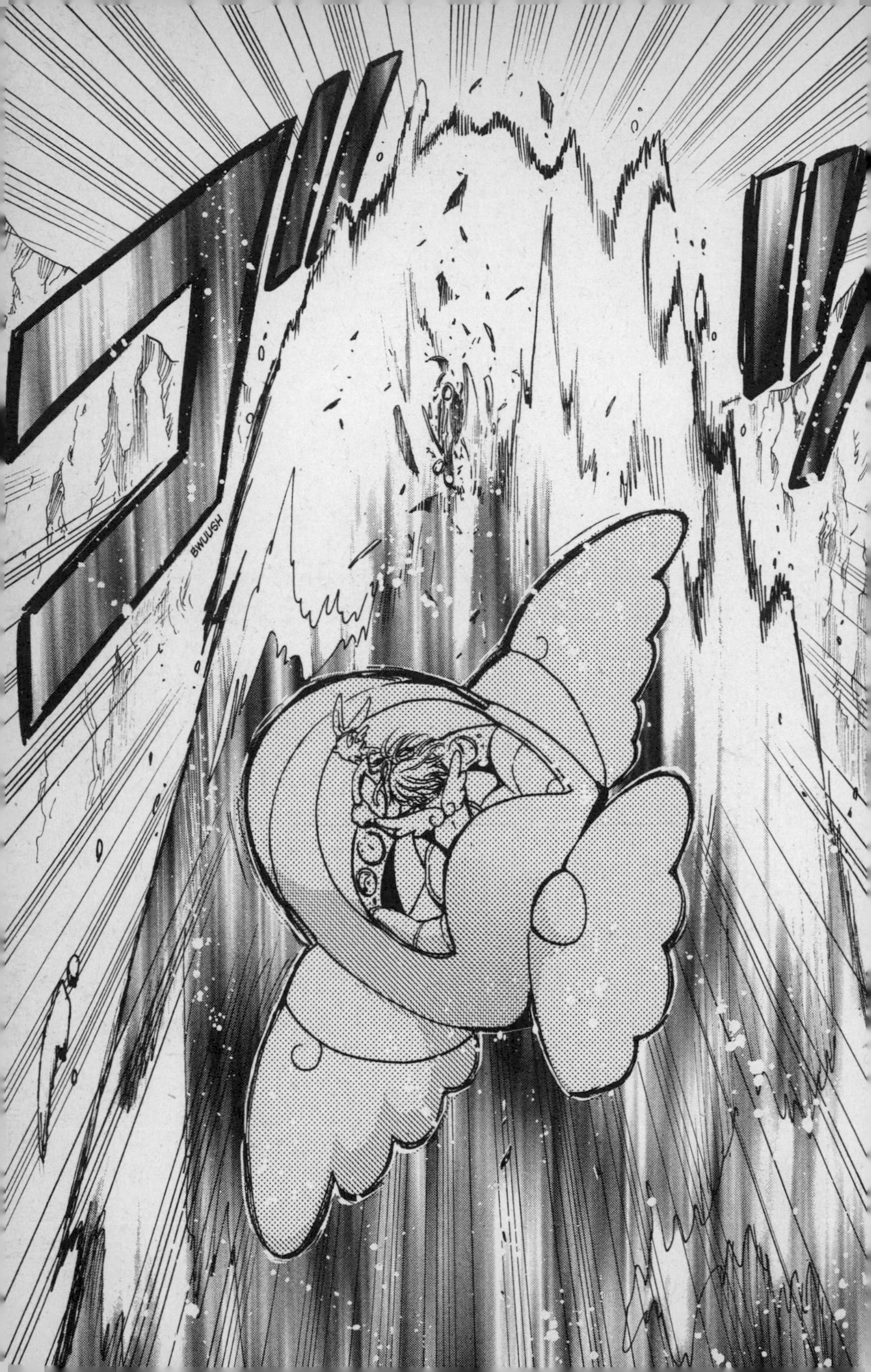
BWUUSH

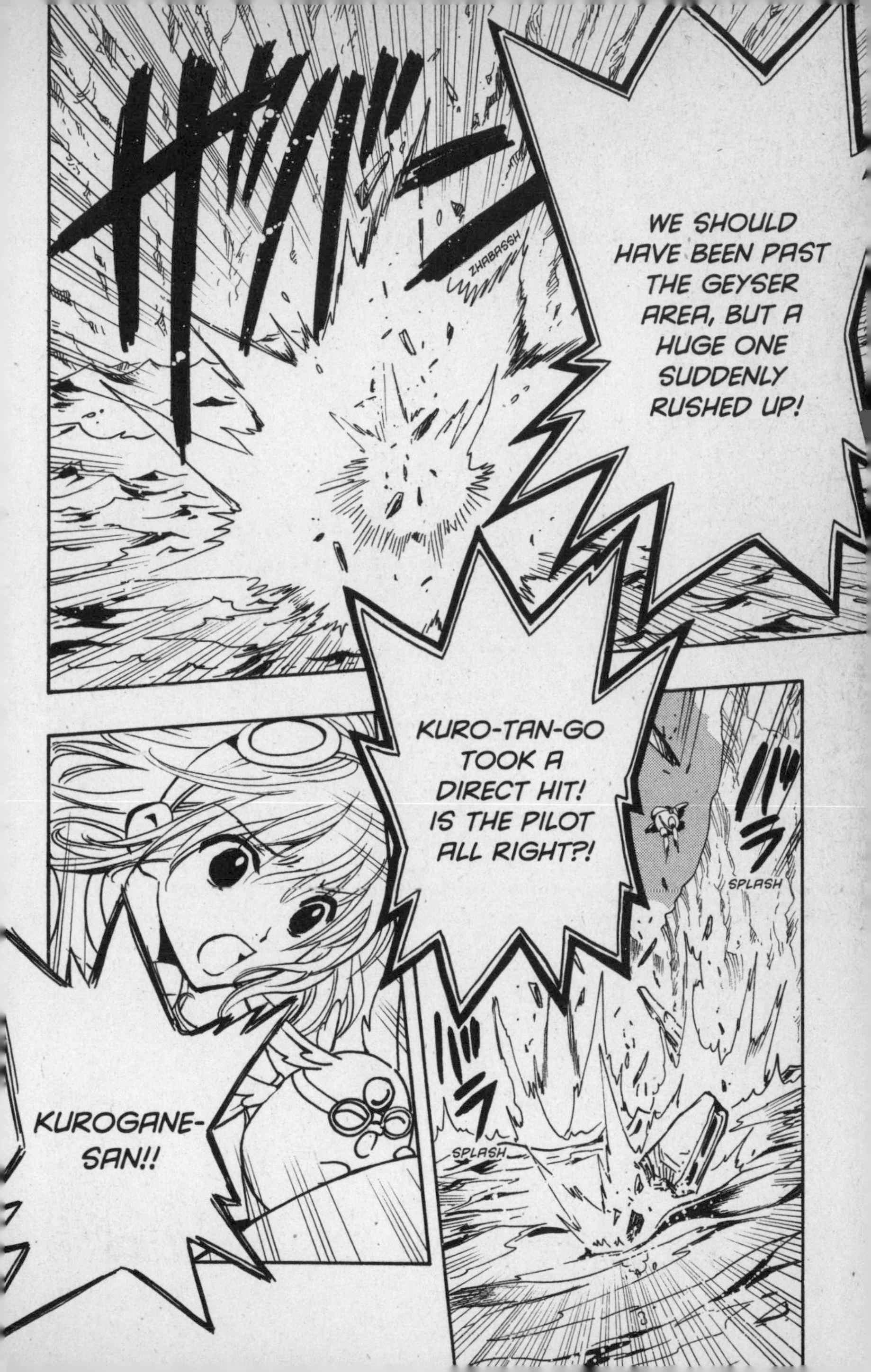
ZHABASSH
WE SHOULD HAVE BEEN PAST THE GEYSER AREA, BUT A HUGE ONE SUDDENLY RUSHED UP!
KURO-TAN-GO TOOK A DIRECT HIT! IS THE PILOT ALL RIGHT?!
SPLASH
SPLASH
KUROGANE-SAN!!

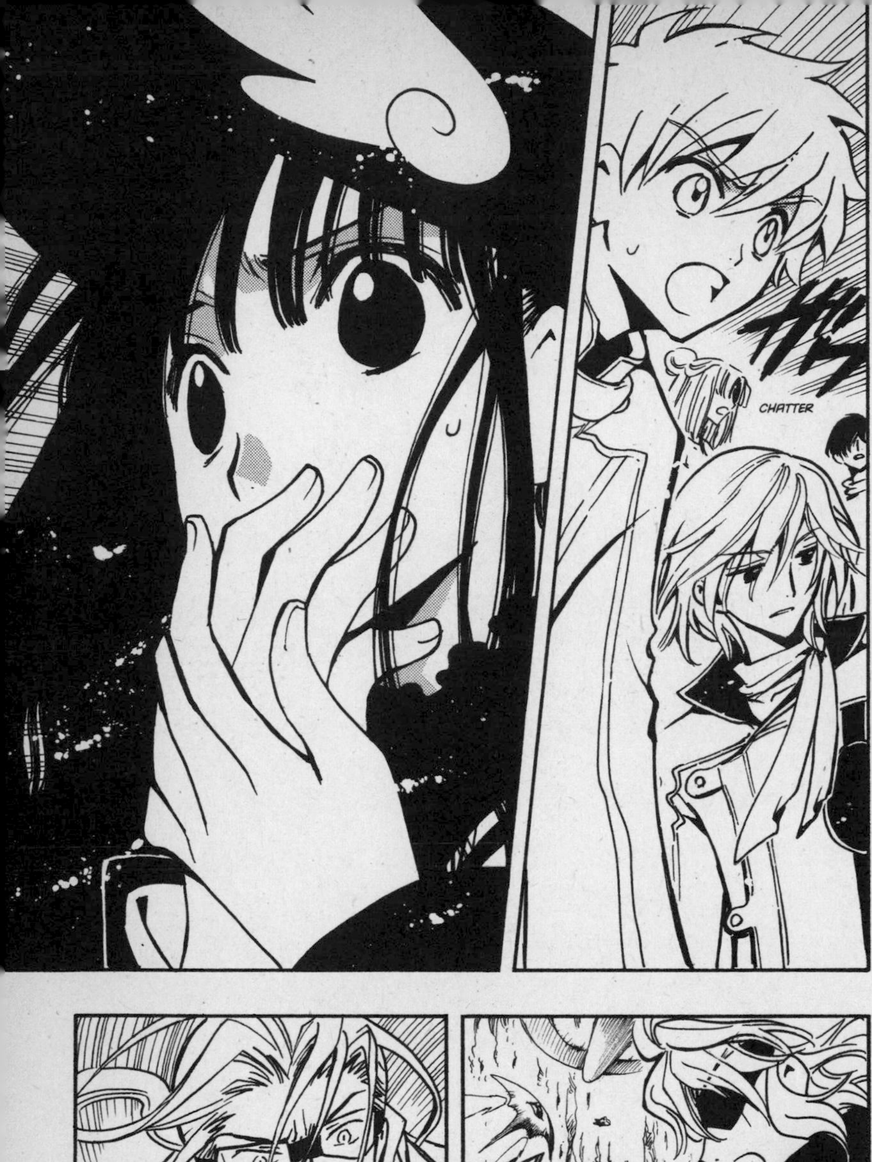
CHATTER
?!

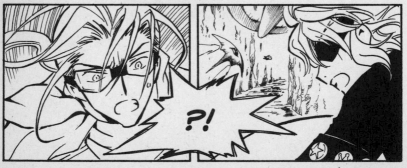

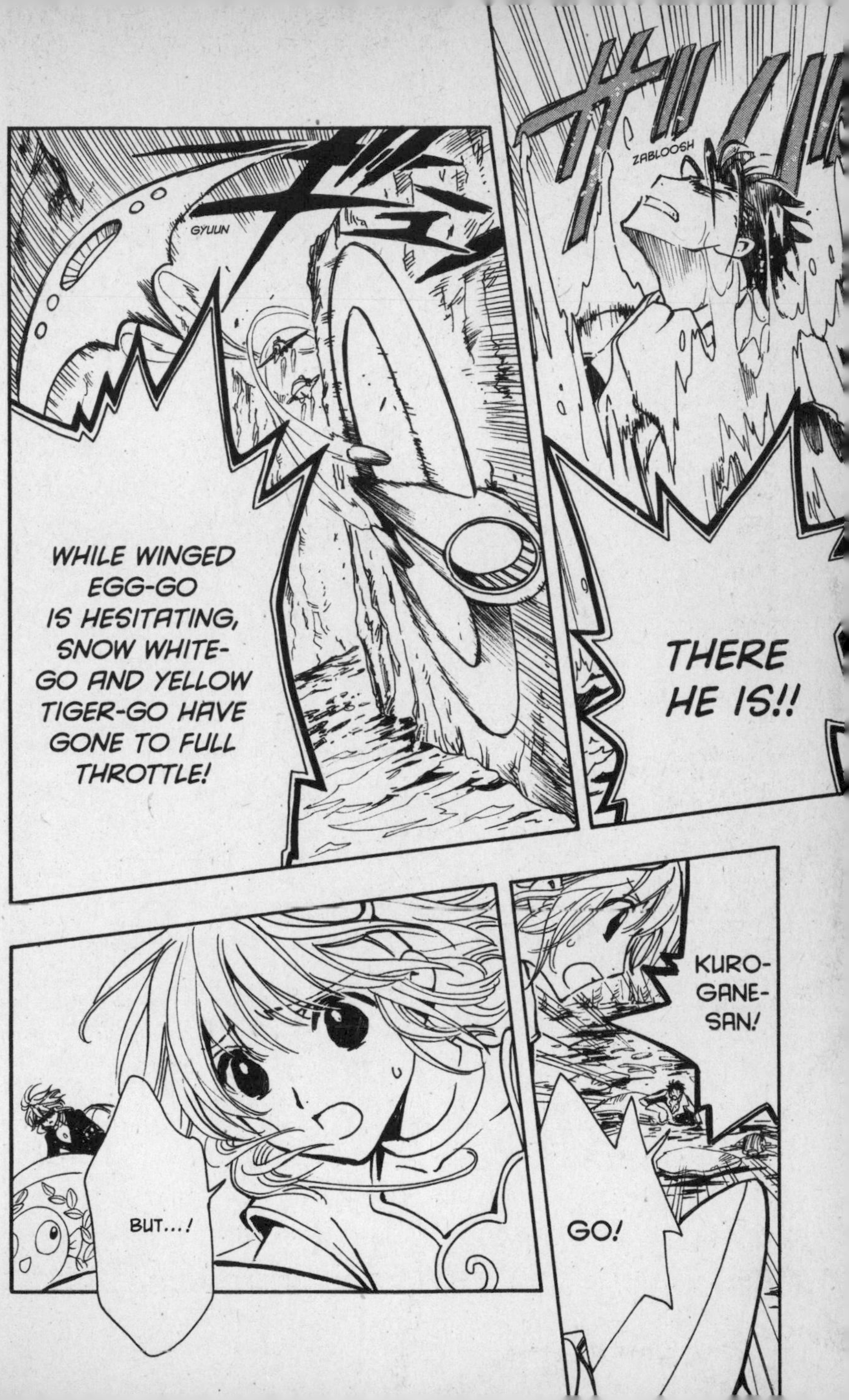
ZABLOOSH
THERE HE IS!!
GYUUN
WHILE WINGED EGG-GO IS HESITATING, SNOW WHITE-GO AND YELLOW TIGER-GO HAVE GONE TO FULL THROTTLE!
KURO-GANE-SAN!
GO!
BUT...!

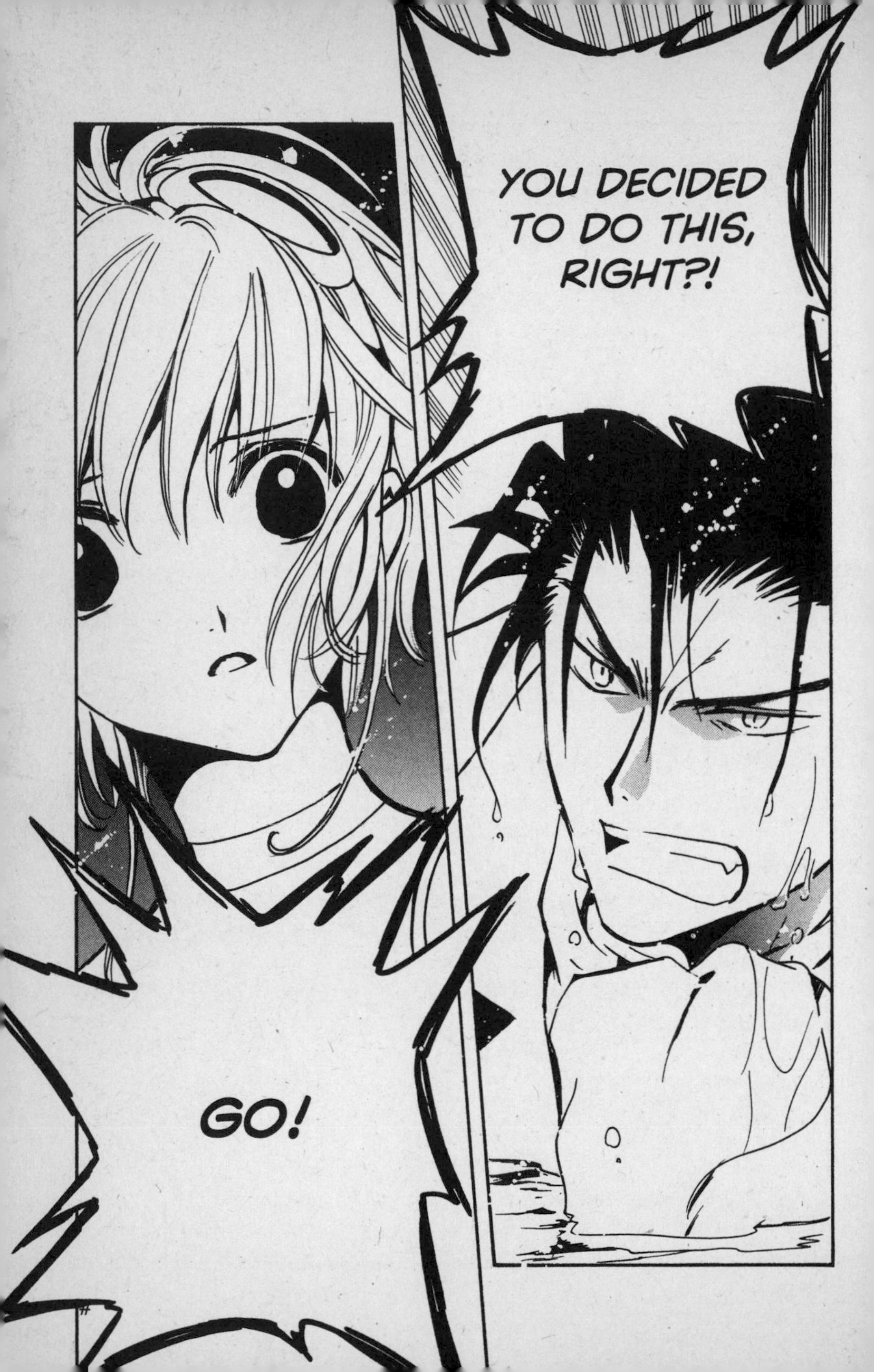
YOU DECIDED TO DO THIS, RIGHT?!
GO!

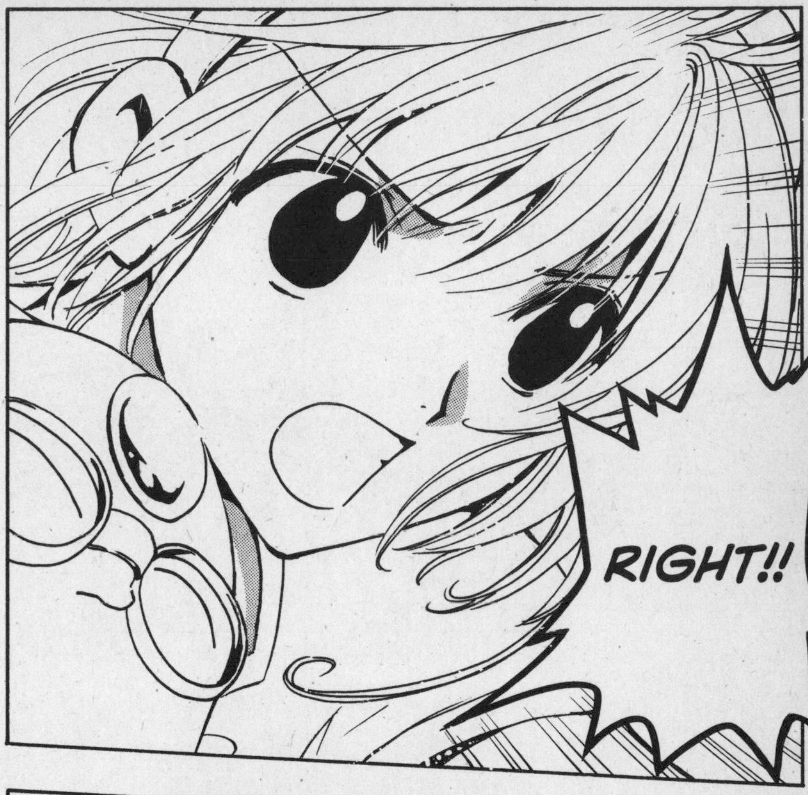
RIGHT!!

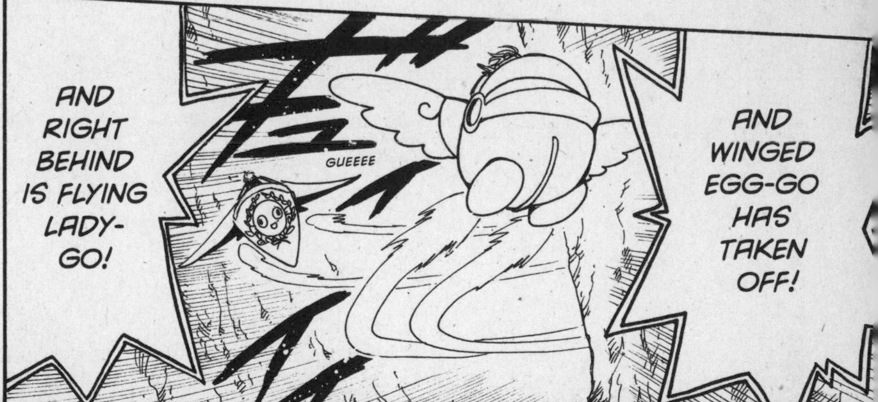
AND WINGED EGG-GO HAS TAKEN OFF!
GUEEEE
AND RIGHT BEHIND IS FLYING LADY-GO!

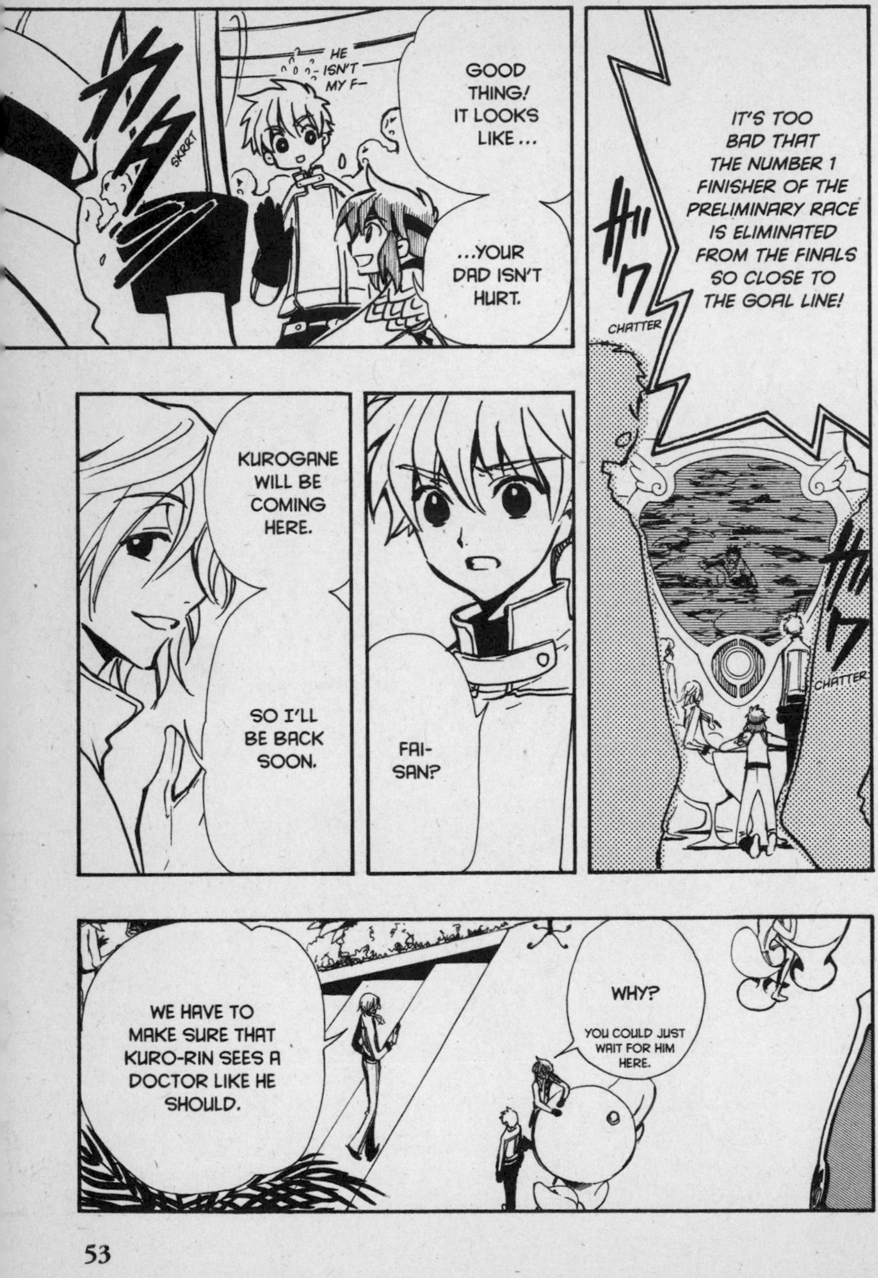
IT'S TOO BAD THAT THE NUMBER 1 FINISHER OF THE PRELIMINARY RACE IS ELIMINATED FROM THE FINALS SO CLOSE TO THE GOAL LINE!
CHATTER
CHATTER
GOOD THING! IT LOOKS LIKE...
...YOUR DAD ISN'T HURT.
HE ISN'T MY F—
SKRRT
FAI-SAN?
KUROGANE WILL BE COMING HERE.
SO I'LL BE BACK SOON.
WHY?
YOU COULD JUST WAIT FOR HIM HERE.
WE HAVE TO MAKE SURE THAT KURO-RIN SEES A DOCTOR LIKE HE SHOULD.

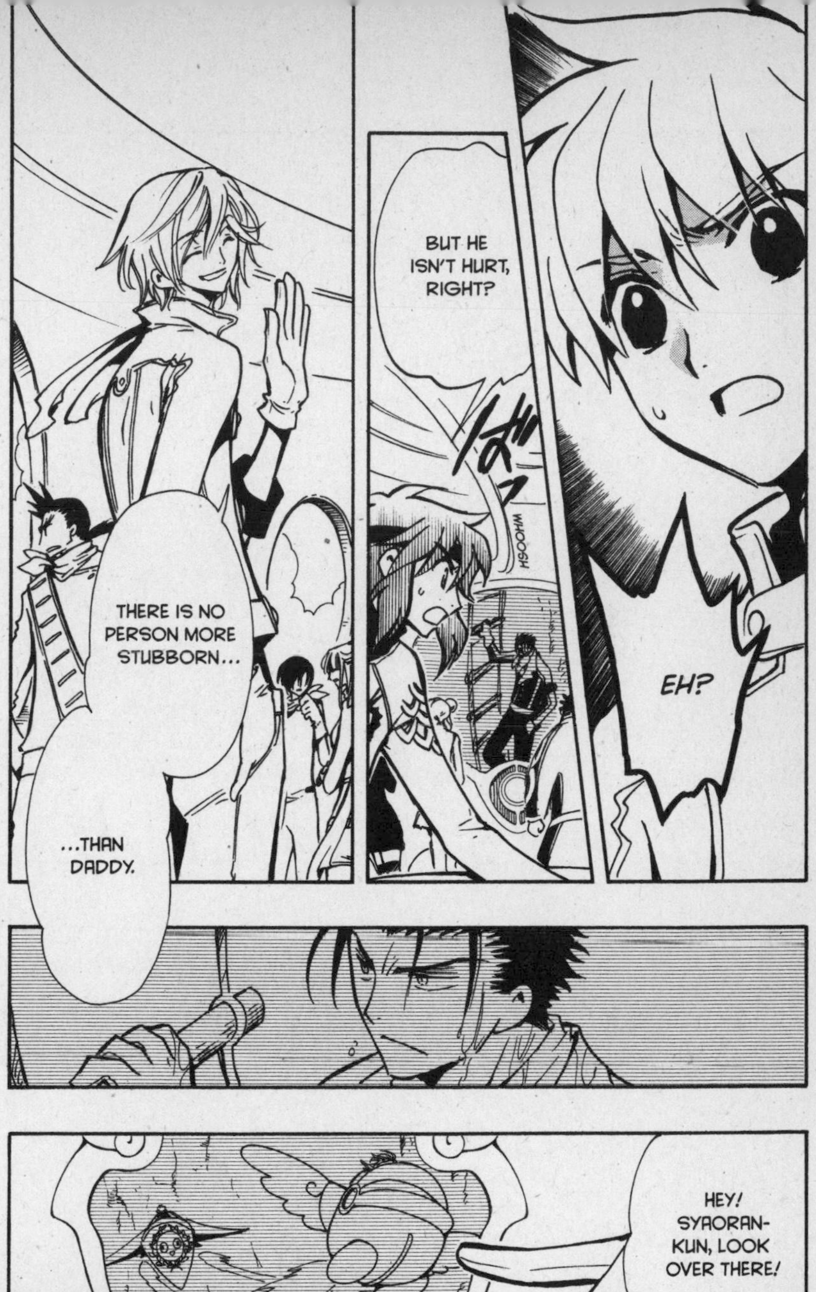
EH?
BUT HE ISN'T HURT, RIGHT?
ぱッ
WHOOSH
THERE IS NO PERSON MORE STUBBORN...
...THAN DADDY.
HEY! SYAORAN-KUN, LOOK OVER THERE!

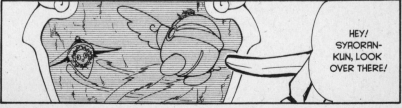

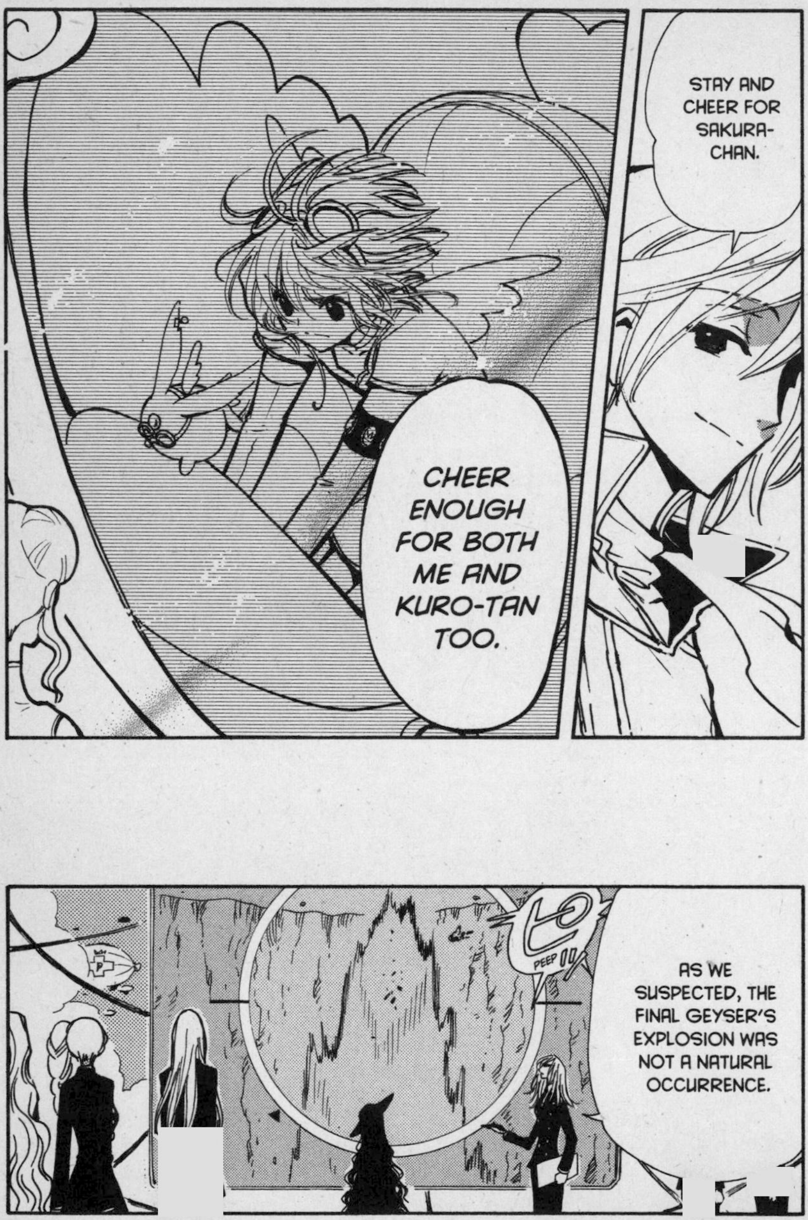
STAY AND CHEER FOR SAKURA-CHAN.
CHEER ENOUGH FOR BOTH ME AND KURO-TAN TOO.
AS WE SUSPECTED, THE FINAL GEYSER'S EXPLOSION WAS NOT A NATURAL OCCURRENCE.
PEEP

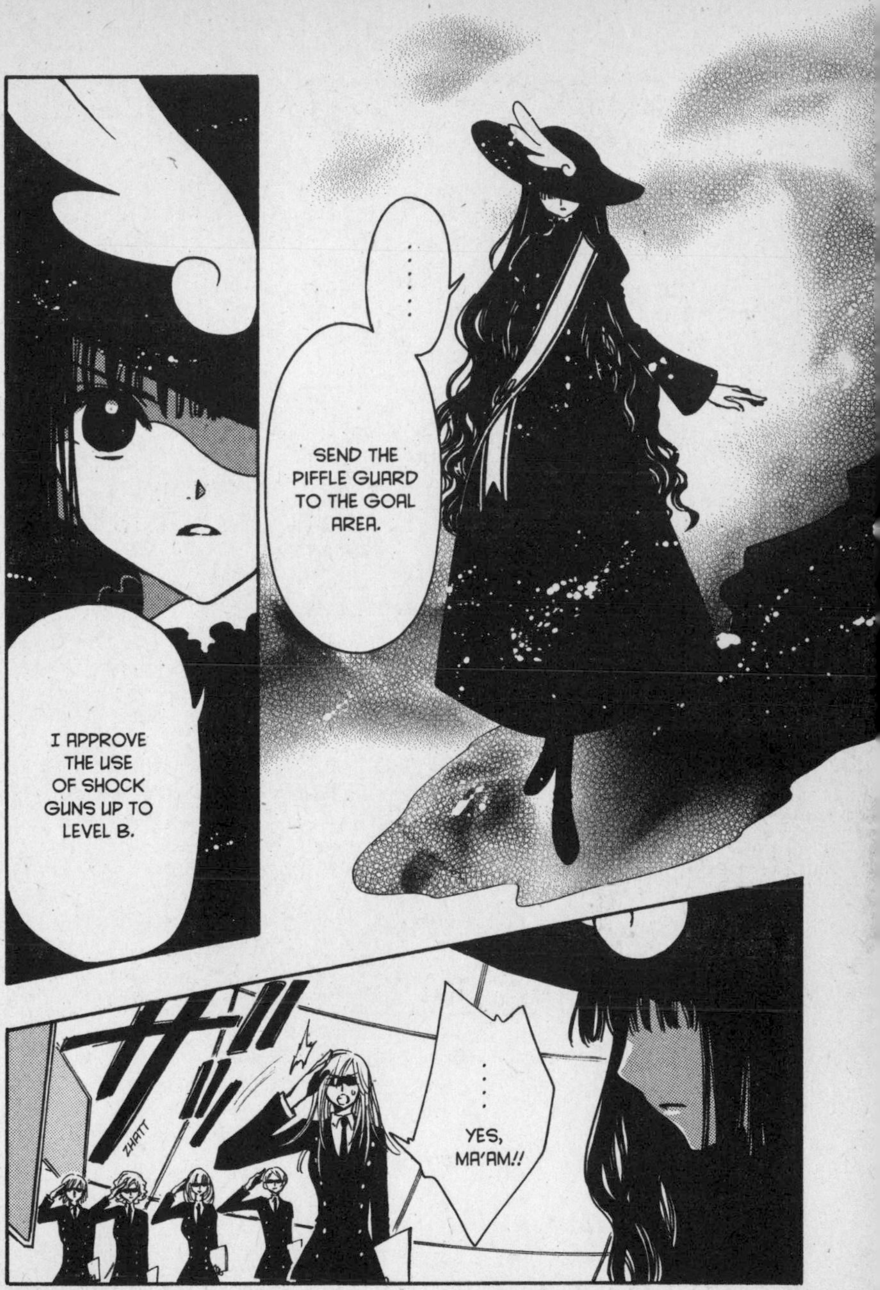
……
SEND THE PIFFLE GUARD TO THE GOAL AREA.
I APPROVE THE USE OF SHOCK GUNS UP TO LEVEL B.
….
YES, MA'AM!!
ZHATT

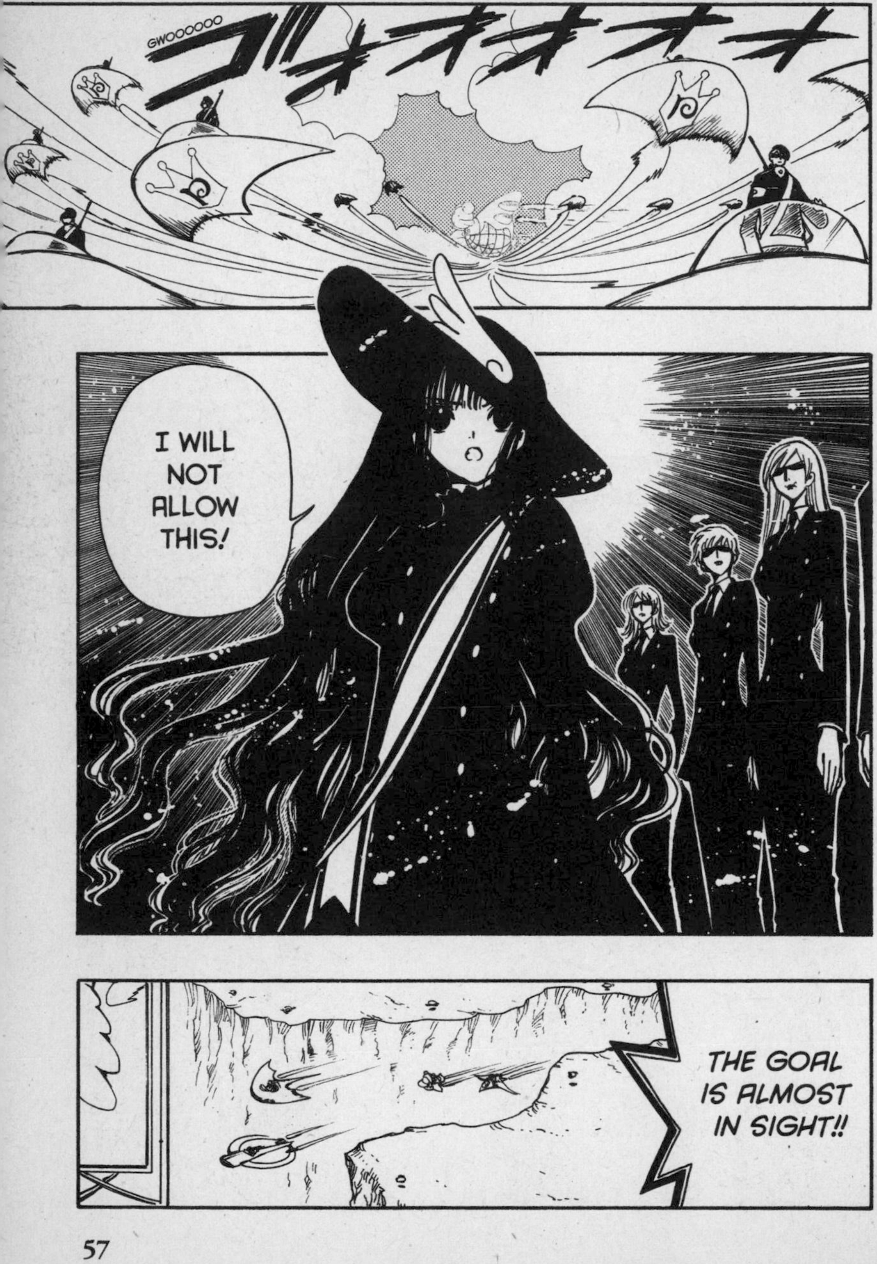
GWOOOOOO
ゴォオオオオ
I WILL NOT ALLOW THIS!
THE GOAL IS ALMOST IN SIGHT!!

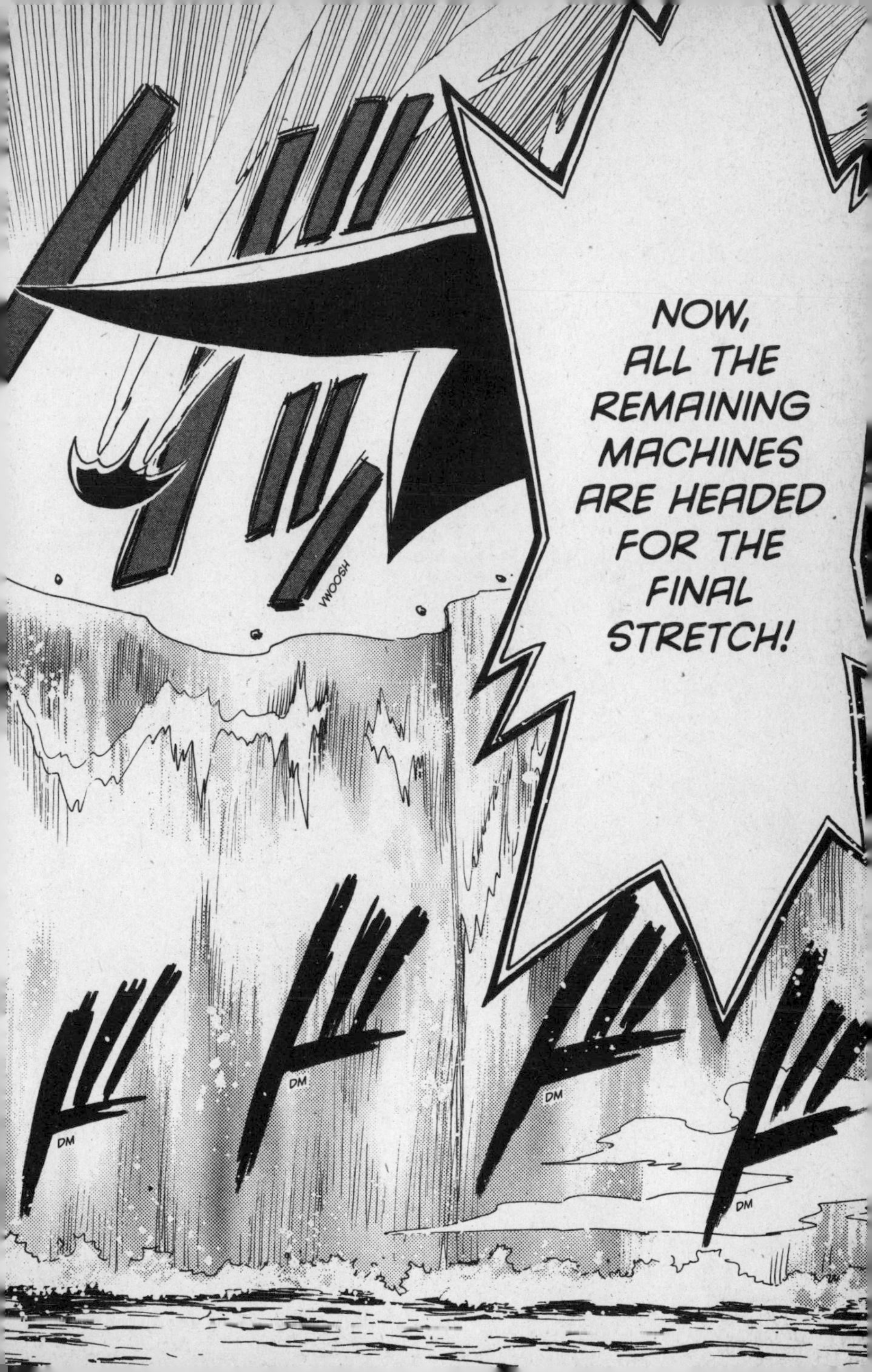
NOW, ALL THE REMAINING MACHINES ARE HEADED FOR THE FINAL STRETCH!
VWOOSH
DM
DM
DM
DM

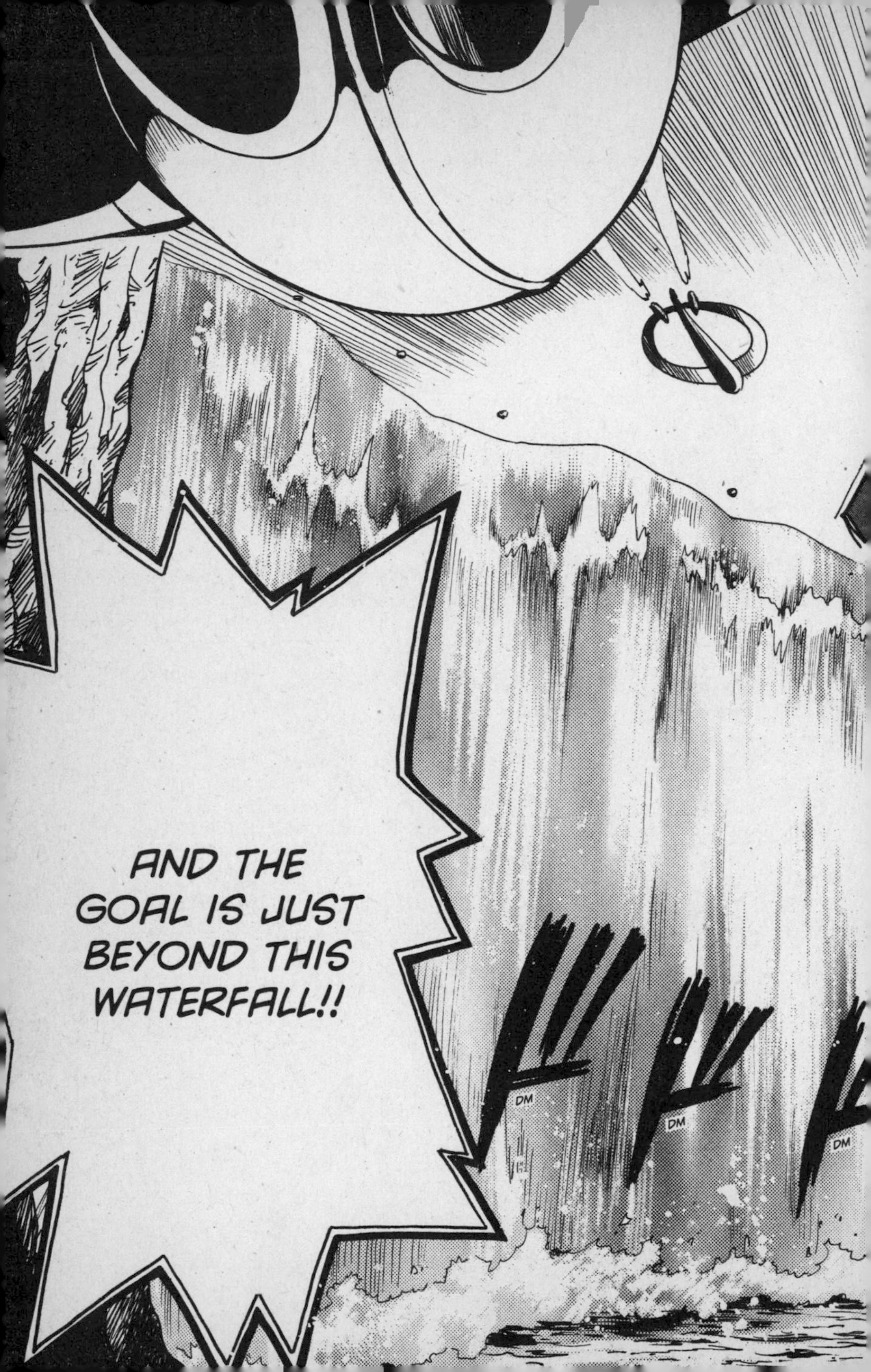
AND THE GOAL IS JUST BEYOND THIS WATERFALL!!
DM
DM
DM

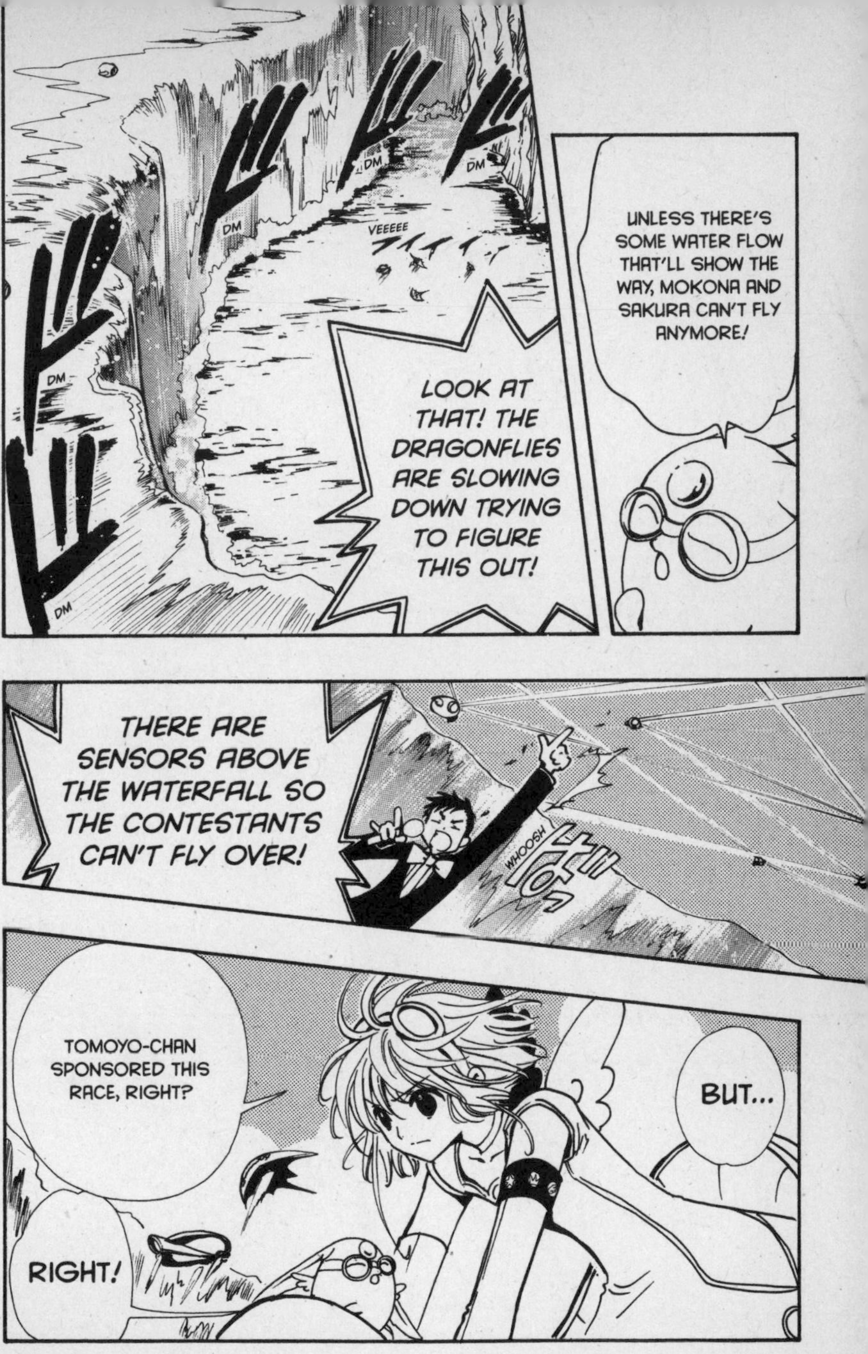
UNLESS THERE'S SOME WATER FLOW THAT'LL SHOW THE WAY, MOKONA AND SAKURA CAN'T FLY ANYMORE!
DM
DM
DM
DM
DM
VEEEEE
LOOK AT THAT! THE DRAGONFLIES ARE SLOWING DOWN TRYING TO FIGURE THIS OUT!
THERE ARE SENSORS ABOVE THE WATERFALL SO THE CONTESTANTS CAN'T FLY OVER!
WHOOSH
BUT...
TOMOYO-CHAN SPONSORED THIS RACE, RIGHT?
RIGHT!

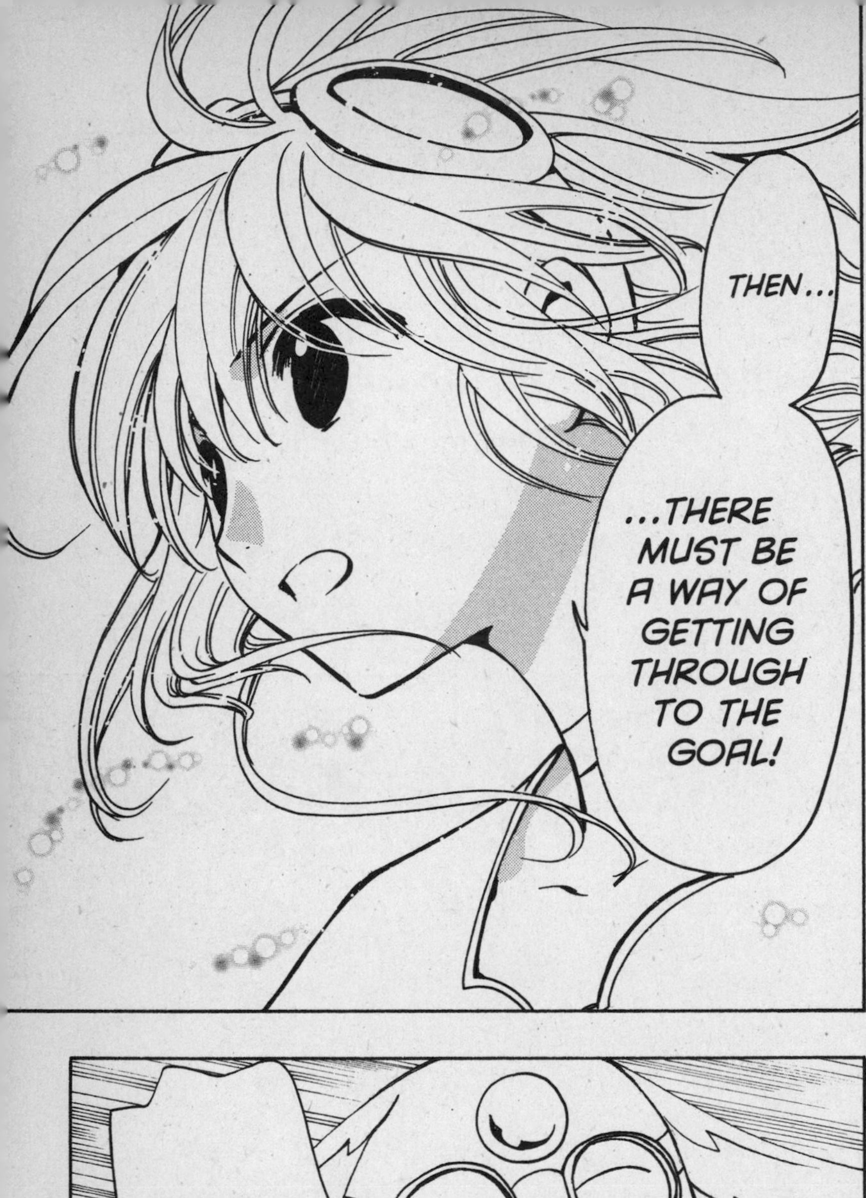
THEN...
...THERE MUST BE A WAY OF GETTING THROUGH TO THE GOAL!
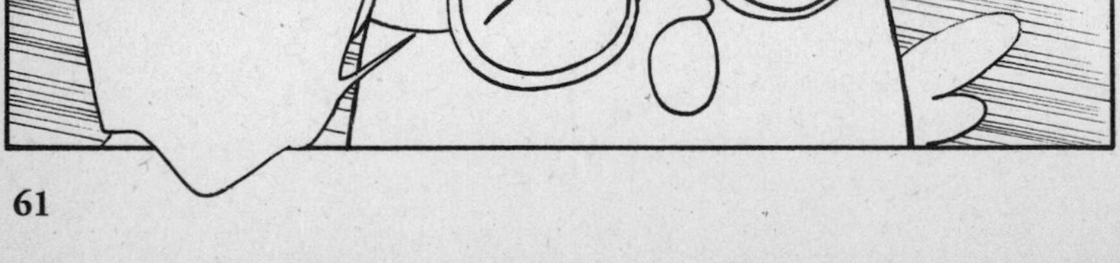
SAKURA?!

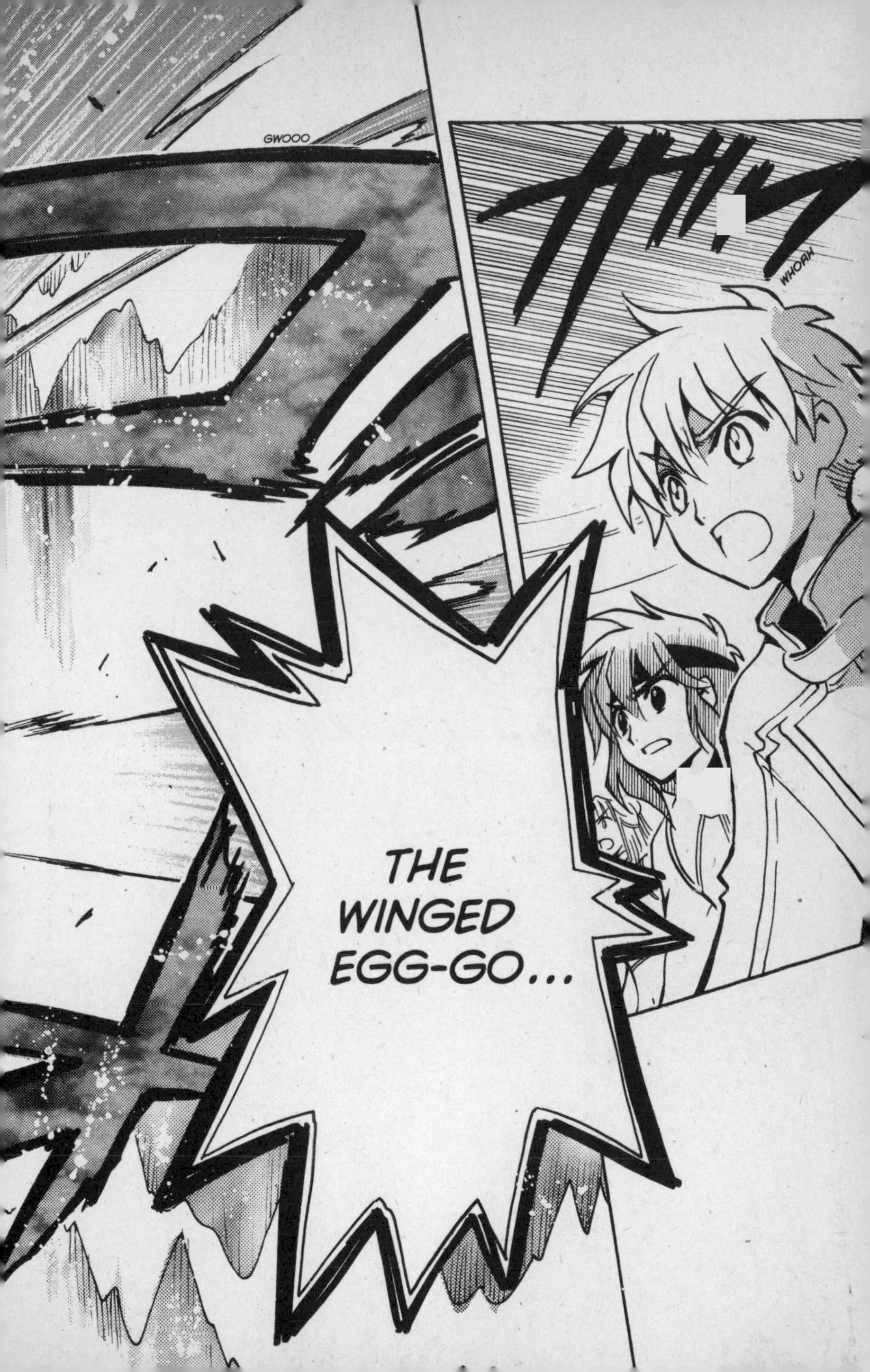
WHOAH
THE WINGED EGG-GO...
GWOOO

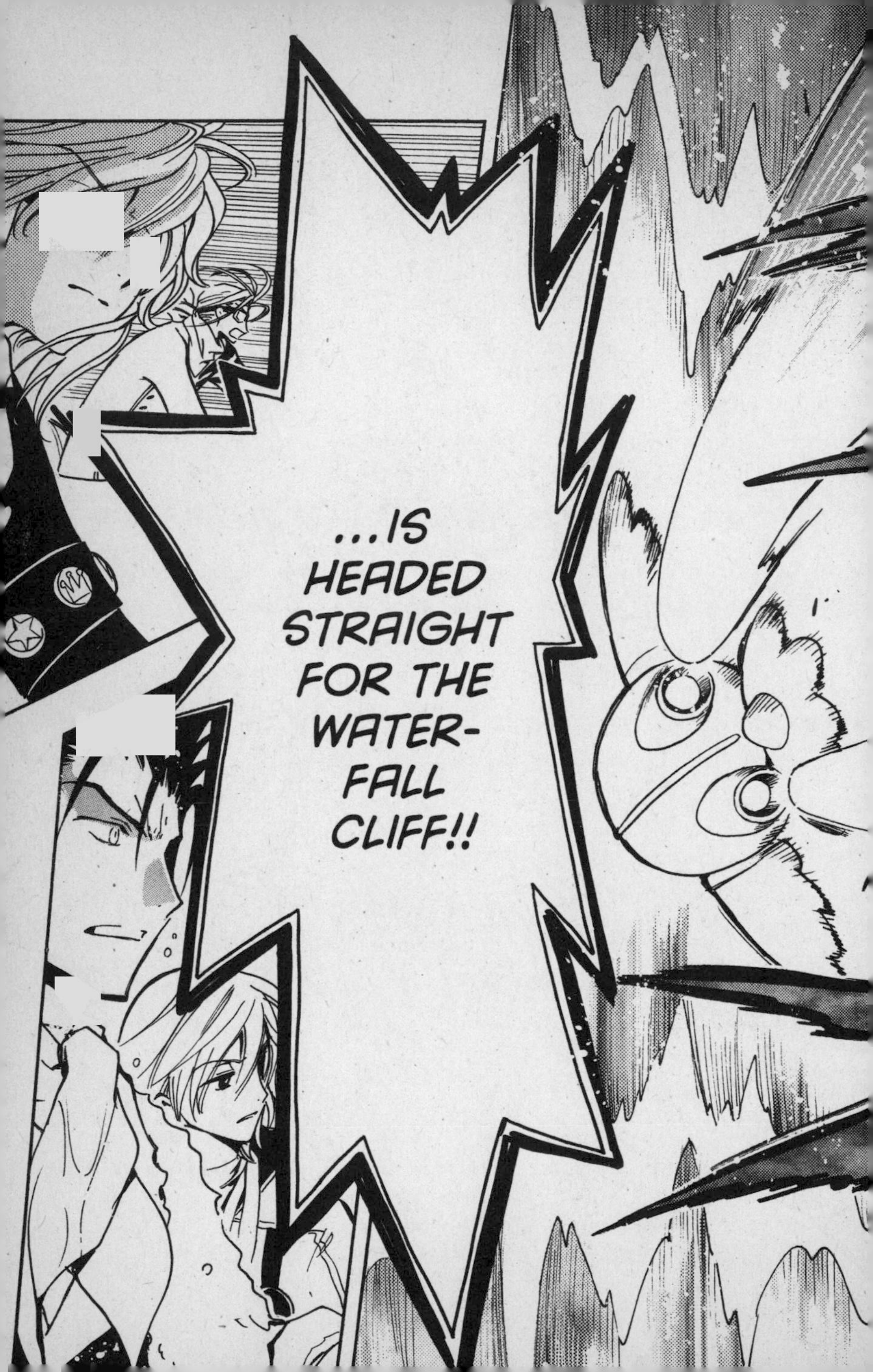
...IS HEADED STRAIGHT FOR THE WATER-FALL CLIFF!!

ツバサ
RESERVoir CHRoNiCLE

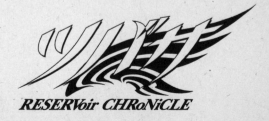

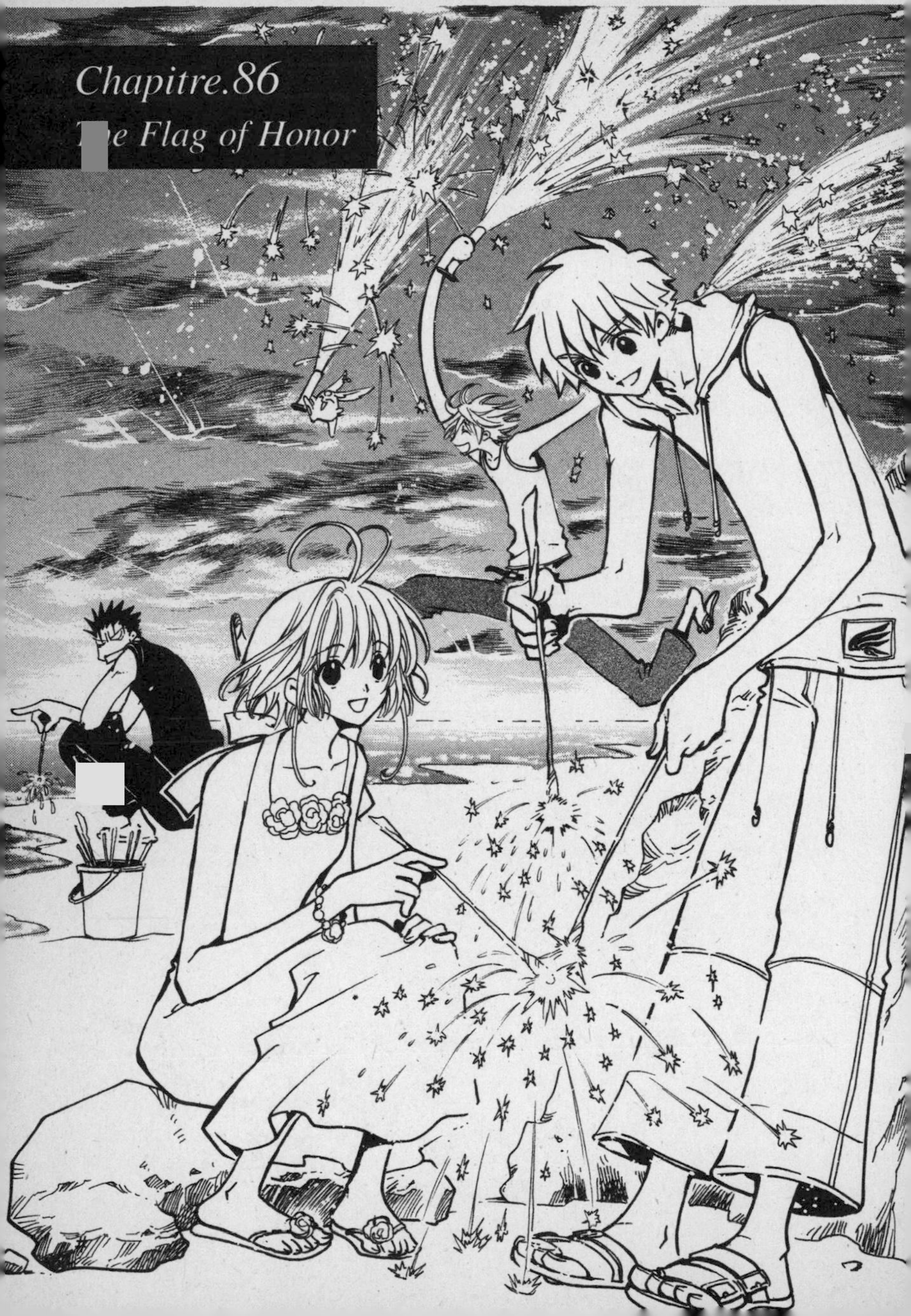
Chapitre.86
The Flag of Honor

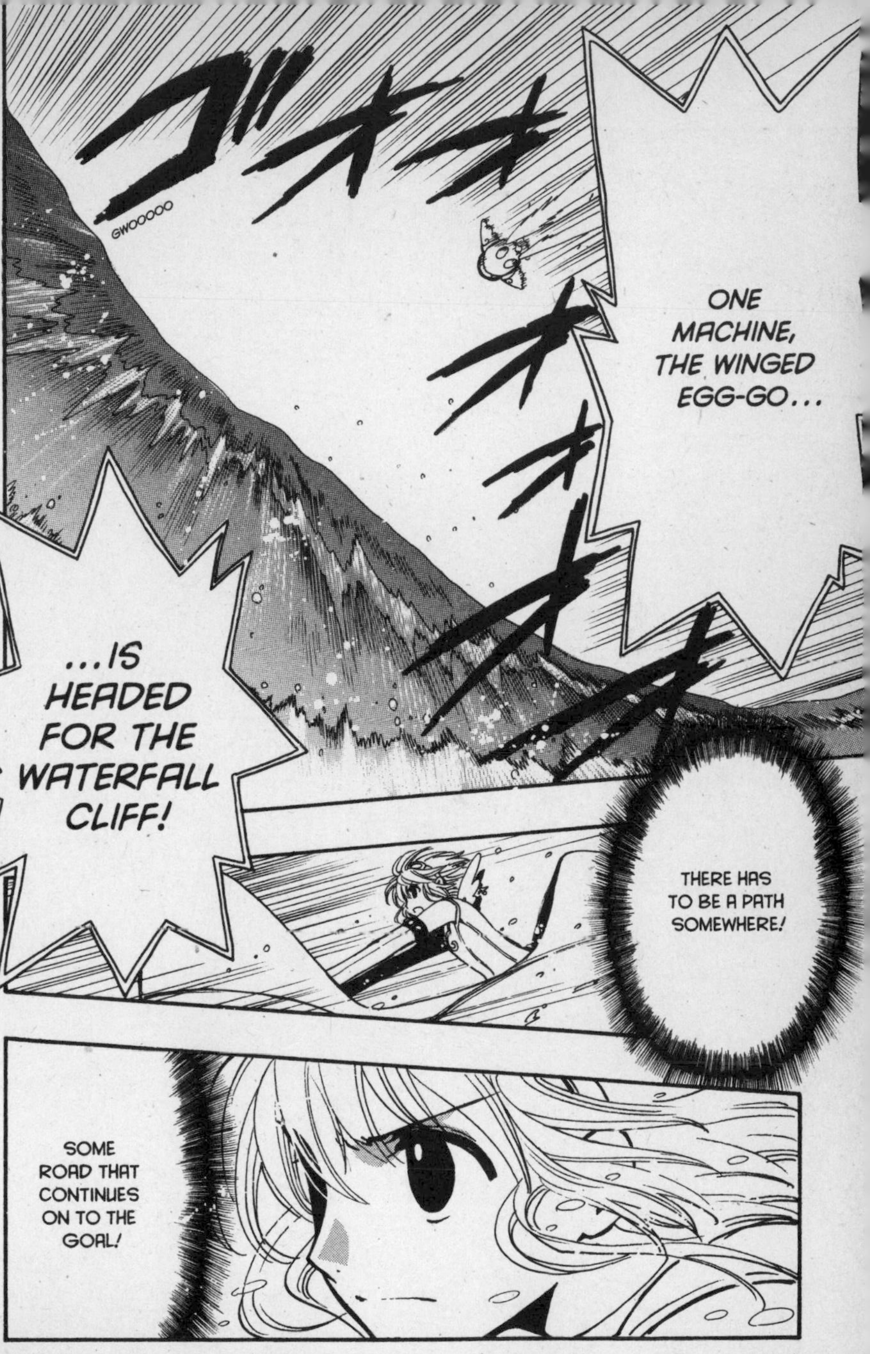
GWOOOOO
ONE MACHINE, THE WINGED EGG-GO...
...IS HEADED FOR THE WATERFALL CLIFF!
THERE HAS TO BE A PATH SOMEWHERE!
SOME ROAD THAT CONTINUES ON TO THE GOAL!

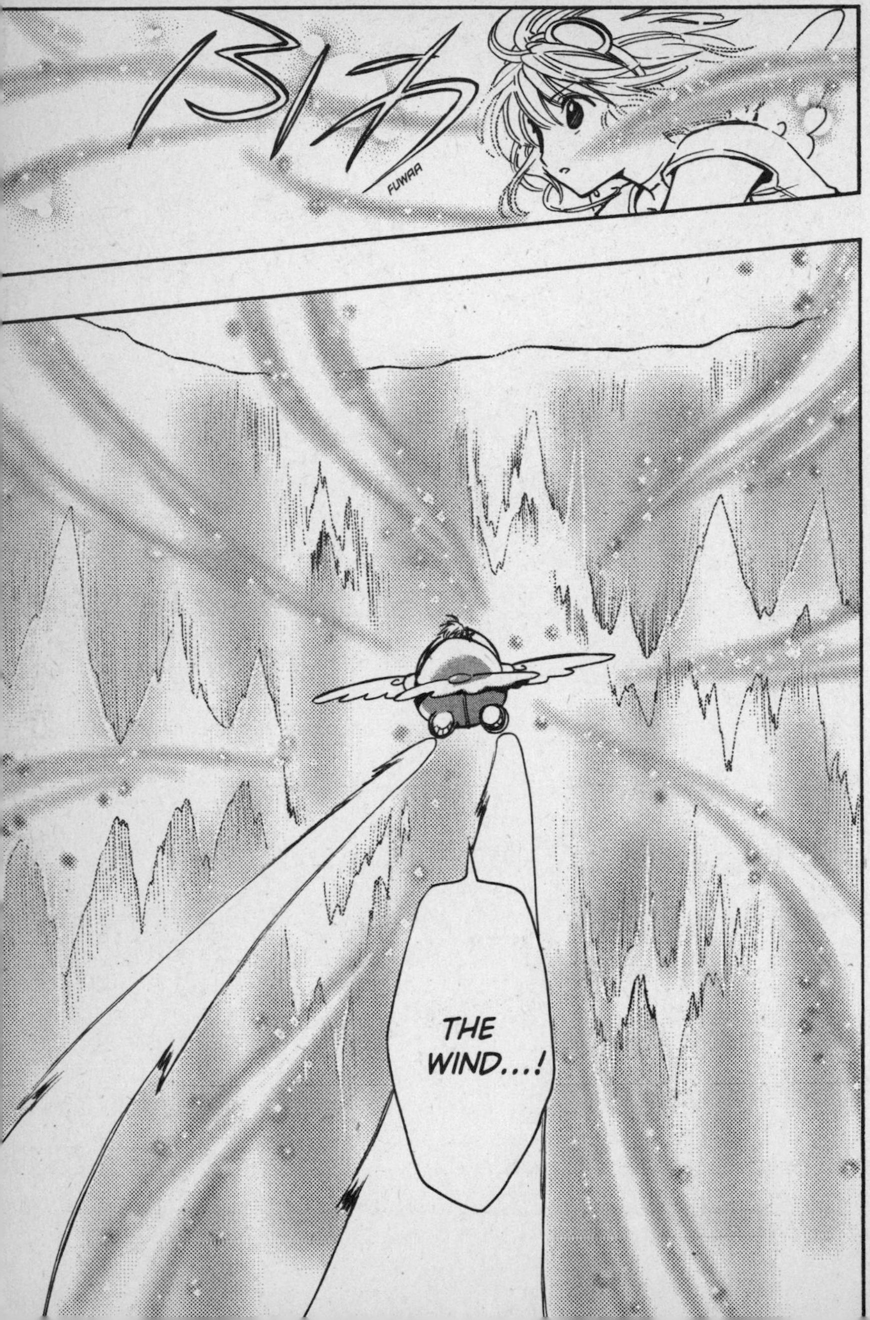
ふわ
FUWAA
THE WIND...!

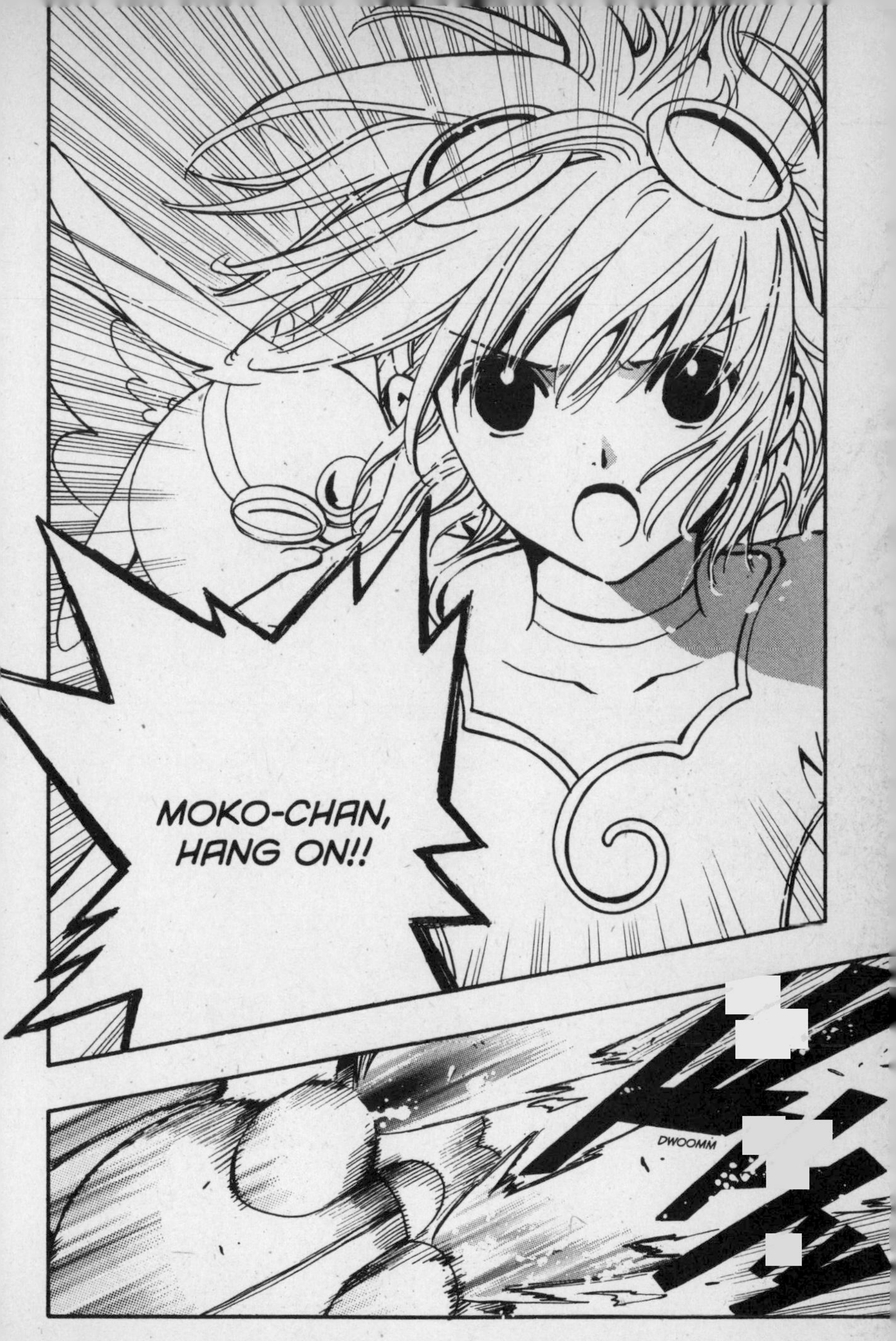
MOKO-CHAN,
HANG ON!!
DWOOMM

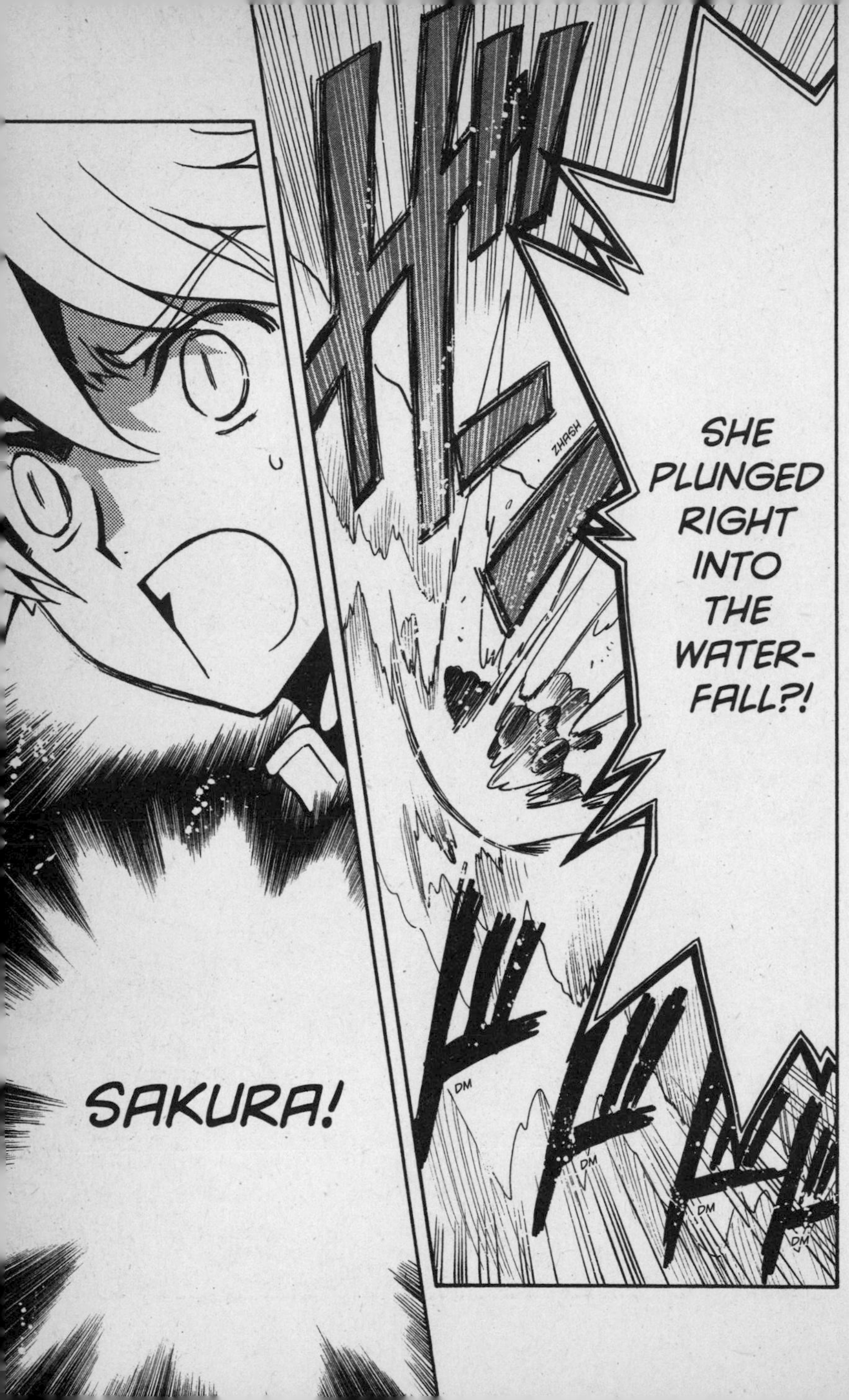
SHE PLUNGED RIGHT INTO THE WATER-FALL?!
ZHASH
DM
DM
DM
DM
SAKURA!

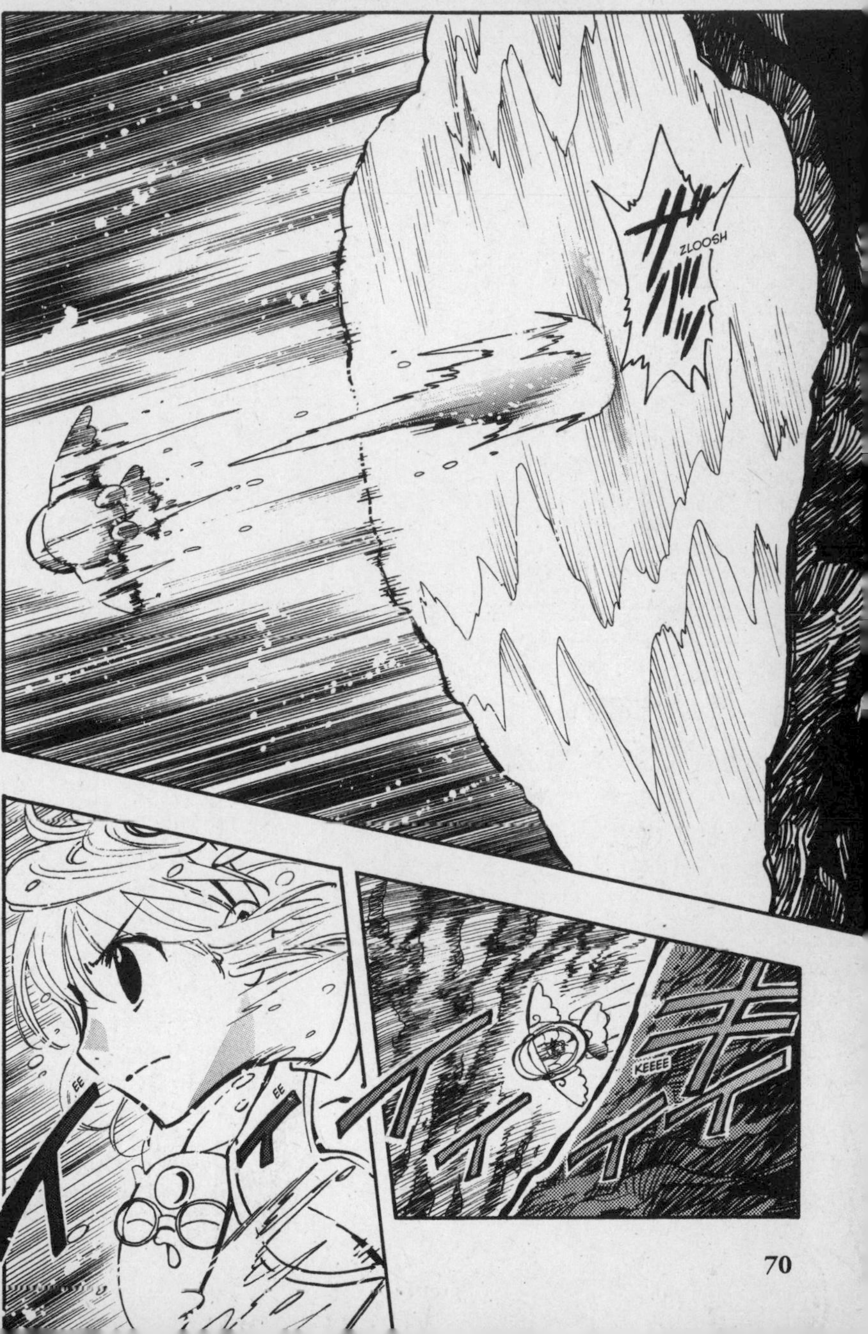
ZLOOSH
KEEEE
EE
EE

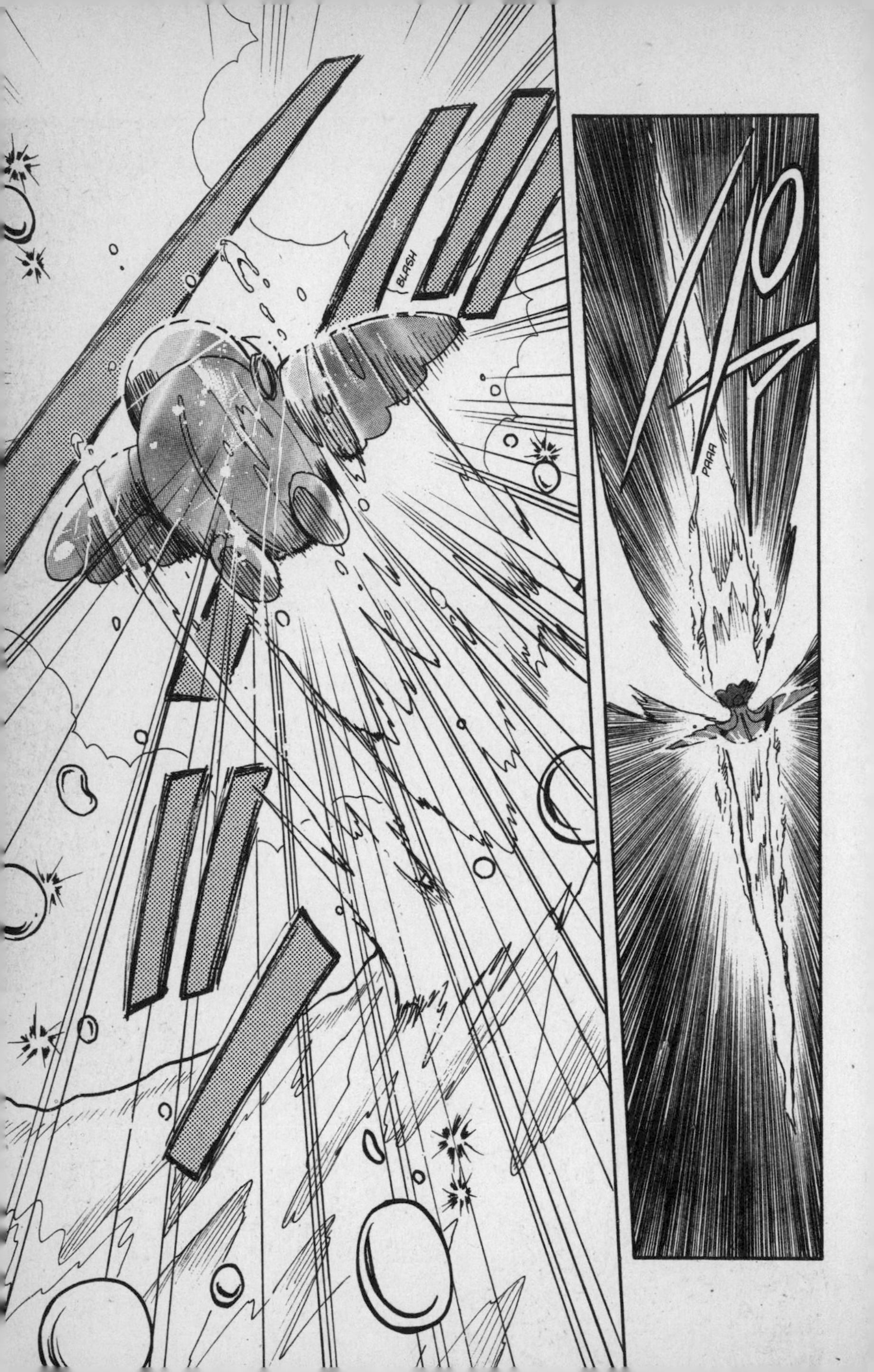
PAAA
BLASH

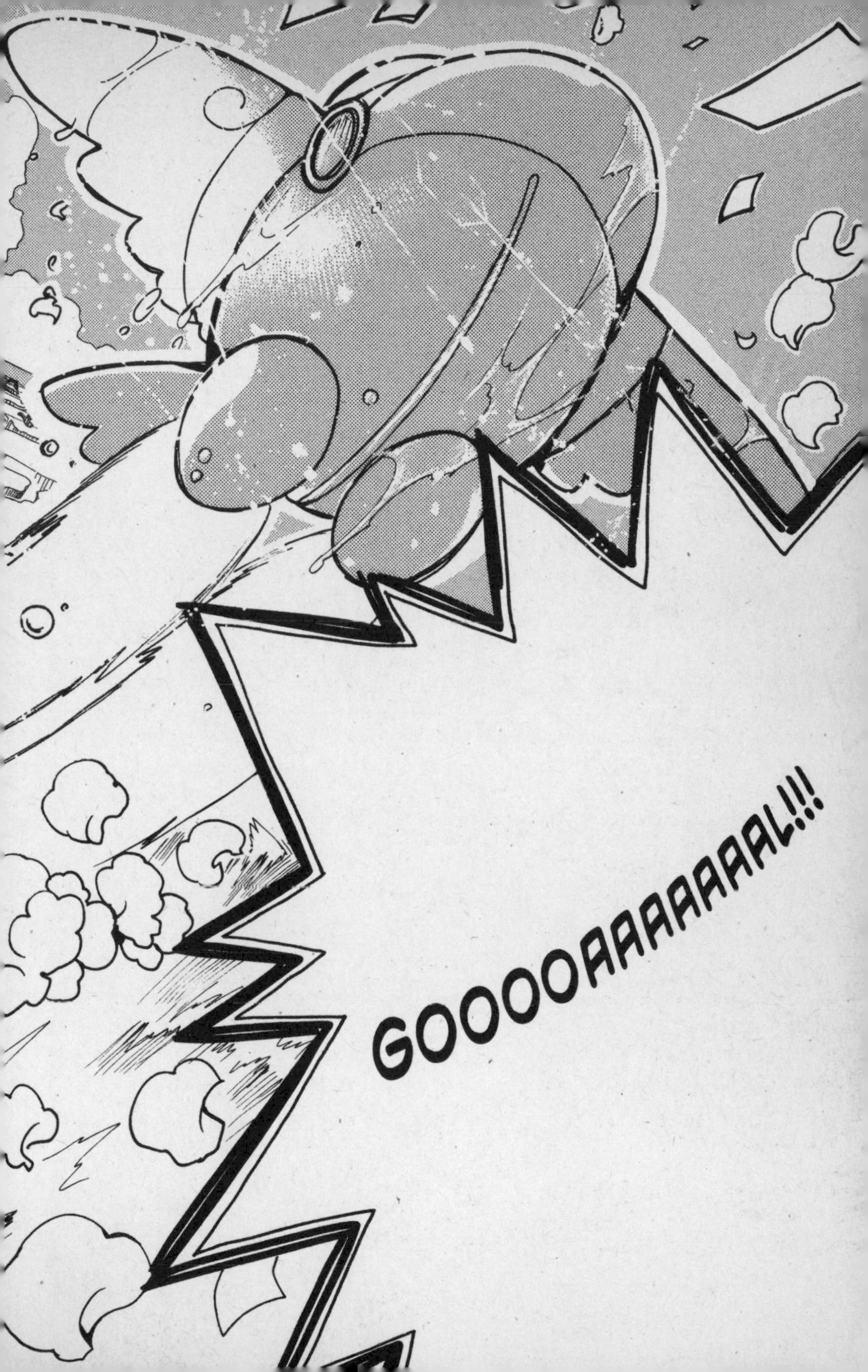
GOOOOAAAAAAAL!!!

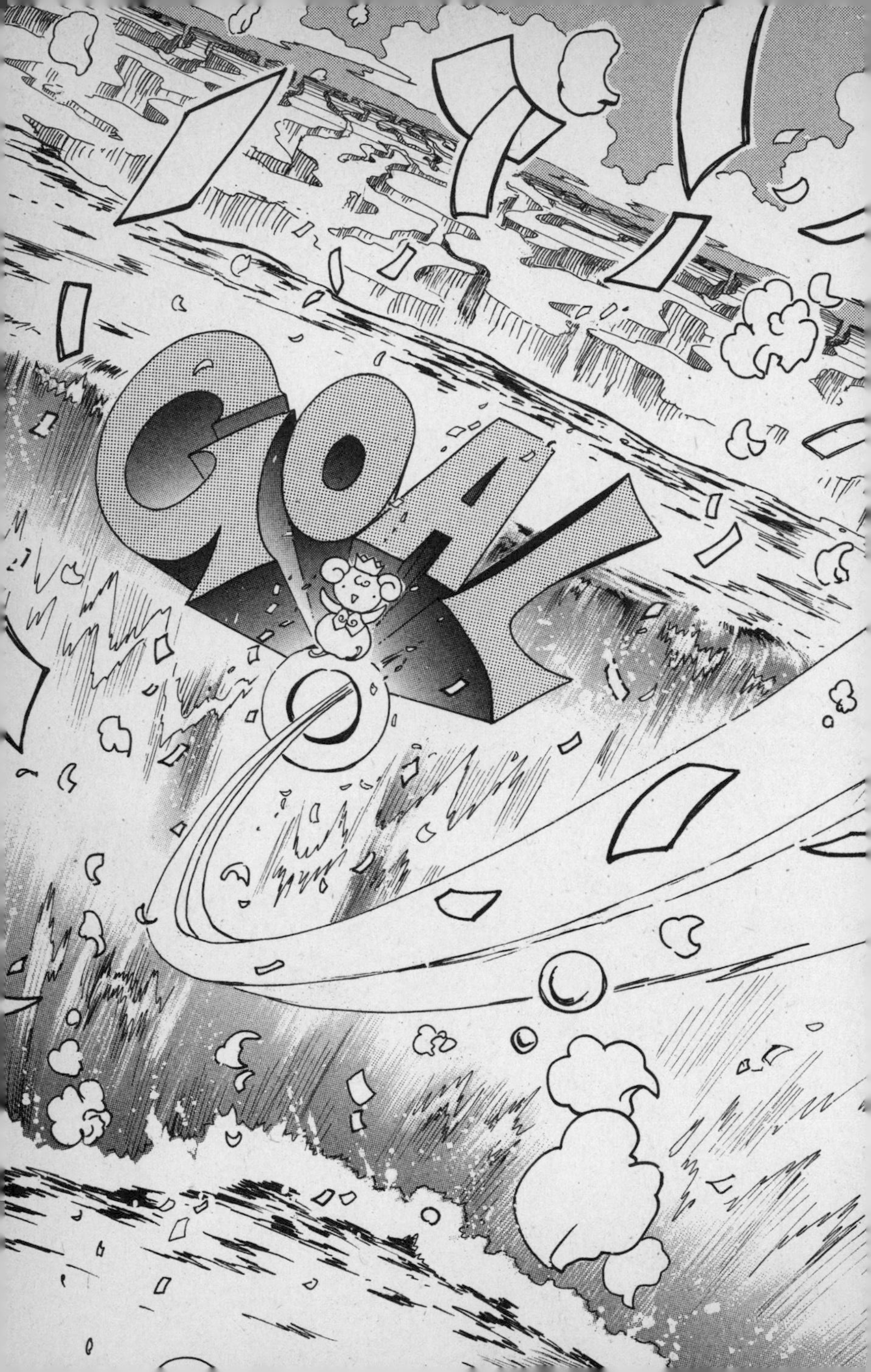
GOAL

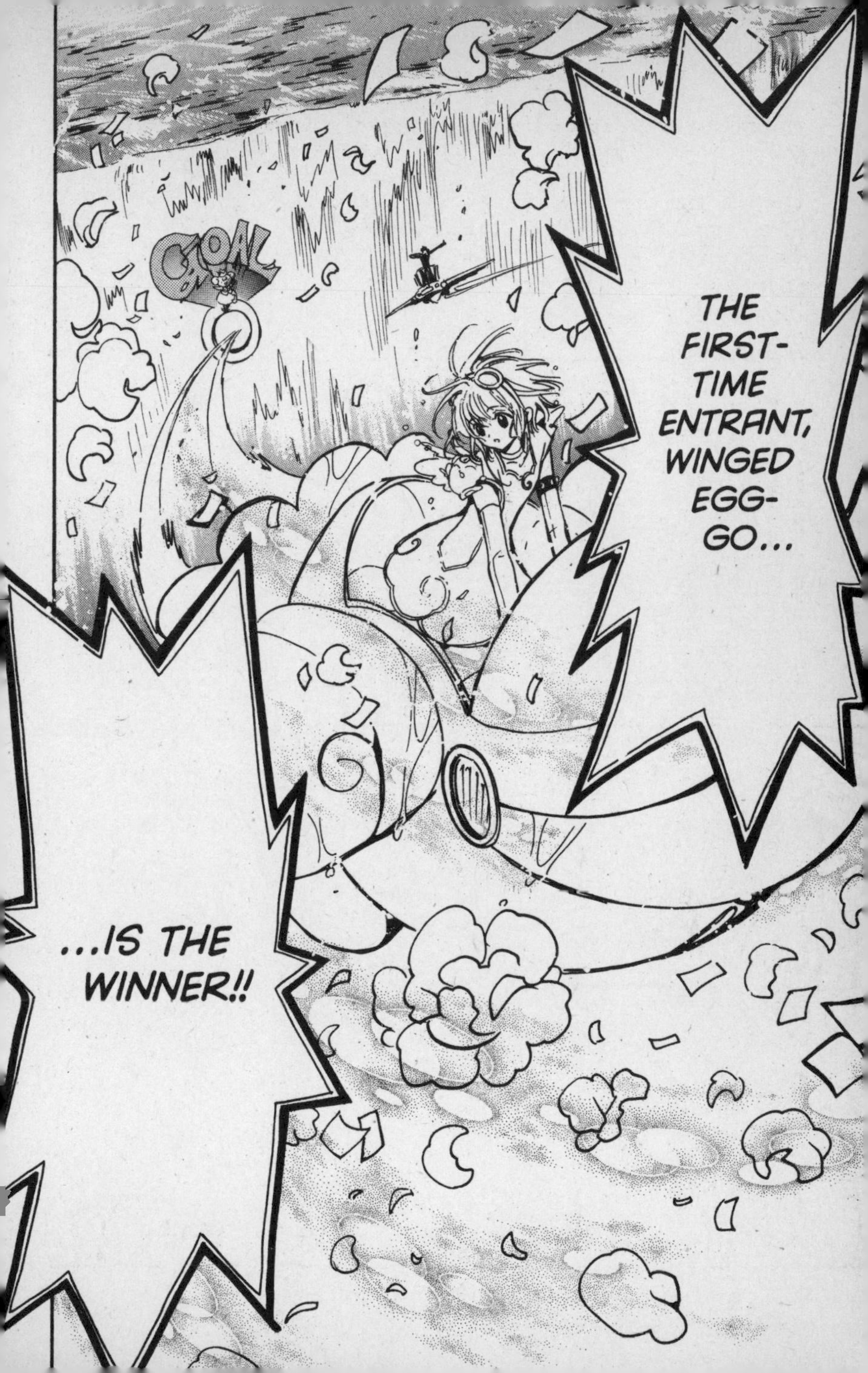
THE FIRST-TIME ENTRANT, WINGED EGG-GO...
GOAL
...IS THE WINNER!!

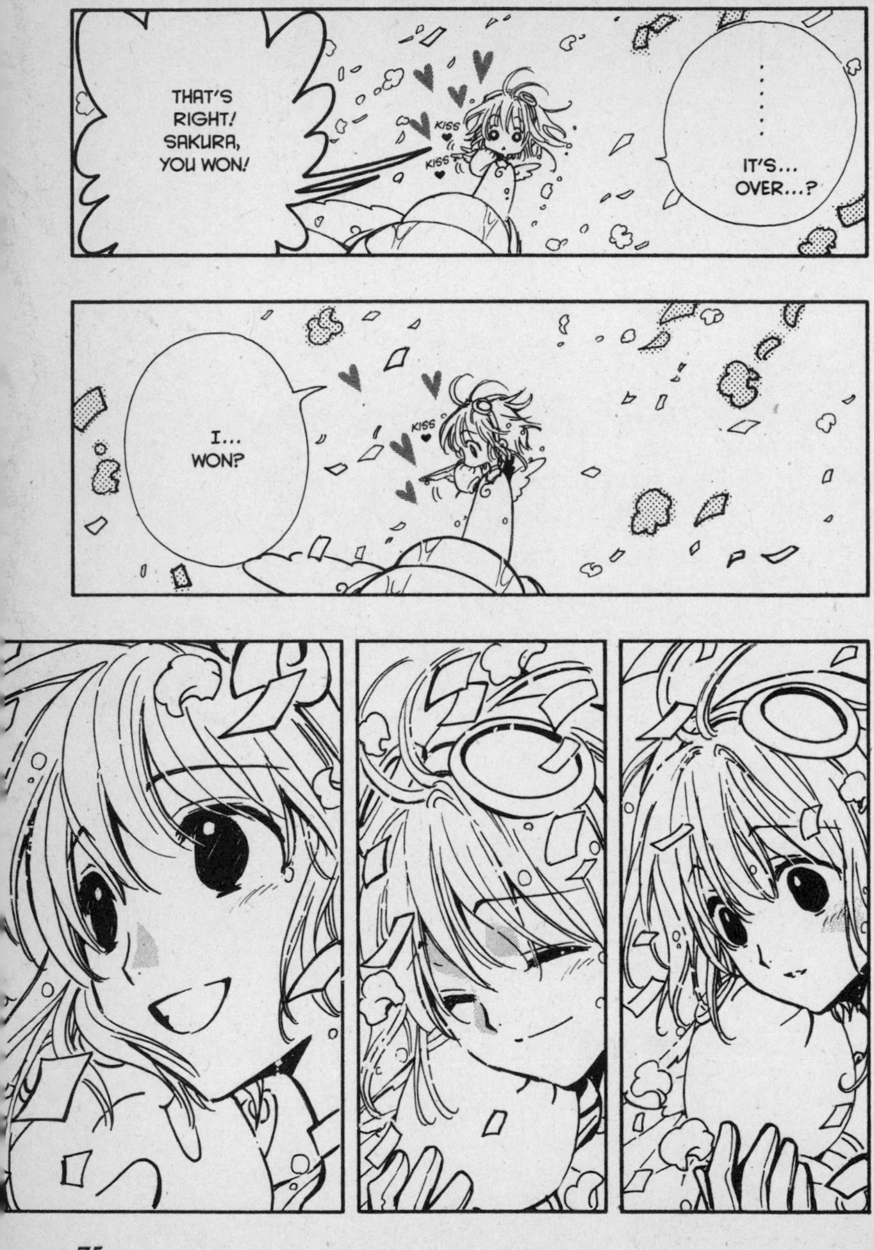
IT'S... OVER...?
THAT'S RIGHT! SAKURA, YOU WON!
KISS
KISS
I... WON?
KISS

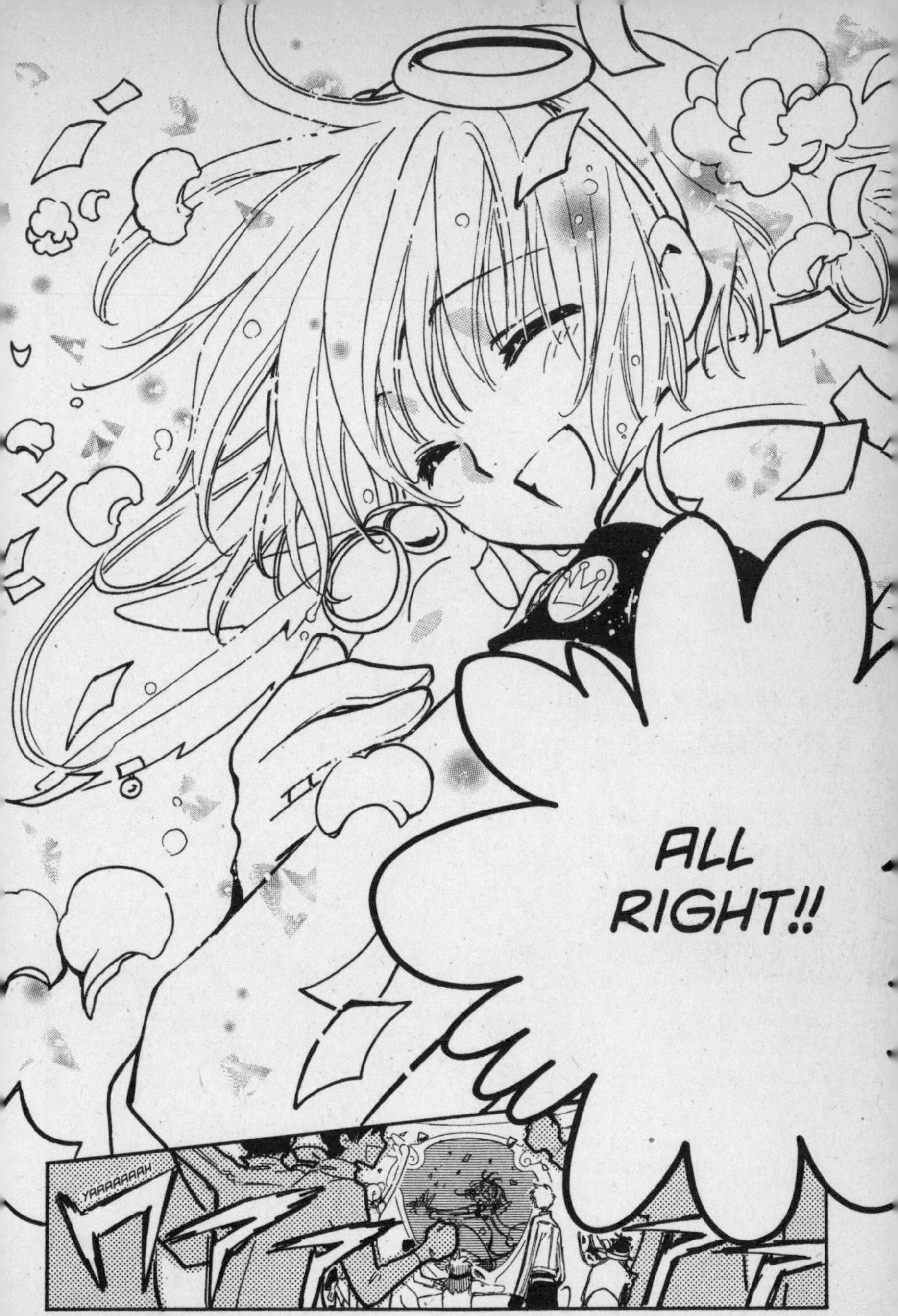
ALL RIGHT!!
YAAAAAAAH

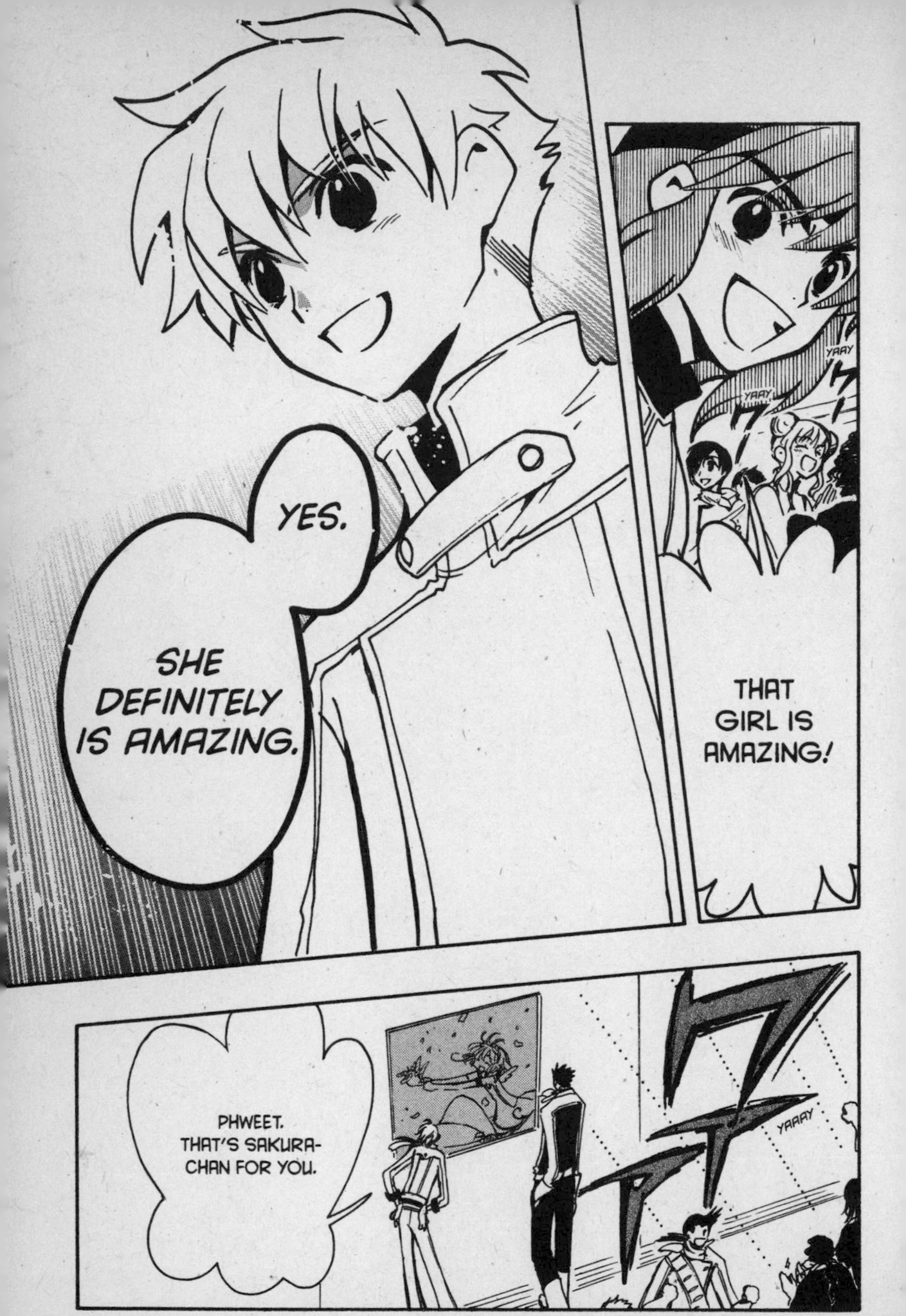
YAAY
YAAY
THAT GIRL IS AMAZING!
YES.
SHE DEFINITELY IS AMAZING.
YAAAY
PHWEET. THAT'S SAKURA-CHAN FOR YOU.

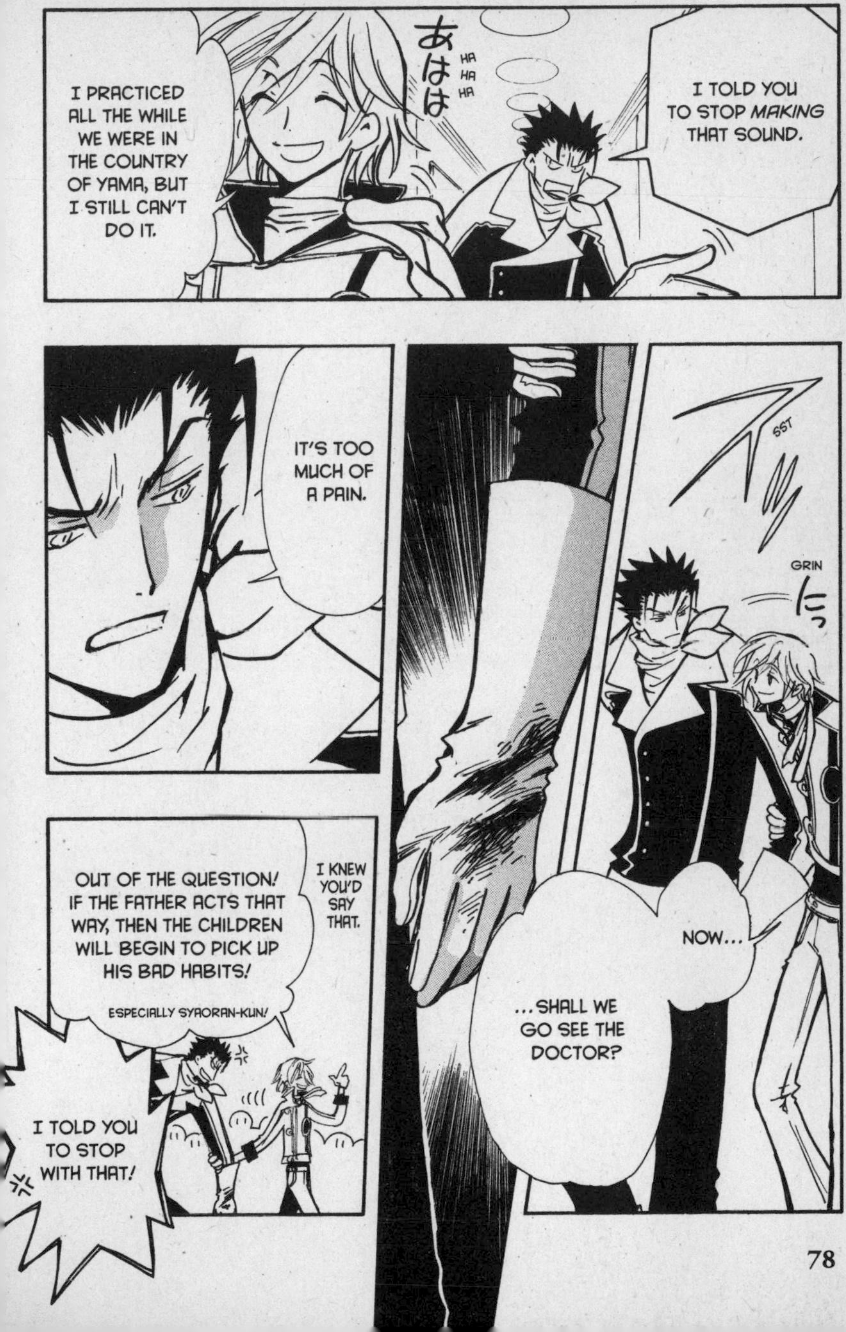
I TOLD YOU TO STOP *MAKING* THAT SOUND.
あはは HA HA HA
I PRACTICED ALL THE WHILE WE WERE IN THE COUNTRY OF YAMA, BUT I STILL CAN'T DO IT.
SST
GRIN
NOW...
...SHALL WE GO SEE THE DOCTOR?
IT'S TOO MUCH OF A PAIN.
I KNEW YOU'D SAY THAT.
OUT OF THE QUESTION! IF THE FATHER ACTS THAT WAY, THEN THE CHILDREN WILL BEGIN TO PICK UP HIS BAD HABITS!
ESPECIALLY SYAORAN-KUN!
I TOLD YOU TO STOP WITH THAT!

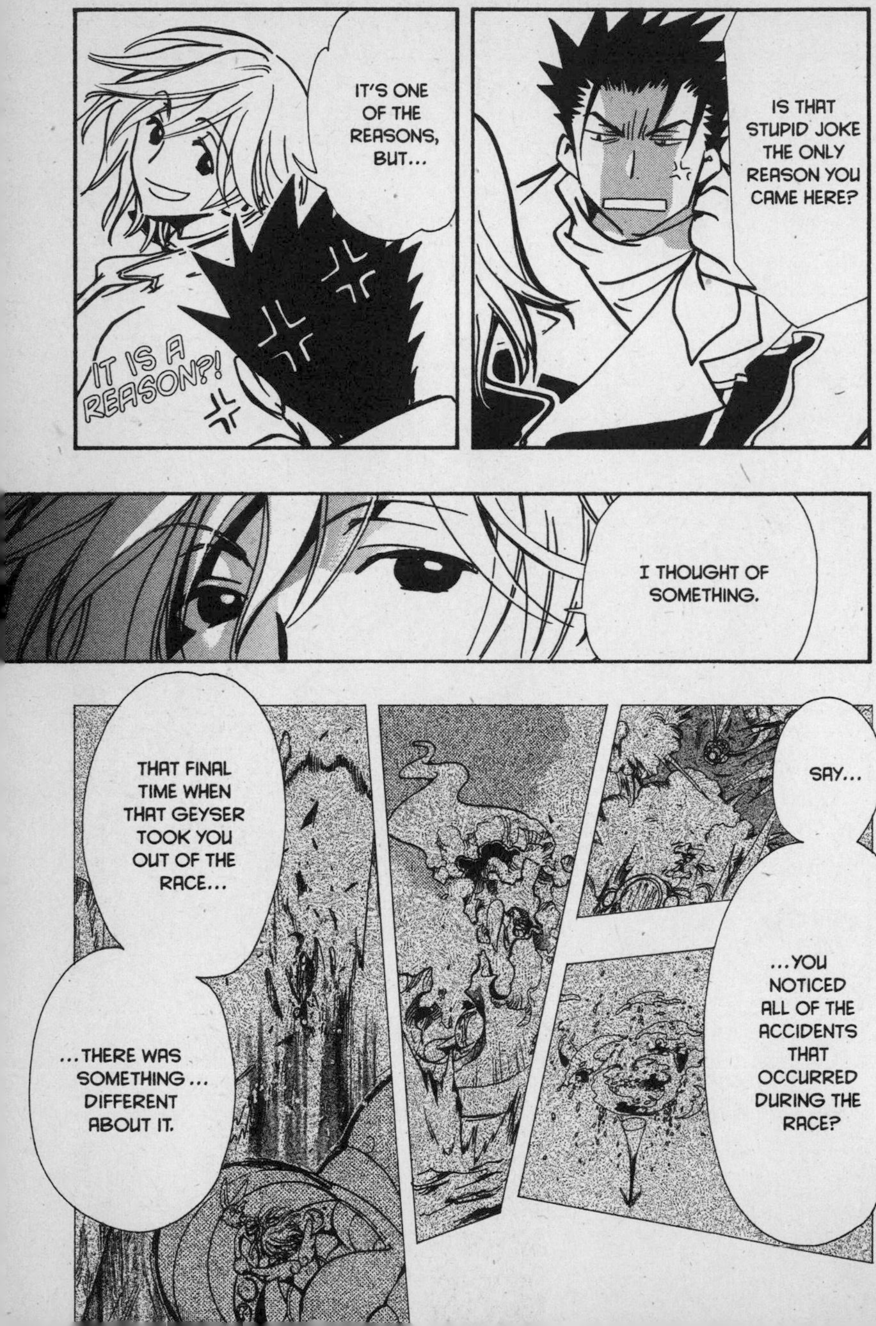
IS THAT STUPID JOKE THE ONLY REASON YOU CAME HERE?
IT'S ONE OF THE REASONS, BUT...
IT IS A REASON?!
I THOUGHT OF SOMETHING.
SAY...
...YOU NOTICED ALL OF THE ACCIDENTS THAT OCCURRED DURING THE RACE?
THAT FINAL TIME WHEN THAT GEYSER TOOK YOU OUT OF THE RACE...
...THERE WAS SOMETHING... DIFFERENT ABOUT IT.

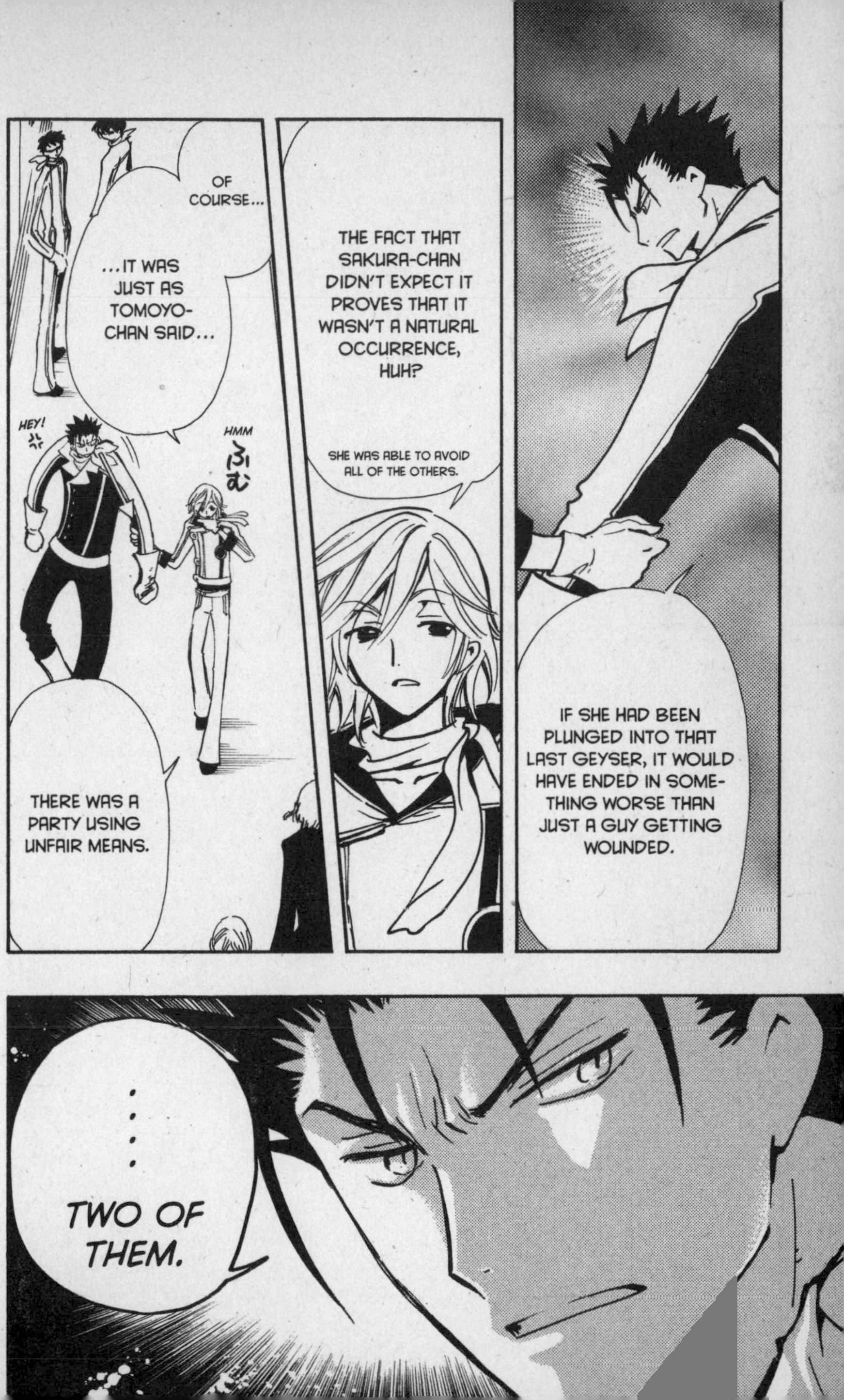
IF SHE HAD BEEN PLUNGED INTO THAT LAST GEYSER, IT WOULD HAVE ENDED IN SOMETHING WORSE THAN JUST A GUY GETTING WOUNDED.
THE FACT THAT SAKURA-CHAN DIDN'T EXPECT IT PROVES THAT IT WASN'T A NATURAL OCCURRENCE, HUH?
SHE WAS ABLE TO AVOID ALL OF THE OTHERS.
OF COURSE...
...IT WAS JUST AS TOMOYO-CHAN SAID...
HMM
ふむ
HEY!
THERE WAS A PARTY USING UNFAIR MEANS.
....
TWO OF THEM.

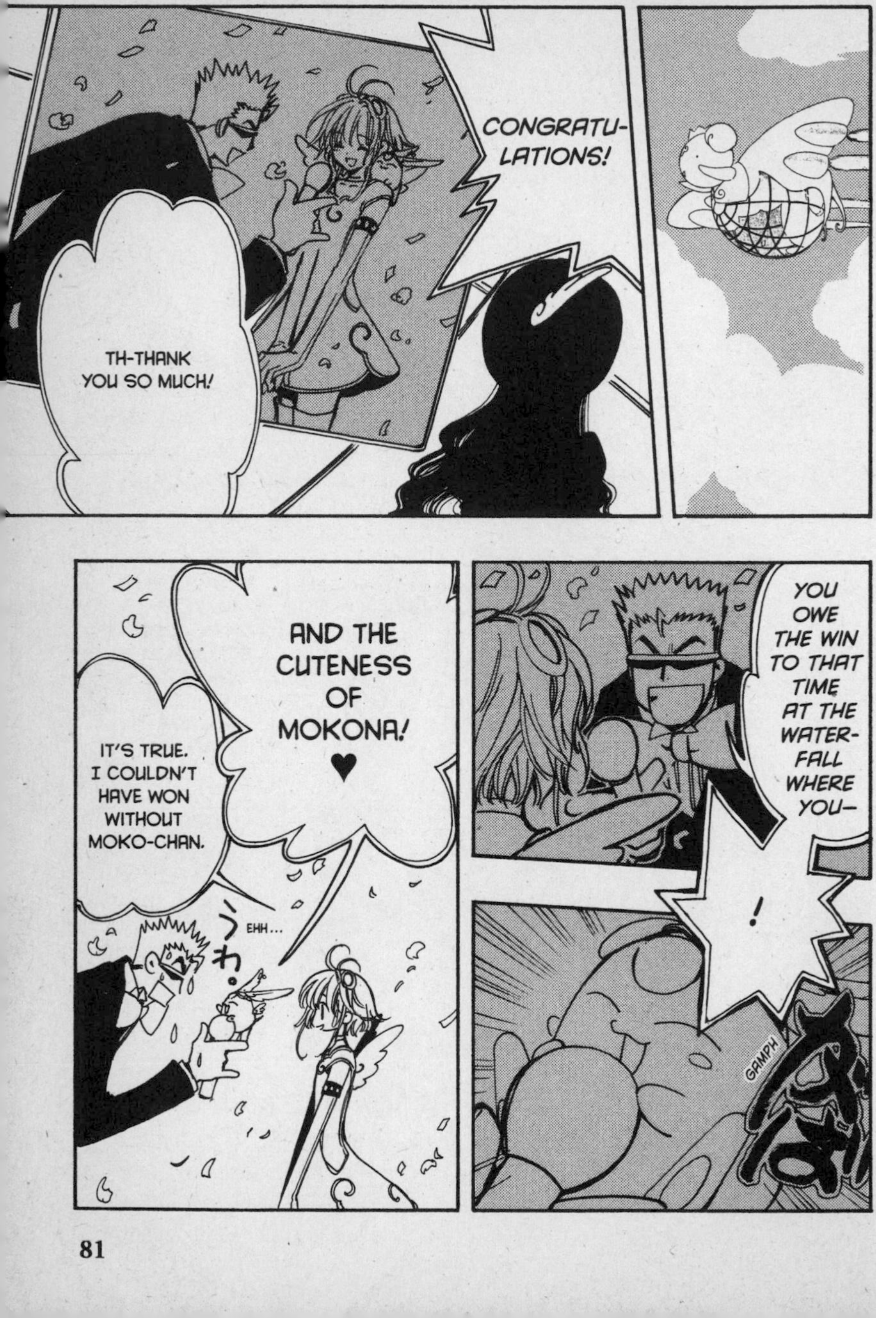
CONGRATULATIONS!
TH-THANK YOU SO MUCH!
YOU OWE THE WIN TO THAT TIME AT THE WATERFALL WHERE YOU—
!
GAMPH
AND THE CUTENESS OF MOKONA! ♥
IT'S TRUE. I COULDN'T HAVE WON WITHOUT MOKO-CHAN.
うわ。
EHH...

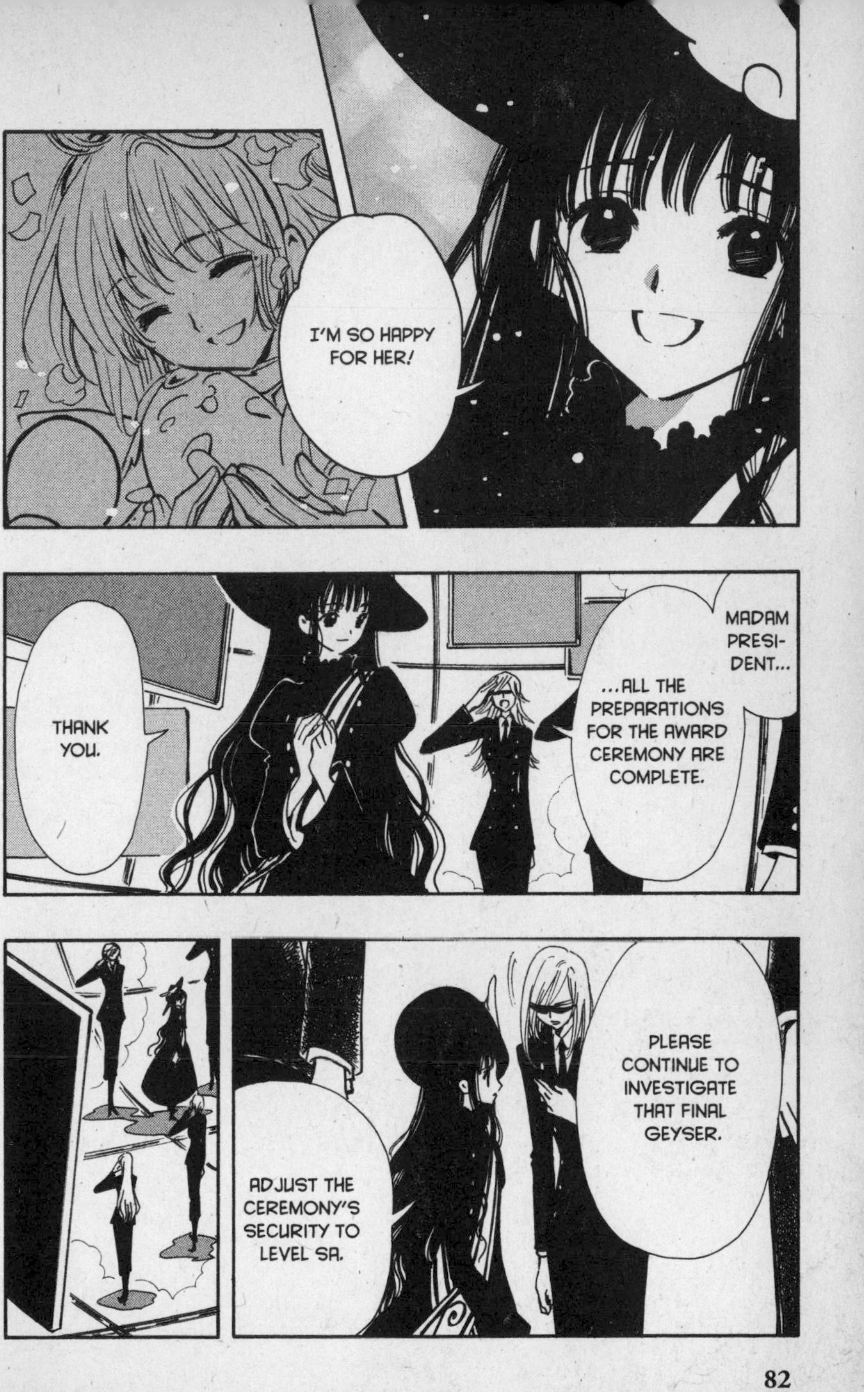
I'M SO HAPPY FOR HER!
MADAM PRESI-DENT...
...ALL THE PREPARATIONS FOR THE AWARD CEREMONY ARE COMPLETE.
THANK YOU.
PLEASE CONTINUE TO INVESTIGATE THAT FINAL GEYSER.
ADJUST THE CEREMONY'S SECURITY TO LEVEL SA.

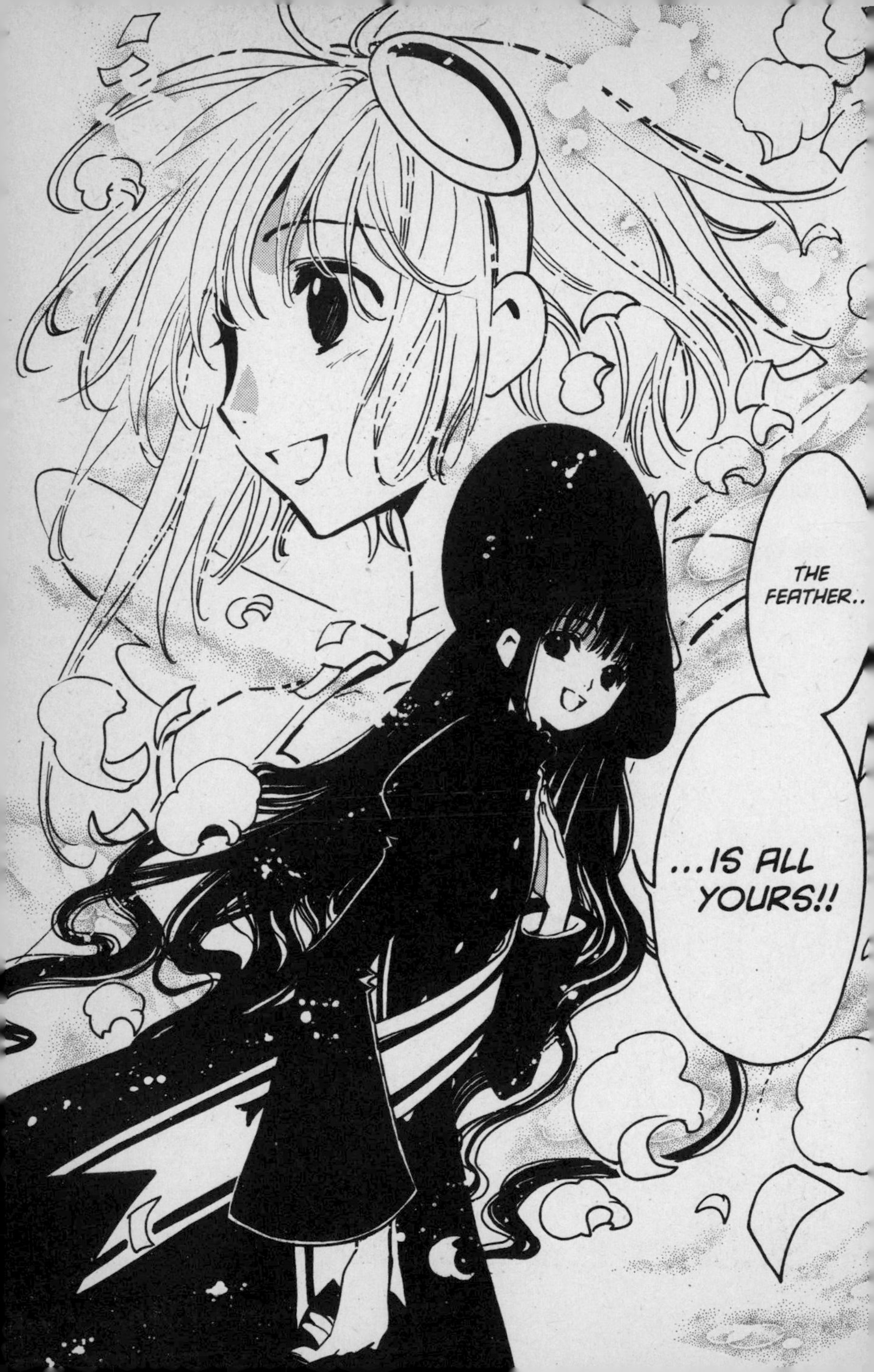
THE FEATHER..
...IS ALL YOURS!!

ツバサ
RESERVoir CHRoNiCLE

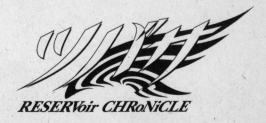

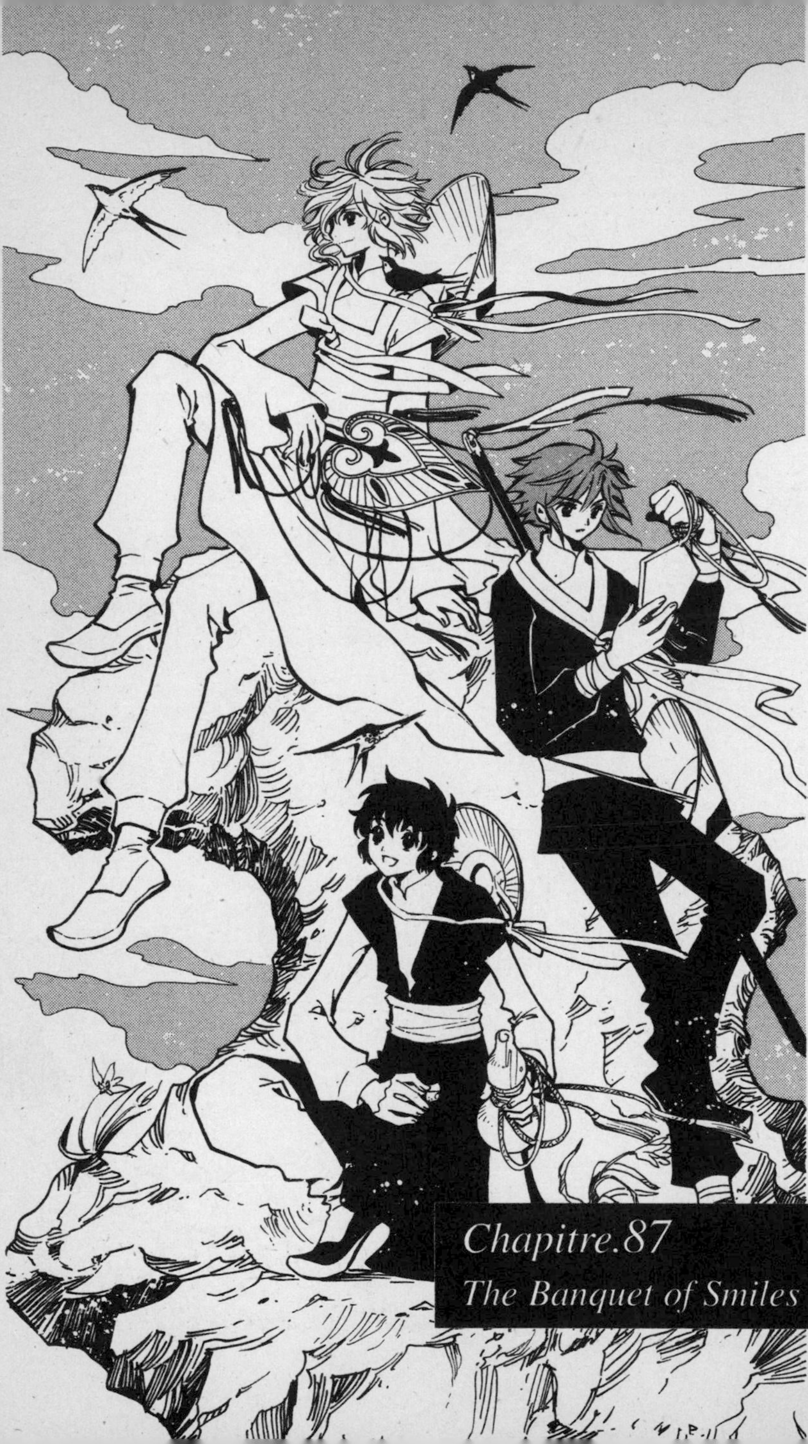
Chapitre.87
The Banquet of Smiles

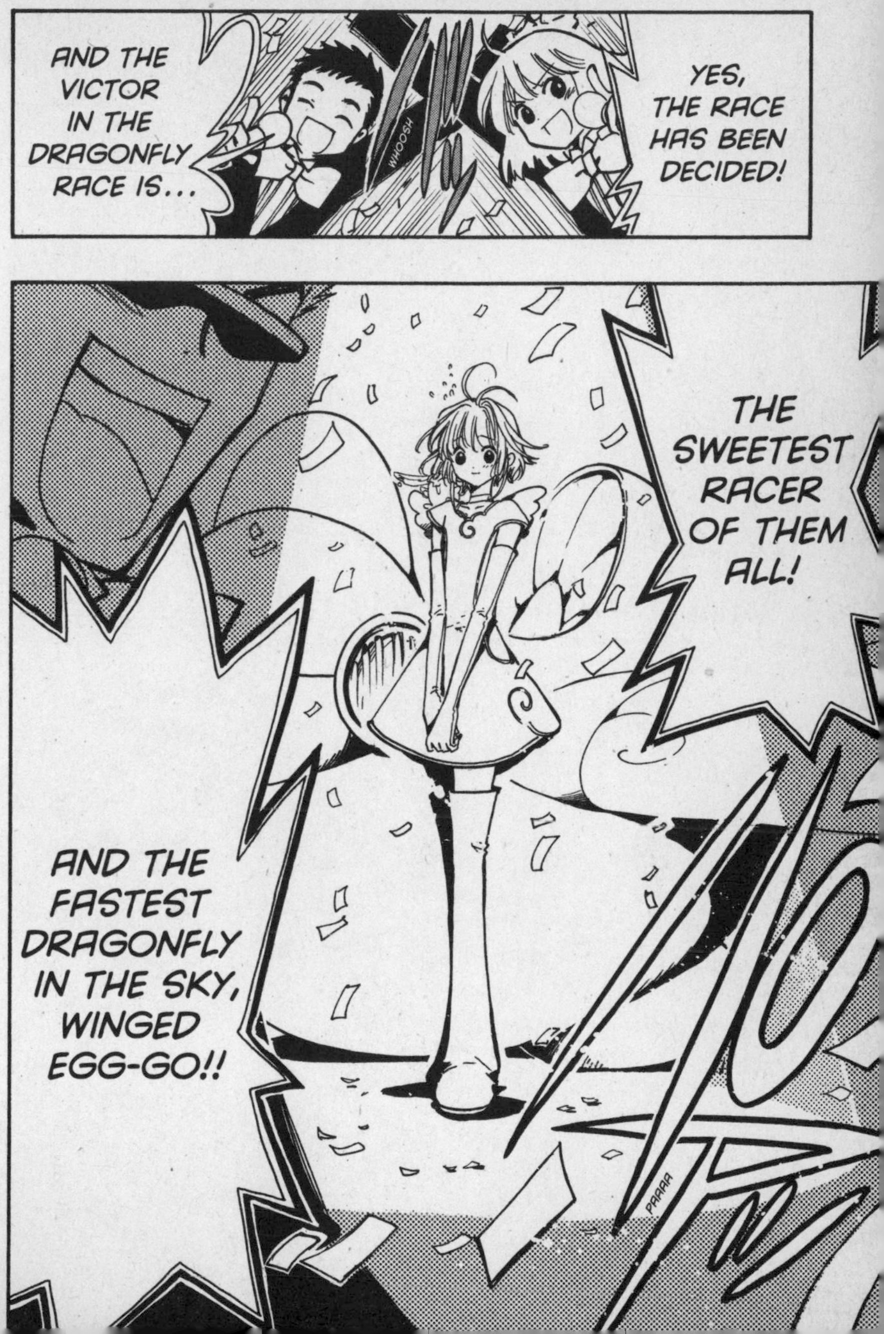
YES, THE RACE HAS BEEN DECIDED!
AND THE VICTOR IN THE DRAGONFLY RACE IS...
WHOOSH
THE SWEETEST RACER OF THEM ALL!
AND THE FASTEST DRAGONFLY IN THE SKY, WINGED EGG-GO!!
PAAAA

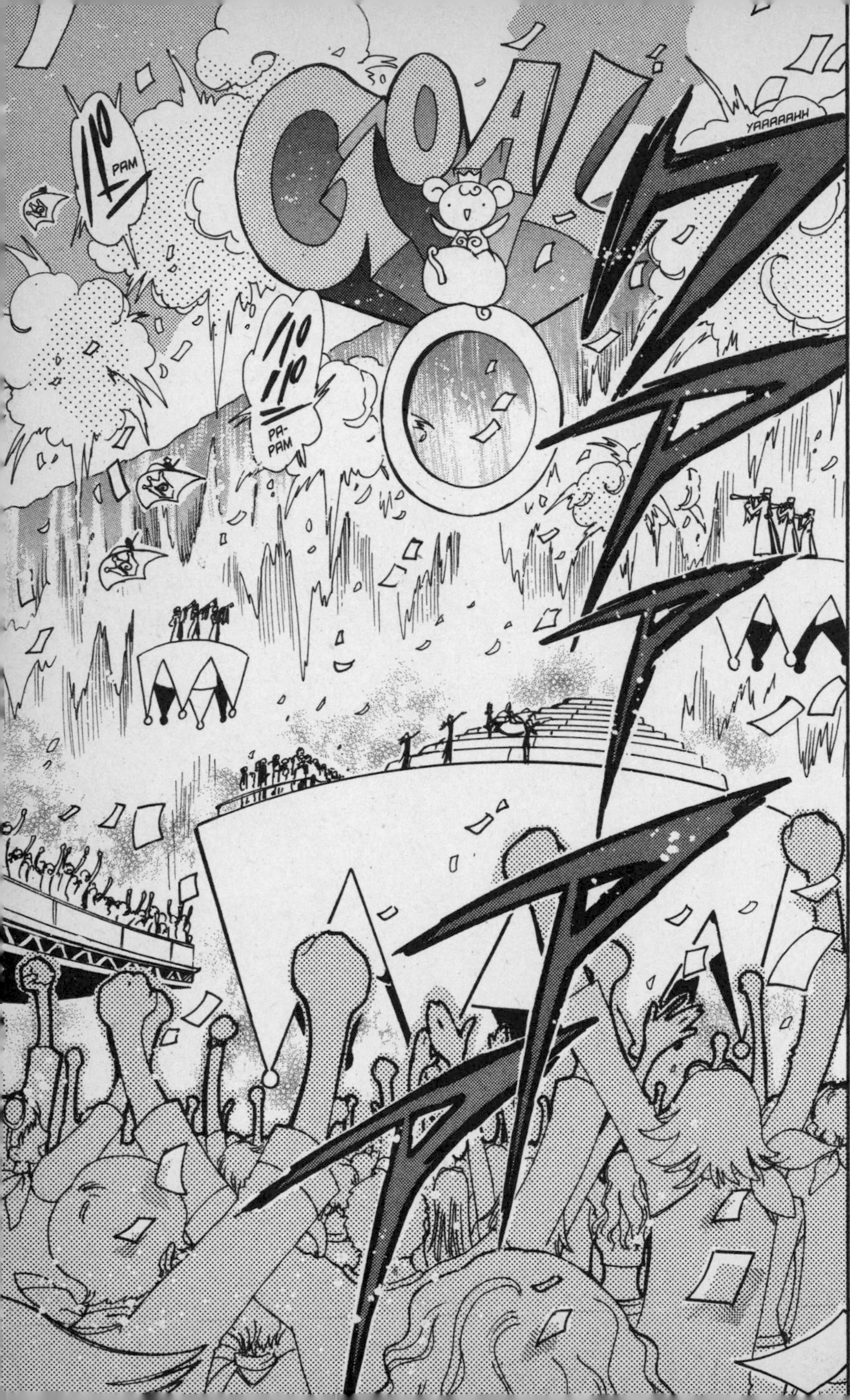
YAAAAAHH
GOAL
PA-PAM
PAM

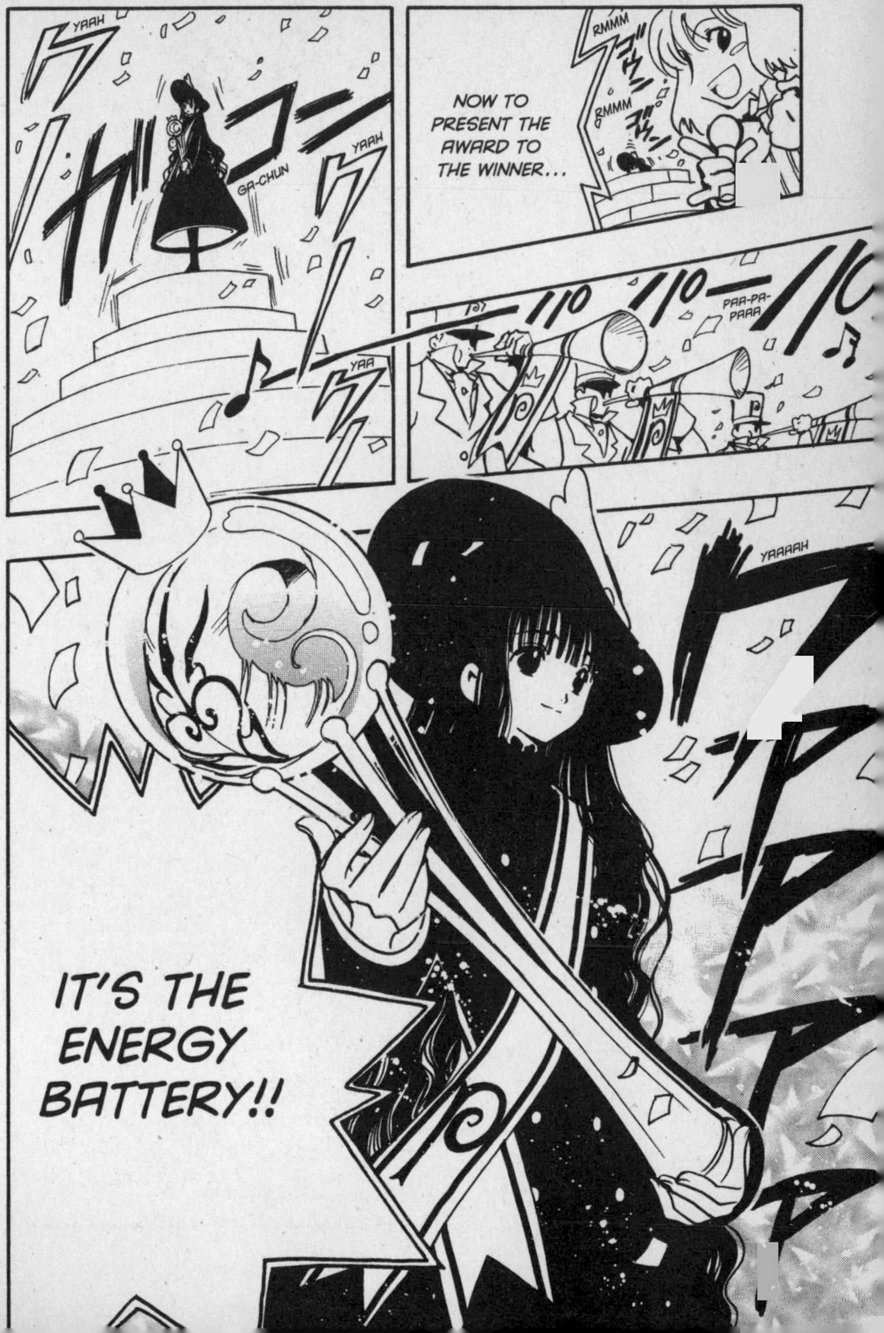
RMMM
RMMM
NOW TO PRESENT THE AWARD TO THE WINNER...
PAA-PA-PAAA
YAAH
YAAH
GA-CHUN
YAA
YAAAAH
IT'S THE ENERGY BATTERY!!

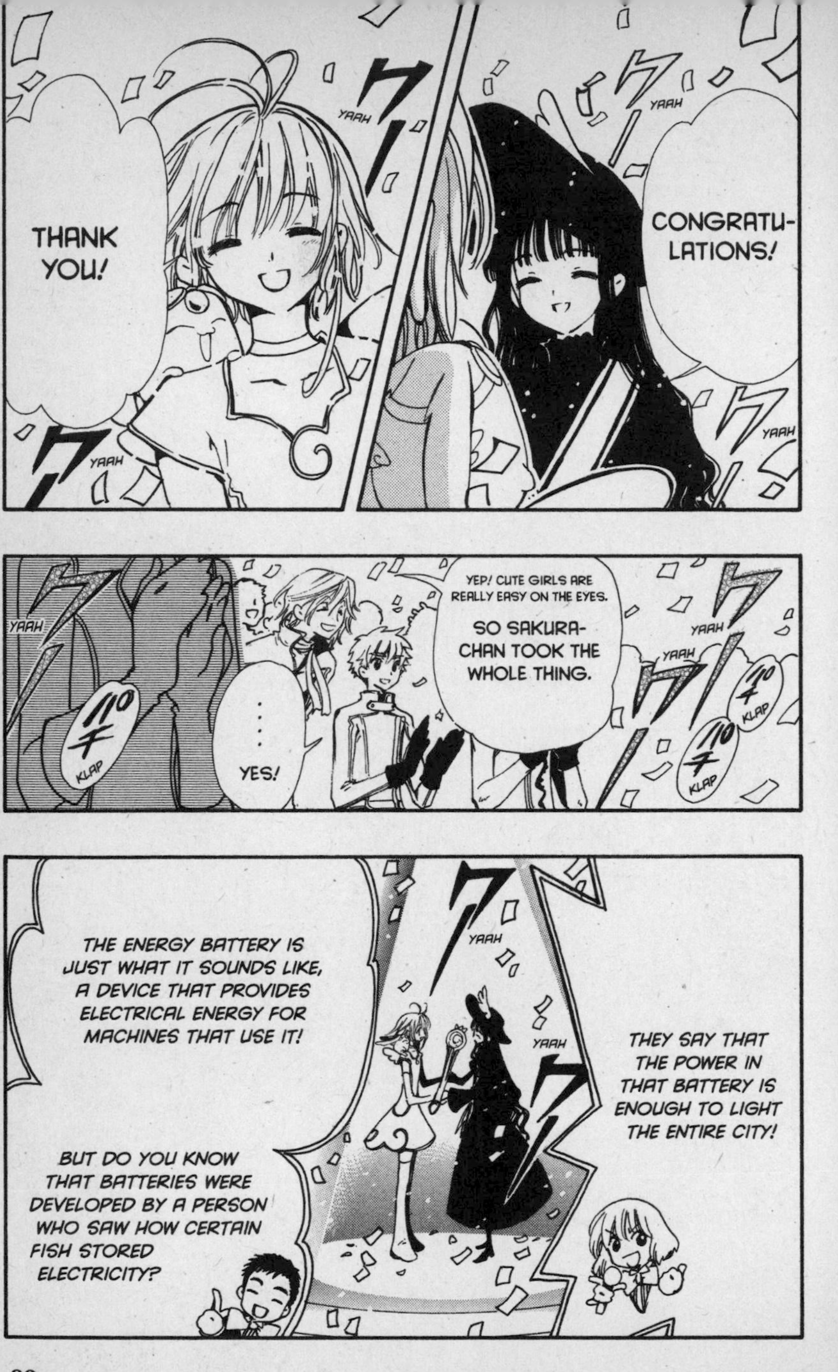
YAAH
CONGRATU-LATIONS!
YAAH
YAAH
THANK YOU!
YAAH
YAAH
YAAH
KLAP
KLAP
YEP! CUTE GIRLS ARE REALLY EASY ON THE EYES.
SO SAKURA-CHAN TOOK THE WHOLE THING.
...YES!
YAAH
KLAP
THEY SAY THAT THE POWER IN THAT BATTERY IS ENOUGH TO LIGHT THE ENTIRE CITY!
YAAH
YAAH
THE ENERGY BATTERY IS JUST WHAT IT SOUNDS LIKE, A DEVICE THAT PROVIDES ELECTRICAL ENERGY FOR MACHINES THAT USE IT!
BUT DO YOU KNOW THAT BATTERIES WERE DEVELOPED BY A PERSON WHO SAW HOW CERTAIN FISH STORED ELECTRICITY?

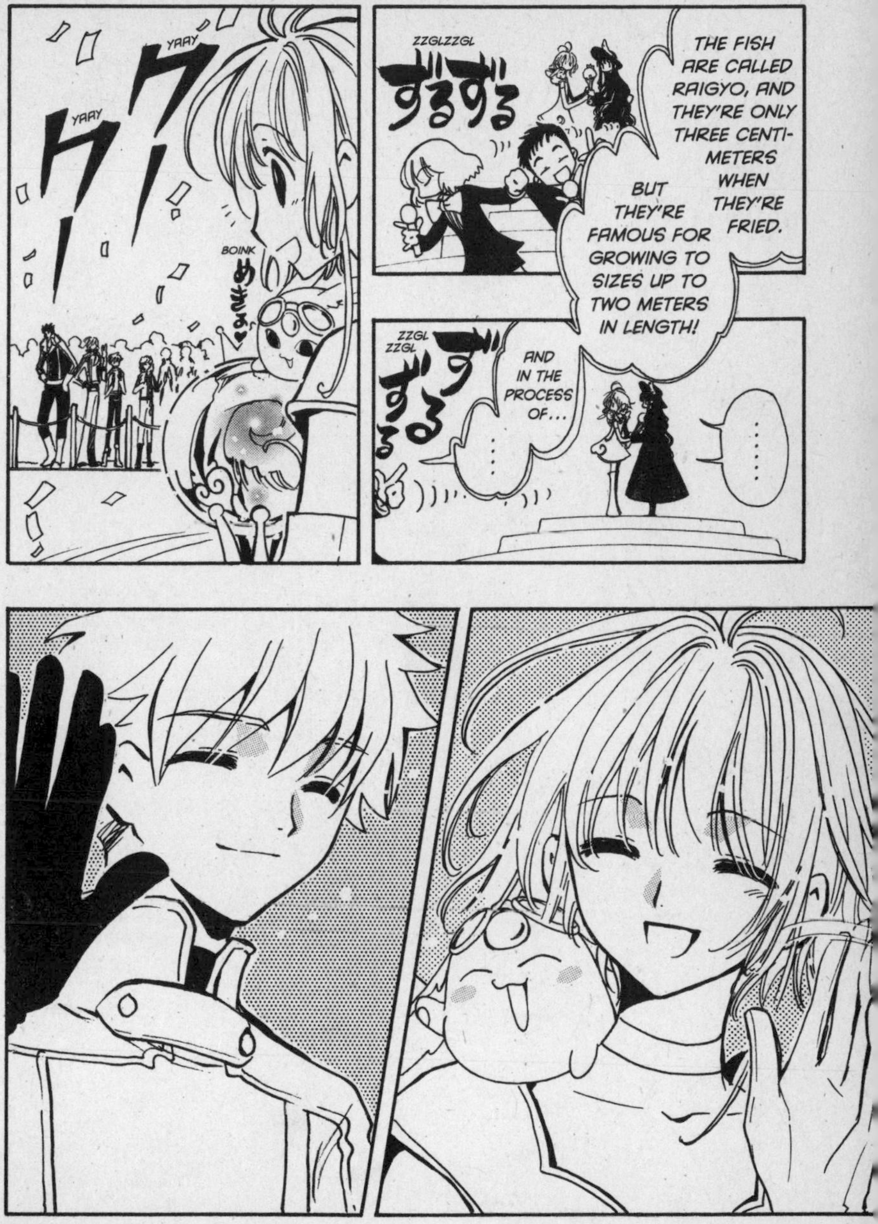
ZZGLZZGL
ずるずる
THE FISH ARE CALLED RAIGYO, AND THEY'RE ONLY THREE CENTI-METERS WHEN THEY'RE FRIED.
BUT THEY'RE FAMOUS FOR GROWING TO SIZES UP TO TWO METERS IN LENGTH!
AND IN THE PROCESS OF...
ZZGL ZZGL
......
......
YAAY
YAAY
BOINK

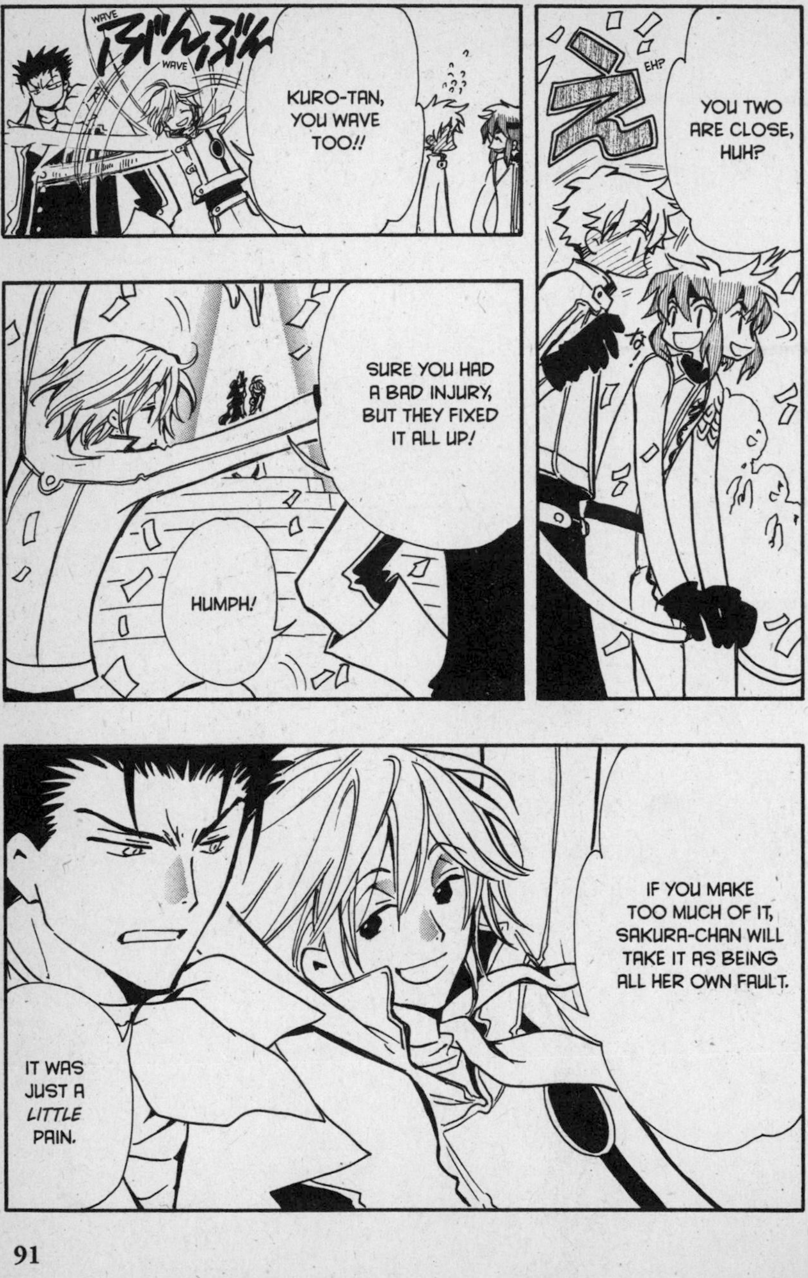
EH?
YOU TWO ARE CLOSE, HUH?
WAVE
WAVE
KURO-TAN, YOU WAVE TOO!!
SURE YOU HAD A BAD INJURY, BUT THEY FIXED IT ALL UP!
HUMPH!
IF YOU MAKE TOO MUCH OF IT, SAKURA-CHAN WILL TAKE IT AS BEING ALL HER OWN FAULT.
IT WAS JUST A *LITTLE* PAIN.

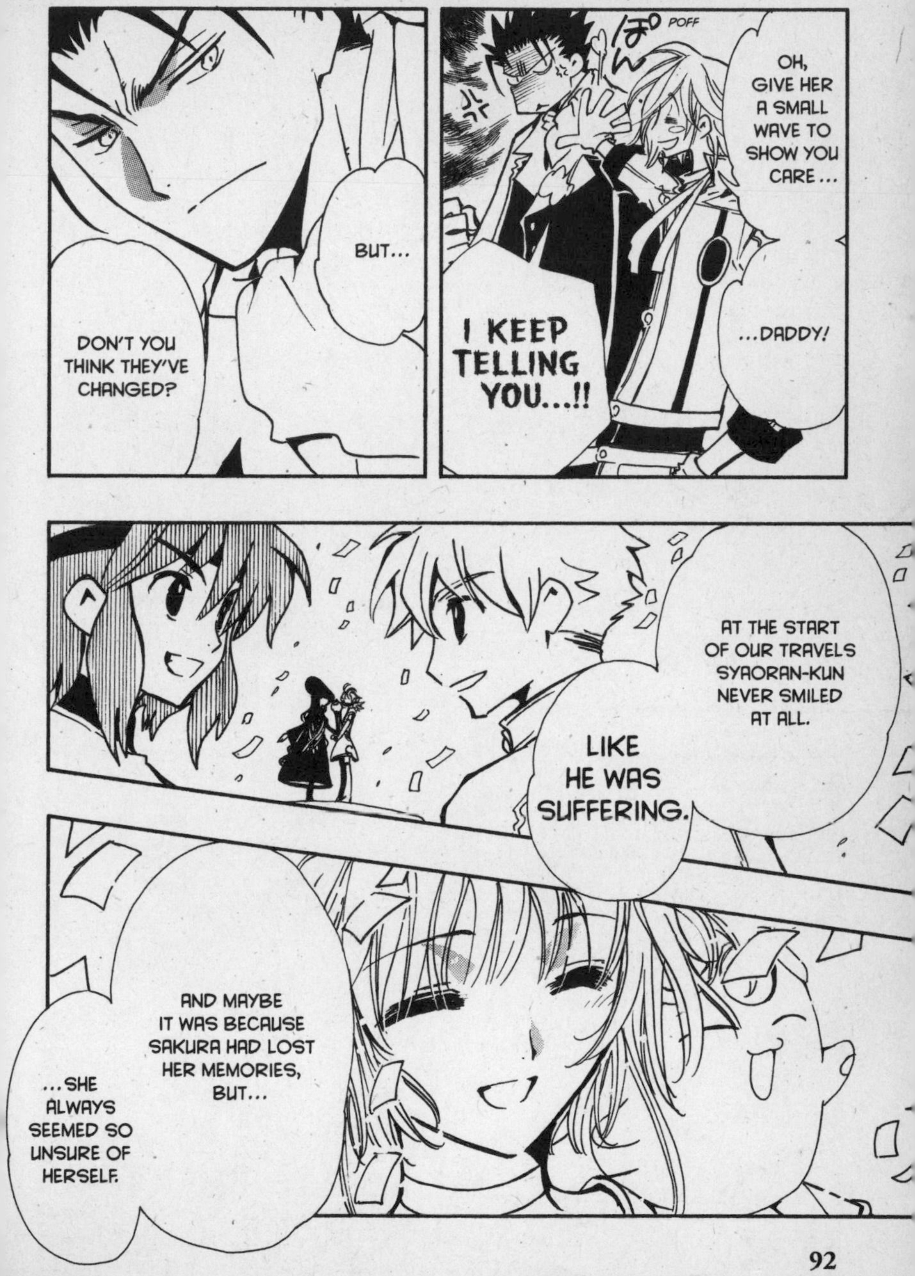
POFF
ぽん
OH, GIVE HER A SMALL WAVE TO SHOW YOU CARE...
...DADDY!
I KEEP TELLING YOU...!!
BUT...
DON'T YOU THINK THEY'VE CHANGED?
AT THE START OF OUR TRAVELS SYAORAN-KUN NEVER SMILED AT ALL.
LIKE HE WAS SUFFERING.
AND MAYBE IT WAS BECAUSE SAKURA HAD LOST HER MEMORIES, BUT...
...SHE ALWAYS SEEMED SO UNSURE OF HERSELF.

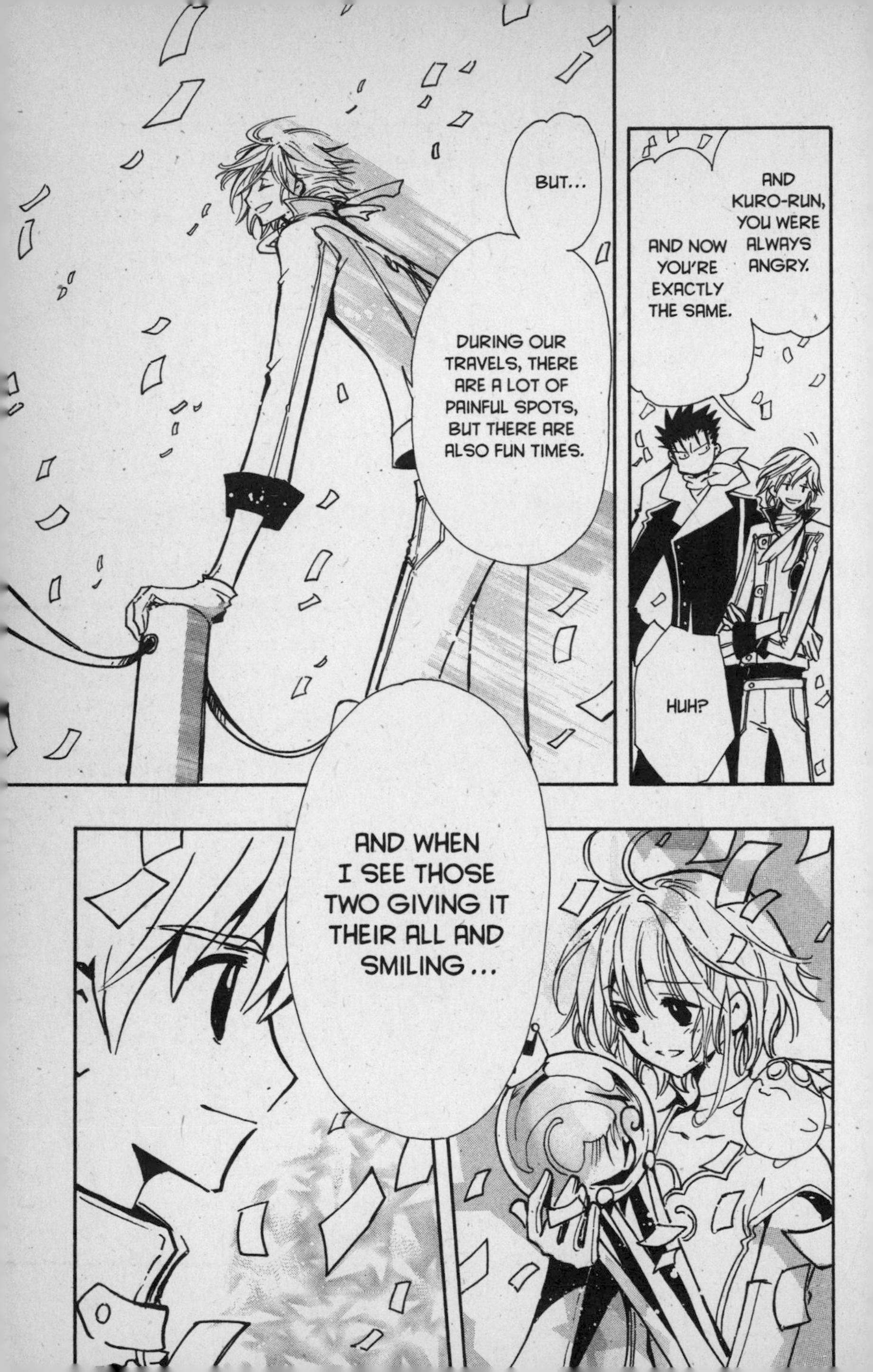
AND KURO-RUN, YOU WERE ALWAYS ANGRY.
AND NOW YOU'RE EXACTLY THE SAME.
HUH?
BUT…
DURING OUR TRAVELS, THERE ARE A LOT OF PAINFUL SPOTS, BUT THERE ARE ALSO FUN TIMES.
AND WHEN I SEE THOSE TWO GIVING IT THEIR ALL AND SMILING…

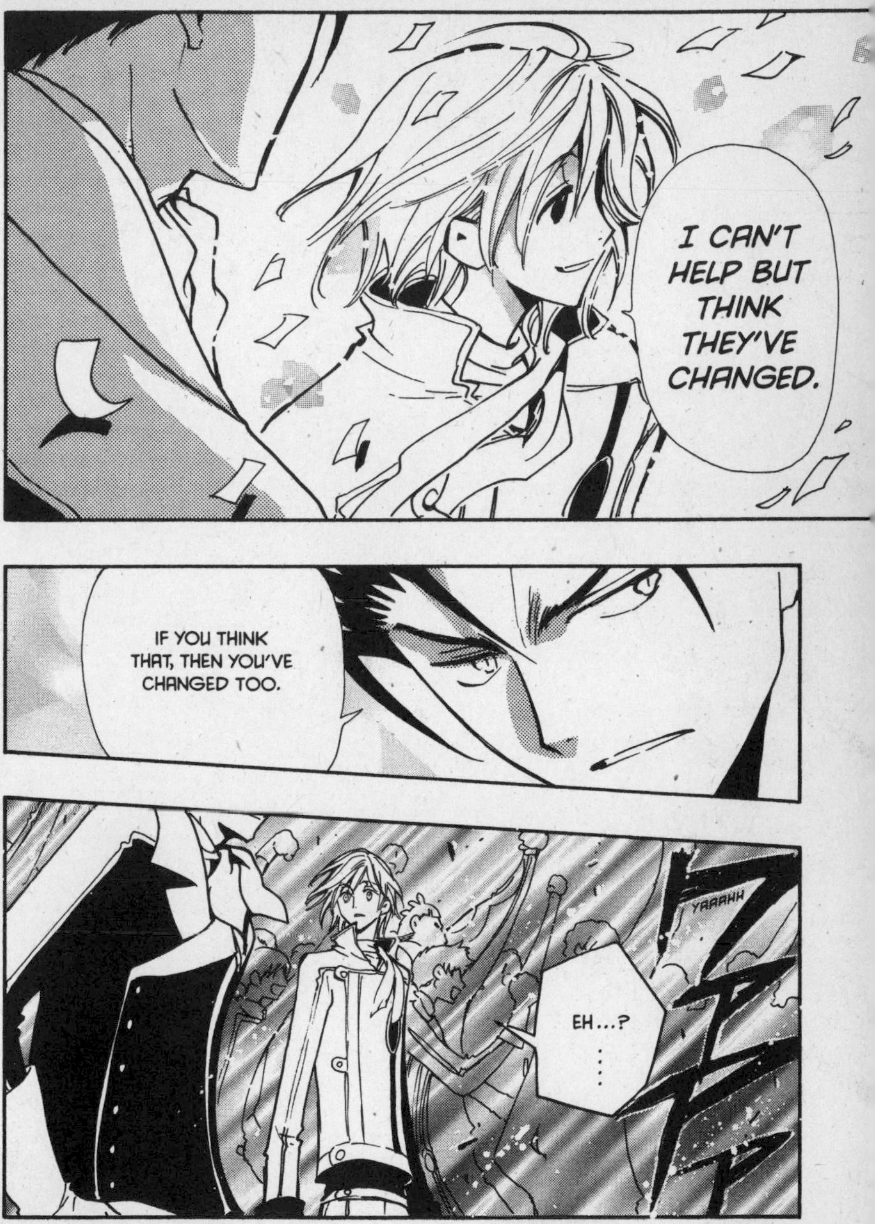
I CAN'T HELP BUT THINK THEY'VE CHANGED.
IF YOU THINK THAT, THEN YOU'VE CHANGED TOO.
YAAAHH
EH...?
....

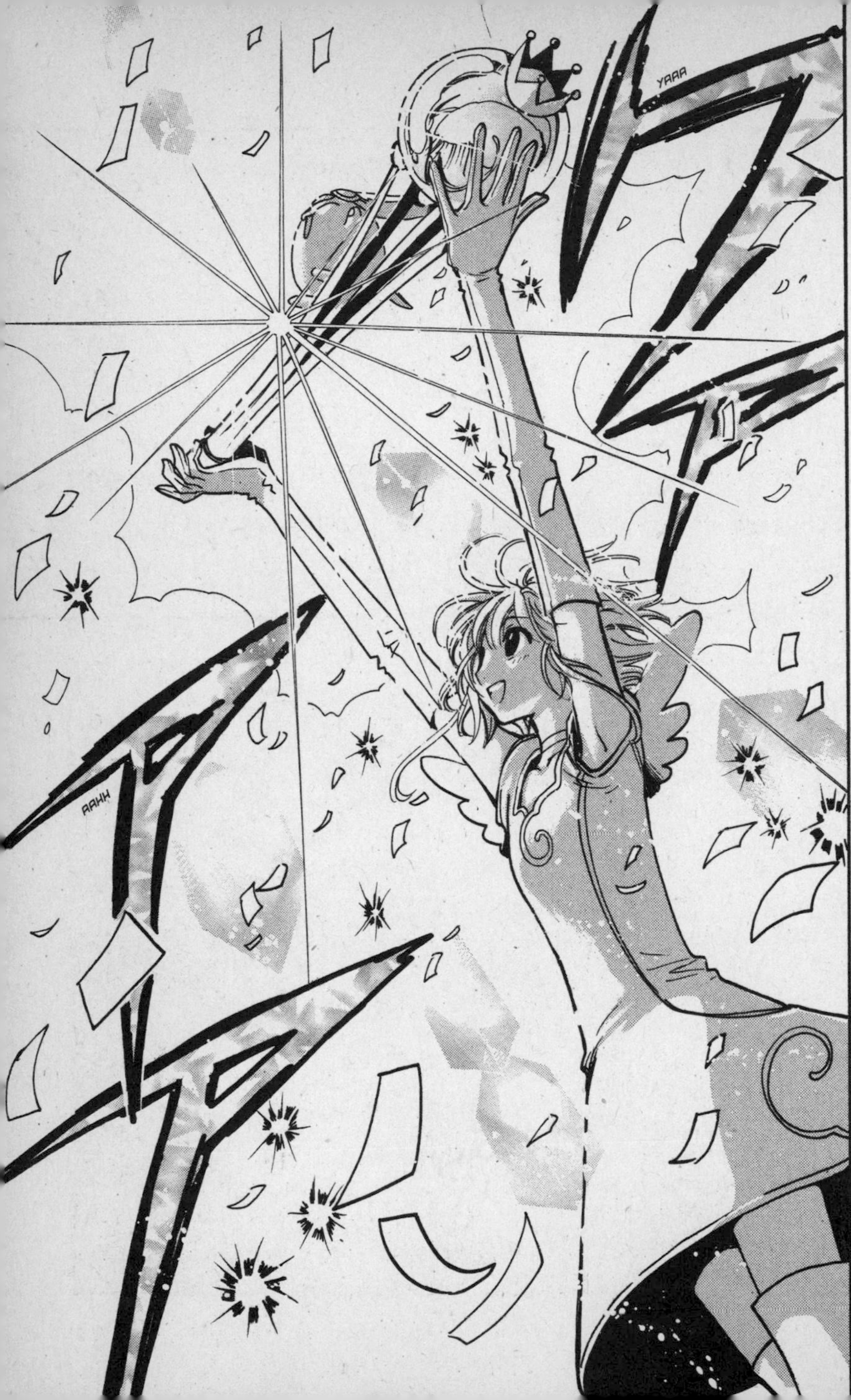
YAAA
AAHH

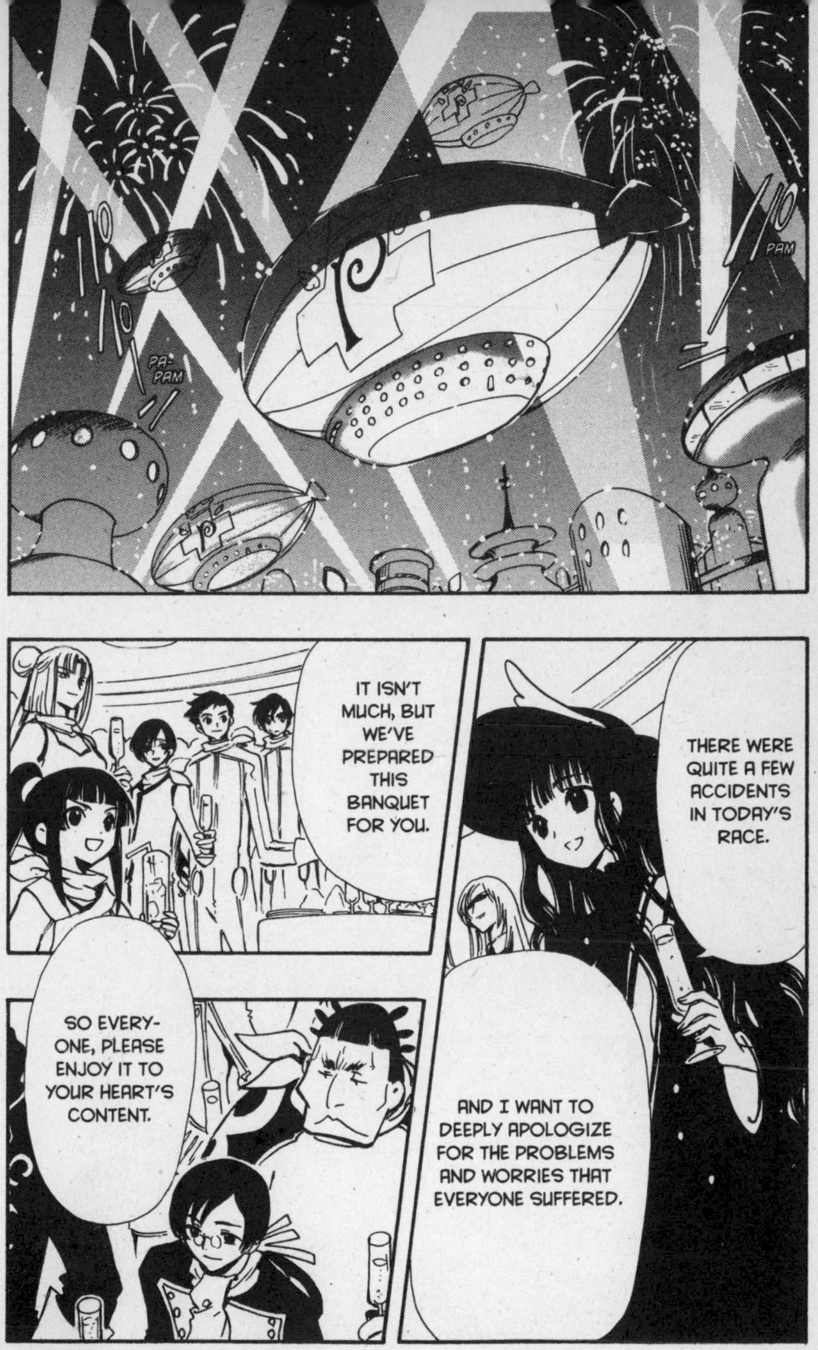
PAM
PA-PAM
THERE WERE QUITE A FEW ACCIDENTS IN TODAY'S RACE.
AND I WANT TO DEEPLY APOLOGIZE FOR THE PROBLEMS AND WORRIES THAT EVERYONE SUFFERED.
IT ISN'T MUCH, BUT WE'VE PREPARED THIS BANQUET FOR YOU.
SO EVERY-ONE, PLEASE ENJOY IT TO YOUR HEART'S CONTENT.

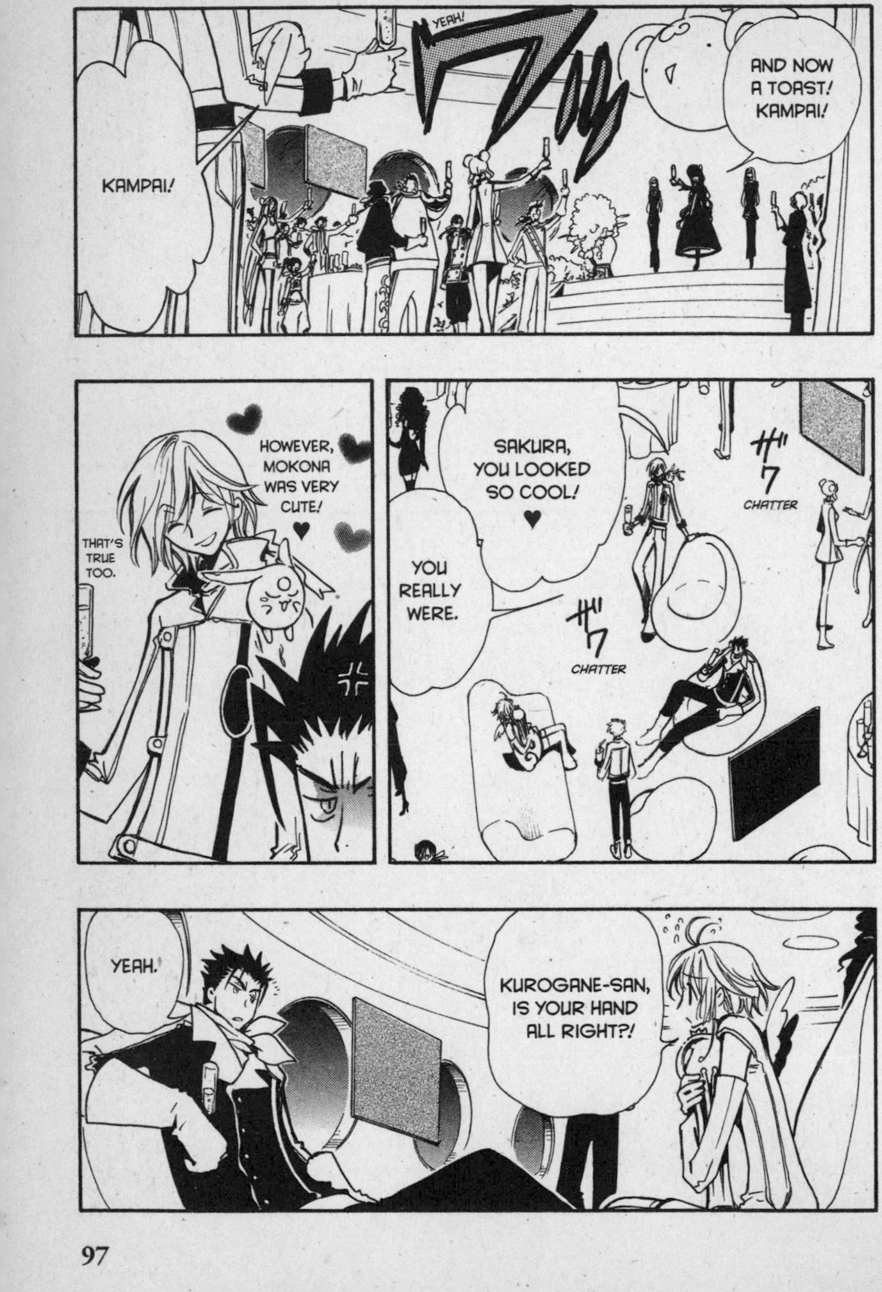
AND NOW A TOAST! KAMPAI!
YEAH!
KAMPAI!
SAKURA, YOU LOOKED SO COOL! ♥
ザワ
CHATTER
YOU REALLY WERE.
ザワ
CHATTER
HOWEVER, MOKONA WAS VERY CUTE! ♥
THAT'S TRUE TOO.
KUROGANE-SAN, IS YOUR HAND ALL RIGHT?!
YEAH.

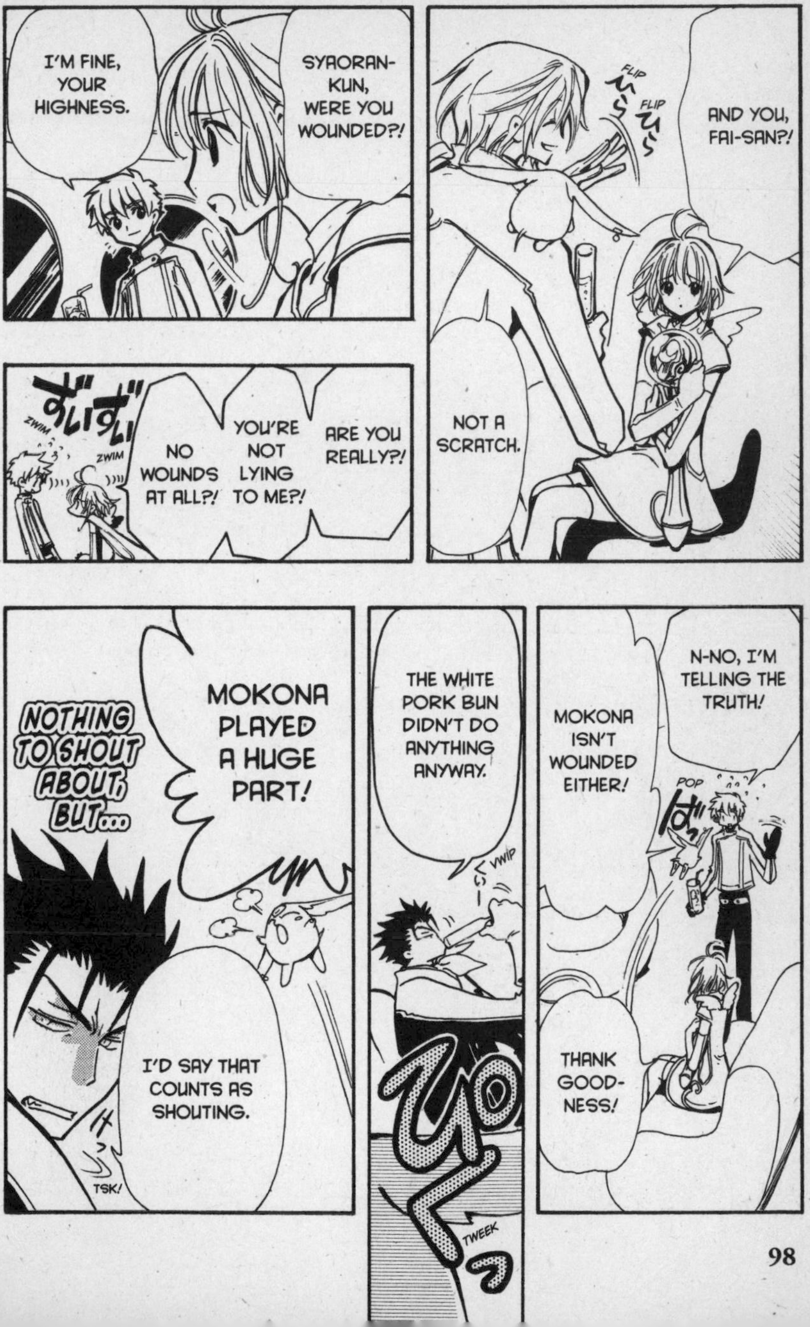
FLIP
ひら
FLIP
ひら
AND YOU, FAI-SAN?!
NOT A SCRATCH.
SYAORAN-KUN, WERE YOU WOUNDED?!
I'M FINE, YOUR HIGHNESS.
ARE YOU REALLY?!
YOU'RE NOT LYING TO ME?!
NO WOUNDS AT ALL?!
ずいずい
ZWIM
ZWIM
N-NO, I'M TELLING THE TRUTH!
MOKONA ISN'T WOUNDED EITHER!
POP
ぱっ
THANK GOOD-NESS!
THE WHITE PORK BUN DIDN'T DO ANYTHING ANYWAY.
VWIP
くいー
TWEEK
MOKONA PLAYED A HUGE PART!
NOTHING TO SHOUT ABOUT, BUT...
I'D SAY THAT COUNTS AS SHOUTING.
けっ
TSK!

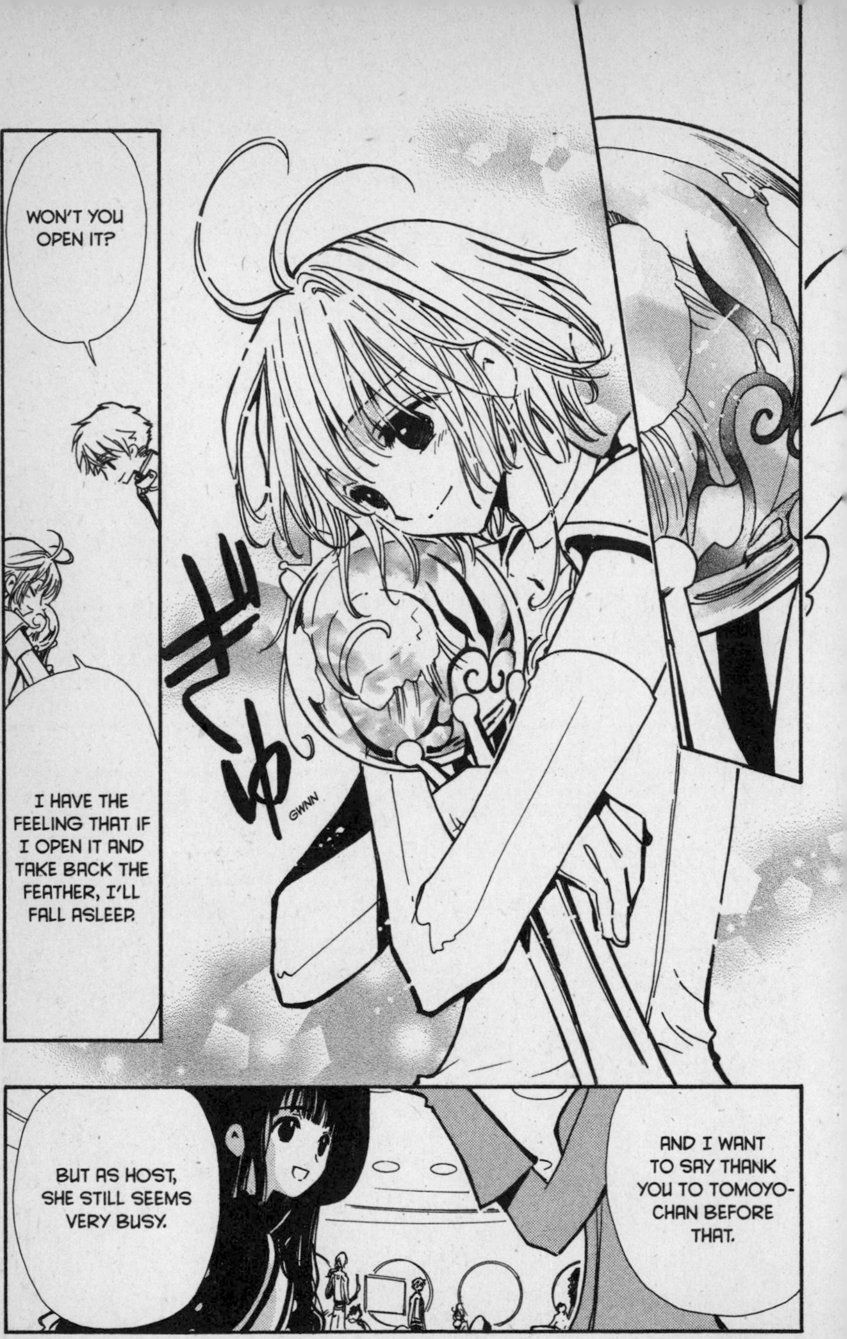
ぎゅ
GWNN
WON'T YOU OPEN IT?
I HAVE THE FEELING THAT IF I OPEN IT AND TAKE BACK THE FEATHER, I'LL FALL ASLEEP.
AND I WANT TO SAY THANK YOU TO TOMOYO-CHAN BEFORE THAT.
BUT AS HOST, SHE STILL SEEMS VERY BUSY.

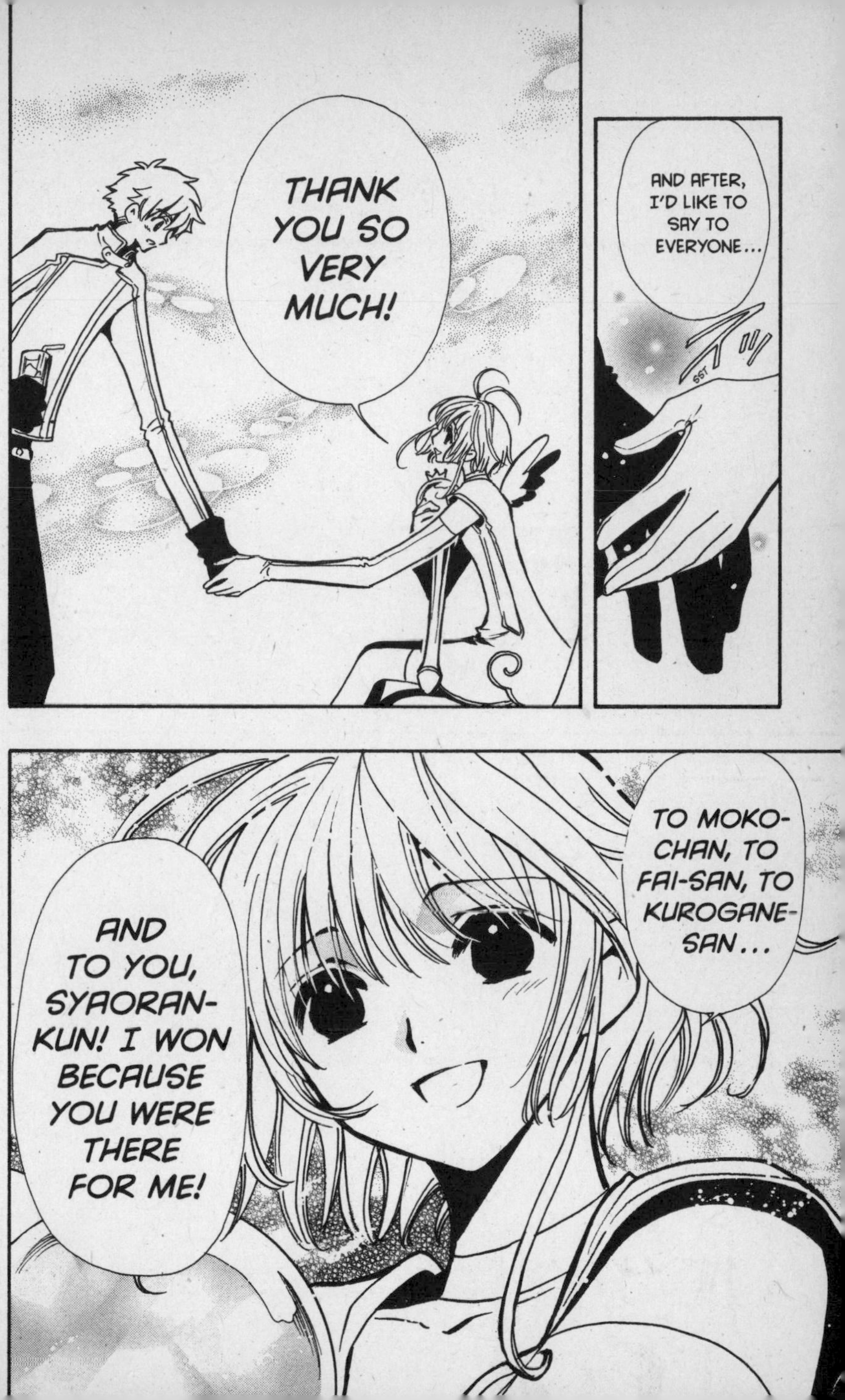
AND AFTER, I'D LIKE TO SAY TO EVERYONE...
SST
THANK YOU SO VERY MUCH!
TO MOKO-CHAN, TO FAI-SAN, TO KUROGANE-SAN...
AND TO YOU, SYAORAN-KUN! I WON BECAUSE YOU WERE THERE FOR ME!

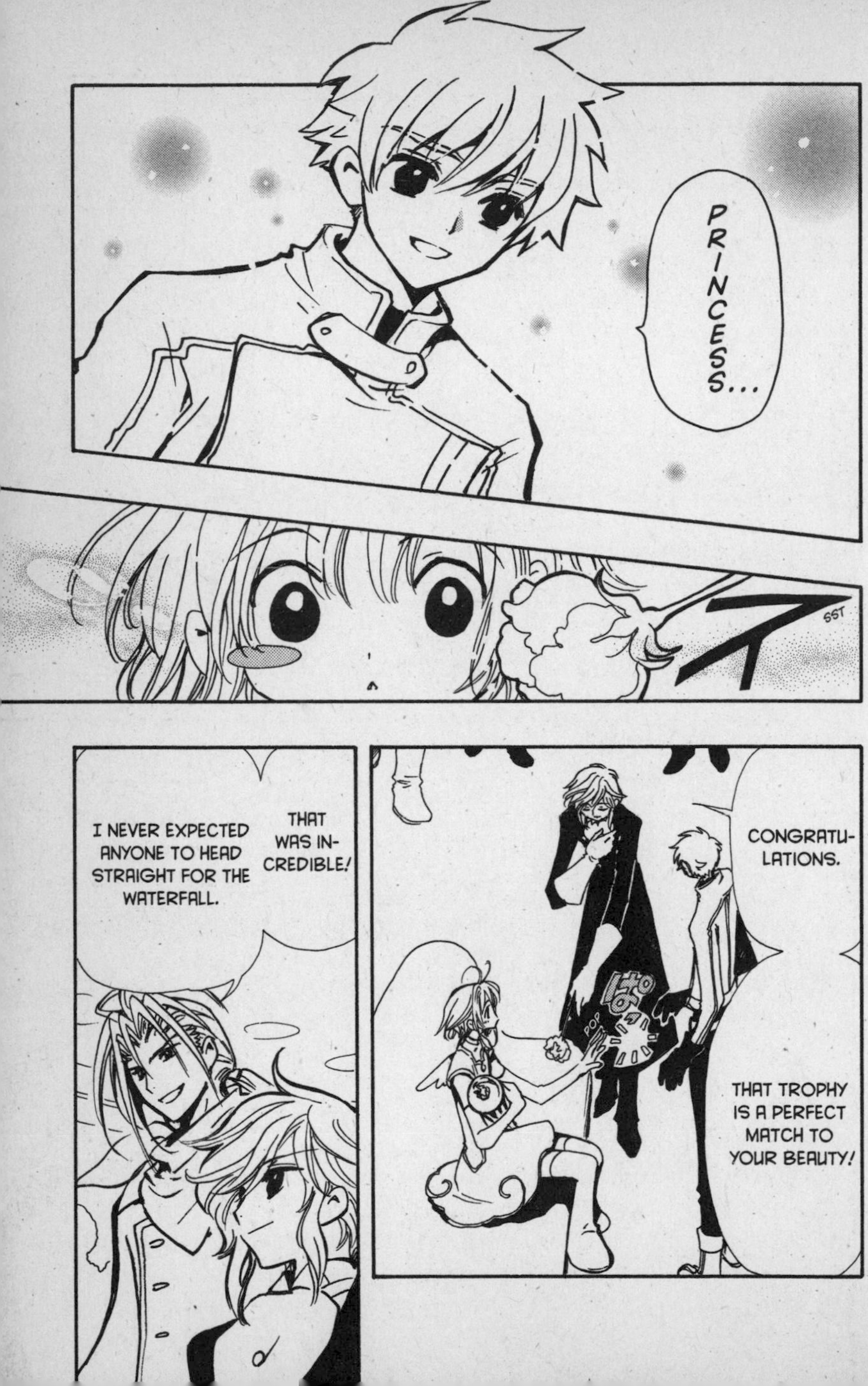
PRINCESS...
SST
CONGRATU-LATIONS.
ぽっ
POP
THAT TROPHY IS A PERFECT MATCH TO YOUR BEAUTY!
THAT WAS IN-CREDIBLE!
I NEVER EXPECTED ANYONE TO HEAD STRAIGHT FOR THE WATERFALL.

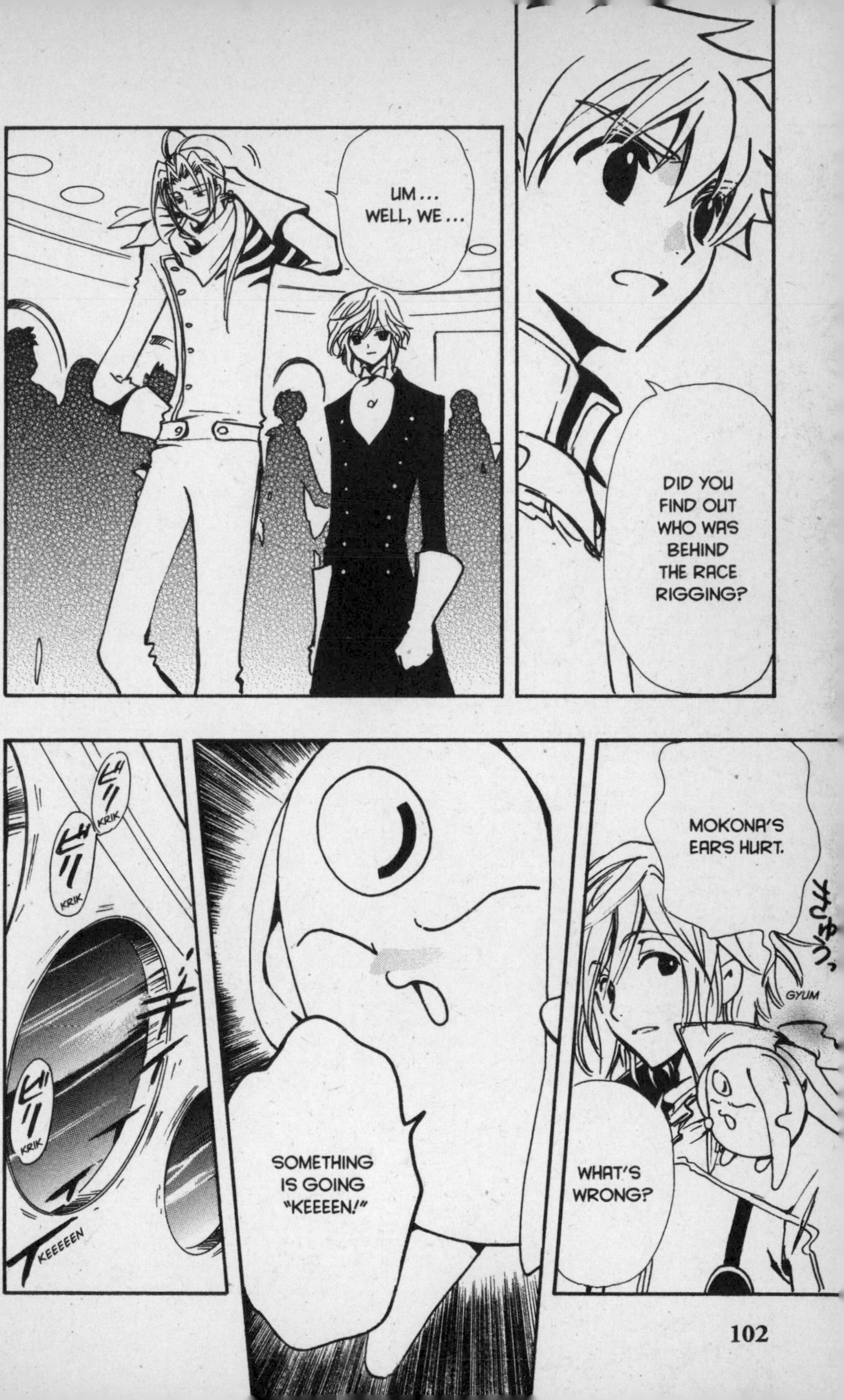
DID YOU FIND OUT WHO WAS BEHIND THE RACE RIGGING?
UM... WELL, WE...
MOKONA'S EARS HURT.
GYUM
WHAT'S WRONG?
SOMETHING IS GOING "KEEEEN!"
KRIK
KRIK
KRIK
KEEEEEN

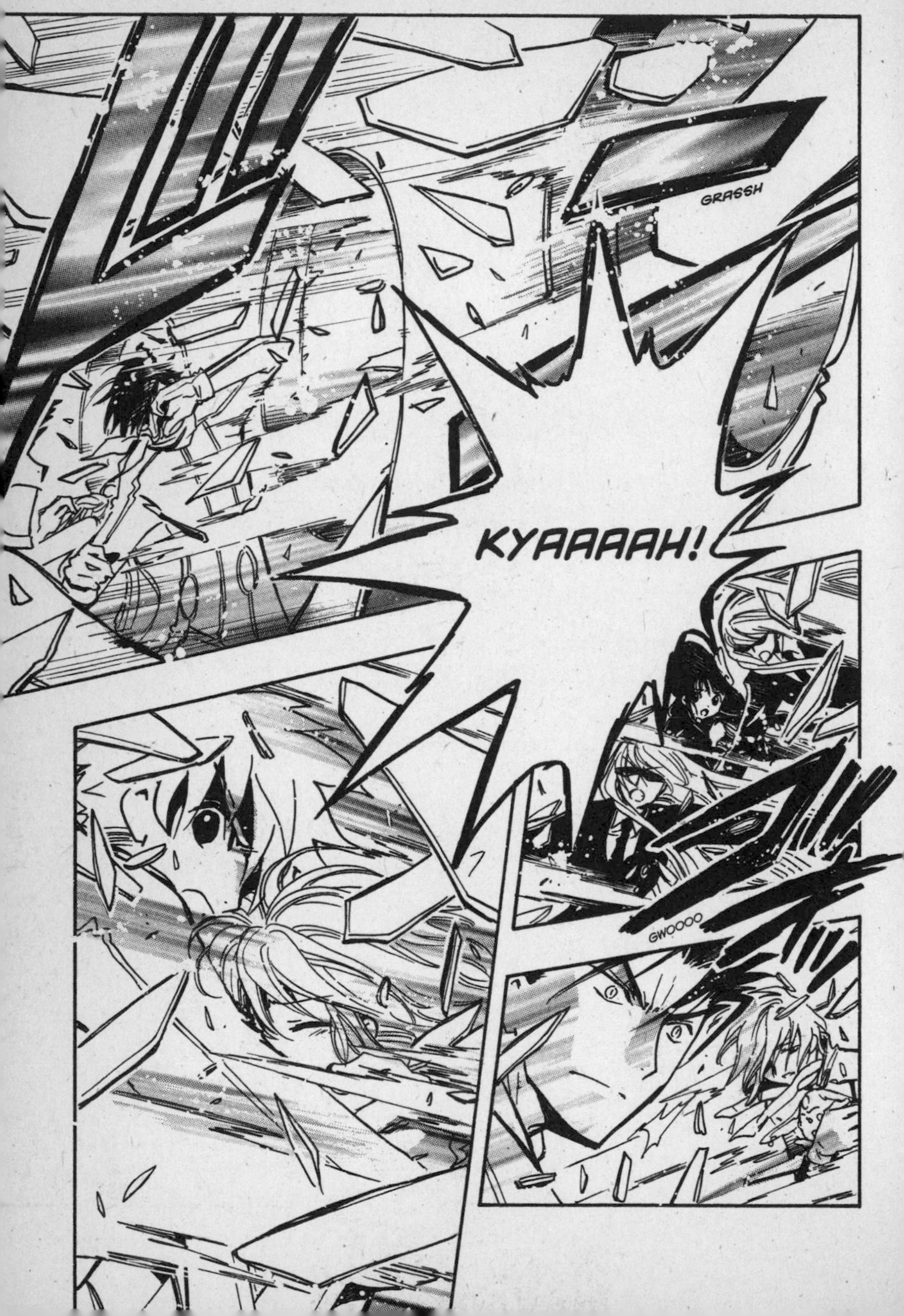
GRASSH
KYAAAAH!
GWOOOO

ツバサ

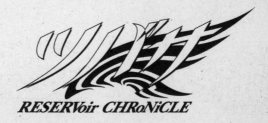

RESERVoir CHRoNiCLE

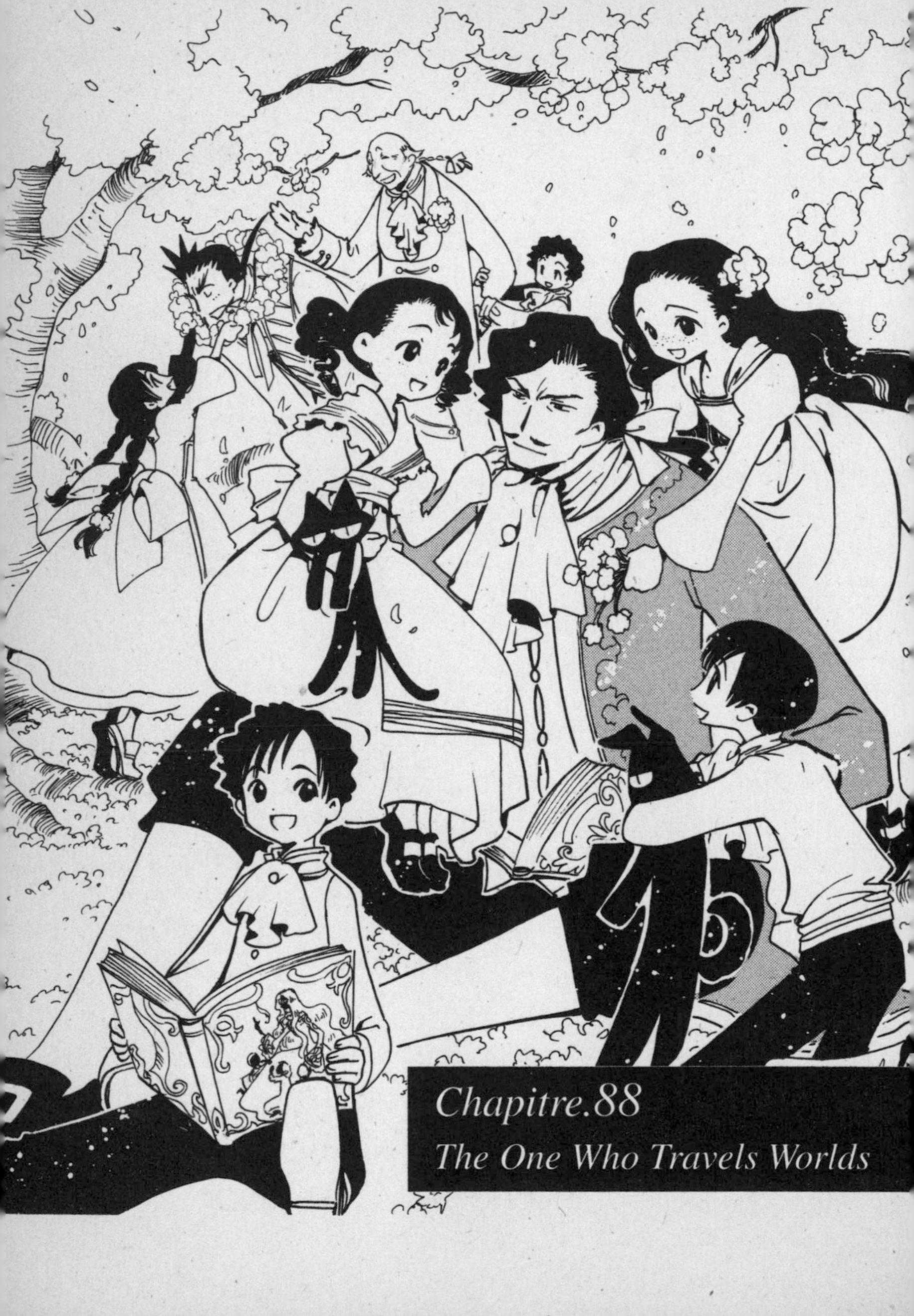

Chapitre.88
The One Who Travels Worlds

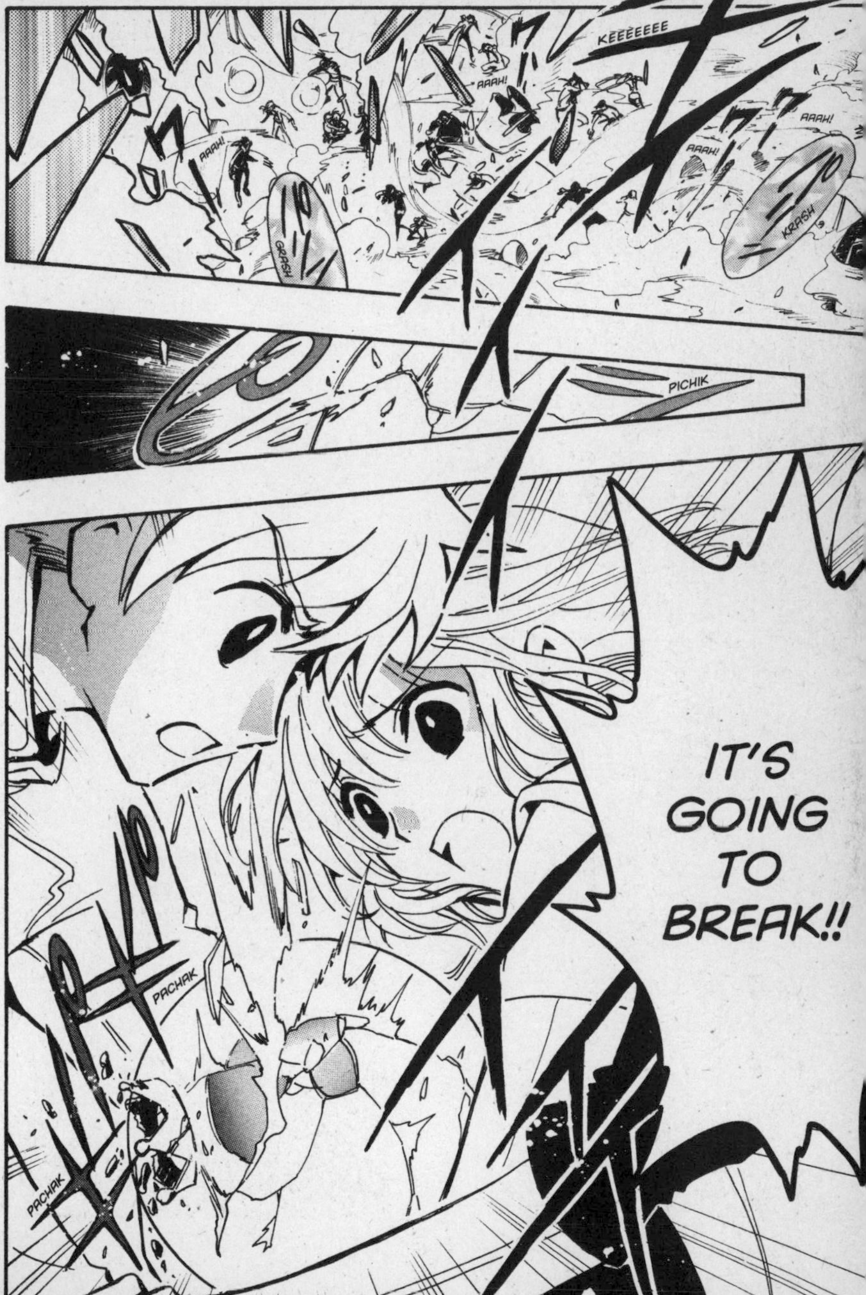
KEEEEEEE
AAAH!
AAAH!
KRASH
AAAH!
AAAH!
CRASH
PICHIK
IT'S GOING TO BREAK!!
PACHAK
PACHAK

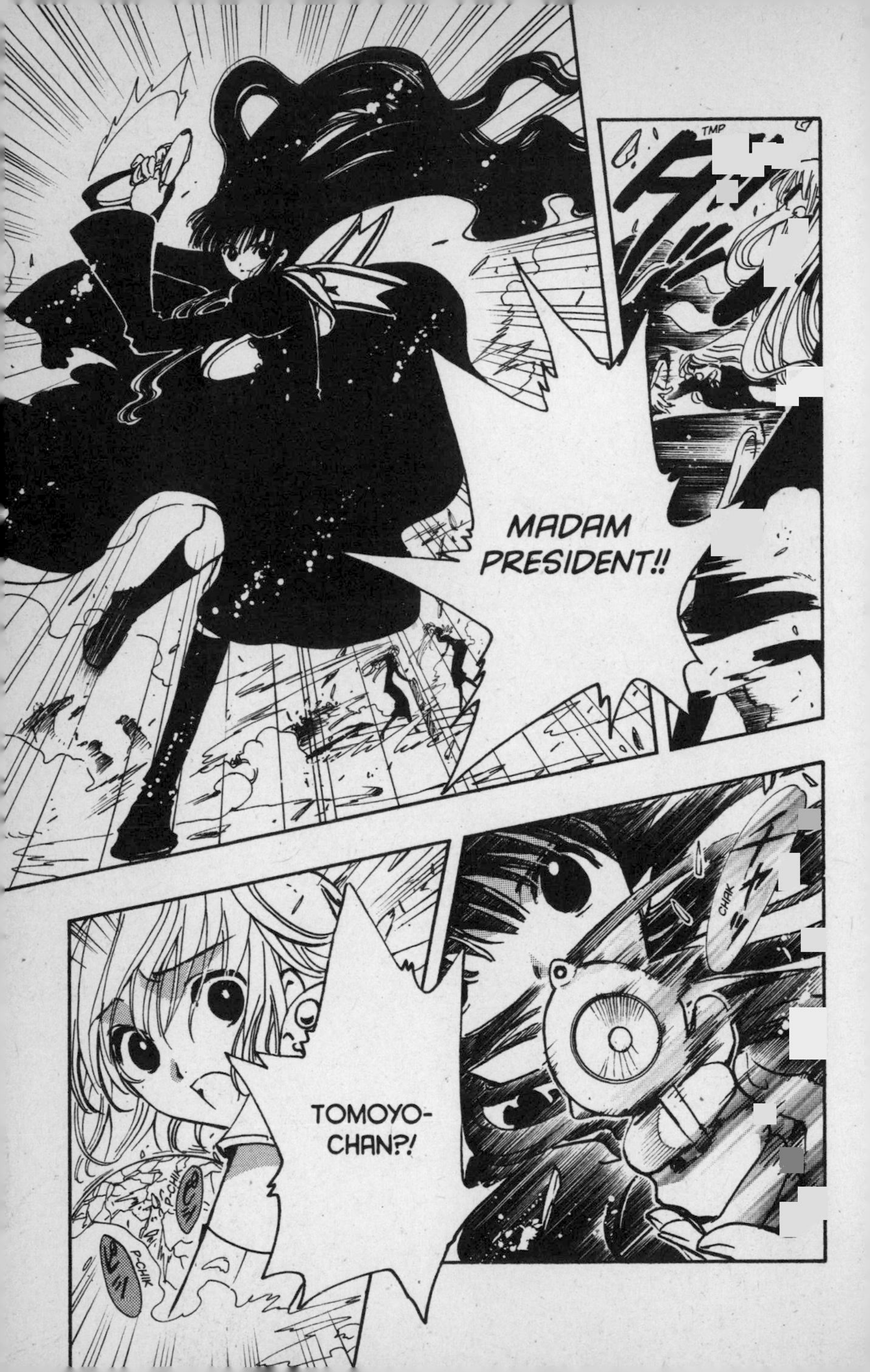
TMP
MADAM PRESIDENT!!
CHAK
TOMOYO-CHAN?!
P-CHIK
P-CHIK

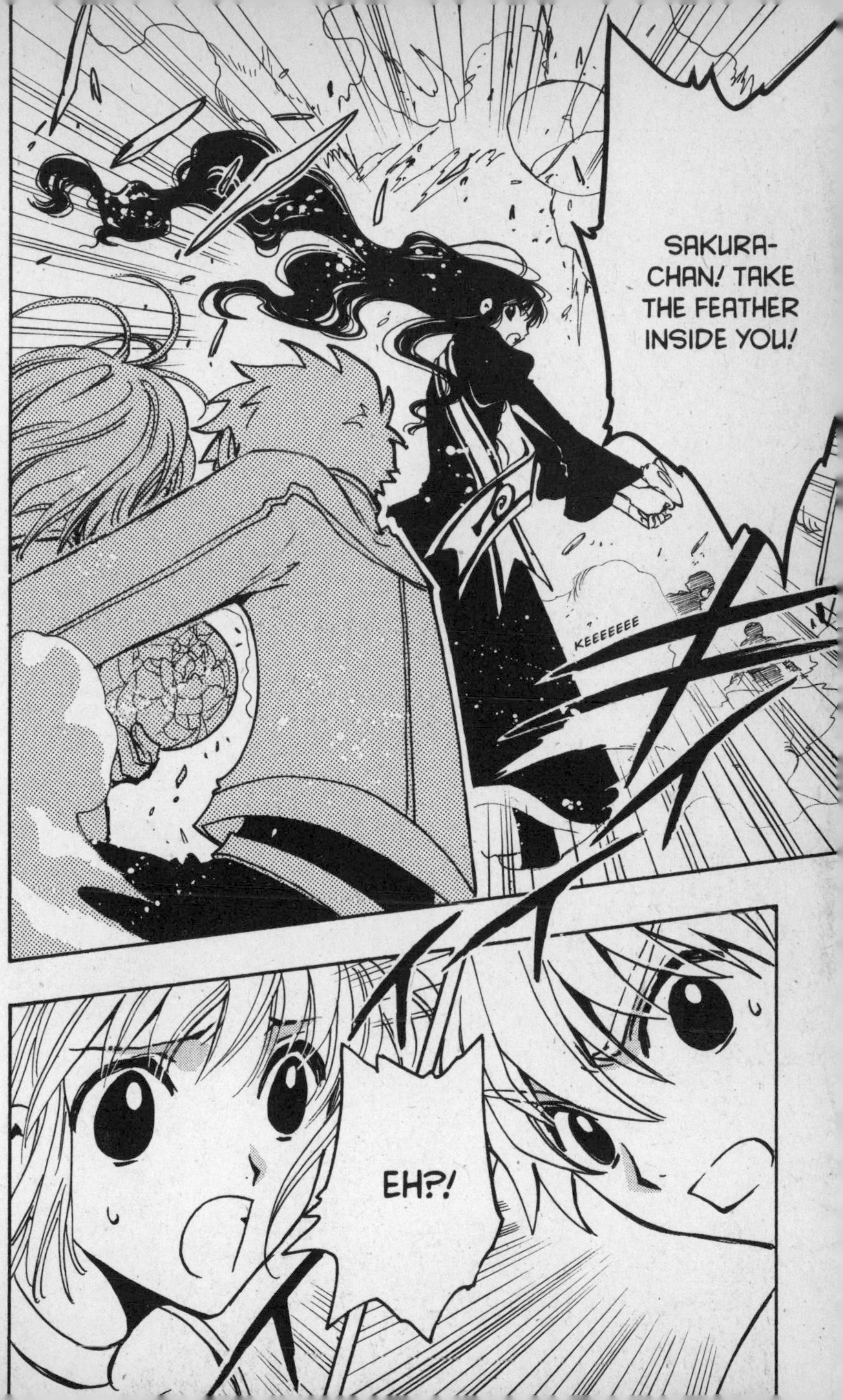
SAKURA-CHAN! TAKE THE FEATHER INSIDE YOU!
KEEEEEEE
EH?!

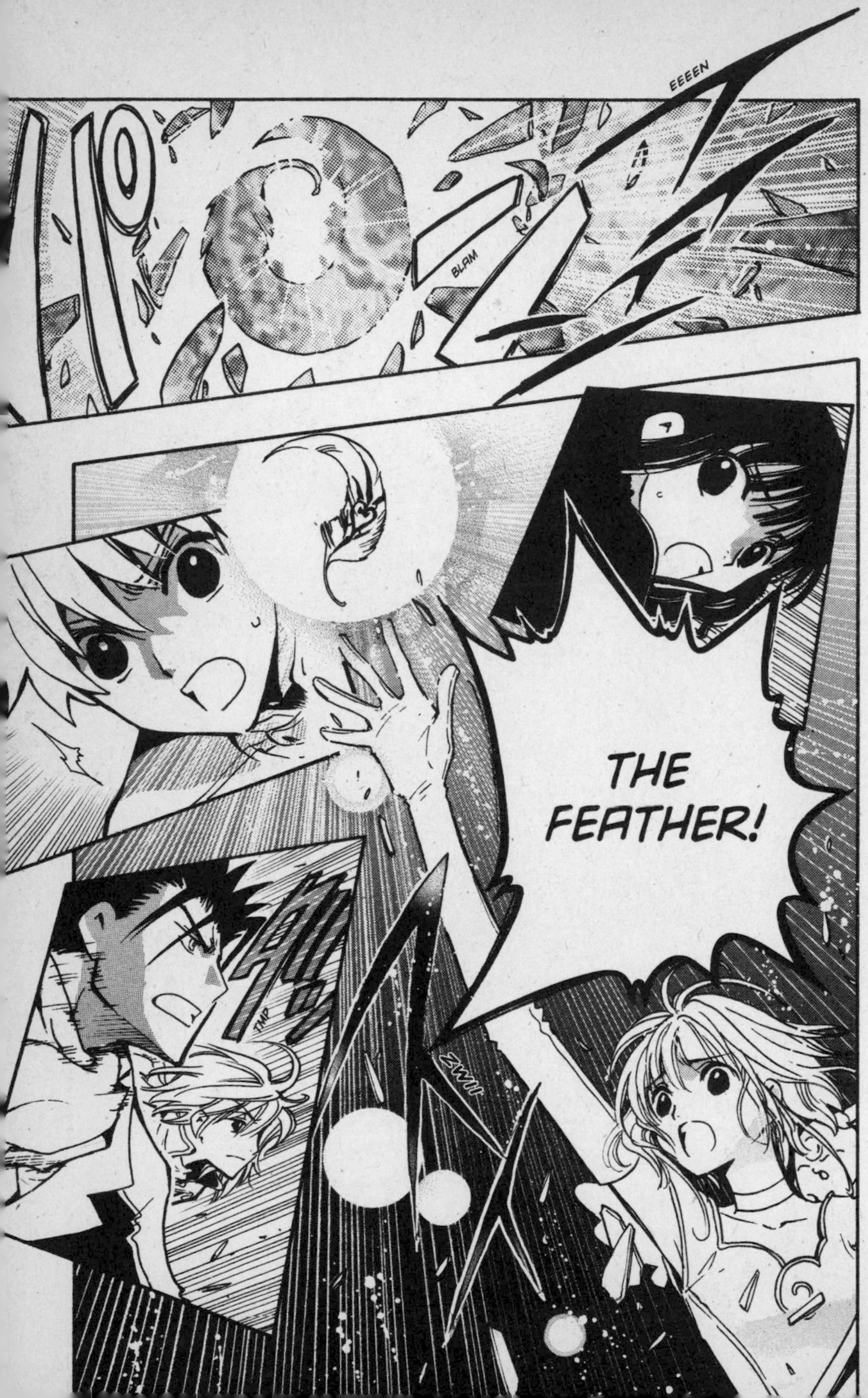
EEEEN
BLAM
THE FEATHER!
ZWII
TMP

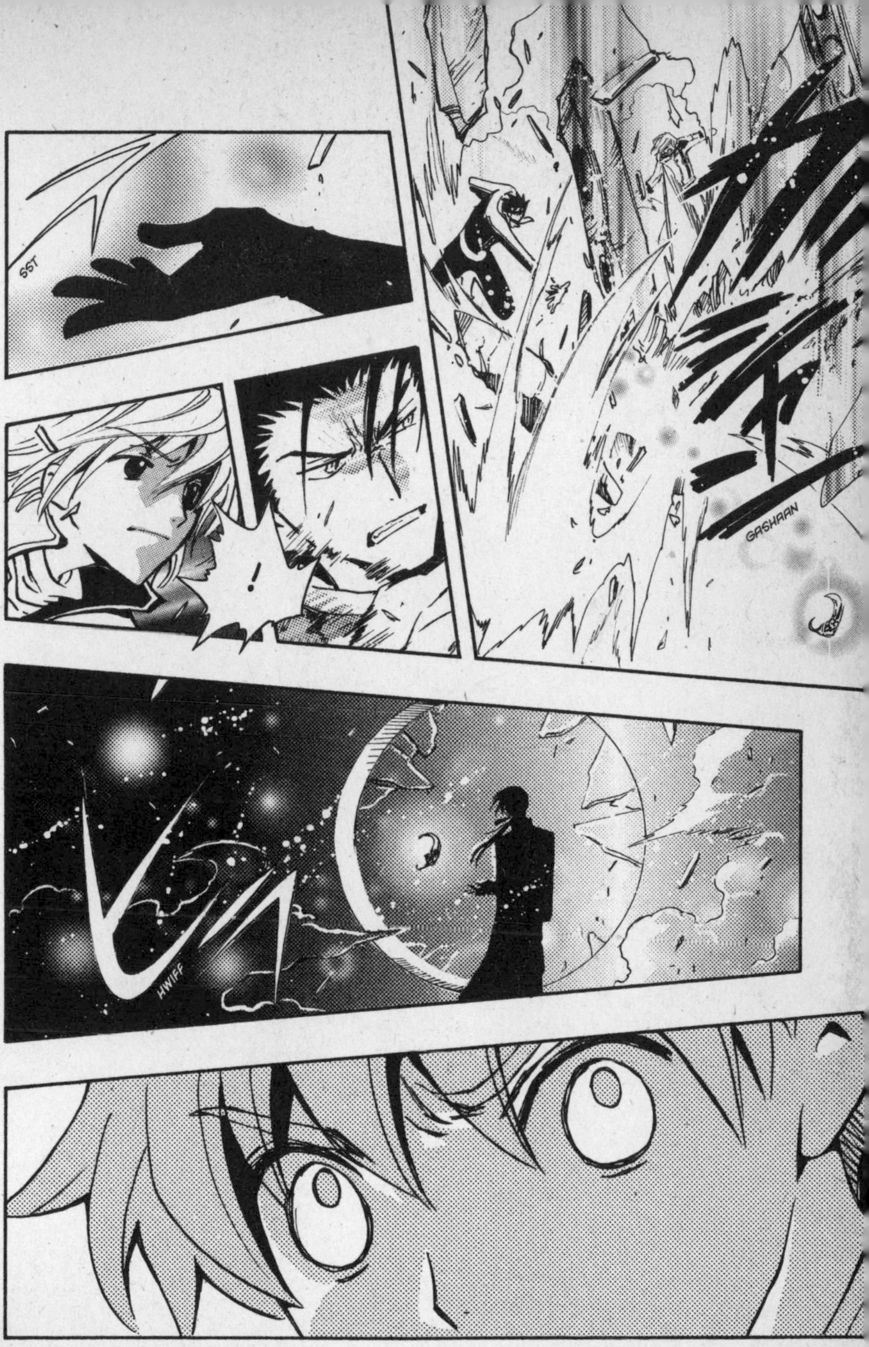
GASHAAN
SST
HWIFF

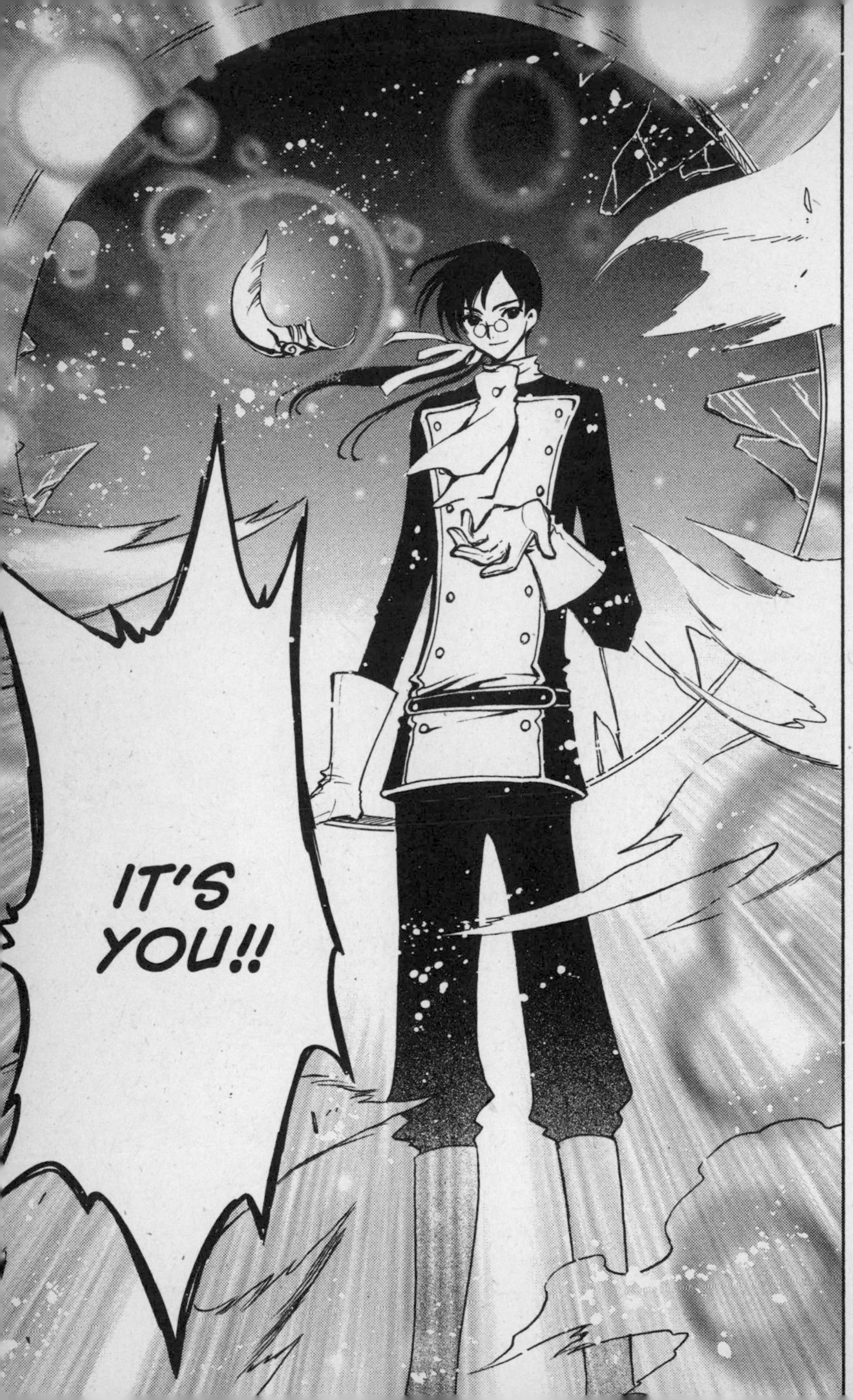
IT'S YOU!!

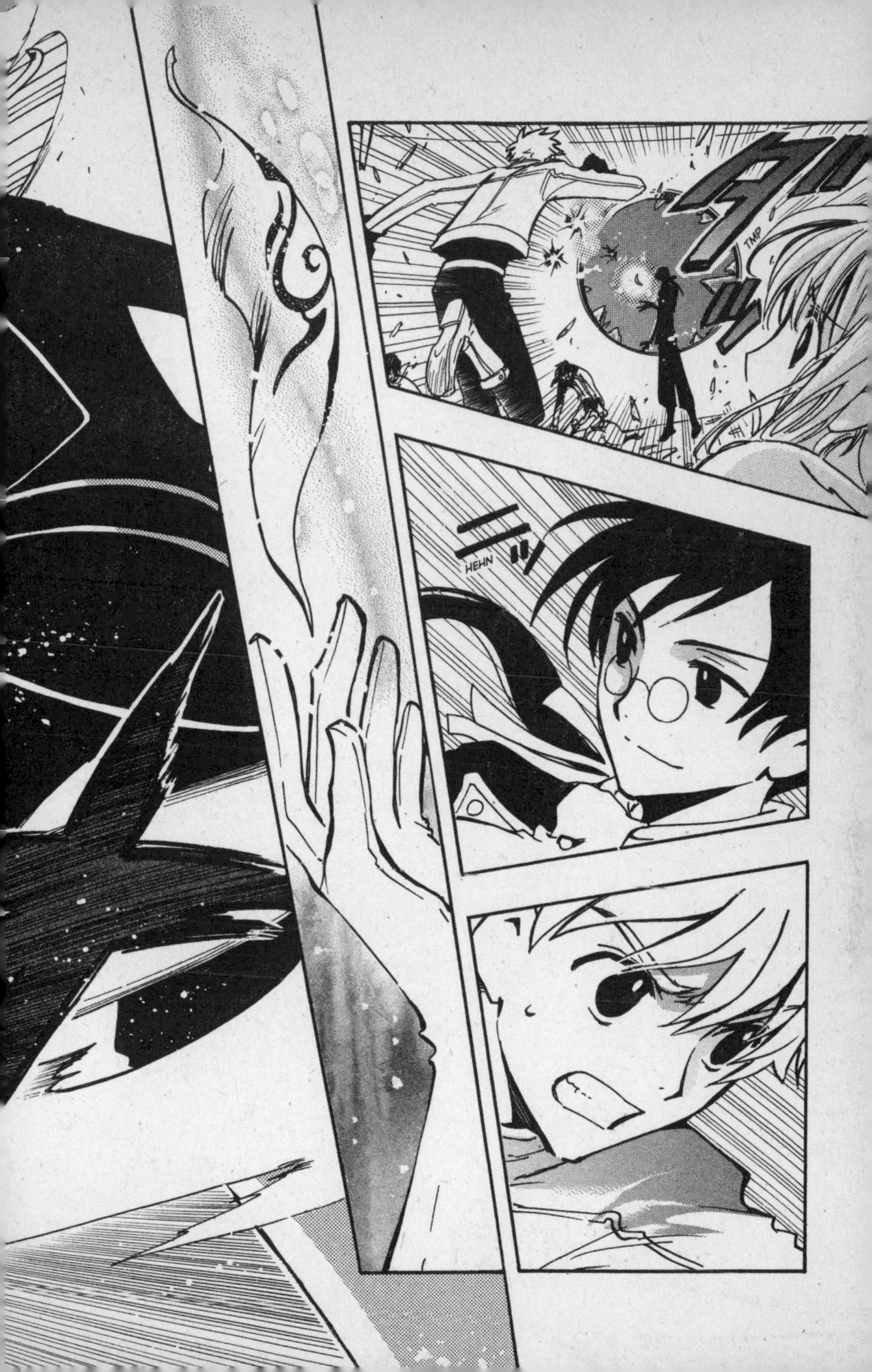
TMP
HEHN

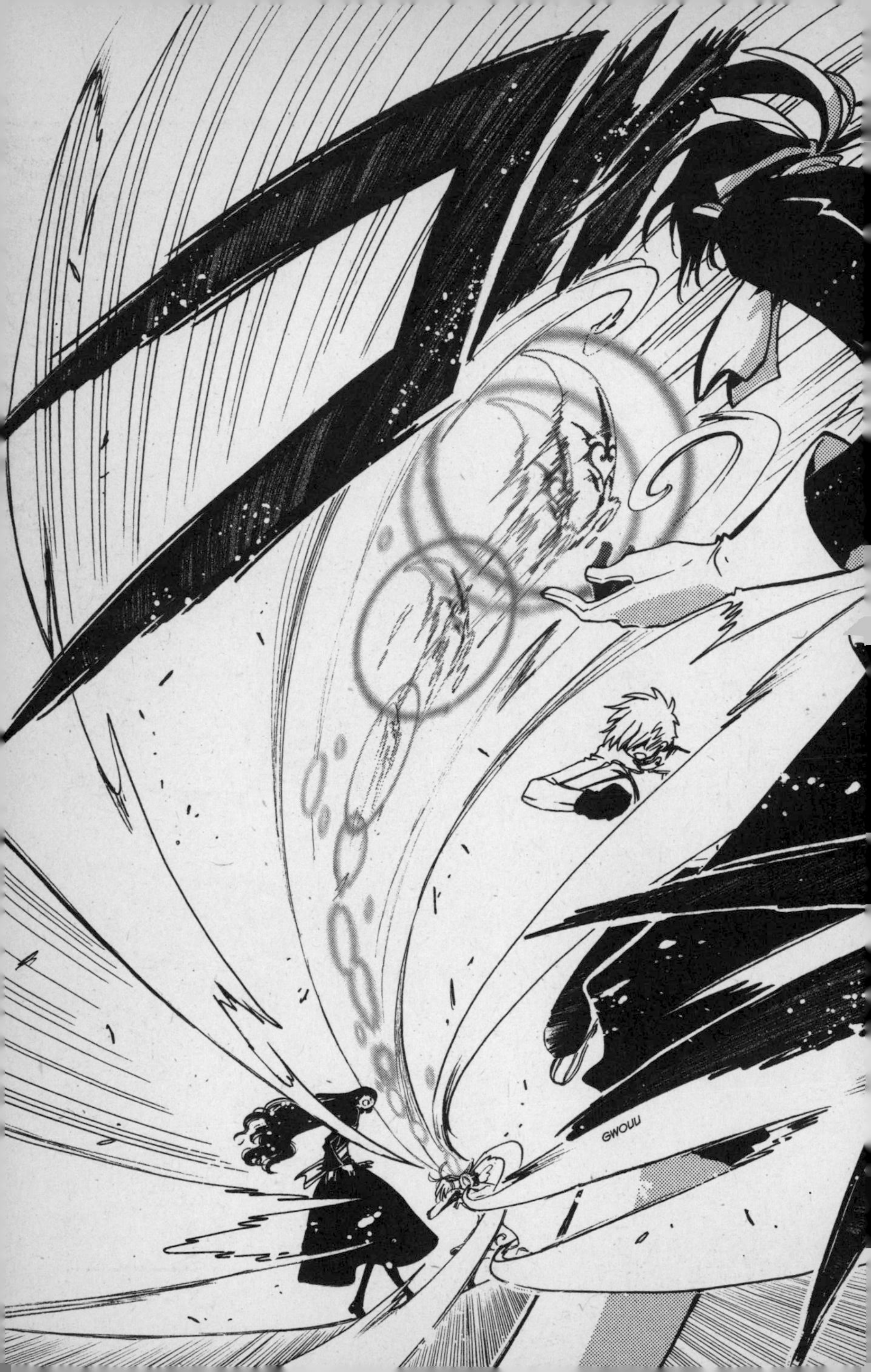
GWOUU

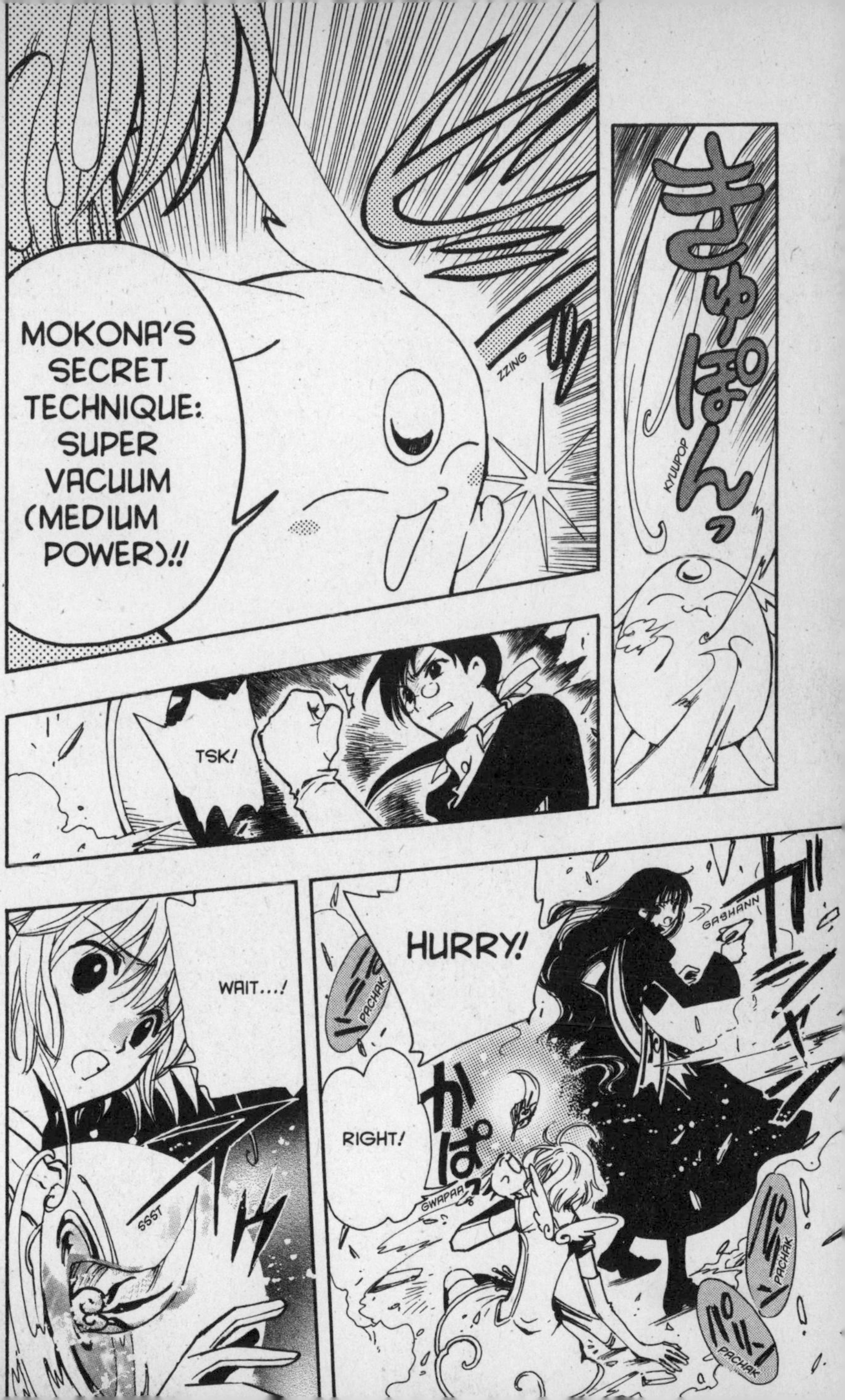

きゅぽんっ
KYUUPOP
MOKONA'S SECRET TECHNIQUE: SUPER VACUUM (MEDIUM POWER)!!
ZZING
TSK!
GASHANN
HURRY!
PACHAK
RIGHT!
かぱっ
GWAPAA
PACHAK
PACHAK
WAIT...!
SSST

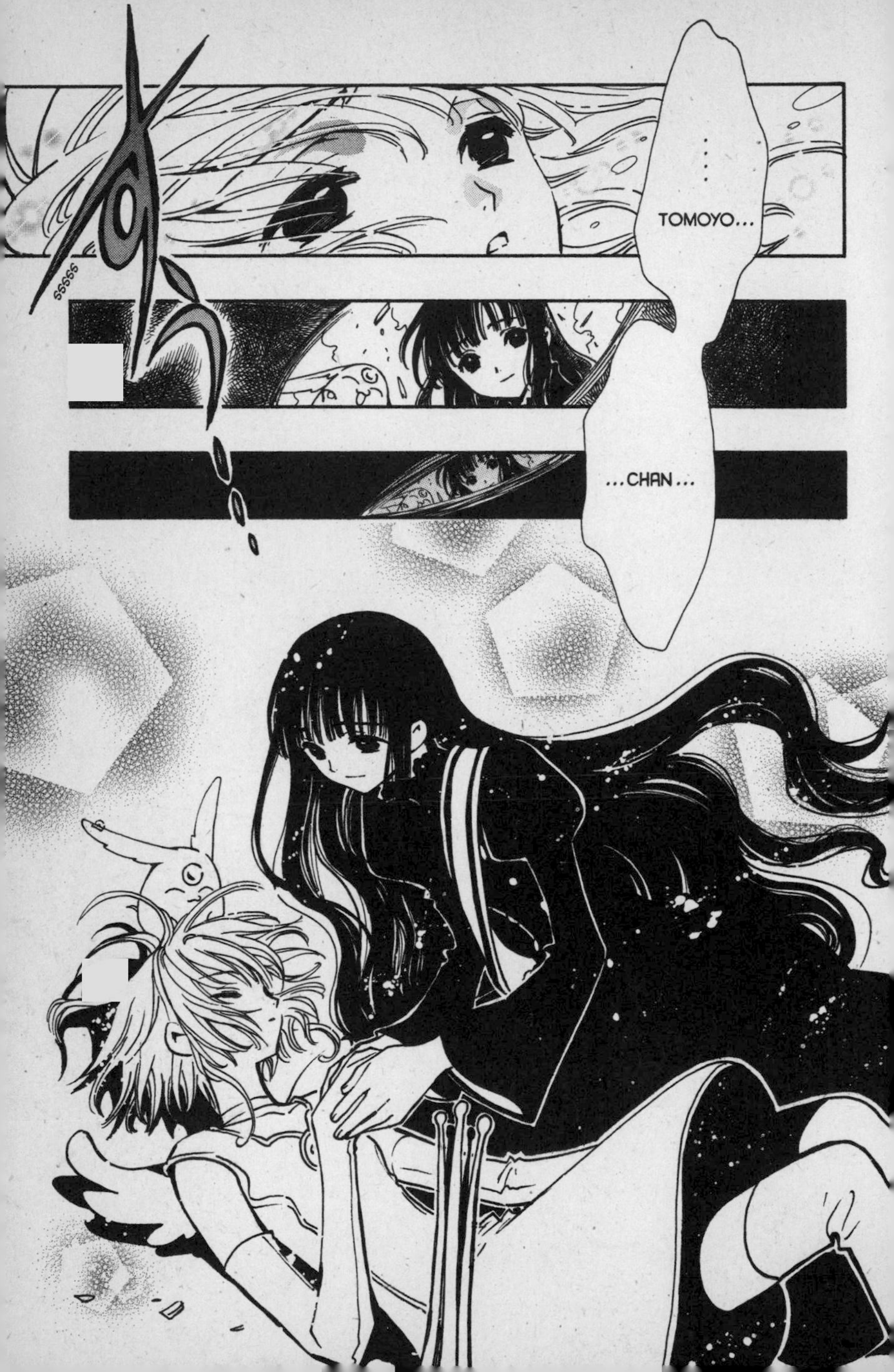
SSSSS
. . .
TOMOYO...
...CHAN...

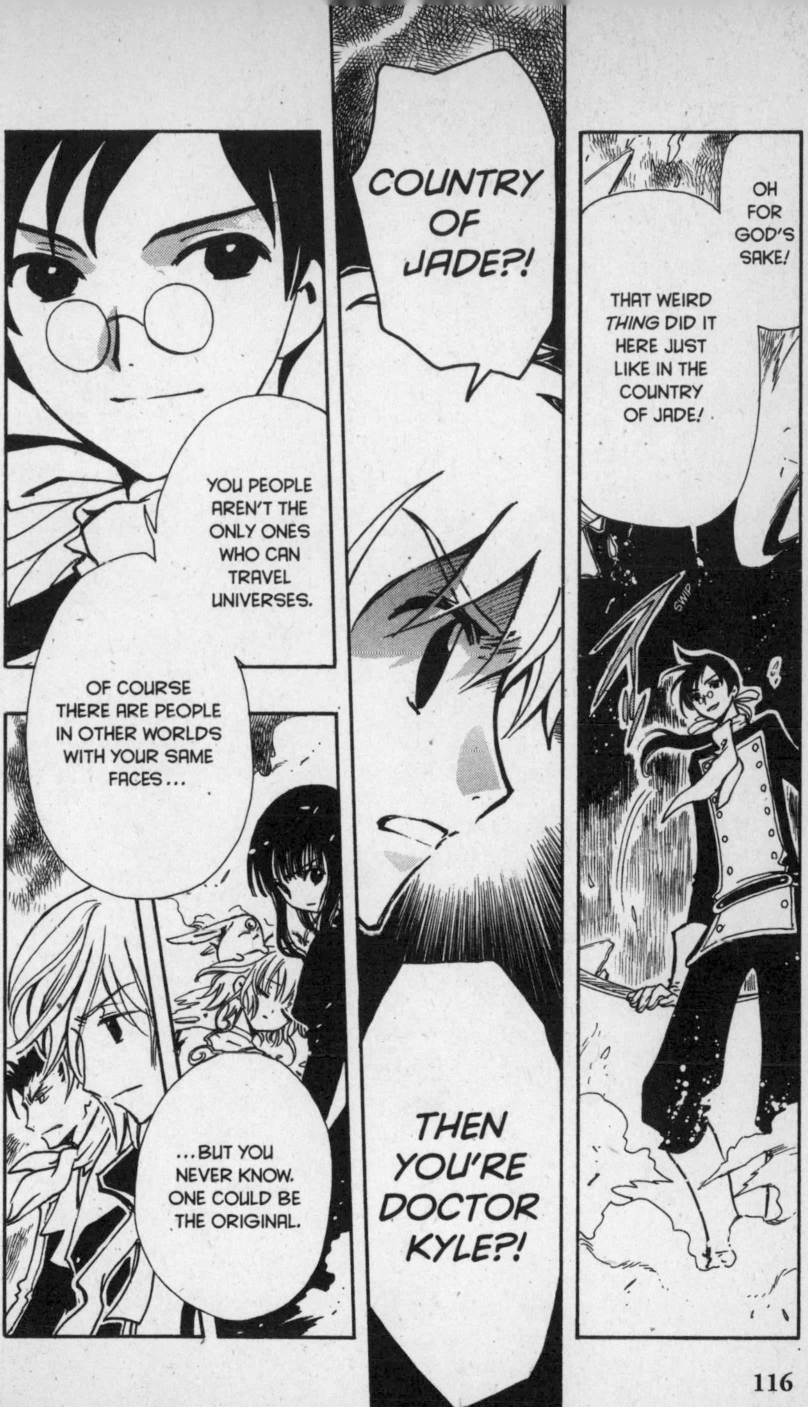
OH FOR GOD'S SAKE!
THAT WEIRD *THING* DID IT HERE JUST LIKE IN THE COUNTRY OF JADE!
SWIP
...
COUNTRY OF JADE?!
THEN YOU'RE DOCTOR KYLE?!
YOU PEOPLE AREN'T THE ONLY ONES WHO CAN TRAVEL UNIVERSES.
OF COURSE THERE ARE PEOPLE IN OTHER WORLDS WITH YOUR SAME FACES...
...BUT YOU NEVER KNOW. ONE COULD BE THE ORIGINAL.

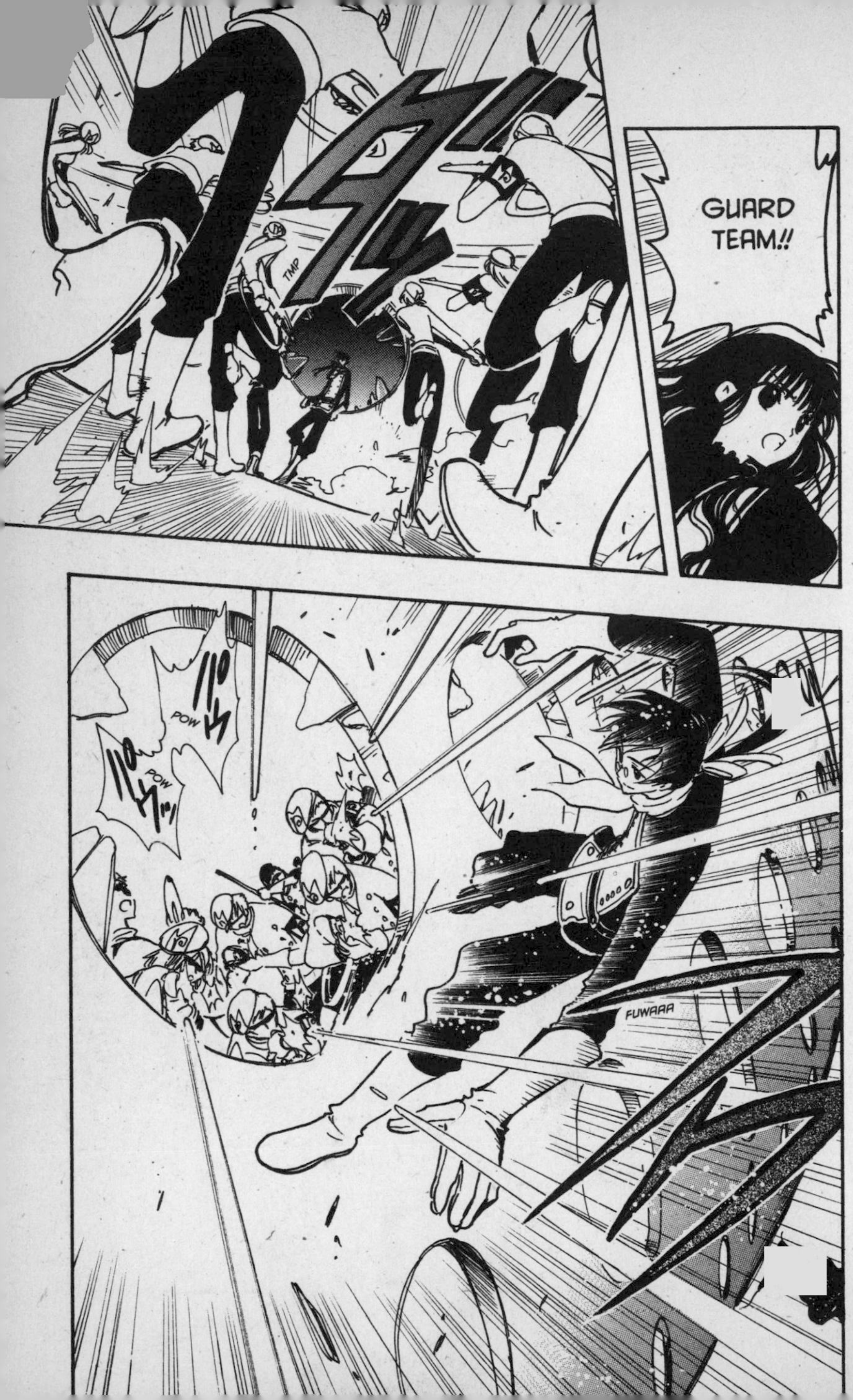
GUARD TEAM!!
TMP
POW
POW
FUWAAA

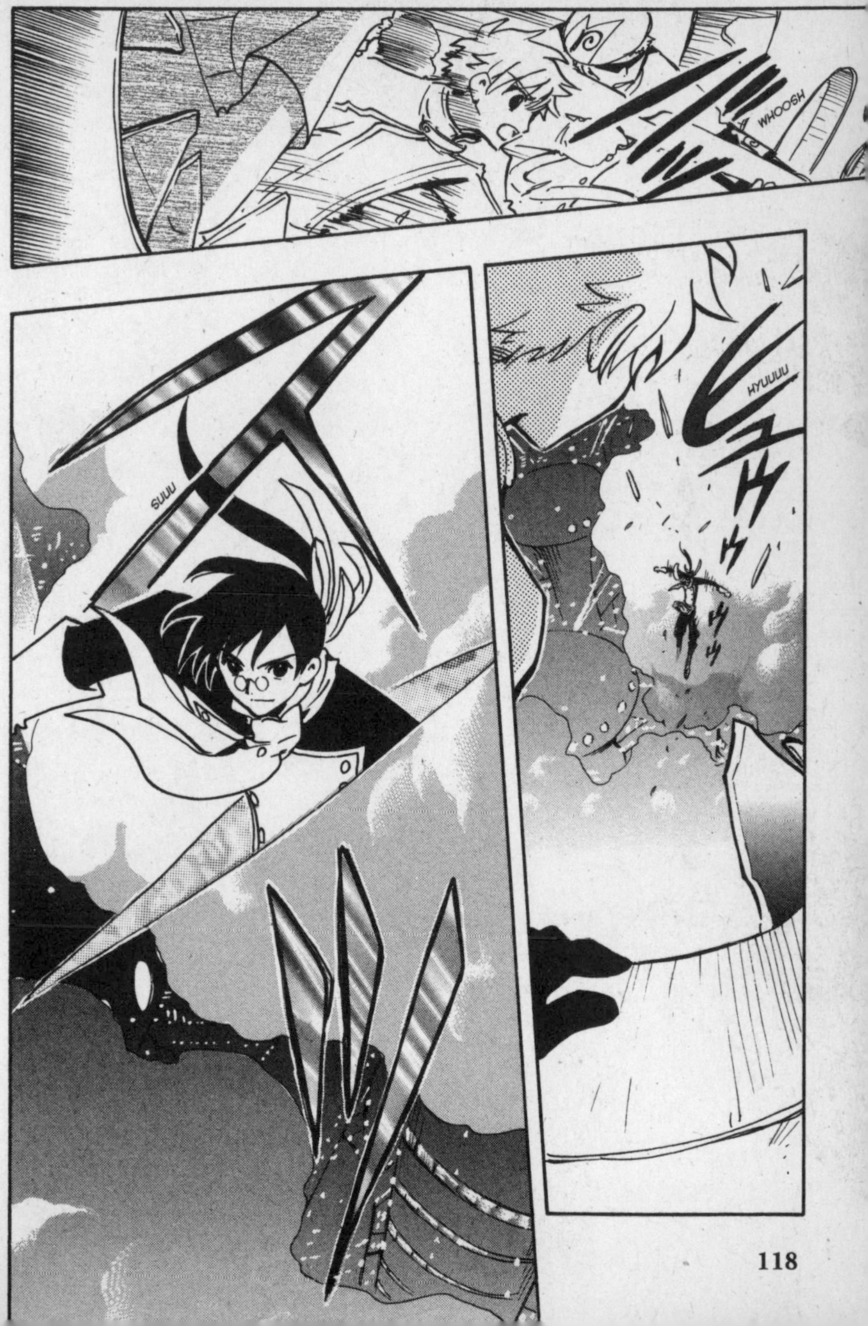
WHOOSH
HYUUUU
SUUU

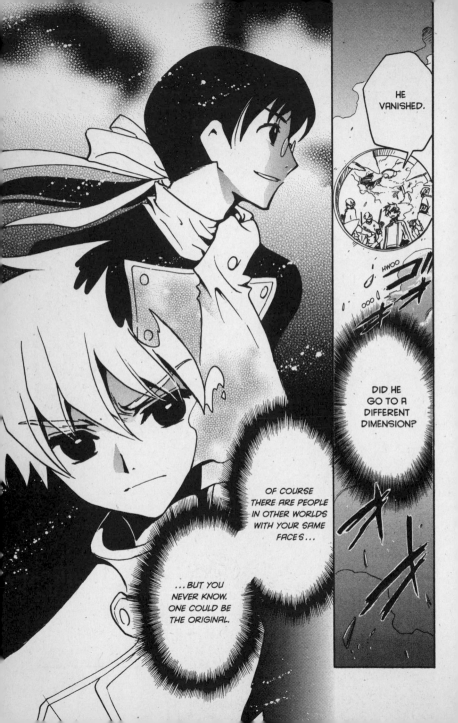

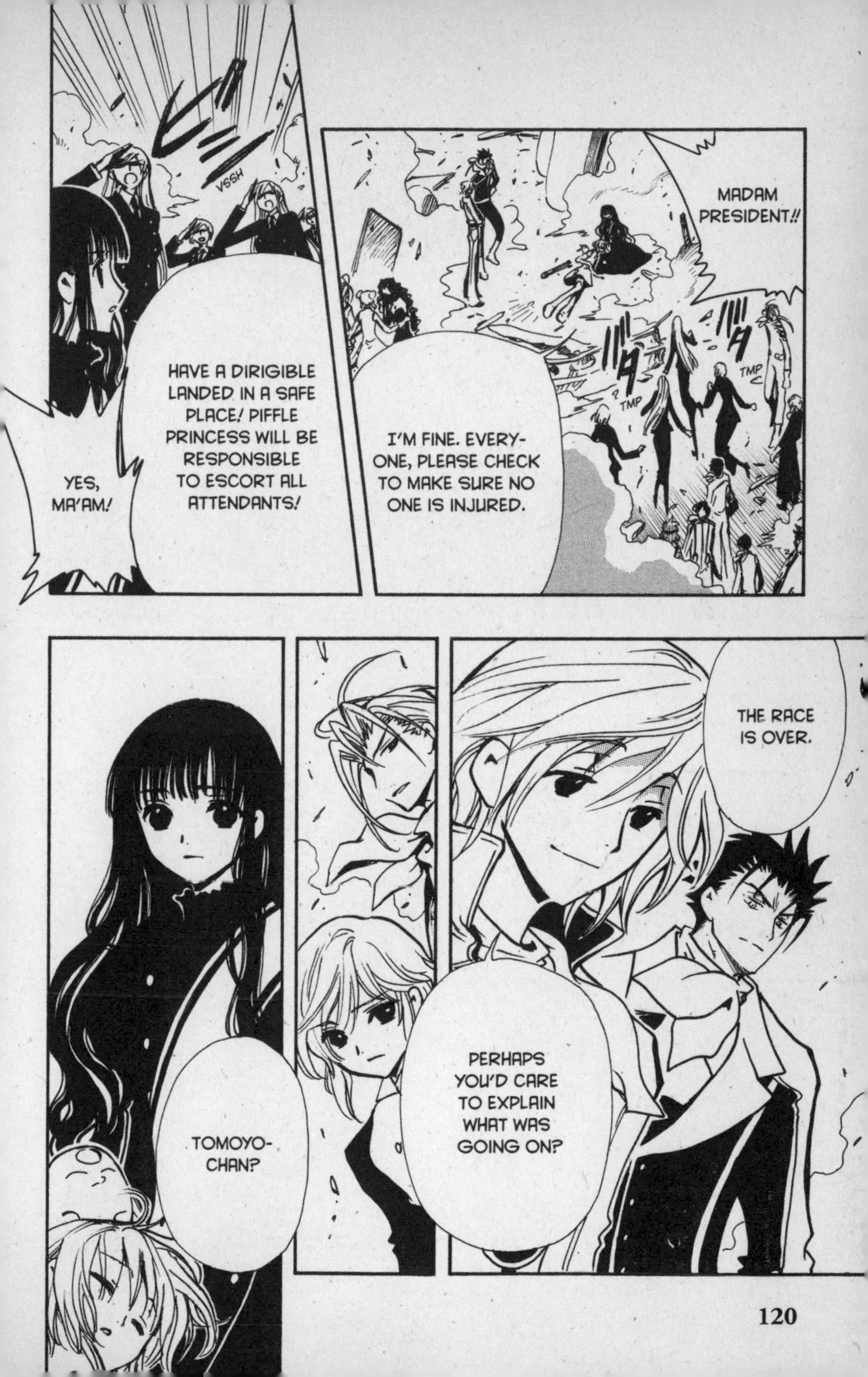
MADAM PRESIDENT!!
TMP
TMP
I'M FINE. EVERY-ONE, PLEASE CHECK TO MAKE SURE NO ONE IS INJURED.
VSSH
HAVE A DIRIGIBLE LANDED IN A SAFE PLACE! PIFFLE PRINCESS WILL BE RESPONSIBLE TO ESCORT ALL ATTENDANTS!
YES, MA'AM!
THE RACE IS OVER.
PERHAPS YOU'D CARE TO EXPLAIN WHAT WAS GOING ON?
TOMOYO-CHAN?

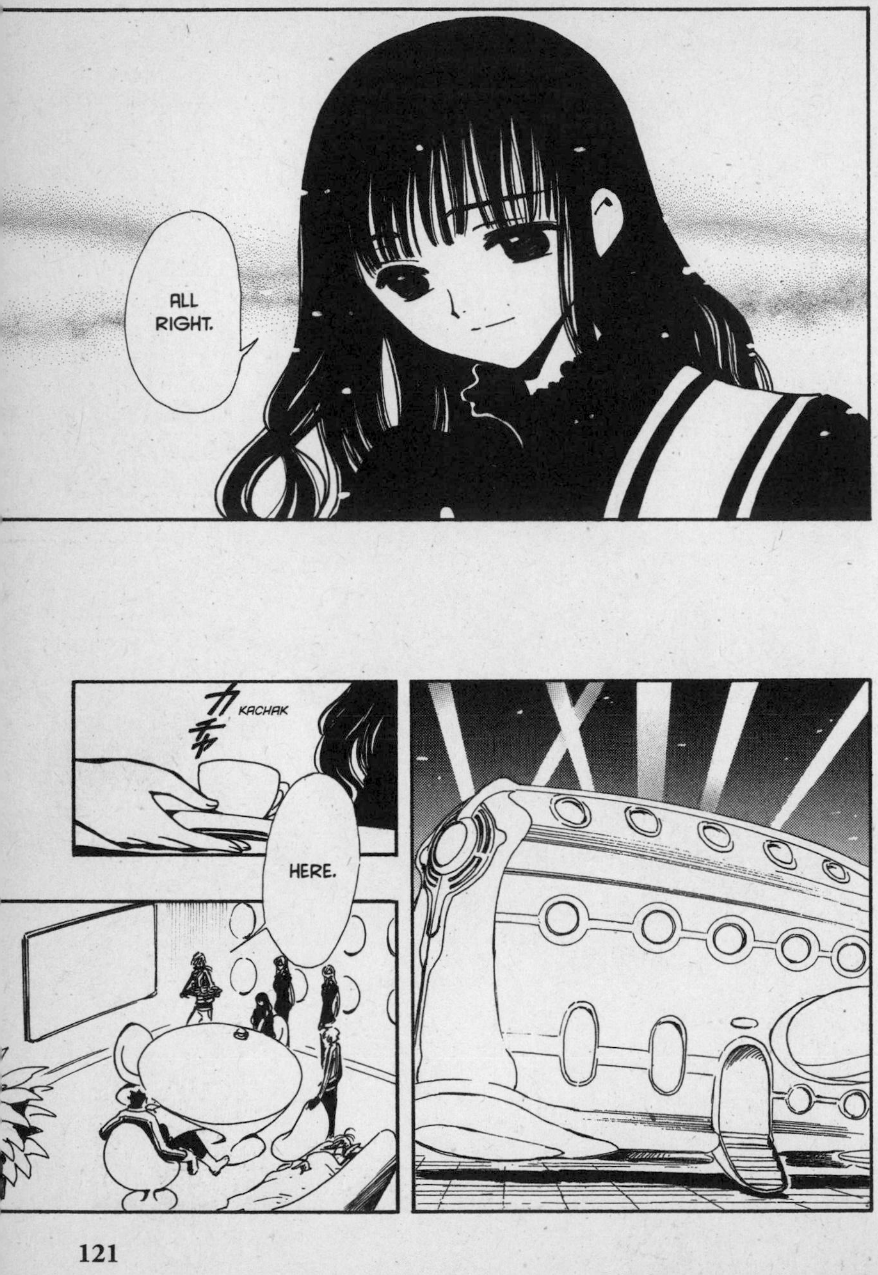
ALL RIGHT.
カチャ
KACHAK
HERE.

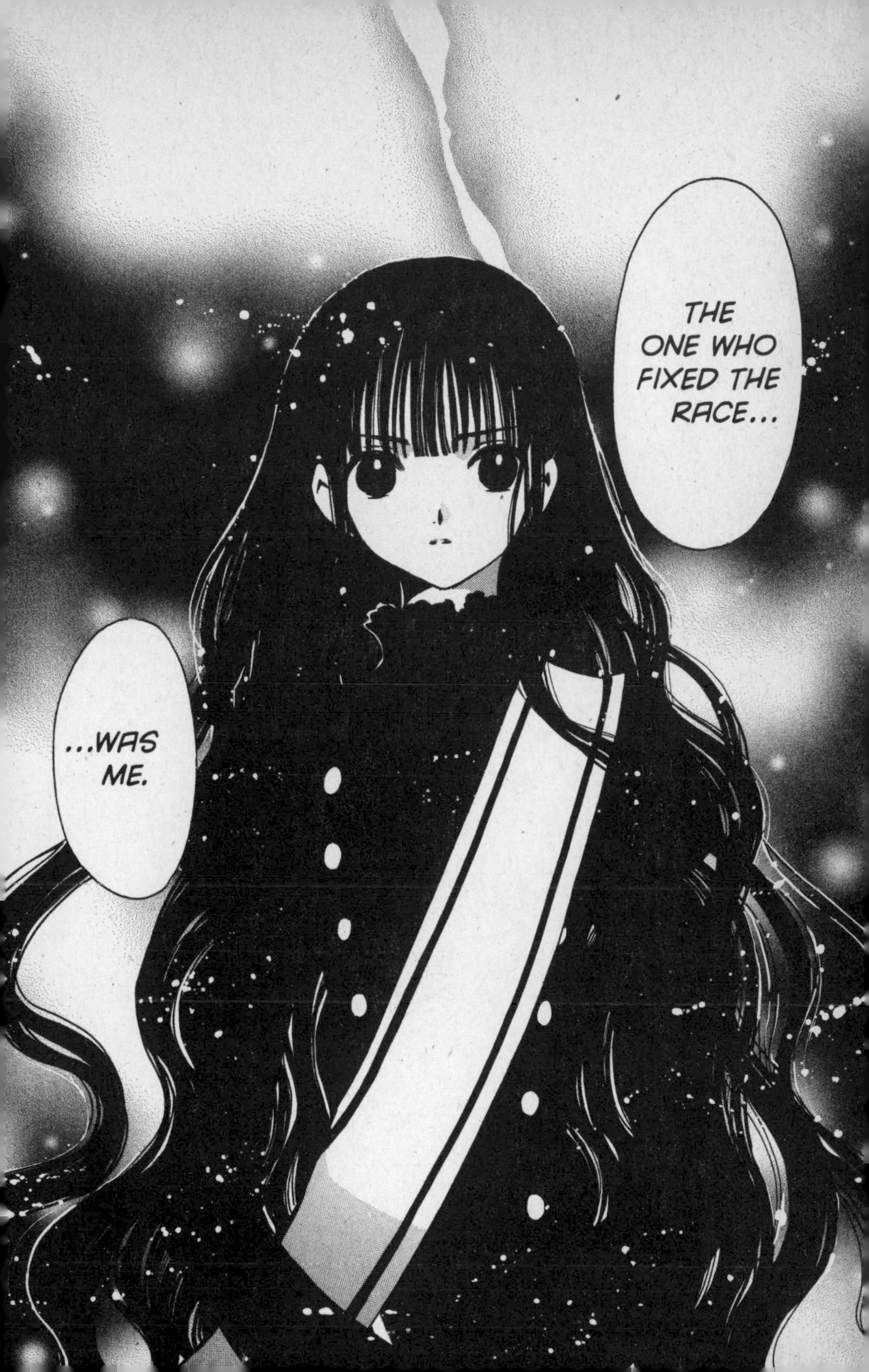
THE ONE WHO FIXED THE RACE...
...WAS ME.

Chapitre.89
The False Reason

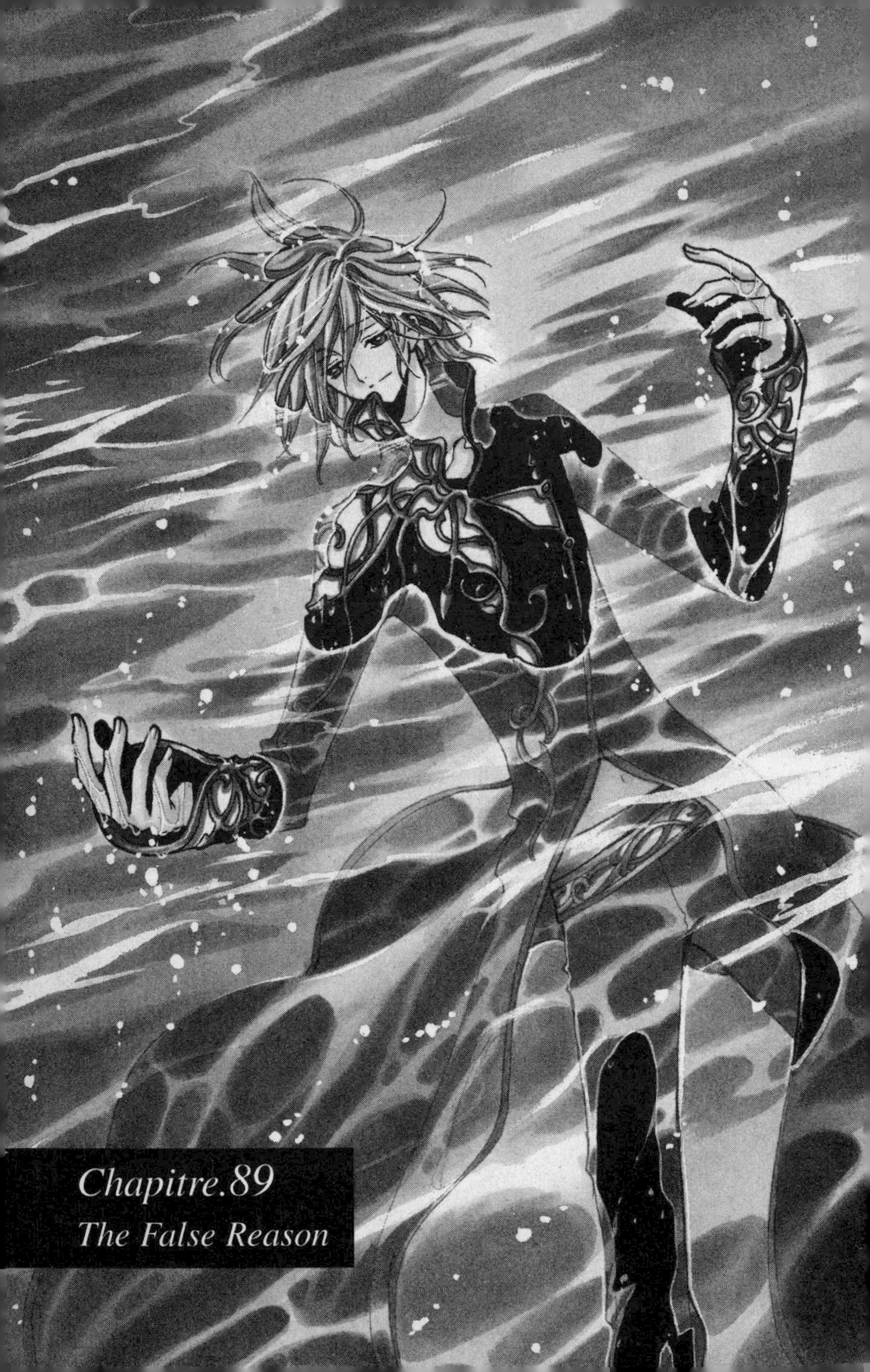

ツバサ

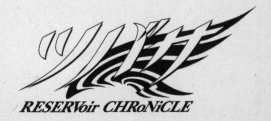

RESERVoir CHRoNiCLE

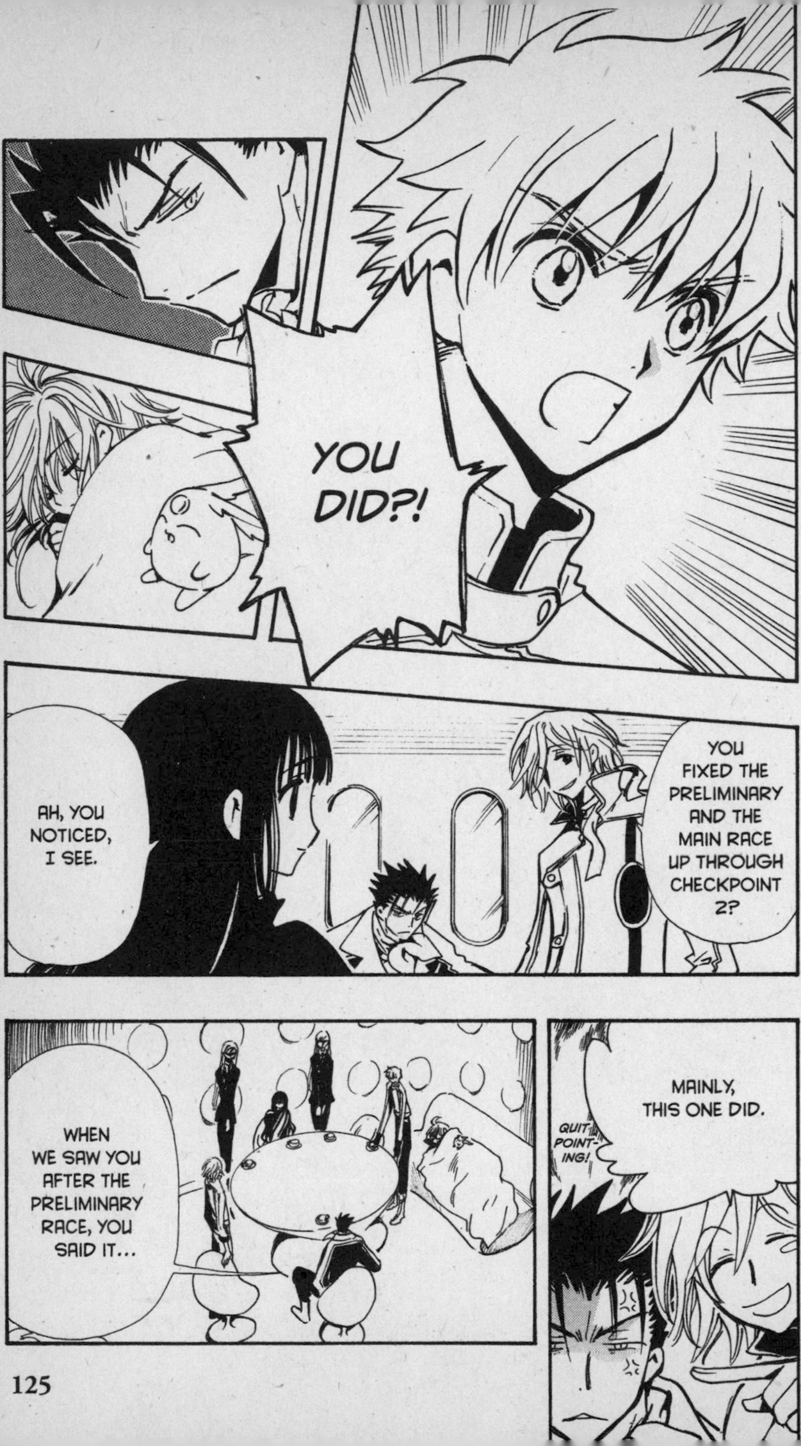

YOU DID?!
YOU FIXED THE PRELIMINARY AND THE MAIN RACE UP THROUGH CHECKPOINT 2?
AH, YOU NOTICED, I SEE.
MAINLY, THIS ONE DID.
QUIT POINTING!
WHEN WE SAW YOU AFTER THE PRELIMINARY RACE, YOU SAID IT...

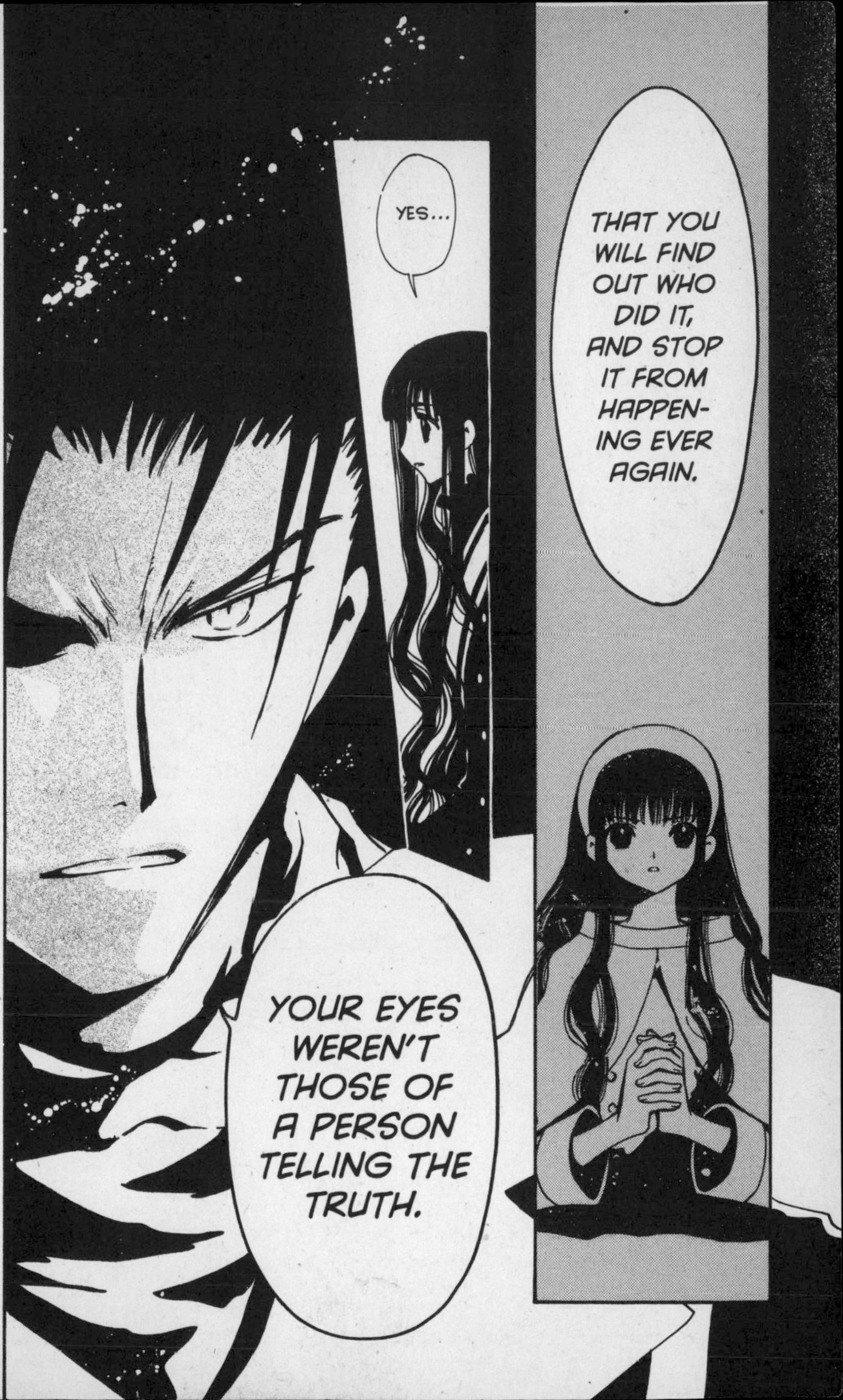
THAT YOU WILL FIND OUT WHO DID IT, AND STOP IT FROM HAPPEN-ING EVER AGAIN.
YES...
YOUR EYES WEREN'T THOSE OF A PERSON TELLING THE TRUTH.

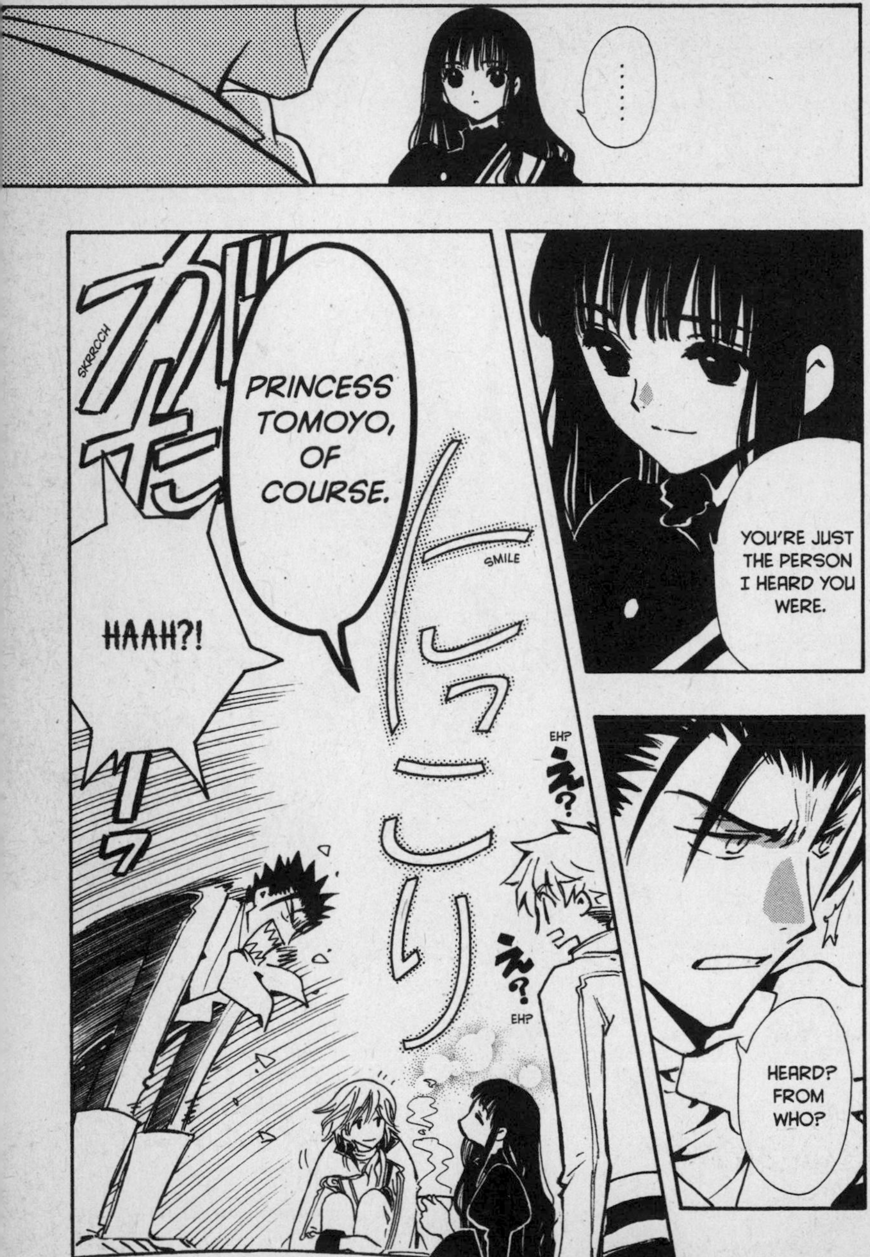
......
YOU'RE JUST THE PERSON I HEARD YOU WERE.
HEARD? FROM WHO?
PRINCESS TOMOYO, OF COURSE.
SMILE
SKRRCCH
HAAH?!
EH?
EH?

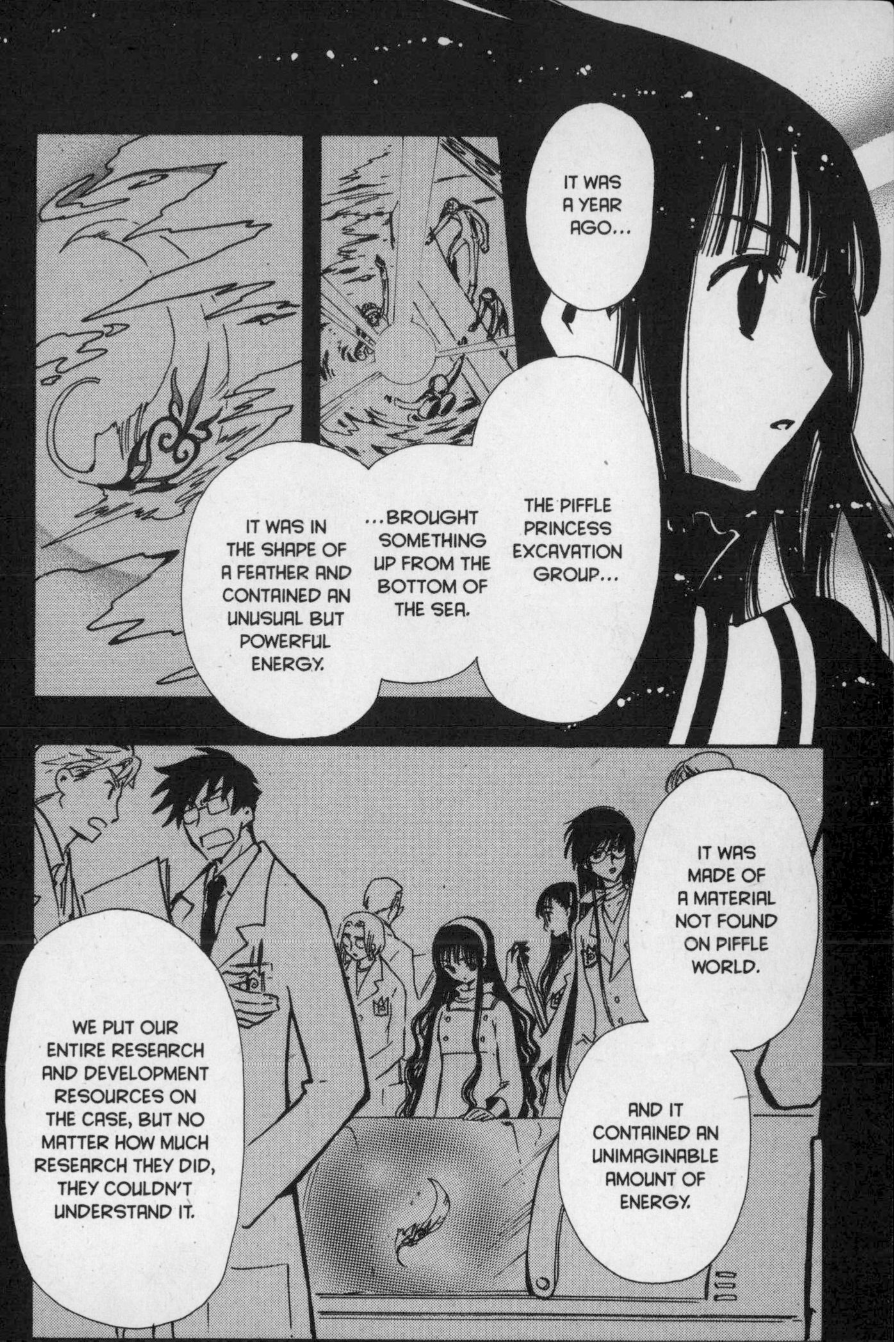
IT WAS A YEAR AGO...
THE PIFFLE PRINCESS EXCAVATION GROUP...
...BROUGHT SOMETHING UP FROM THE BOTTOM OF THE SEA.
IT WAS IN THE SHAPE OF A FEATHER AND CONTAINED AN UNUSUAL BUT POWERFUL ENERGY.
IT WAS MADE OF A MATERIAL NOT FOUND ON PIFFLE WORLD.
AND IT CONTAINED AN UNIMAGINABLE AMOUNT OF ENERGY.
WE PUT OUR ENTIRE RESEARCH AND DEVELOPMENT RESOURCES ON THE CASE, BUT NO MATTER HOW MUCH RESEARCH THEY DID, THEY COULDN'T UNDERSTAND IT.

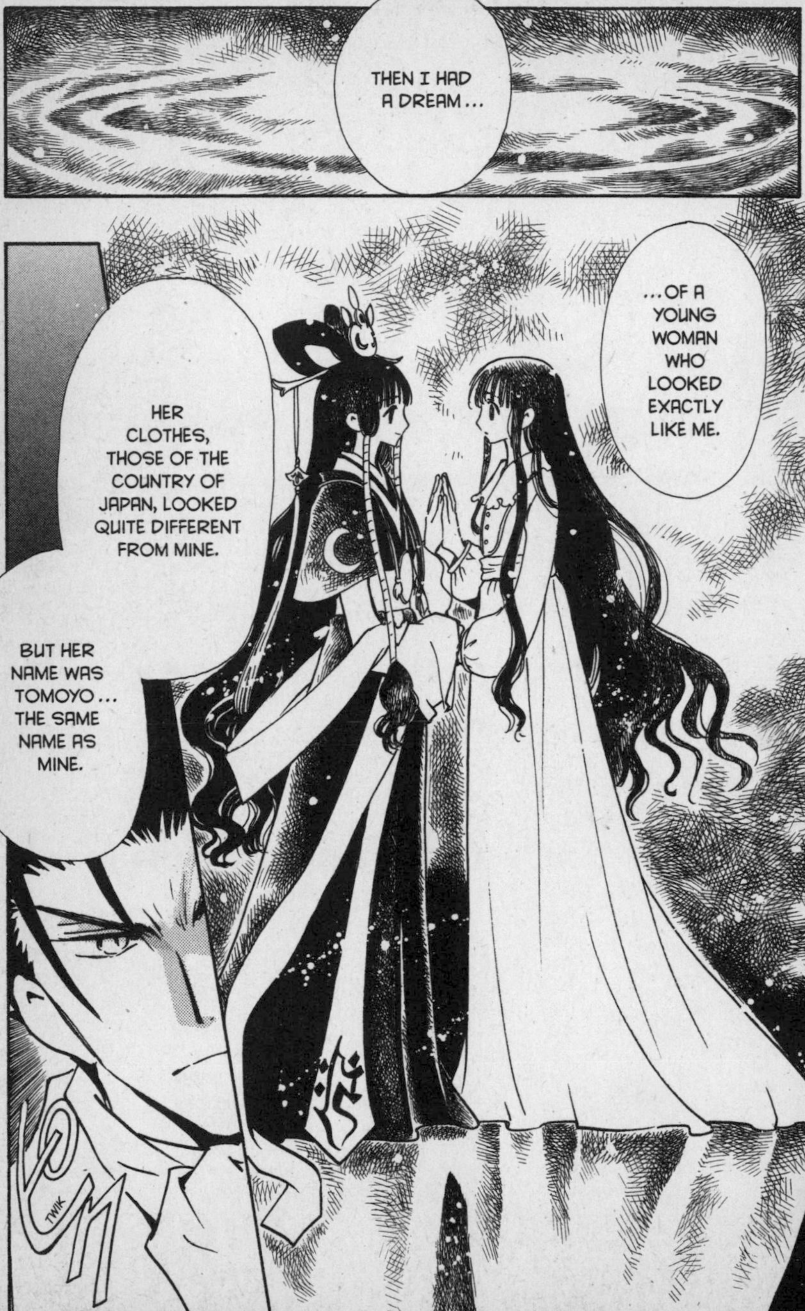
THEN I HAD A DREAM...
...OF A YOUNG WOMAN WHO LOOKED EXACTLY LIKE ME.
HER CLOTHES, THOSE OF THE COUNTRY OF JAPAN, LOOKED QUITE DIFFERENT FROM MINE.
BUT HER NAME WAS TOMOYO... THE SAME NAME AS MINE.
TWIK

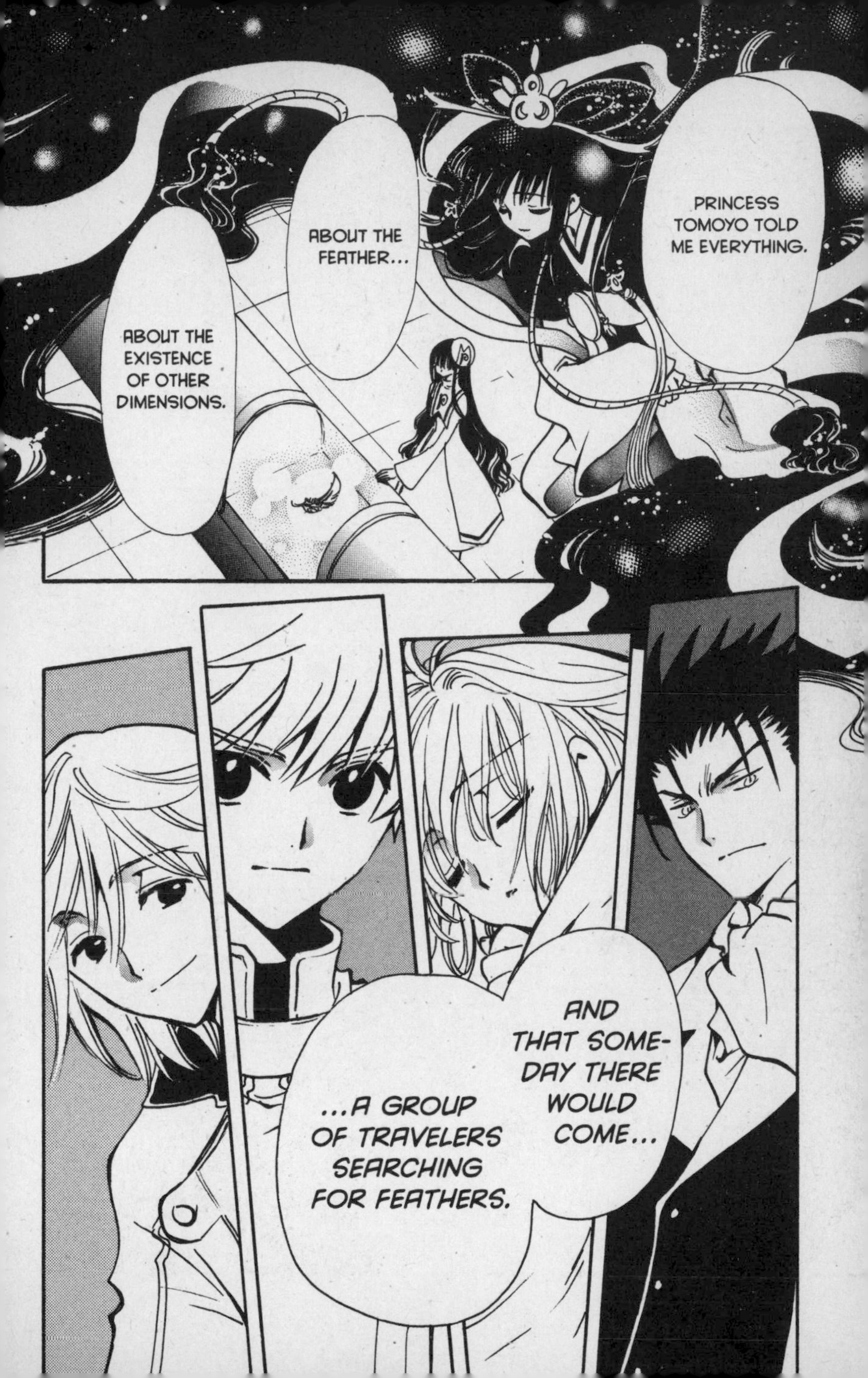
PRINCESS TOMOYO TOLD ME EVERYTHING.
ABOUT THE FEATHER...
ABOUT THE EXISTENCE OF OTHER DIMENSIONS.
AND THAT SOME-DAY THERE WOULD COME...
...A GROUP OF TRAVELERS SEARCHING FOR FEATHERS.

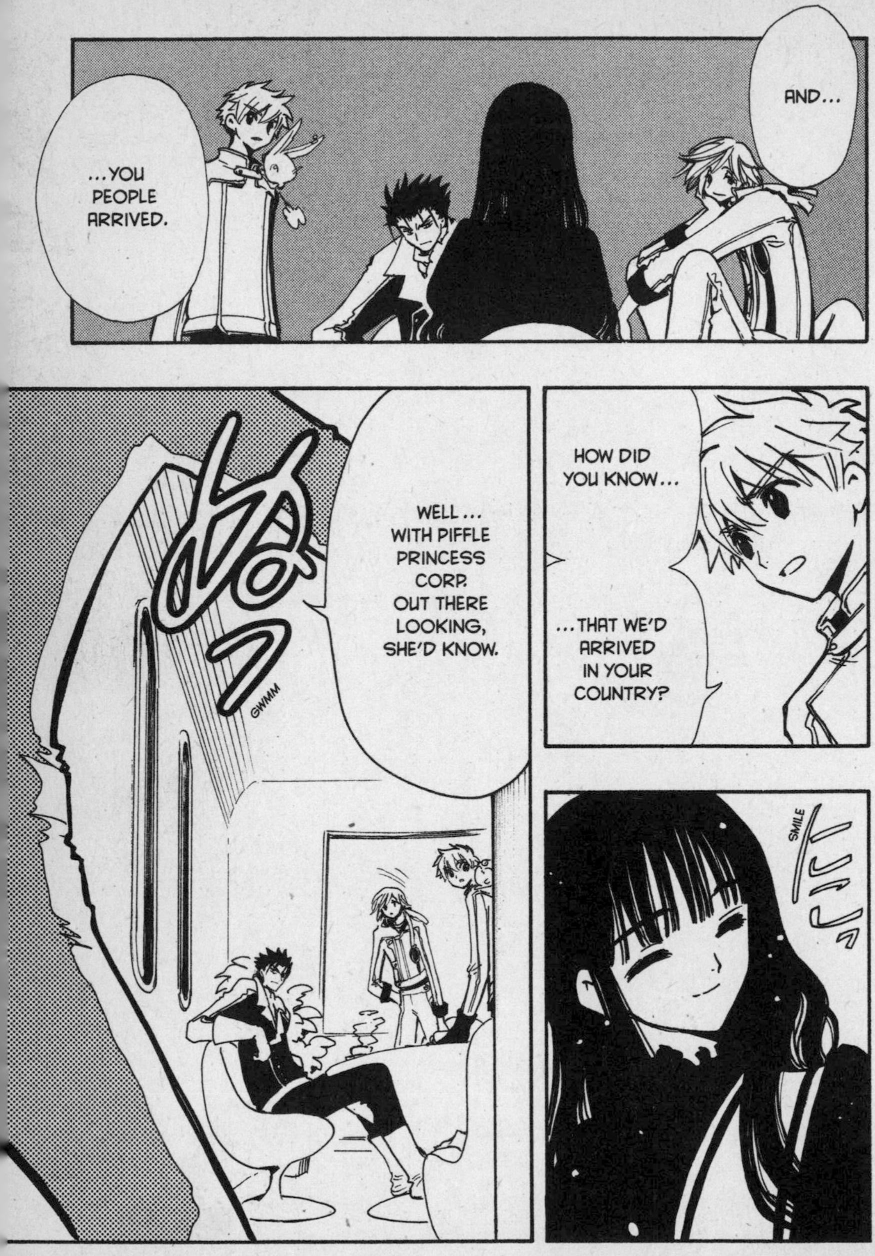
AND...
...YOU PEOPLE ARRIVED.
HOW DID YOU KNOW...
...THAT WE'D ARRIVED IN YOUR COUNTRY?
SMILE
WELL... WITH PIFFLE PRINCESS CORP. OUT THERE LOOKING, SHE'D KNOW.
GWMM

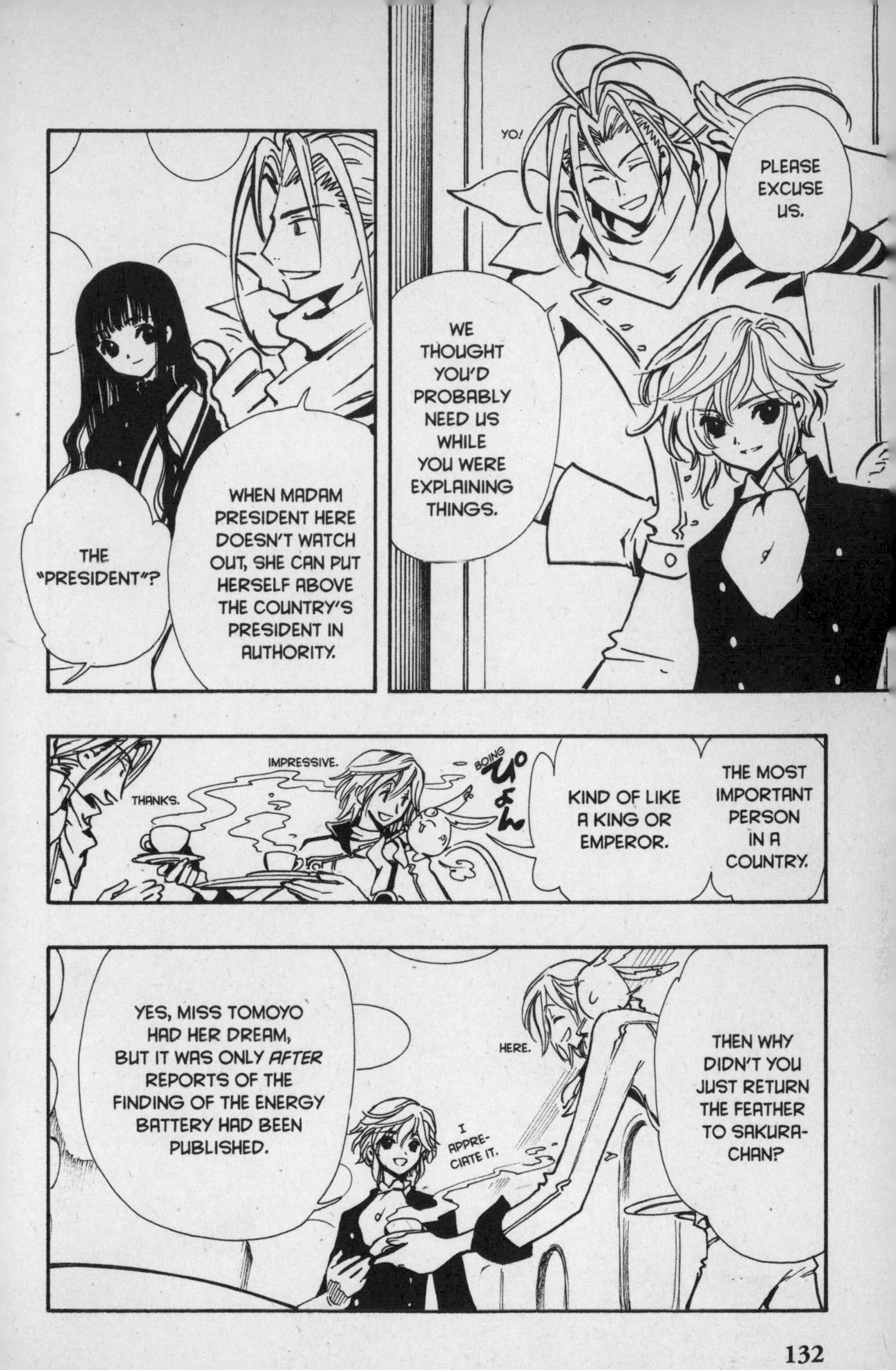
PLEASE EXCUSE US.
YO!
WE THOUGHT YOU'D PROBABLY NEED US WHILE YOU WERE EXPLAINING THINGS.
WHEN MADAM PRESIDENT HERE DOESN'T WATCH OUT, SHE CAN PUT HERSELF ABOVE THE COUNTRY'S PRESIDENT IN AUTHORITY.
THE "PRESIDENT"?
THE MOST IMPORTANT PERSON IN A COUNTRY.
KIND OF LIKE A KING OR EMPEROR.
BOING
IMPRESSIVE.
THANKS.
THEN WHY DIDN'T YOU JUST RETURN THE FEATHER TO SAKURA-CHAN?
HERE.
I APPRECIATE IT.
YES, MISS TOMOYO HAD HER DREAM, BUT IT WAS ONLY *AFTER* REPORTS OF THE FINDING OF THE ENERGY BATTERY HAD BEEN PUBLISHED.

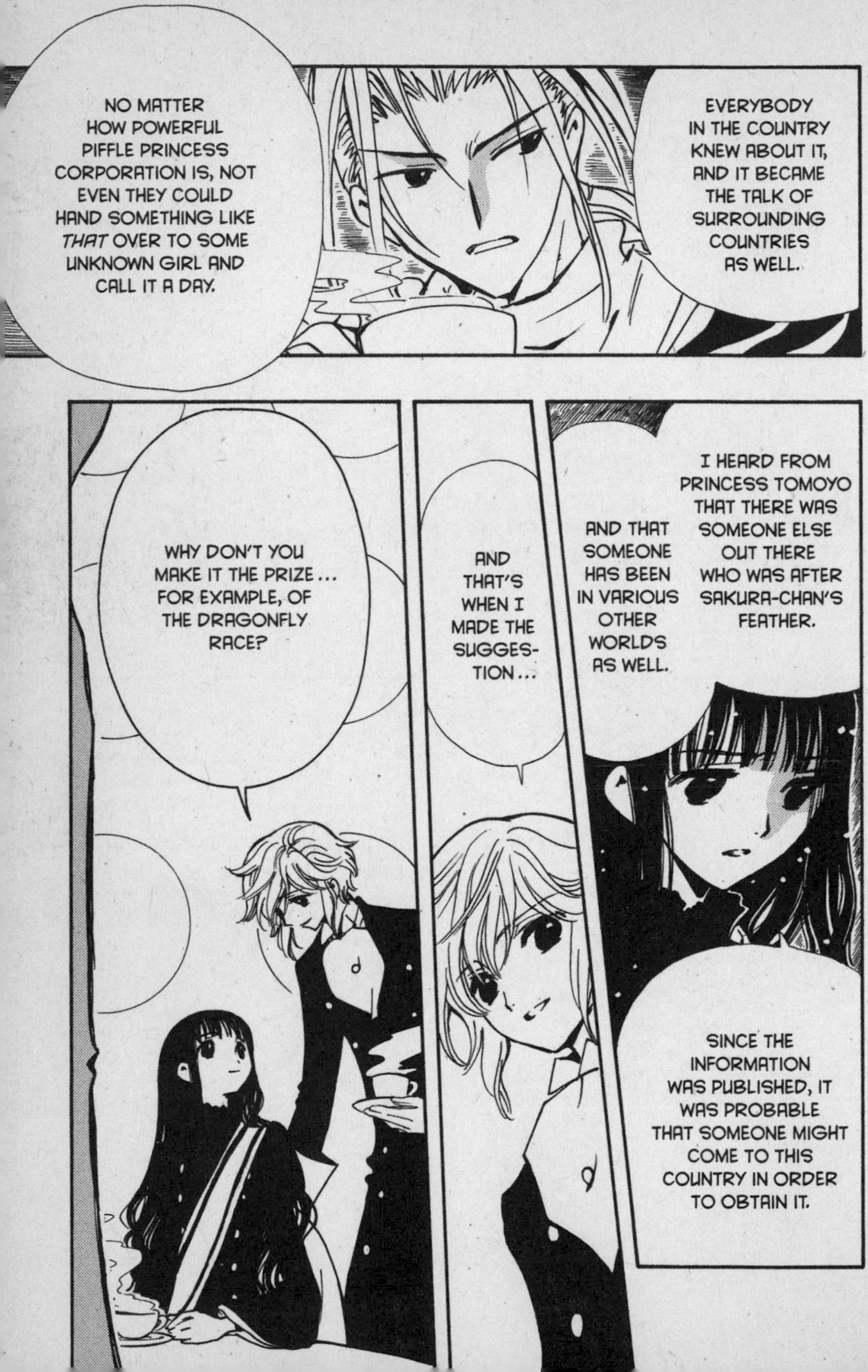
EVERYBODY IN THE COUNTRY KNEW ABOUT IT, AND IT BECAME THE TALK OF SURROUNDING COUNTRIES AS WELL.
NO MATTER HOW POWERFUL PIFFLE PRINCESS CORPORATION IS, NOT EVEN THEY COULD HAND SOMETHING LIKE *THAT* OVER TO SOME UNKNOWN GIRL AND CALL IT A DAY.
I HEARD FROM PRINCESS TOMOYO THAT THERE WAS SOMEONE ELSE OUT THERE WHO WAS AFTER SAKURA-CHAN'S FEATHER.
AND THAT SOMEONE HAS BEEN IN VARIOUS OTHER WORLDS AS WELL.
SINCE THE INFORMATION WAS PUBLISHED, IT WAS PROBABLE THAT SOMEONE MIGHT COME TO THIS COUNTRY IN ORDER TO OBTAIN IT.
AND THAT'S WHEN I MADE THE SUGGES-TION...
WHY DON'T YOU MAKE IT THE PRIZE... FOR EXAMPLE, OF THE DRAGONFLY RACE?

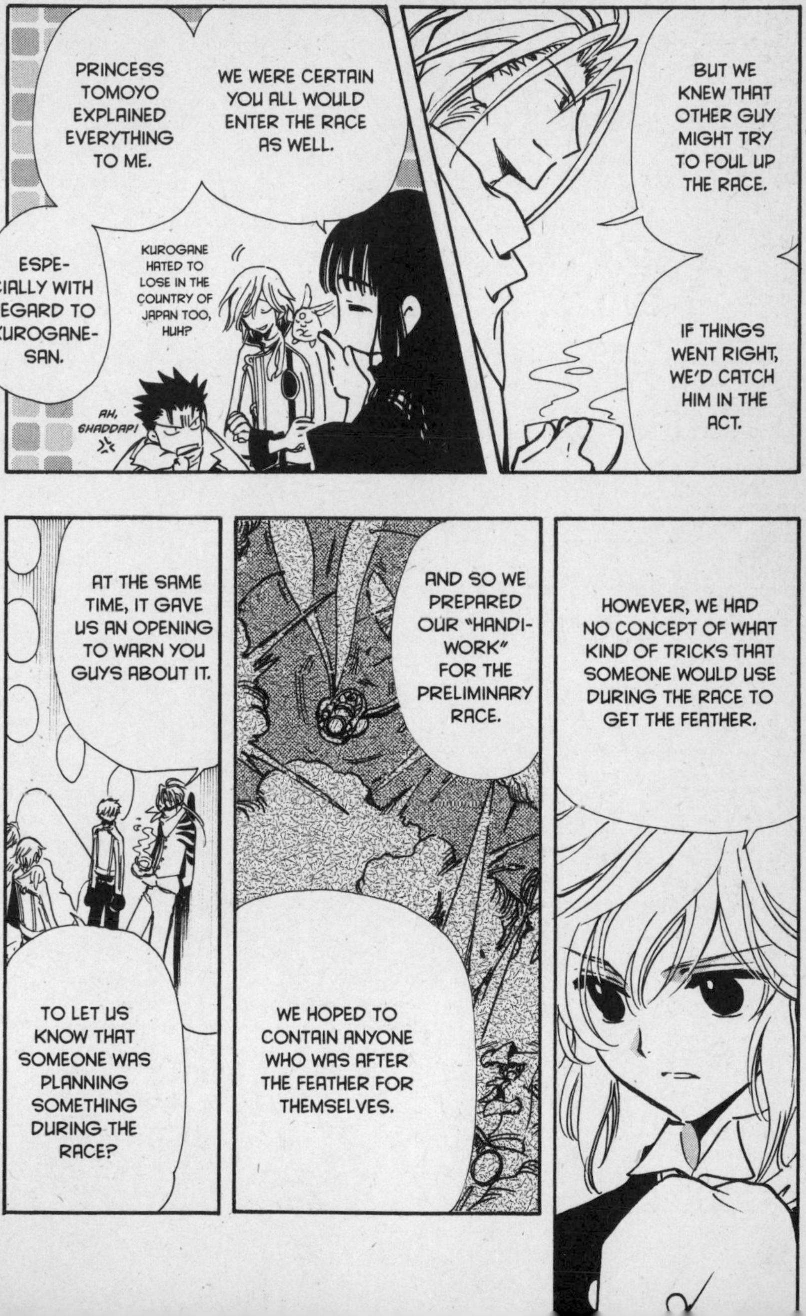
BUT WE KNEW THAT OTHER GUY MIGHT TRY TO FOUL UP THE RACE.
IF THINGS WENT RIGHT, WE'D CATCH HIM IN THE ACT.
WE WERE CERTAIN YOU ALL WOULD ENTER THE RACE AS WELL.
PRINCESS TOMOYO EXPLAINED EVERYTHING TO ME.
ESPE-CIALLY WITH REGARD TO KUROGANE-SAN.
KUROGANE HATED TO LOSE IN THE COUNTRY OF JAPAN TOO, HUH?
AH, SHADDAP!
HOWEVER, WE HAD NO CONCEPT OF WHAT KIND OF TRICKS THAT SOMEONE WOULD USE DURING THE RACE TO GET THE FEATHER.
AND SO WE PREPARED OUR "HANDI-WORK" FOR THE PRELIMINARY RACE.
WE HOPED TO CONTAIN ANYONE WHO WAS AFTER THE FEATHER FOR THEMSELVES.
AT THE SAME TIME, IT GAVE US AN OPENING TO WARN YOU GUYS ABOUT IT.
TO LET US KNOW THAT SOMEONE WAS PLANNING SOMETHING DURING THE RACE?

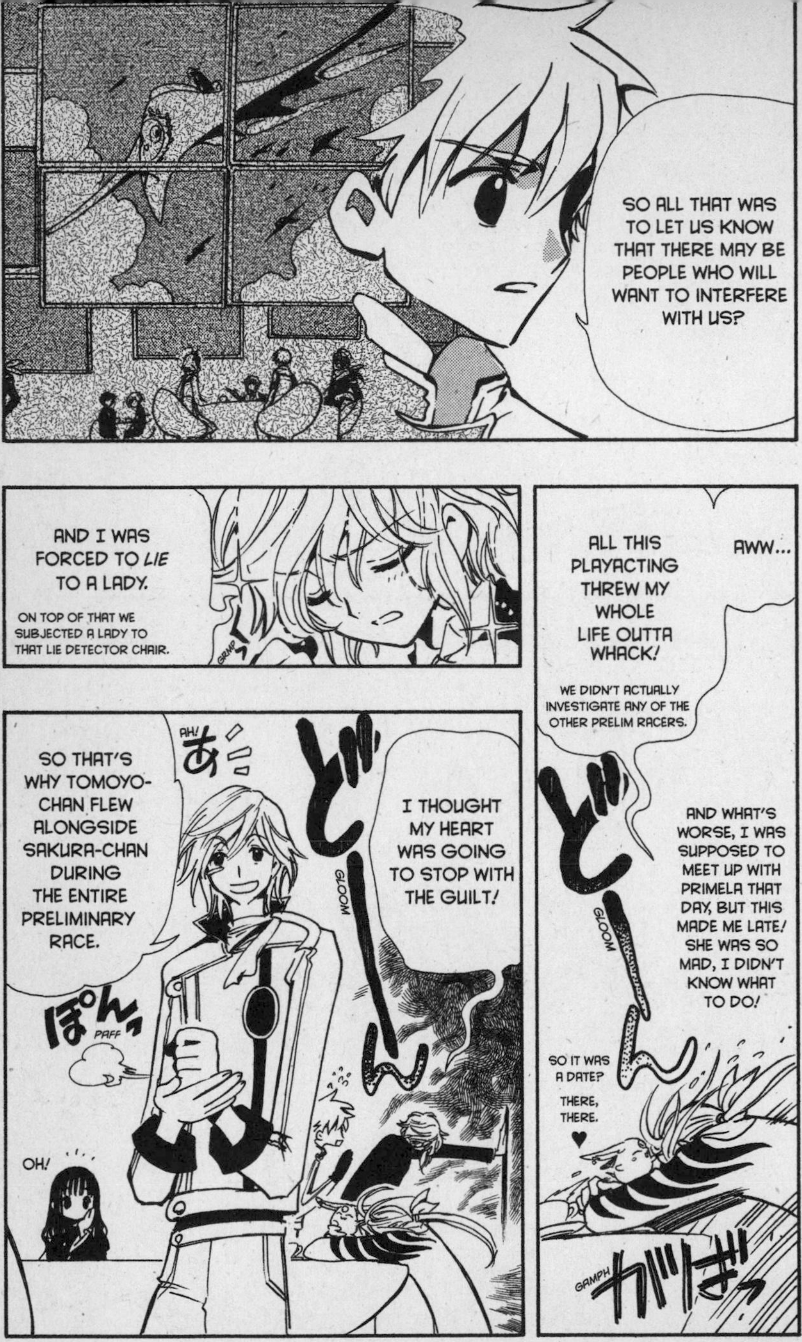
SO ALL THAT WAS TO LET US KNOW THAT THERE MAY BE PEOPLE WHO WILL WANT TO INTERFERE WITH US?
AWW...
ALL THIS PLAYACTING THREW MY WHOLE LIFE OUTTA WHACK!
WE DIDN'T ACTUALLY INVESTIGATE ANY OF THE OTHER PRELIM RACERS.
どーん
GLOOM
AND WHAT'S WORSE, I WAS SUPPOSED TO MEET UP WITH PRIMELA THAT DAY, BUT THIS MADE ME LATE! SHE WAS SO MAD, I DIDN'T KNOW WHAT TO DO!
SO IT WAS A DATE?
THERE, THERE.
GAMPH
がぶっ
AND I WAS FORCED TO *LIE* TO A LADY.
ON TOP OF THAT WE SUBJECTED A LADY TO THAT LIE DETECTOR CHAIR.
GRMP
AH!
あ
I THOUGHT MY HEART WAS GOING TO STOP WITH THE GUILT!
どーん
GLOOM
SO THAT'S WHY TOMOYO-CHAN FLEW ALONGSIDE SAKURA-CHAN DURING THE ENTIRE PRELIMINARY RACE.
ぽん
PAFF
OH!

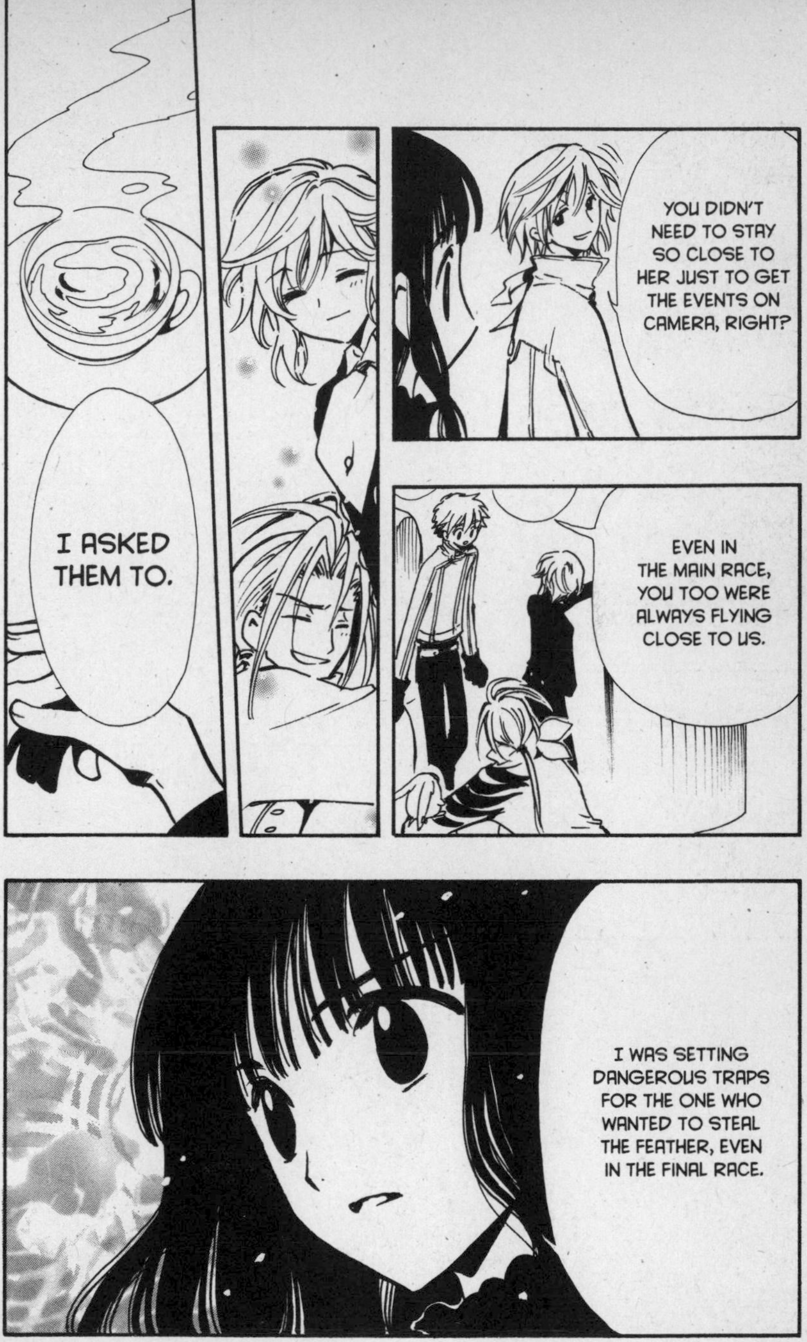
YOU DIDN'T NEED TO STAY SO CLOSE TO HER JUST TO GET THE EVENTS ON CAMERA, RIGHT?
EVEN IN THE MAIN RACE, YOU TOO WERE ALWAYS FLYING CLOSE TO US.
I ASKED THEM TO.
I WAS SETTING DANGEROUS TRAPS FOR THE ONE WHO WANTED TO STEAL THE FEATHER, EVEN IN THE FINAL RACE.

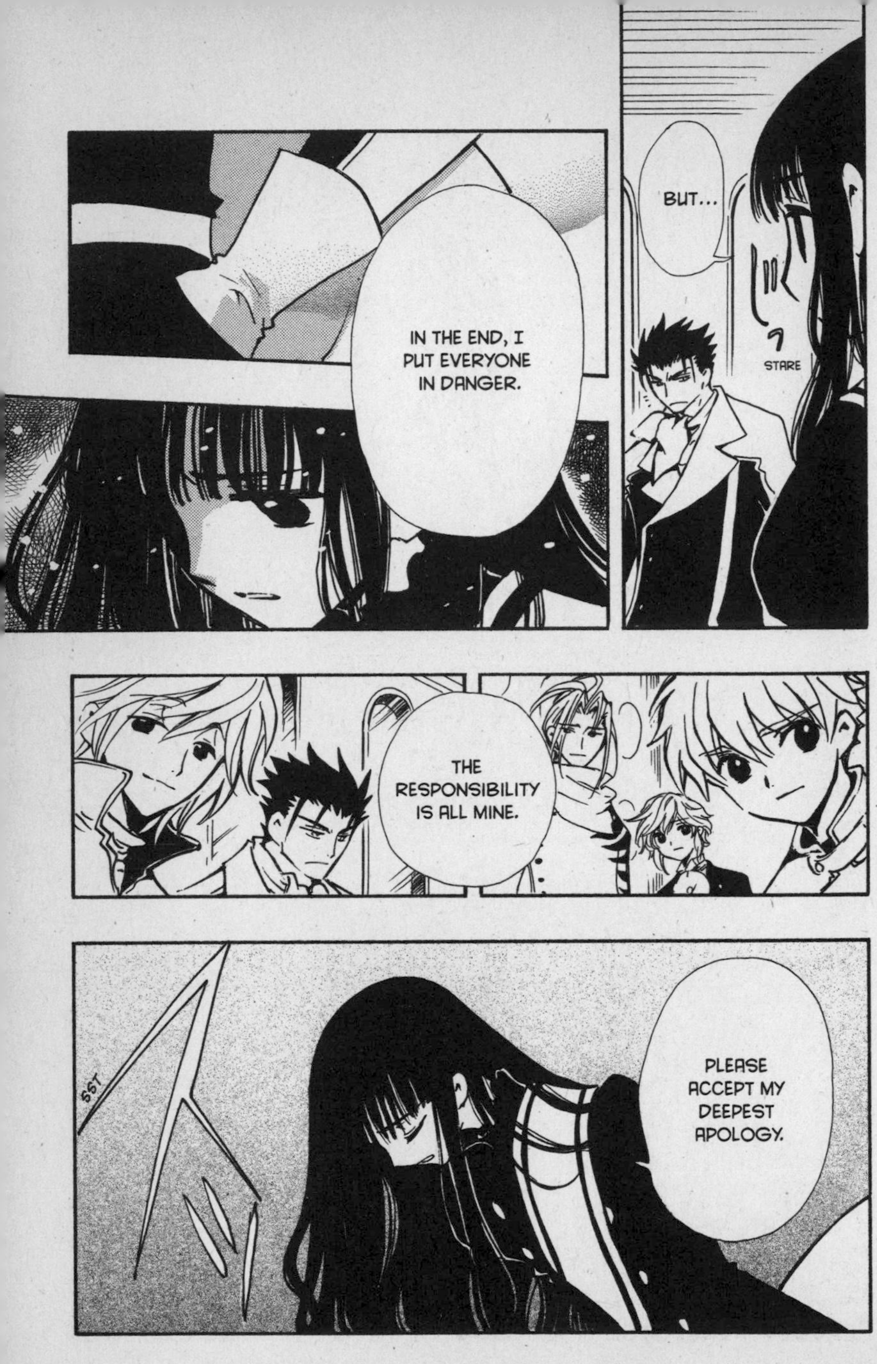
BUT...
STARE
IN THE END, I PUT EVERYONE IN DANGER.
THE RESPONSIBILITY IS ALL MINE.
PLEASE ACCEPT MY DEEPEST APOLOGY.
SST

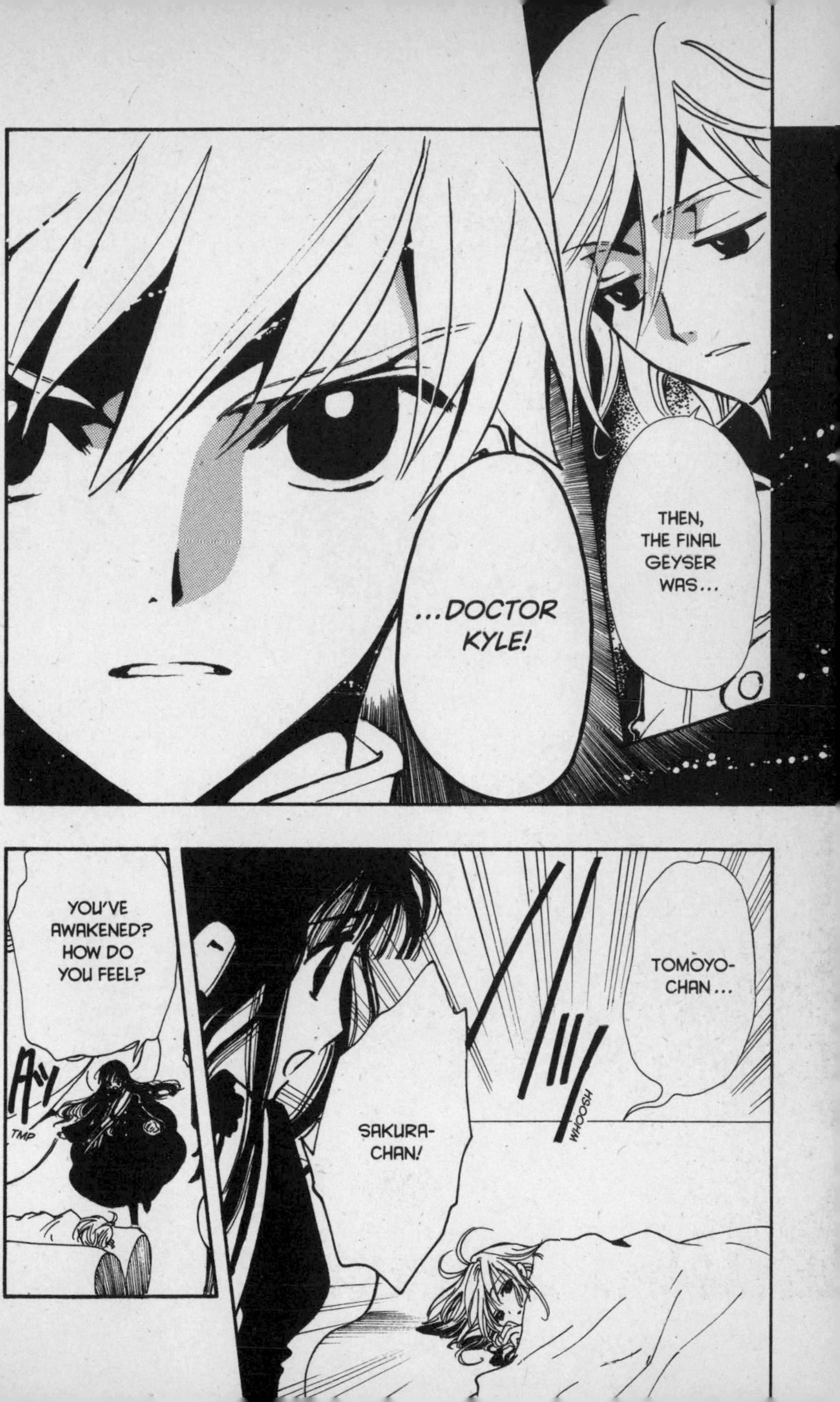
THEN, THE FINAL GEYSER WAS...
...DOCTOR KYLE!
TOMOYO-CHAN...
WHOOSH
SAKURA-CHAN!
YOU'VE AWAKENED? HOW DO YOU FEEL?
TMP

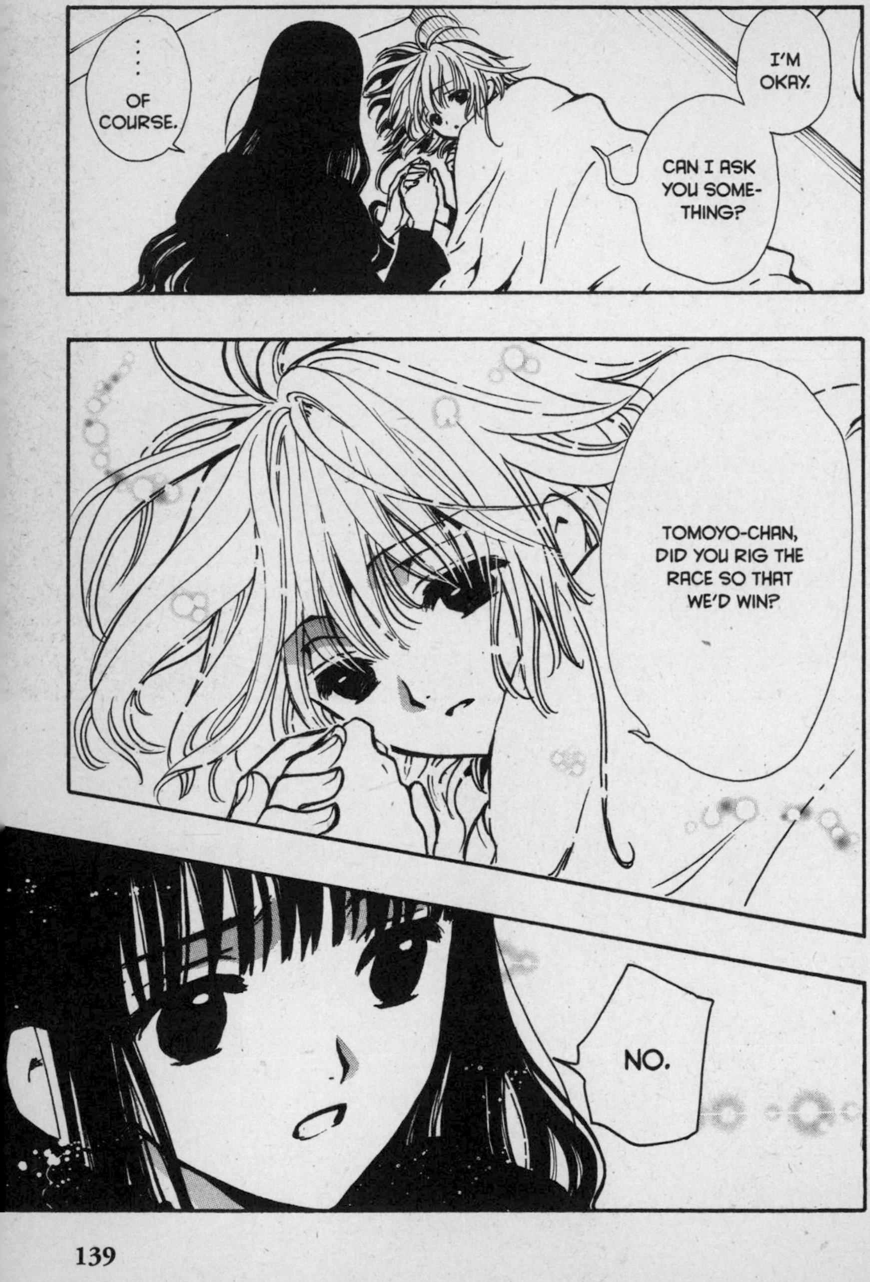
I'M OKAY.
CAN I ASK YOU SOME-THING?
.... OF COURSE.
TOMOYO-CHAN, DID YOU RIG THE RACE SO THAT WE'D WIN?
NO.

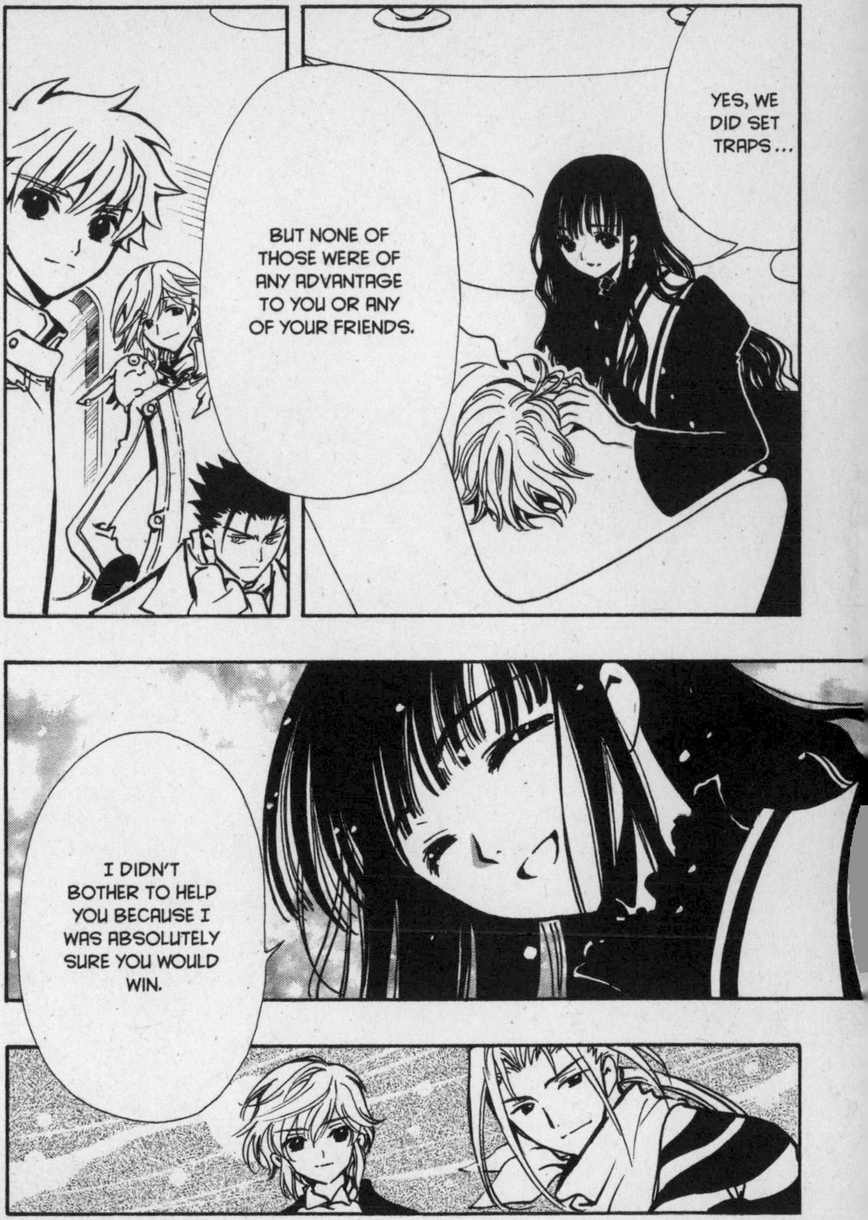
YES, WE DID SET TRAPS...
BUT NONE OF THOSE WERE OF ANY ADVANTAGE TO YOU OR ANY OF YOUR FRIENDS.
I DIDN'T BOTHER TO HELP YOU BECAUSE I WAS ABSOLUTELY SURE YOU WOULD WIN.

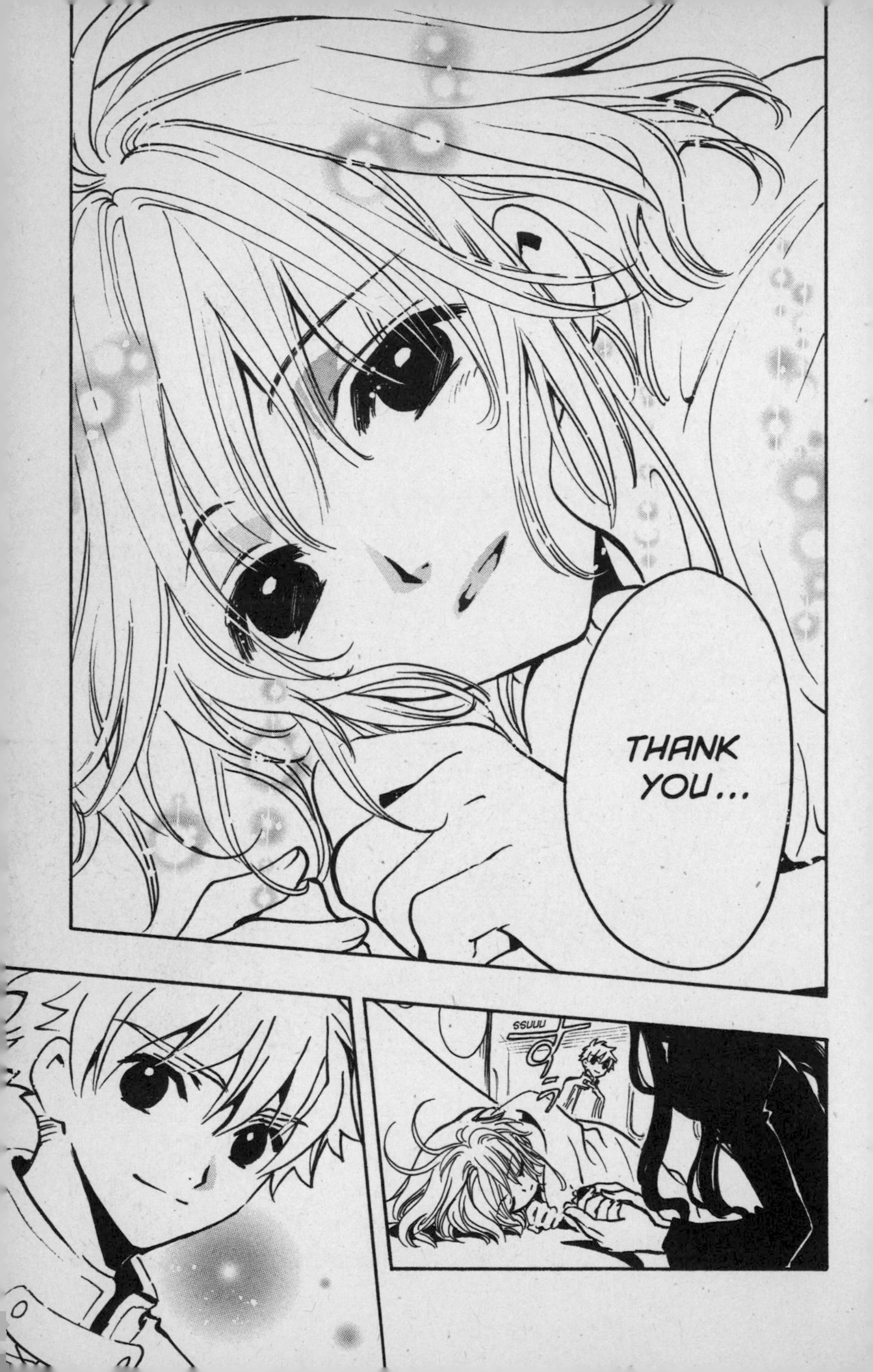
THANK YOU...
SSUUU

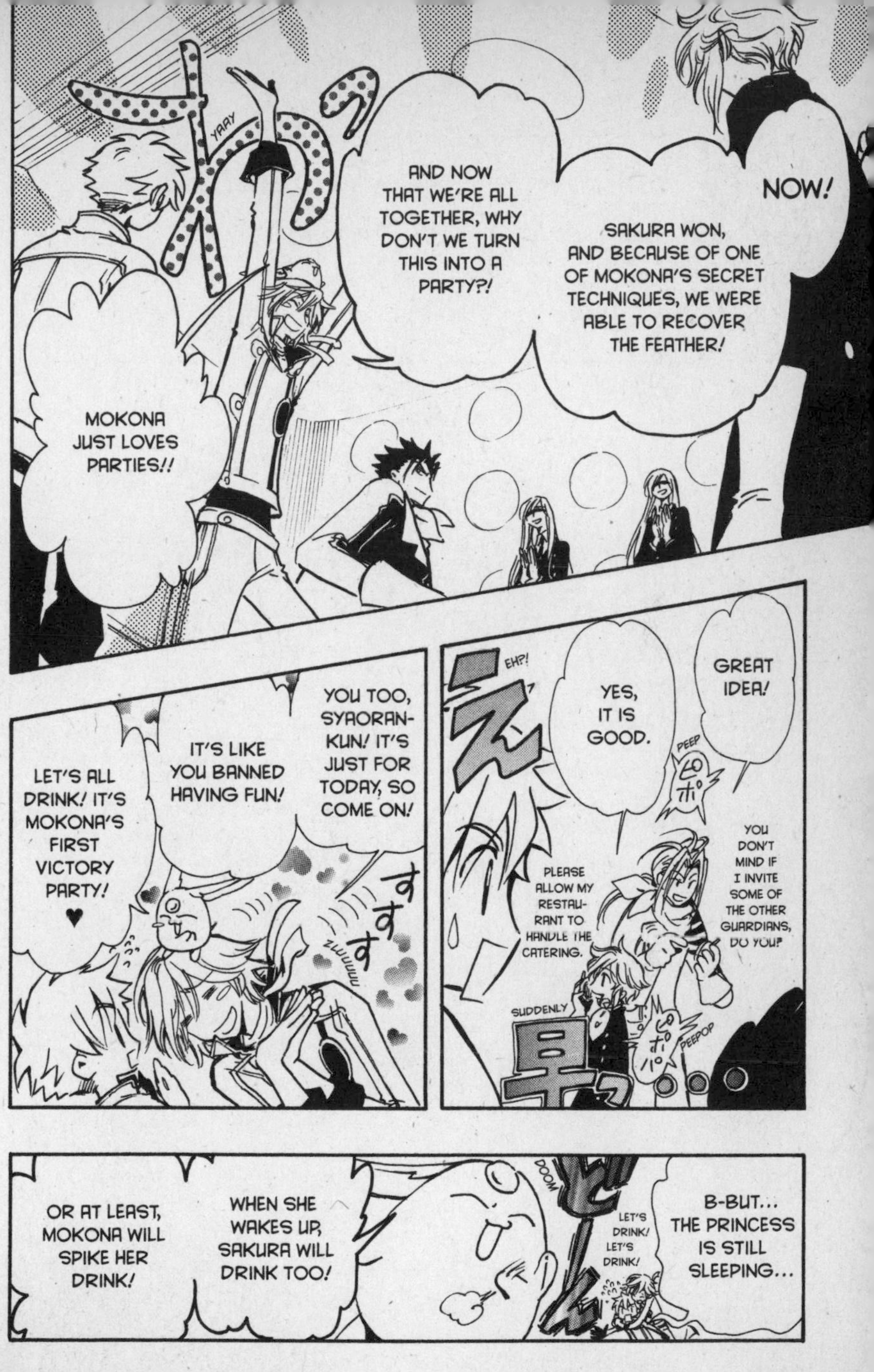
NOW!
SAKURA WON, AND BECAUSE OF ONE OF MOKONA'S SECRET TECHNIQUES, WE WERE ABLE TO RECOVER THE FEATHER!
AND NOW THAT WE'RE ALL TOGETHER, WHY DON'T WE TURN THIS INTO A PARTY?!
YAAY
MOKONA JUST LOVES PARTIES!!
GREAT IDEA!
YES, IT IS GOOD.
EH?!
PEEP
YOU DON'T MIND IF I INVITE SOME OF THE OTHER GUARDIANS, DO YOU?
PLEASE ALLOW MY RESTAURANT TO HANDLE THE CATERING.
SUDDENLY
PEEPOP
YOU TOO, SYAORAN-KUN! IT'S JUST FOR TODAY, SO COME ON!
IT'S LIKE YOU BANNED HAVING FUN!
LET'S ALL DRINK! IT'S MOKONA'S FIRST VICTORY PARTY! ♥
B-BUT... THE PRINCESS IS STILL SLEEPING...
LET'S DRINK! LET'S DRINK!
DOOM
WHEN SHE WAKES UP, SAKURA WILL DRINK TOO!
OR AT LEAST, MOKONA WILL SPIKE HER DRINK!

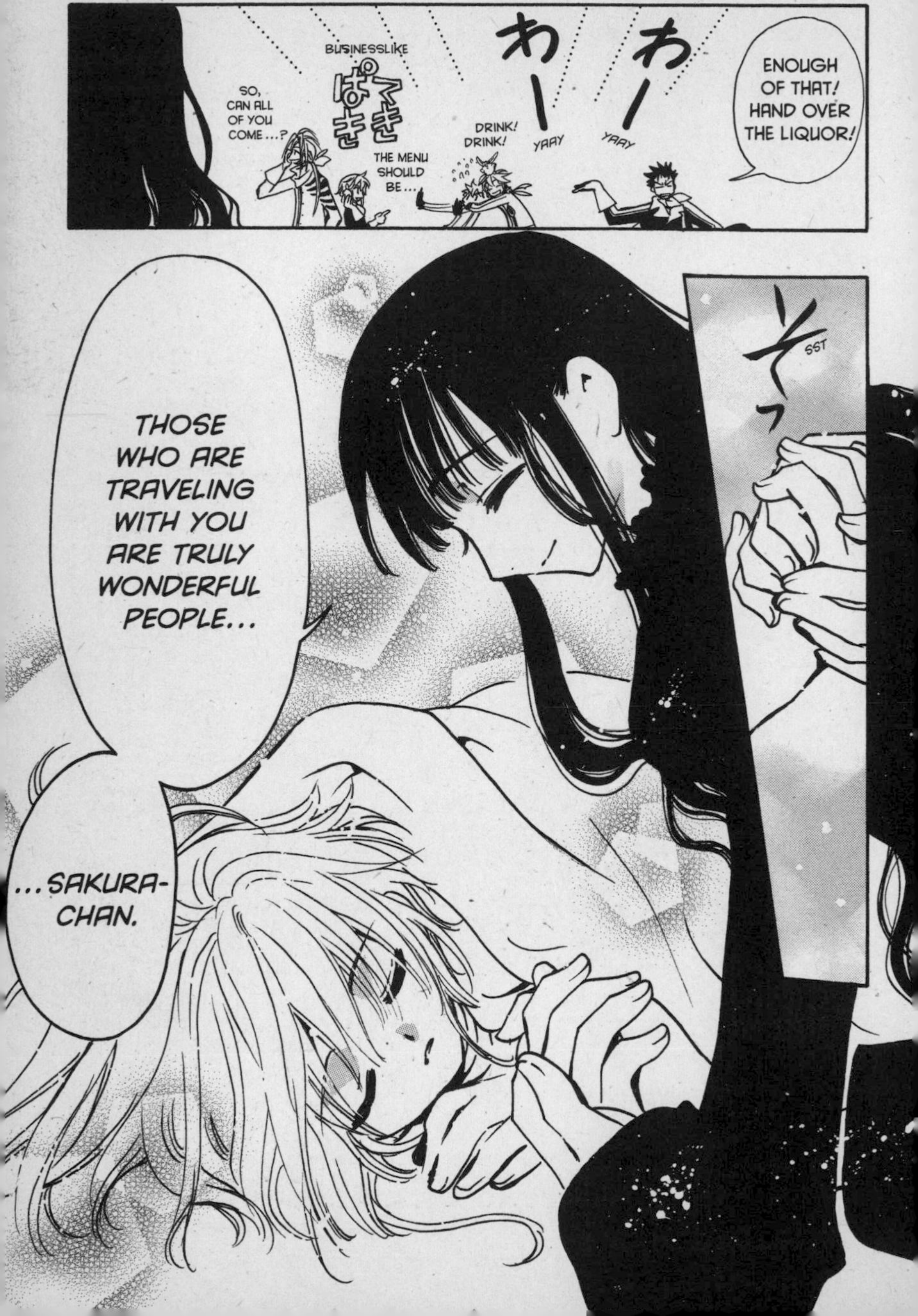
ENOUGH OF THAT! HAND OVER THE LIQUOR!
わー
YAAY
わー
YAAY
DRINK! DRINK!
THE MENU SHOULD BE...
てきぱき
BUSINESSLIKE
SO, CAN ALL OF YOU COME...?
そっ
SST
THOSE WHO ARE TRAVELING WITH YOU ARE TRULY WONDERFUL PEOPLE...
...SAKURA-CHAN.

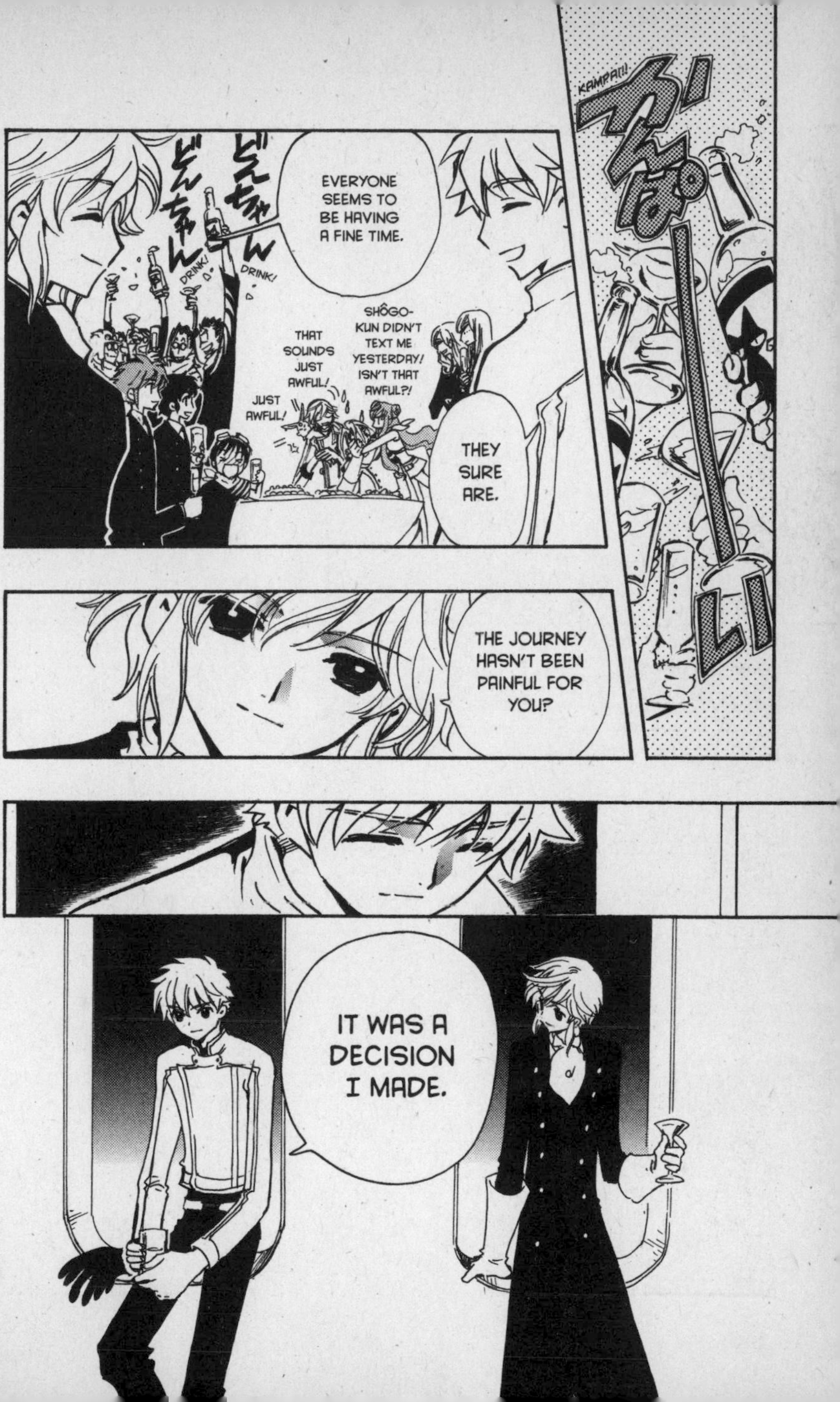
かんぱーい
KAMPAI!!!
EVERYONE SEEMS TO BE HAVING A FINE TIME.
どんちゃん どんちゃん
DRINK! DRINK!
SHÔGO-KUN DIDN'T TEXT ME YESTERDAY! ISN'T THAT AWFUL?!
THAT SOUNDS JUST AWFUL!
JUST AWFUL!
THEY SURE ARE.
THE JOURNEY HASN'T BEEN PAINFUL FOR YOU?
IT WAS A DECISION I MADE.

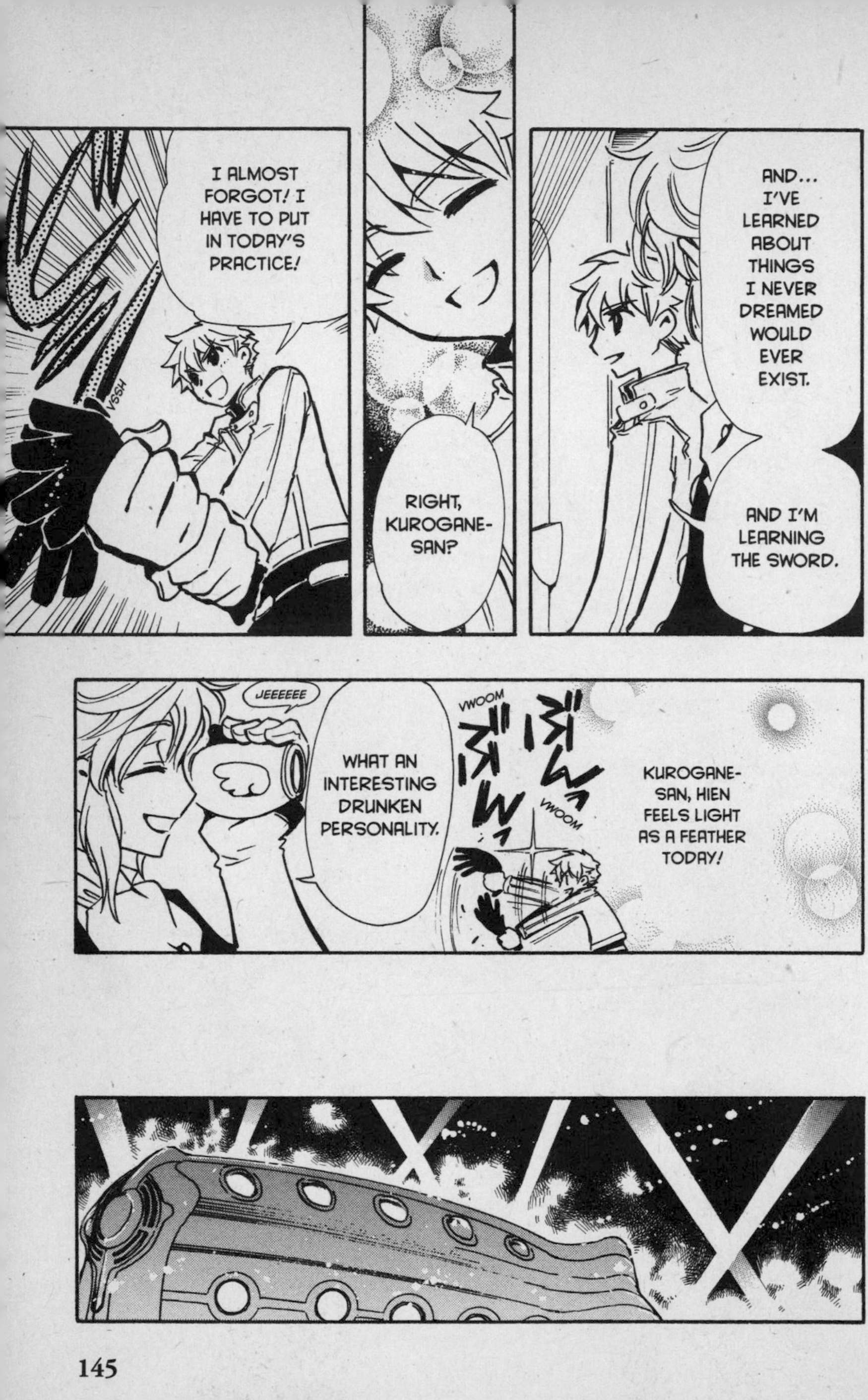
AND... I'VE LEARNED ABOUT THINGS I NEVER DREAMED WOULD EVER EXIST.
AND I'M LEARNING THE SWORD.
RIGHT, KUROGANE-SAN?
I ALMOST FORGOT! I HAVE TO PUT IN TODAY'S PRACTICE!
VSSH
KUROGANE-SAN, HIEN FEELS LIGHT AS A FEATHER TODAY!
VWOOM
VWOOM
WHAT AN INTERESTING DRUNKEN PERSONALITY.
JEEEEEE

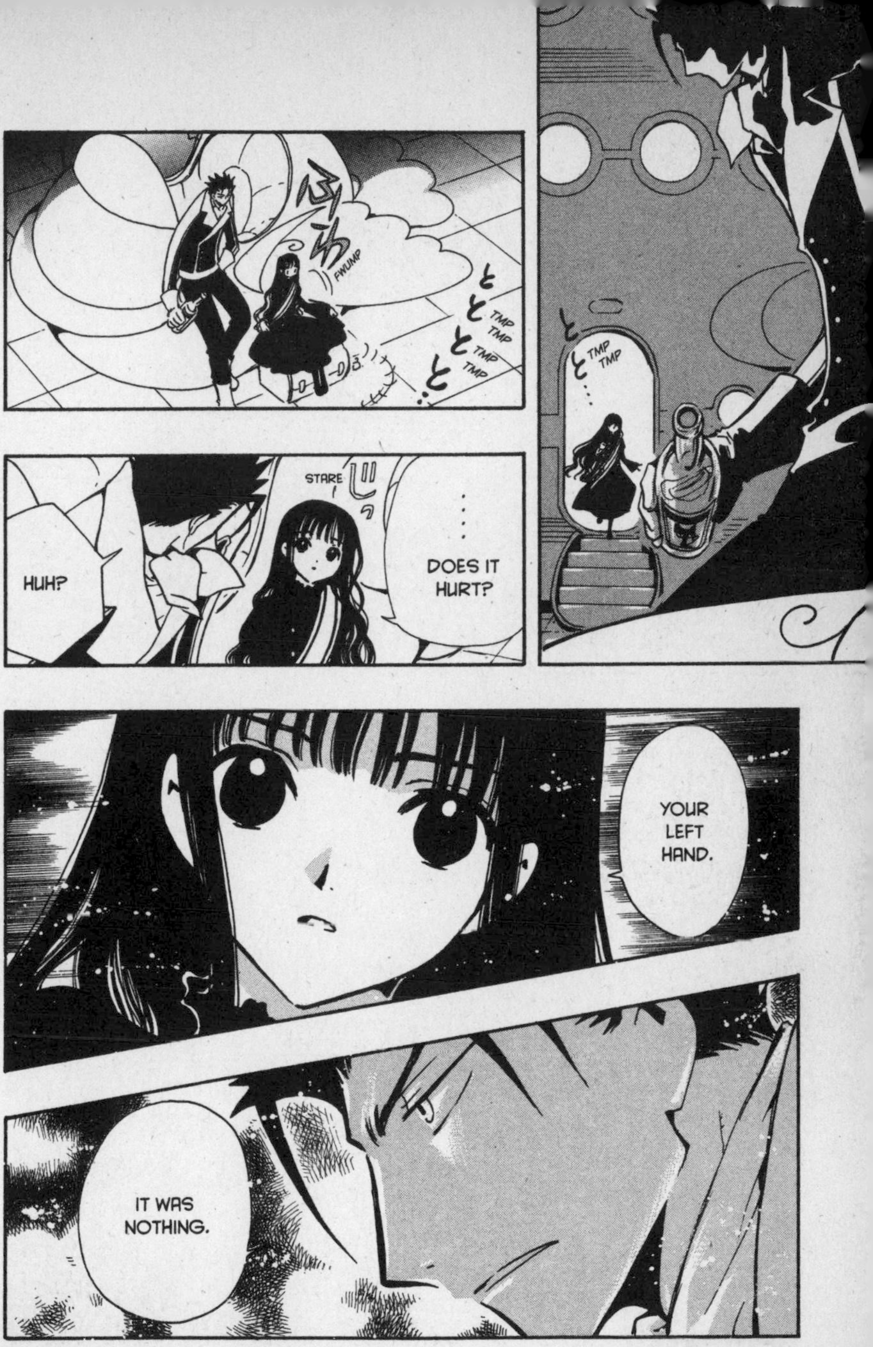

とと
TMP TMP
...
ふわ
FWUMP
とととと
TMP TMP TMP TMP
...
DOES IT HURT?
じっ
STARE
HUH?
YOUR LEFT HAND.
IT WAS NOTHING.

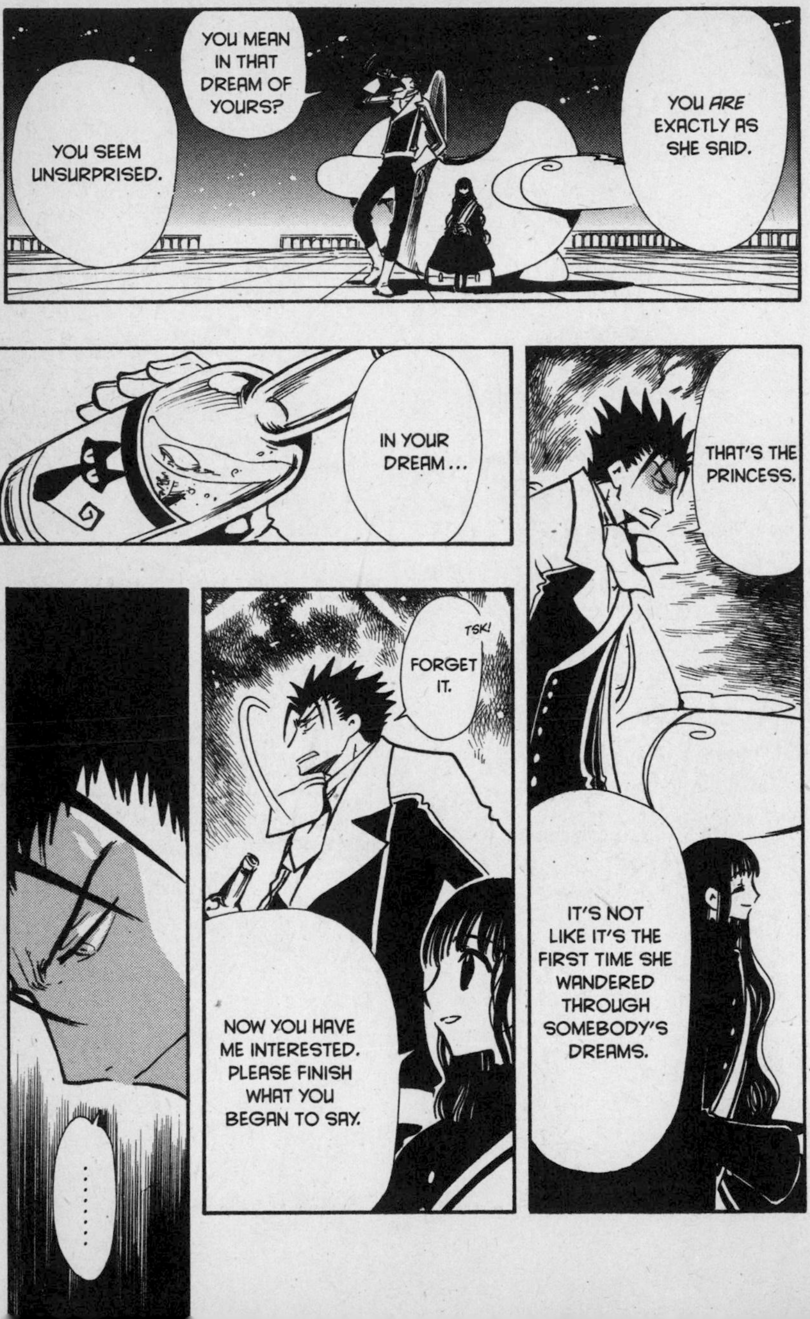
YOU ARE EXACTLY AS SHE SAID.
YOU MEAN IN THAT DREAM OF YOURS?
YOU SEEM UNSURPRISED.
THAT'S THE PRINCESS.
IT'S NOT LIKE IT'S THE FIRST TIME SHE WANDERED THROUGH SOMEBODY'S DREAMS.
IN YOUR DREAM...
TSK!
FORGET IT.
NOW YOU HAVE ME INTERESTED. PLEASE FINISH WHAT YOU BEGAN TO SAY.
......

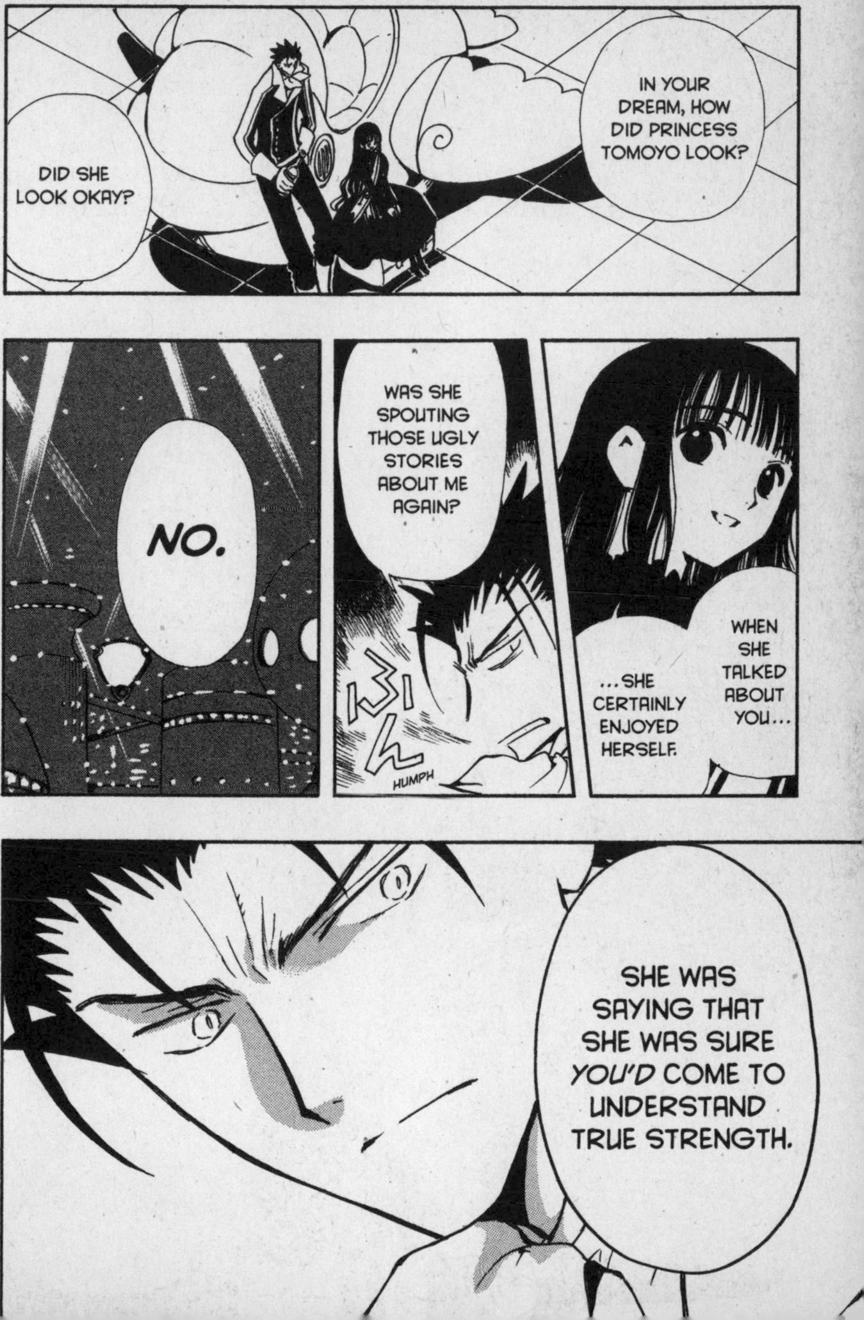
IN YOUR DREAM, HOW DID PRINCESS TOMOYO LOOK?
DID SHE LOOK OKAY?
WHEN SHE TALKED ABOUT YOU...
...SHE CERTAINLY ENJOYED HERSELF.
WAS SHE SPOUTING THOSE UGLY STORIES ABOUT ME AGAIN?
ふん
HUMPH
NO.
SHE WAS SAYING THAT SHE WAS SURE *YOU'D* COME TO UNDERSTAND TRUE STRENGTH.

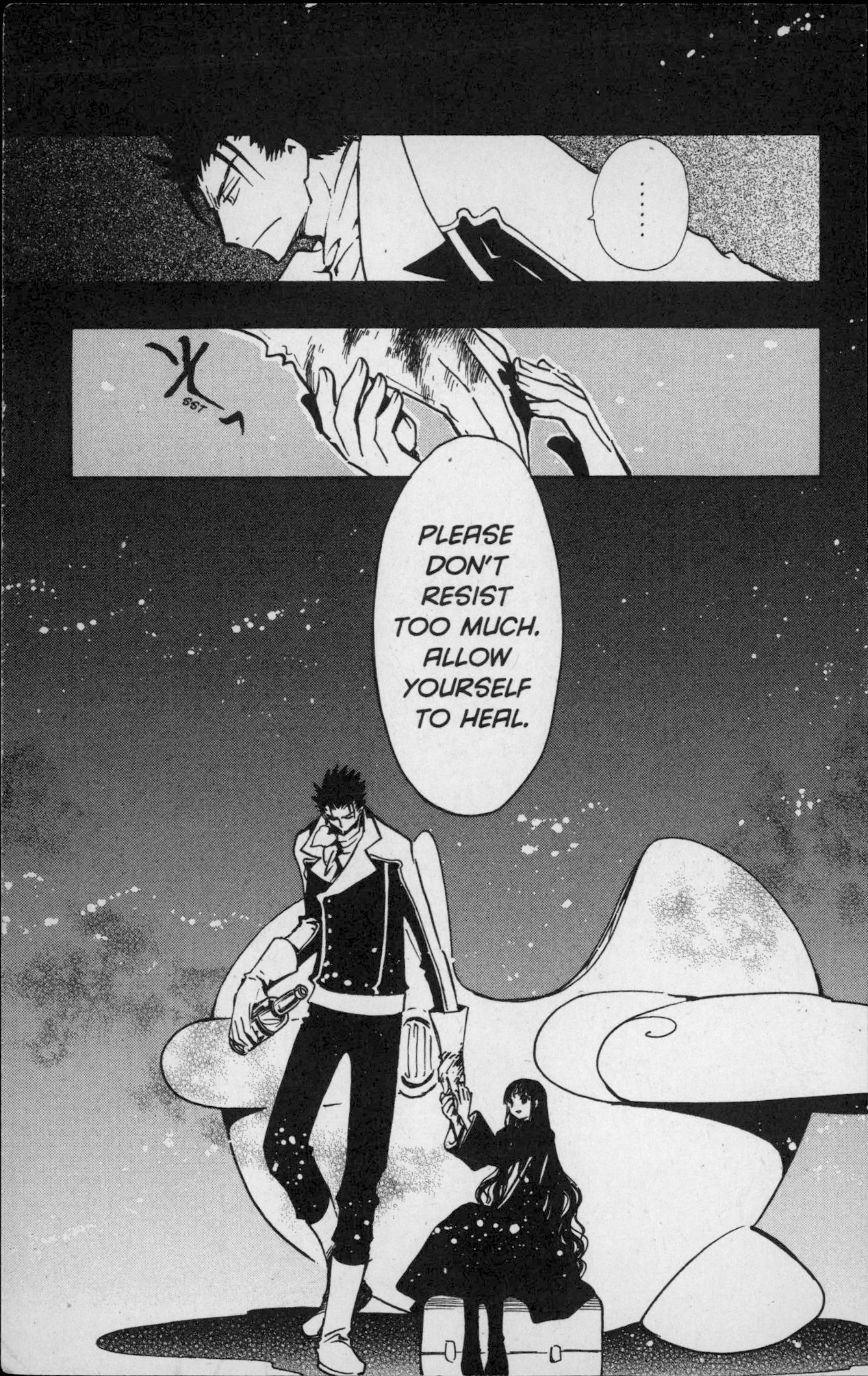
......
SST
PLEASE DON'T RESIST TOO MUCH. ALLOW YOURSELF TO HEAL.

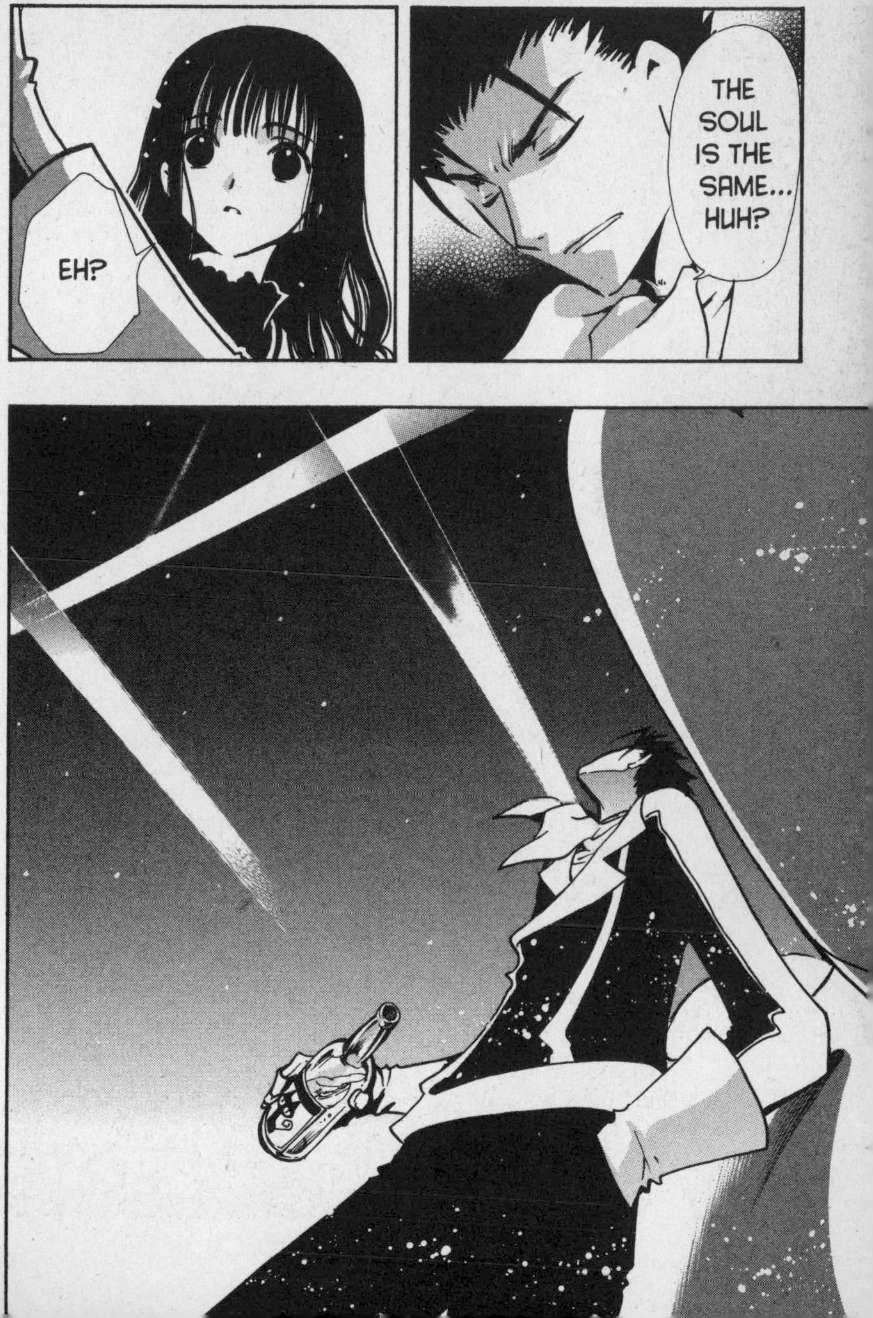
THE SOUL IS THE SAME... HUH?
EH?

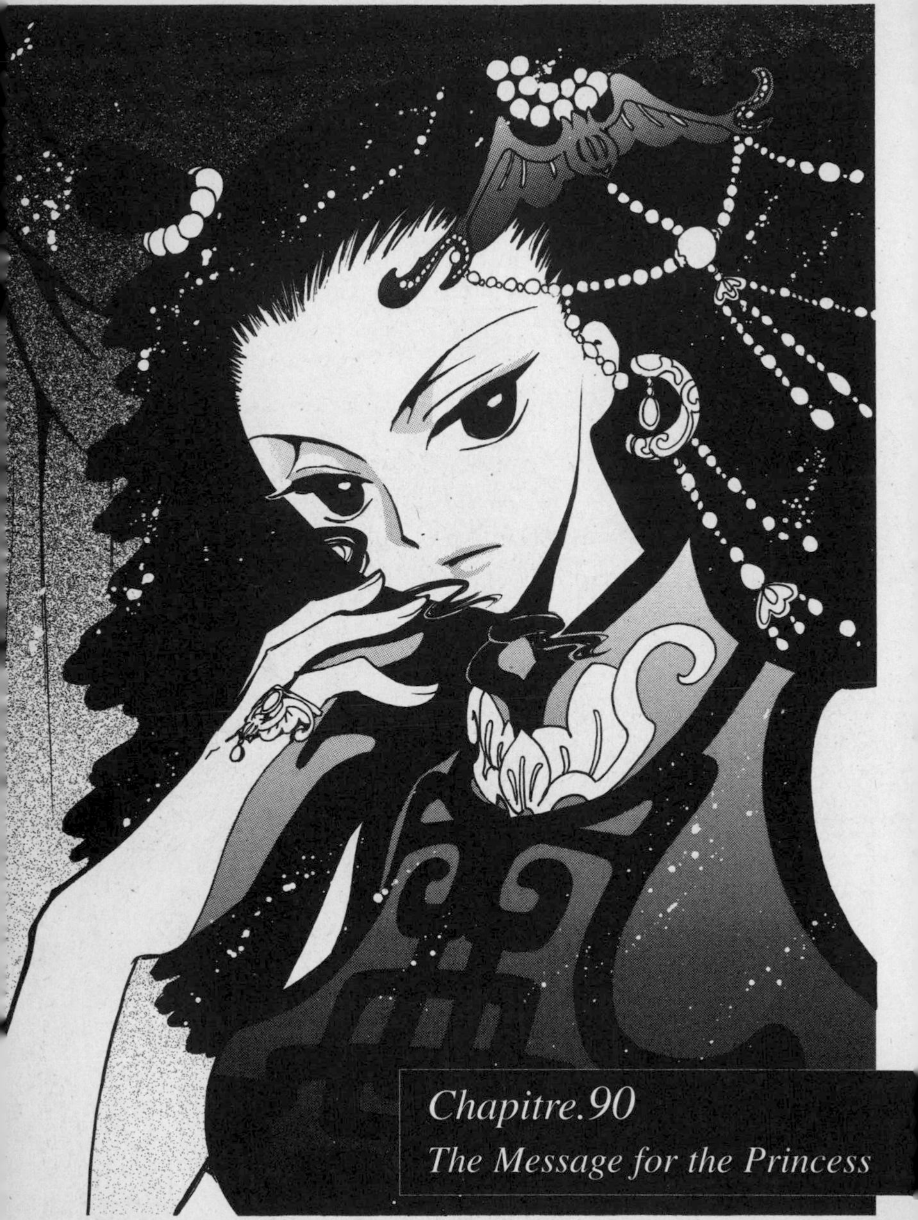
Chapitre.90
The Message for the Princess

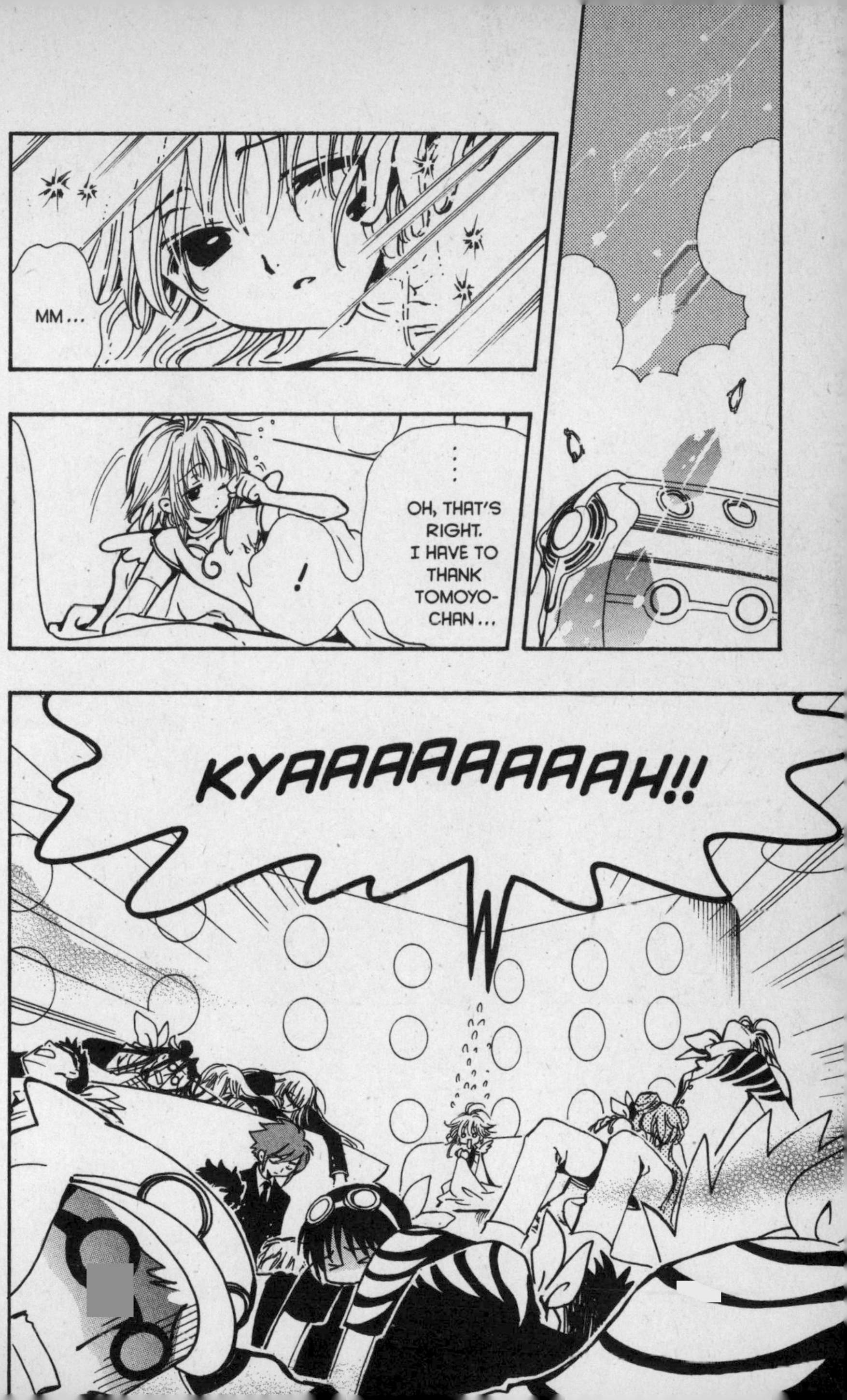
MM...
....
OH, THAT'S RIGHT. I HAVE TO THANK TOMOYO-CHAN...
!
KYAAAAAAAAH!!

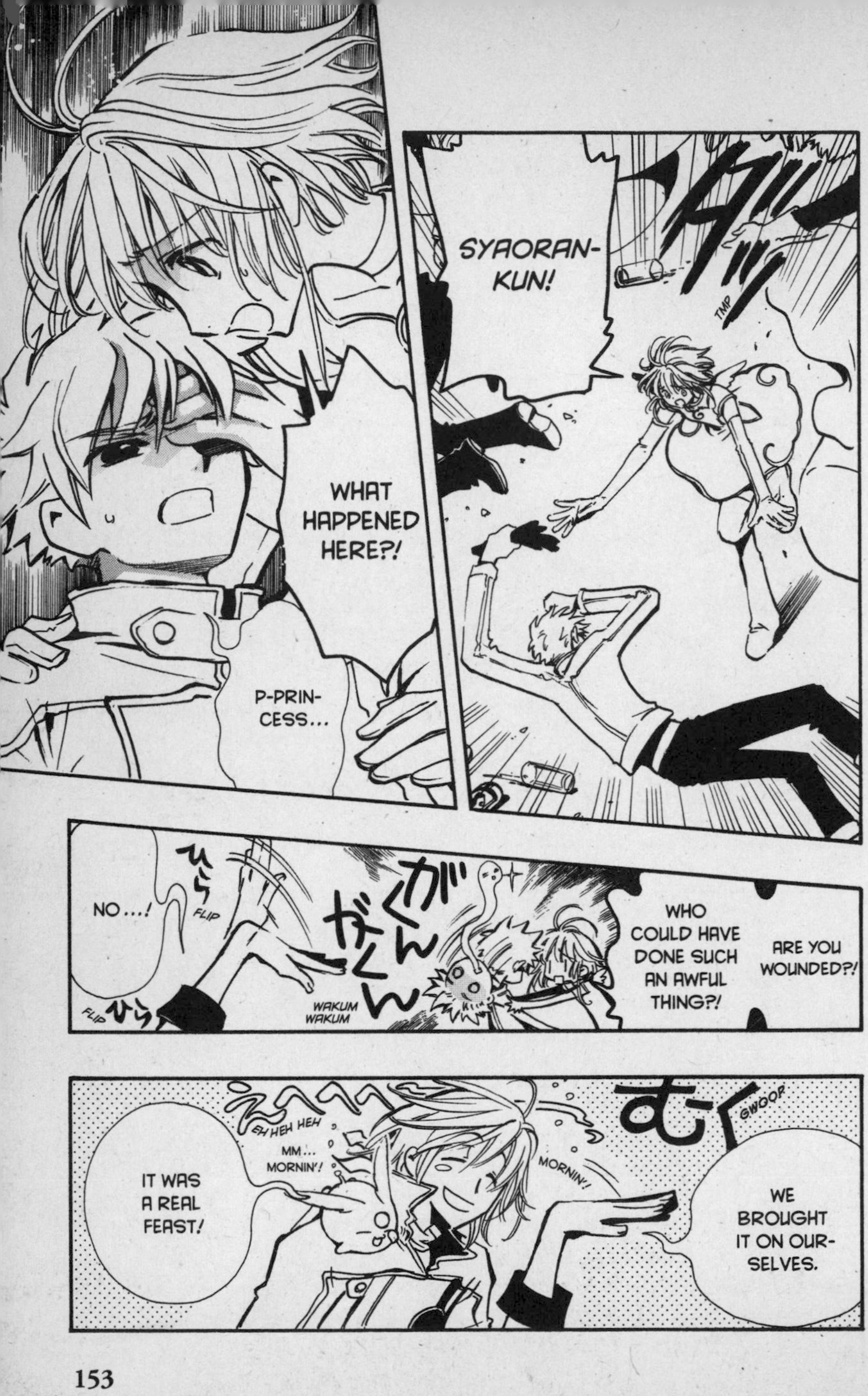
SYAORAN-KUN!
TMP
WHAT HAPPENED HERE?!
P-PRIN-
CESS...
ARE YOU WOUNDED?!
WHO COULD HAVE DONE SUCH AN AWFUL THING?!
がくんがくん
WAKUM WAKUM
ひら
FLIP
NO...!
ひら
FLIP
WE BROUGHT IT ON OUR-SELVES.
むく
GWOOP
MORNIN'!
MM... MORNIN'!
えへへへ
EH HEH HEH
IT WAS A REAL FEAST!

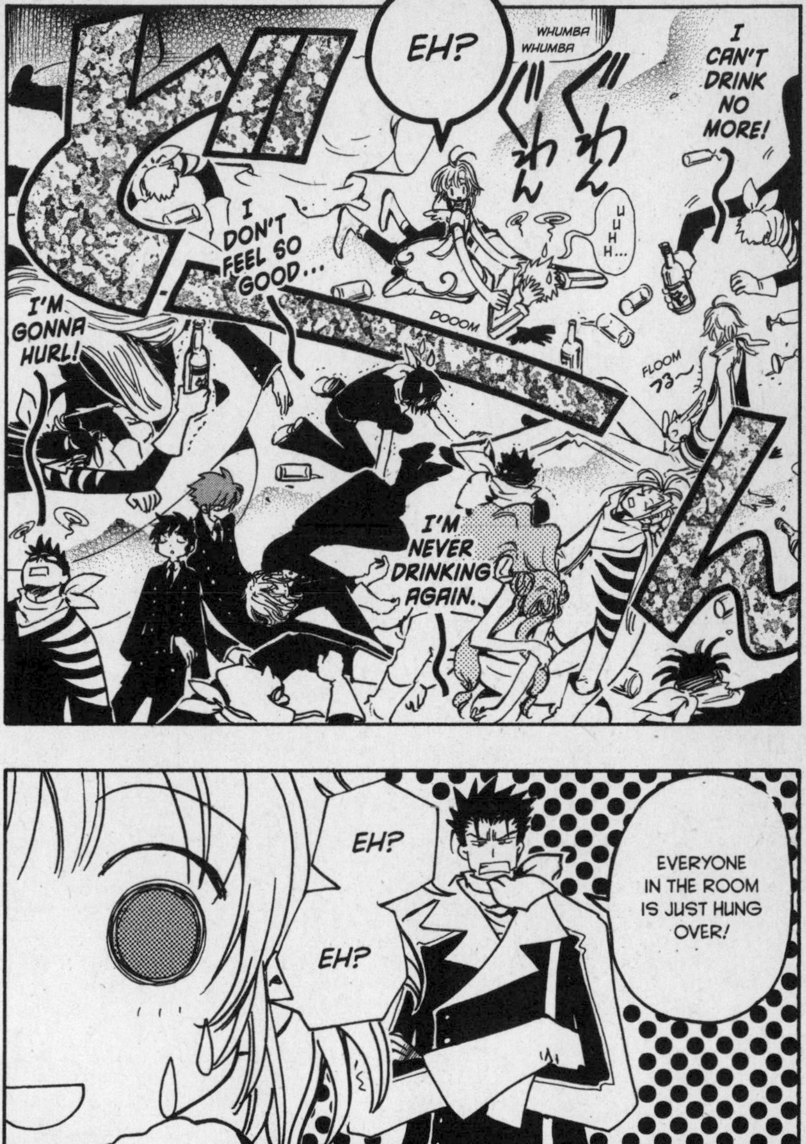

I CAN'T DRINK NO MORE!
WHUMBA WHUMBA
ぐわん ぐわん
EH?
UUHH...
I DON'T FEEL SO GOOD...
DOOOM
FLOOM
I'M GONNA HURL!
I'M NEVER DRINKING AGAIN.
EVERYONE IN THE ROOM IS JUST HUNG OVER!
EH?
EH?

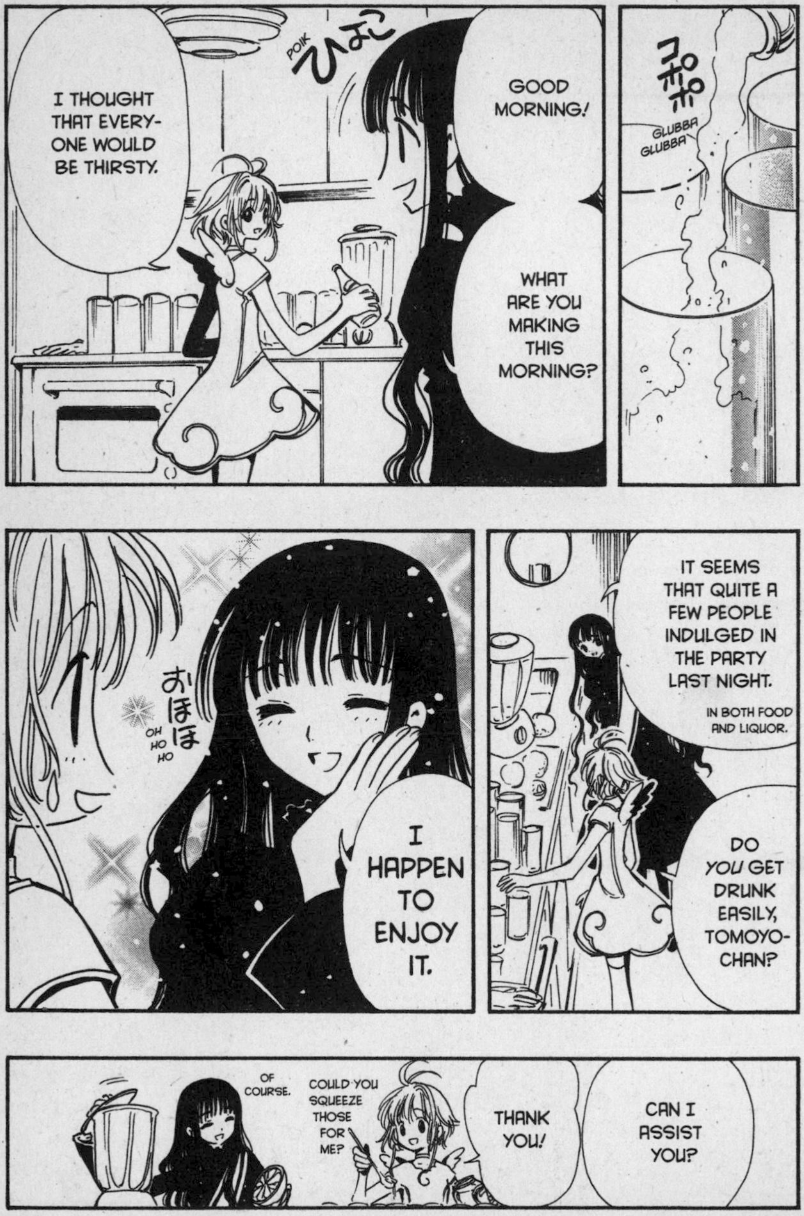
コポポ
GLUBBA GLUBBA
GOOD MORNING!
WHAT ARE YOU MAKING THIS MORNING?
ひよこ
POIK
I THOUGHT THAT EVERY-ONE WOULD BE THIRSTY.
IT SEEMS THAT QUITE A FEW PEOPLE INDULGED IN THE PARTY LAST NIGHT.
IN BOTH FOOD AND LIQUOR.
DO *YOU* GET DRUNK EASILY, TOMOYO-CHAN?
I HAPPEN TO ENJOY IT.
おほほ
OH HO HO
CAN I ASSIST YOU?
THANK YOU!
COULD YOU SQUEEZE THOSE FOR ME?
OF COURSE.

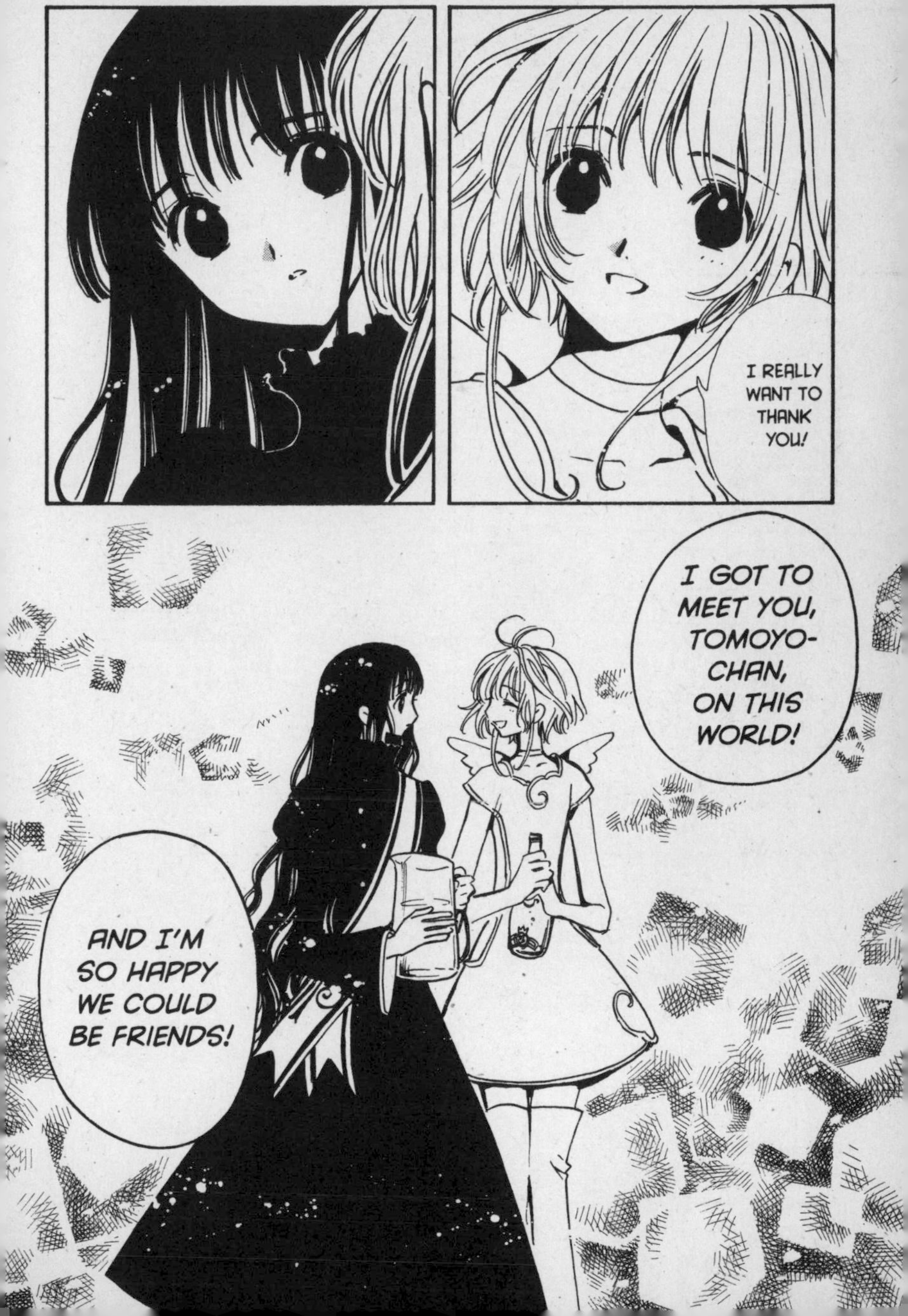
I REALLY WANT TO THANK YOU!
I GOT TO MEET YOU, TOMOYO-CHAN, ON THIS WORLD!
AND I'M SO HAPPY WE COULD BE FRIENDS!

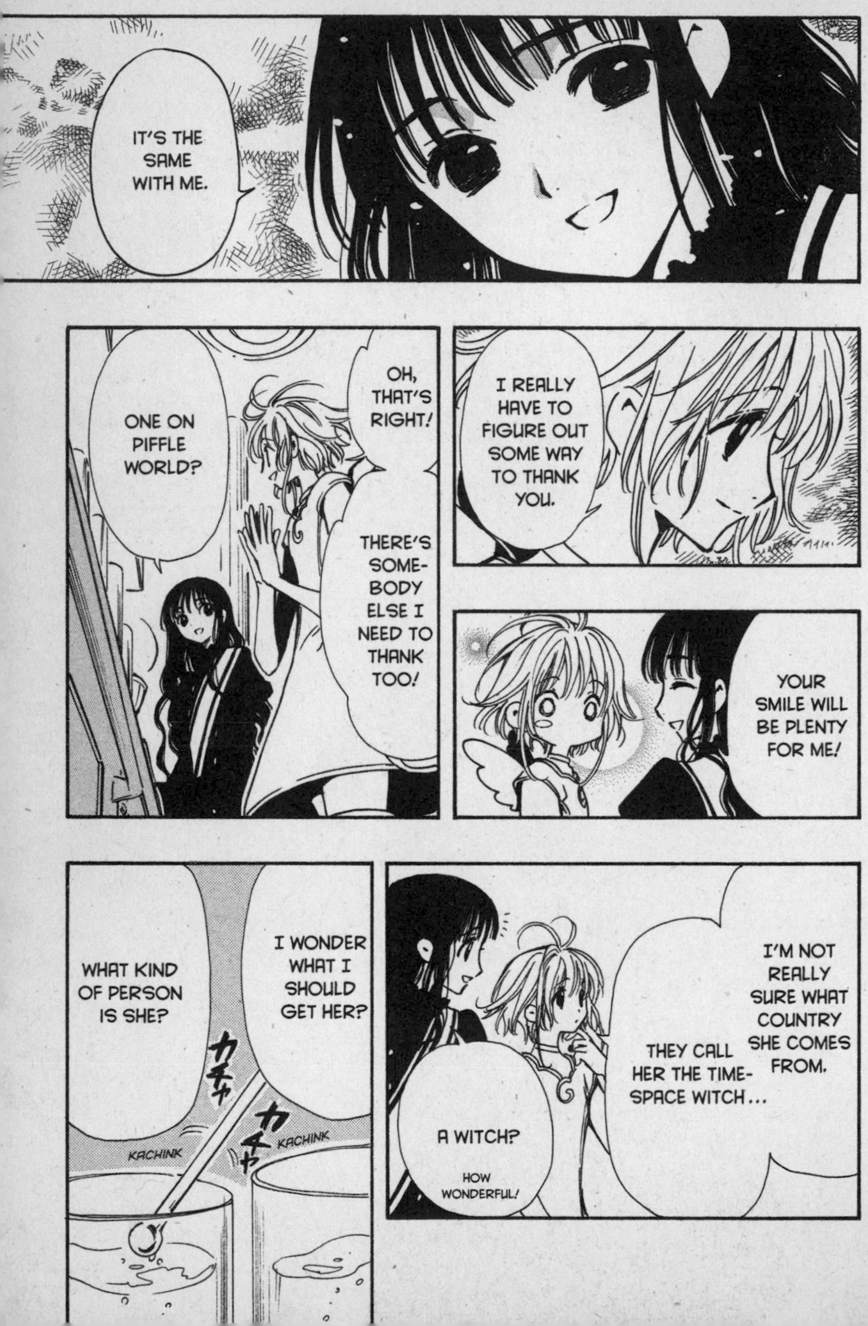

IT'S THE SAME WITH ME.
I REALLY HAVE TO FIGURE OUT SOME WAY TO THANK YOU.
YOUR SMILE WILL BE PLENTY FOR ME!
OH, THAT'S RIGHT!
THERE'S SOME-BODY ELSE I NEED TO THANK TOO!
ONE ON PIFFLE WORLD?
I'M NOT REALLY SURE WHAT COUNTRY SHE COMES FROM.
THEY CALL HER THE TIME-SPACE WITCH...
A WITCH?
HOW WONDERFUL!
I WONDER WHAT I SHOULD GET HER?
WHAT KIND OF PERSON IS SHE?
KACHINK
KACHINK

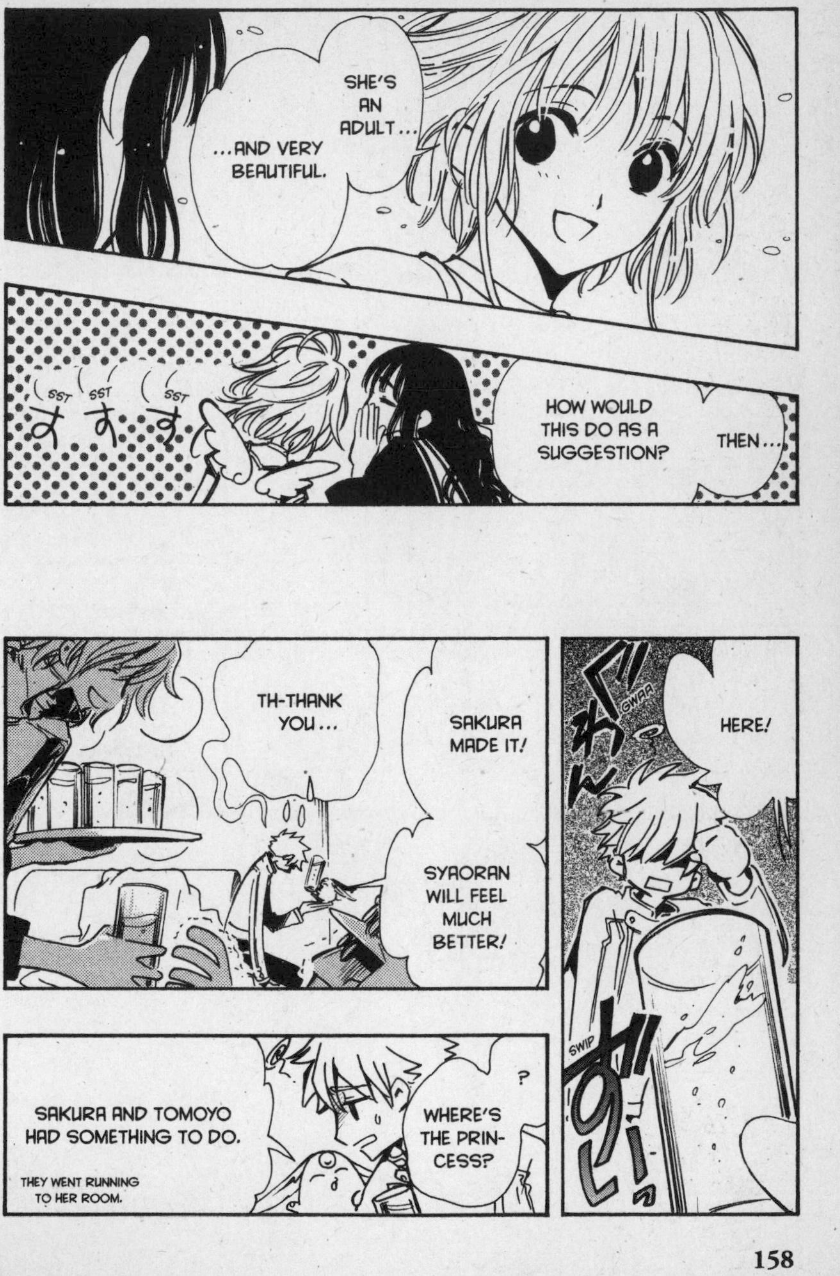
SHE'S AN ADULT...
...AND VERY BEAUTIFUL.
THEN...
HOW WOULD THIS DO AS A SUGGESTION?
SST SST SST
すすす
HERE!
GWAA
SWIP
SAKURA MADE IT!
SYAORAN WILL FEEL MUCH BETTER!
TH-THANK YOU...
?
WHERE'S THE PRIN-CESS?
SAKURA AND TOMOYO HAD SOMETHING TO DO.
THEY WENT RUNNING TO HER ROOM.

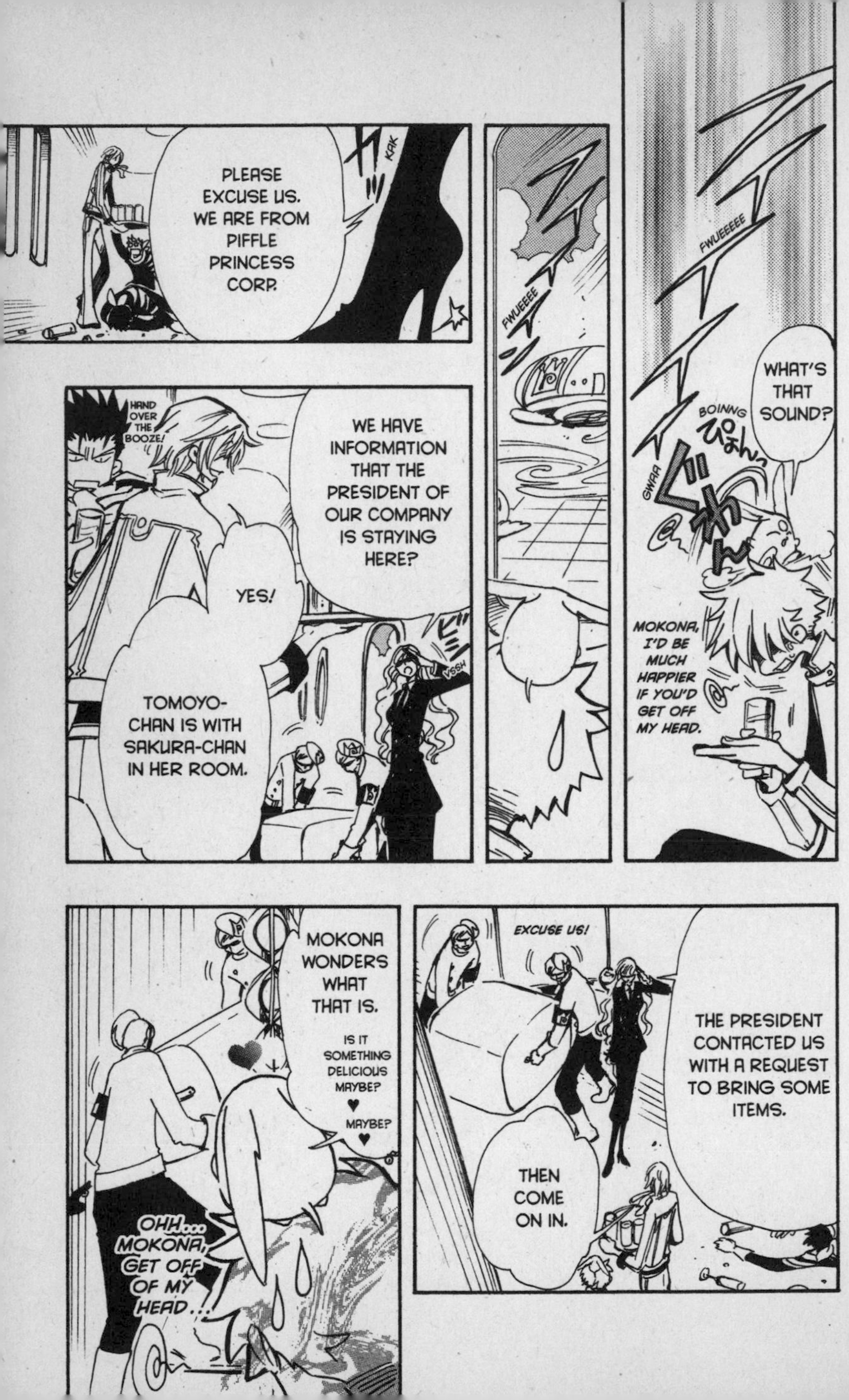
FWUEEEEE
WHAT'S THAT SOUND?
BOING
GWAA
MOKONA, I'D BE MUCH HAPPIER IF YOU'D GET OFF MY HEAD.
FWUEEEE
KAK
PLEASE EXCUSE US. WE ARE FROM PIFFLE PRINCESS CORP.
WE HAVE INFORMATION THAT THE PRESIDENT OF OUR COMPANY IS STAYING HERE?
HAND OVER THE BOOZE!
YES!
VSSH
TOMOYO-CHAN IS WITH SAKURA-CHAN IN HER ROOM.
EXCUSE US!
THE PRESIDENT CONTACTED US WITH A REQUEST TO BRING SOME ITEMS.
THEN COME ON IN.
MOKONA WONDERS WHAT THAT IS.
IS IT SOMETHING DELICIOUS MAYBE? ♥
MAYBE? ♥
OHH... MOKONA, GET OFF OF MY HEAD...

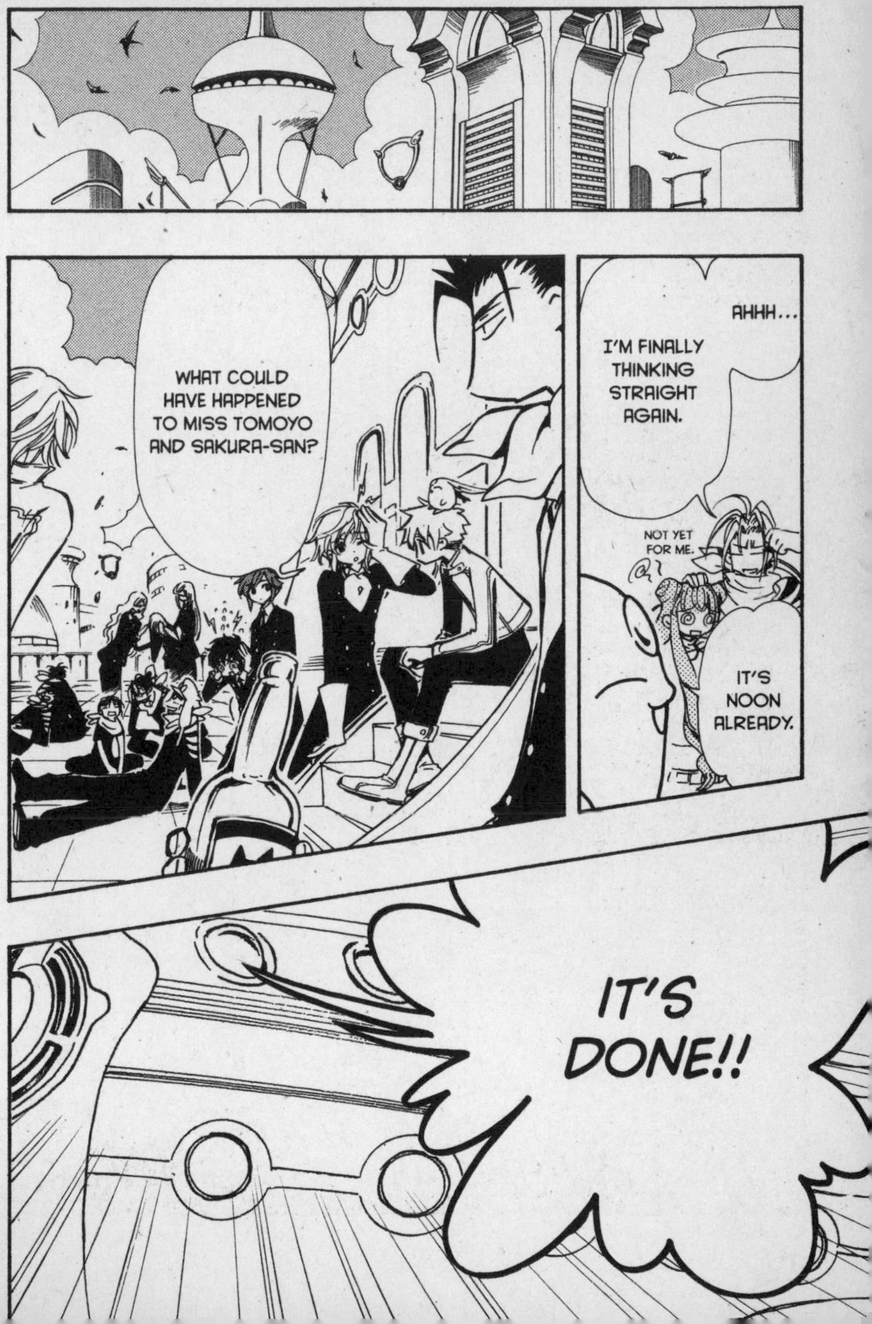
AHHH...
I'M FINALLY THINKING STRAIGHT AGAIN.
NOT YET FOR ME.
IT'S NOON ALREADY.
WHAT COULD HAVE HAPPENED TO MISS TOMOYO AND SAKURA-SAN?
IT'S DONE!!

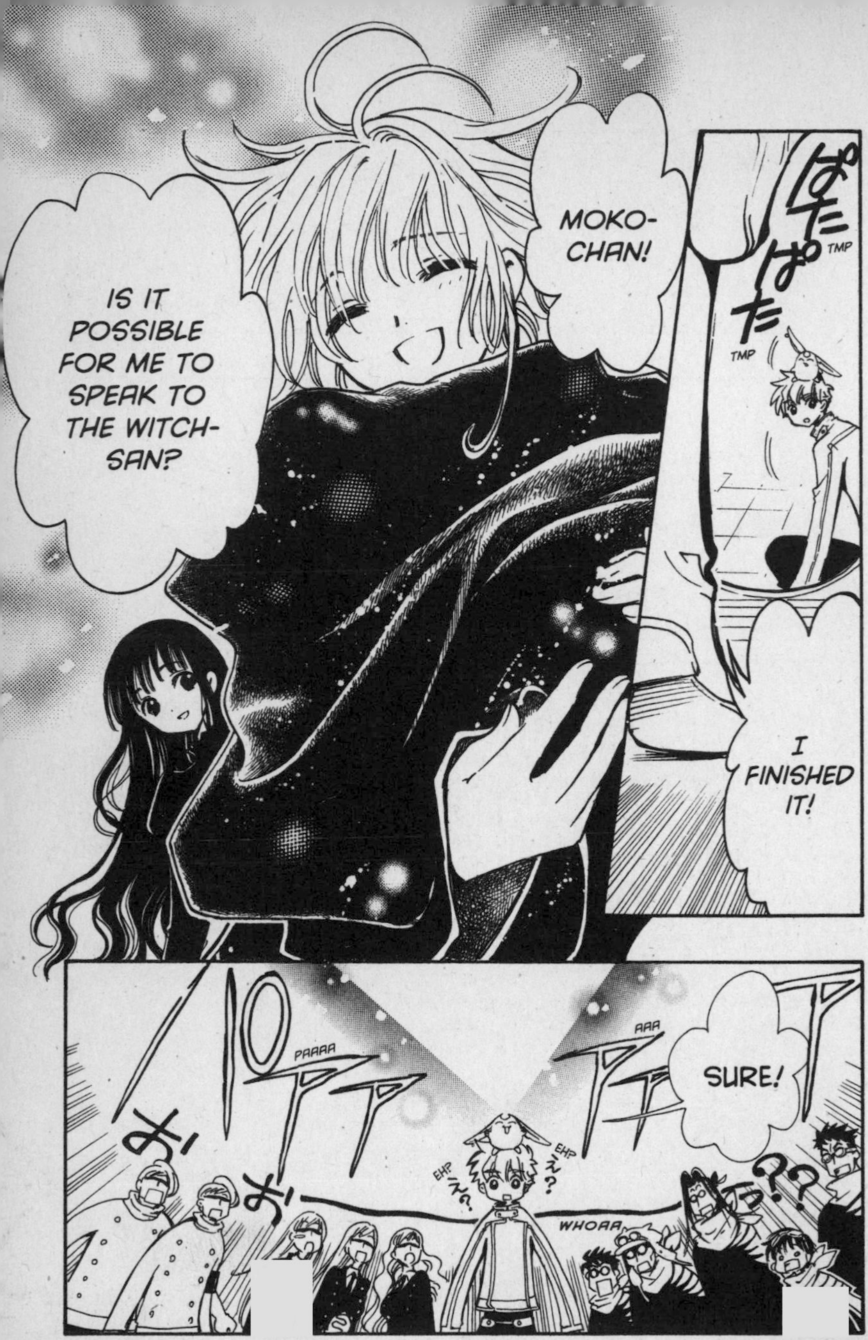

ぱたぱた
TMP
TMP
I FINISHED IT!
MOKO-CHAN!
IS IT POSSIBLE FOR ME TO SPEAK TO THE WITCH-SAN?
SURE!
AAA
PAAAA
EHP
EHP
WHOAA

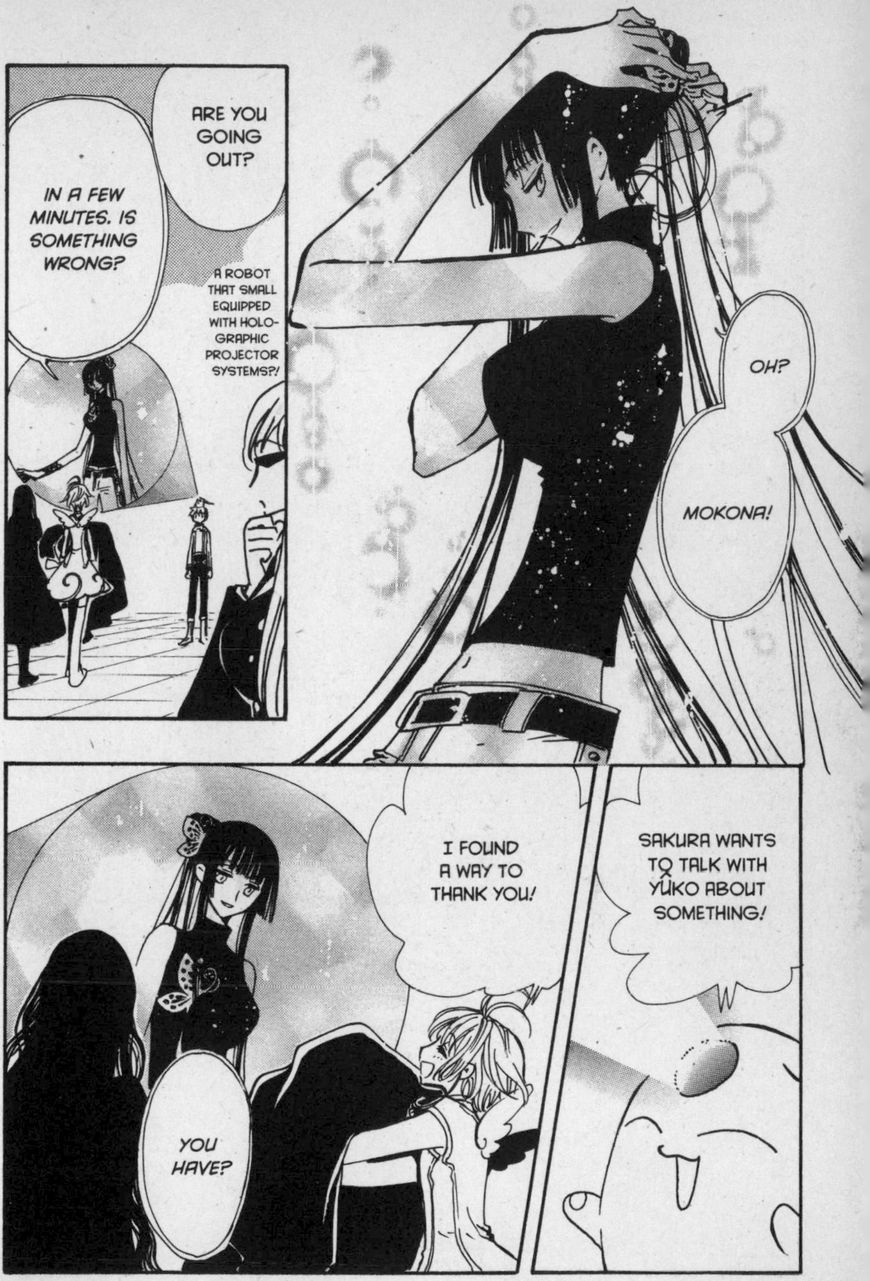
OH?
MOKONA!
ARE YOU GOING OUT?
IN A FEW MINUTES. IS SOMETHING WRONG?
A ROBOT THAT SMALL EQUIPPED WITH HOLO-GRAPHIC PROJECTOR SYSTEMS?!
SAKURA WANTS TO TALK WITH YŪKO ABOUT SOMETHING!
I FOUND A WAY TO THANK YOU!
YOU HAVE?

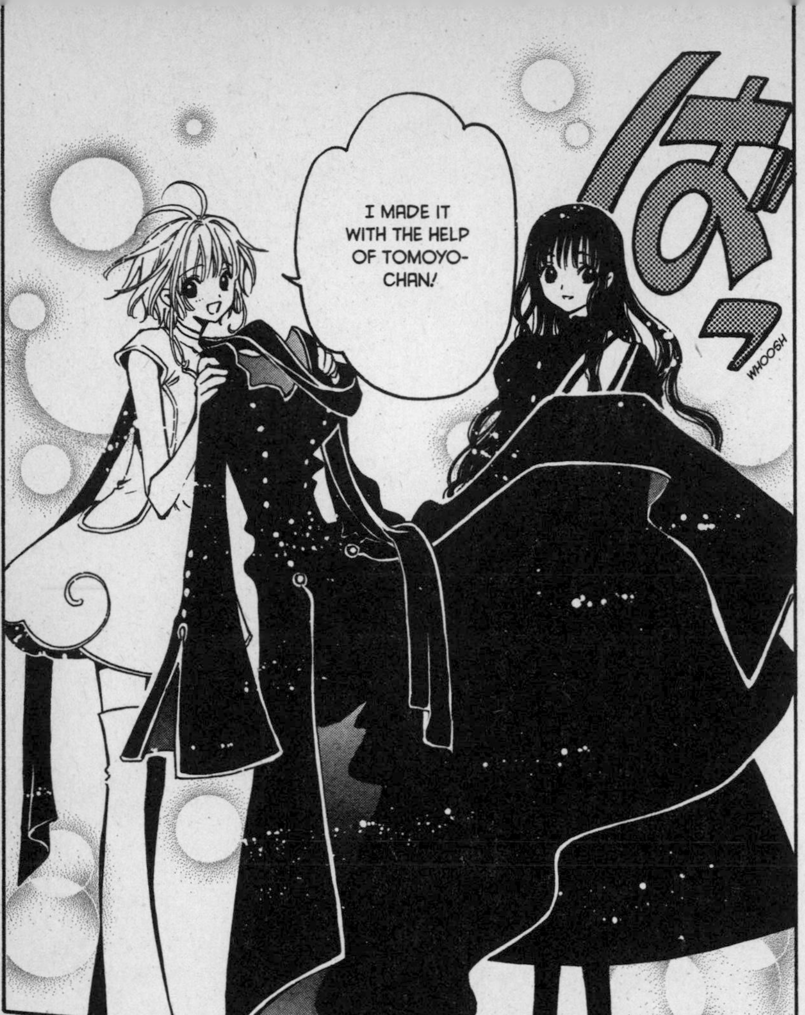
WHOOSH
I MADE IT WITH THE HELP OF TOMOYO-CHAN!

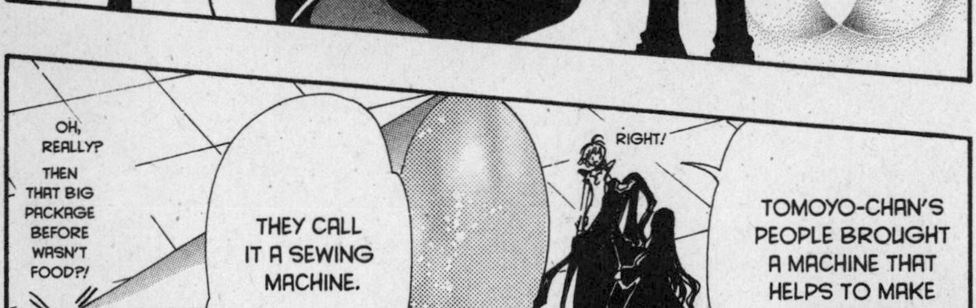
TOMOYO-CHAN'S PEOPLE BROUGHT A MACHINE THAT HELPS TO MAKE CLOTHES.
RIGHT!
THEY CALL IT A SEWING MACHINE.
OH, REALLY? THEN THAT BIG PACKAGE BEFORE WASN'T FOOD?!

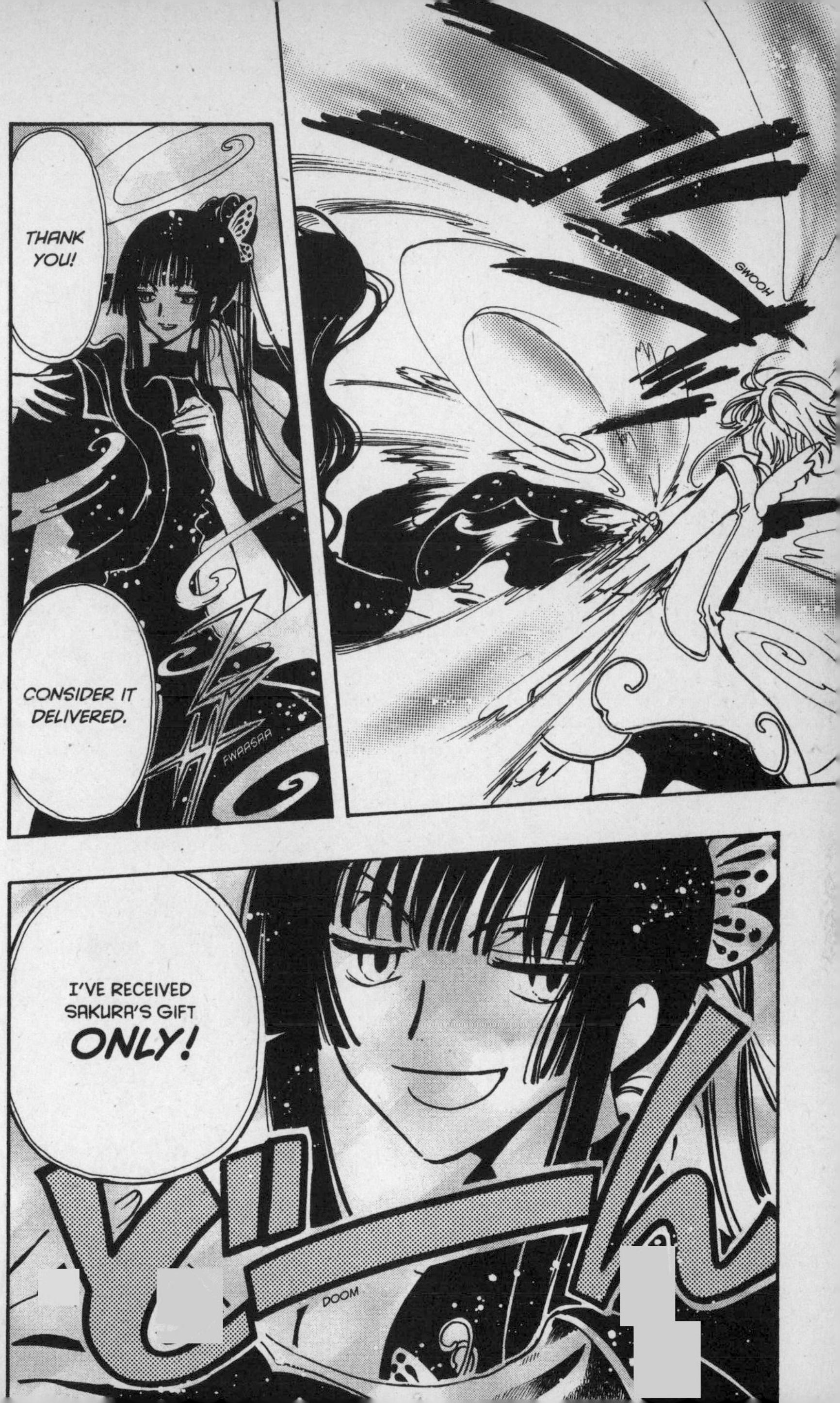
GWOOH
THANK YOU!
CONSIDER IT DELIVERED.
FWAASAA
I'VE RECEIVED SAKURA'S GIFT ONLY!
DOOM

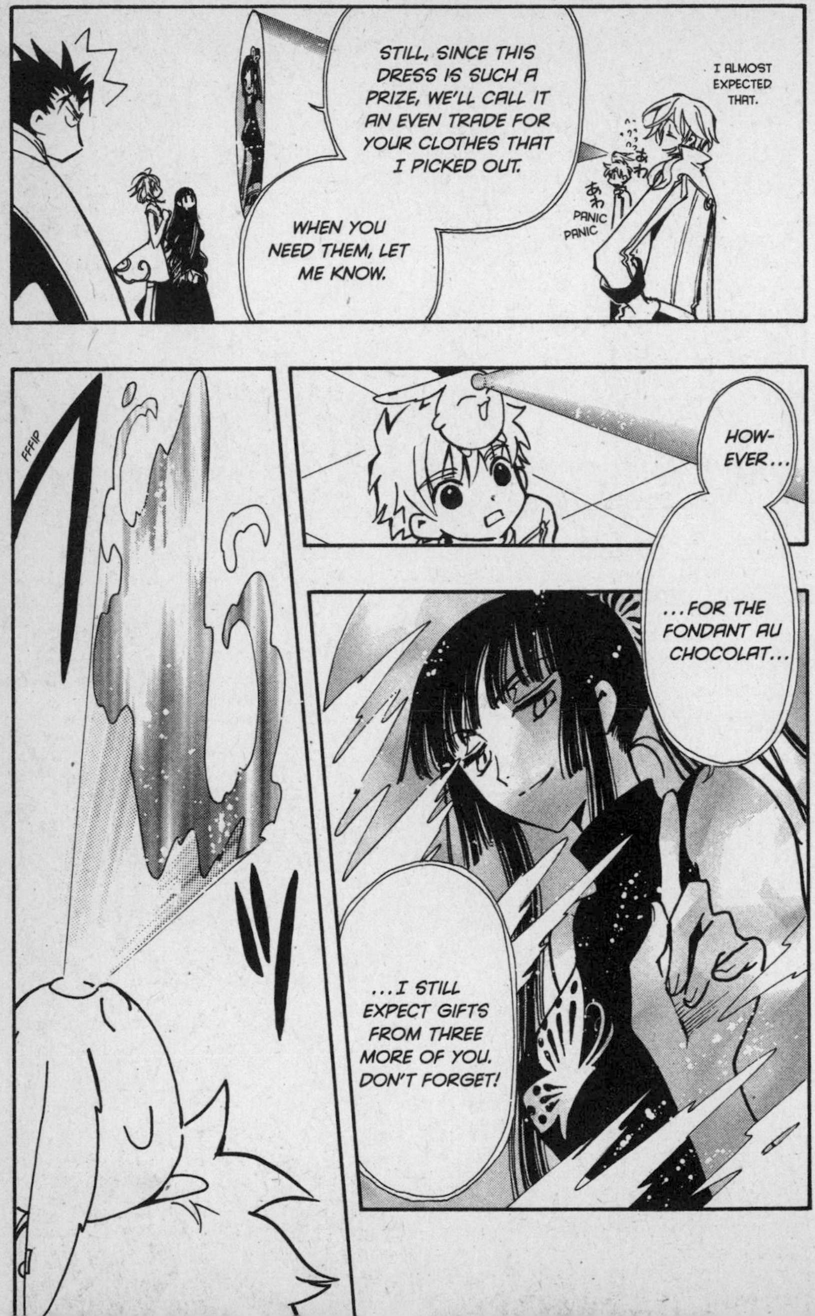
I ALMOST EXPECTED THAT.
あわ あわ
PANIC PANIC
STILL, SINCE THIS DRESS IS SUCH A PRIZE, WE'LL CALL IT AN EVEN TRADE FOR YOUR CLOTHES THAT I PICKED OUT.
WHEN YOU NEED THEM, LET ME KNOW.
HOW-EVER...
...FOR THE FONDANT AU CHOCOLAT...
...I STILL EXPECT GIFTS FROM THREE MORE OF YOU. DON'T FORGET!
FFFIP

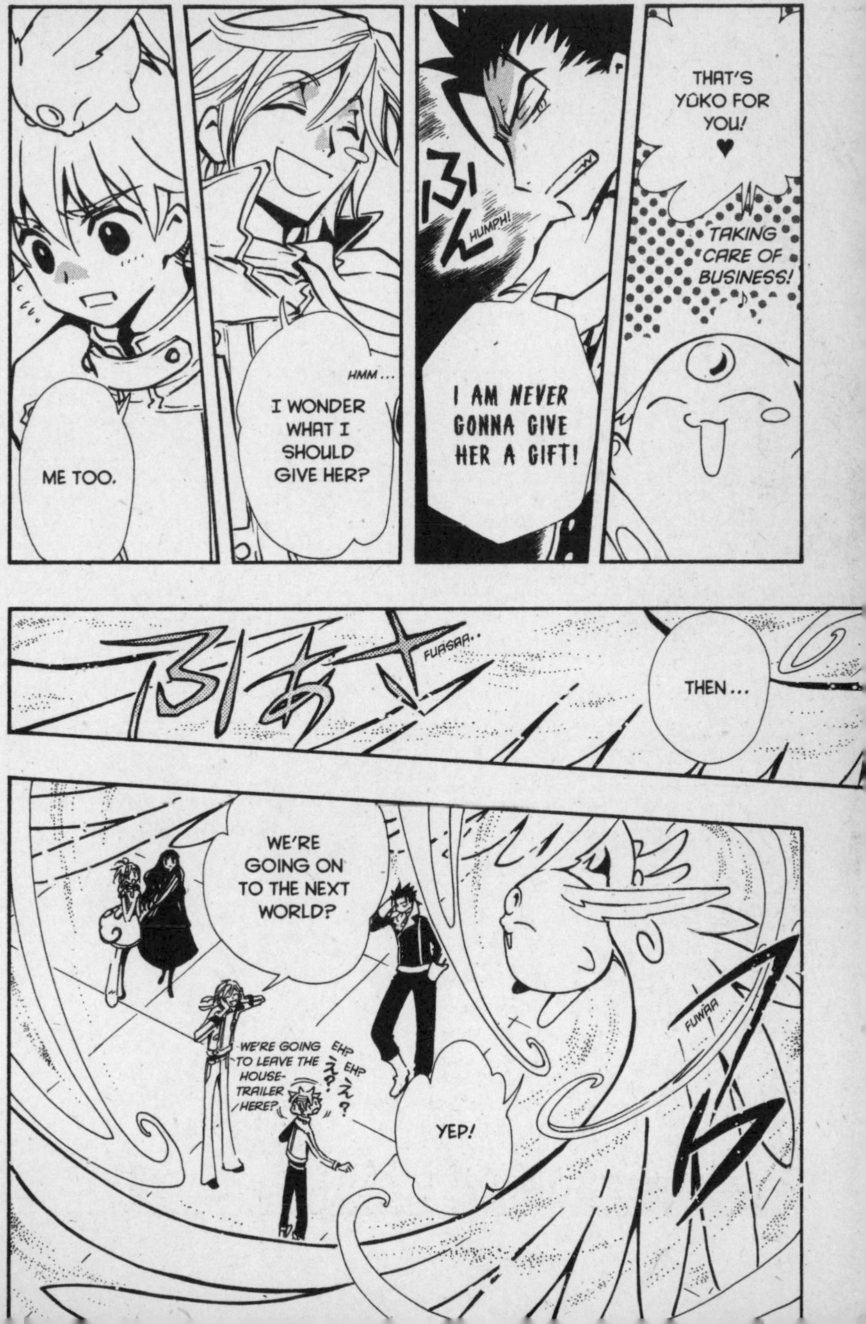
THAT'S YÛKO FOR YOU! ♥
TAKING CARE OF BUSINESS! ♪
ふん
HUMPH!
I AM NEVER GONNA GIVE HER A GIFT!
HMM...
I WONDER WHAT I SHOULD GIVE HER?
ME TOO.
THEN...
ふぁさ
FUASAA..
FUWAA
WE'RE GOING ON TO THE NEXT WORLD?
YEP!
WE'RE GOING TO LEAVE THE HOUSE-TRAILER HERE?
EHP え? EHP え?

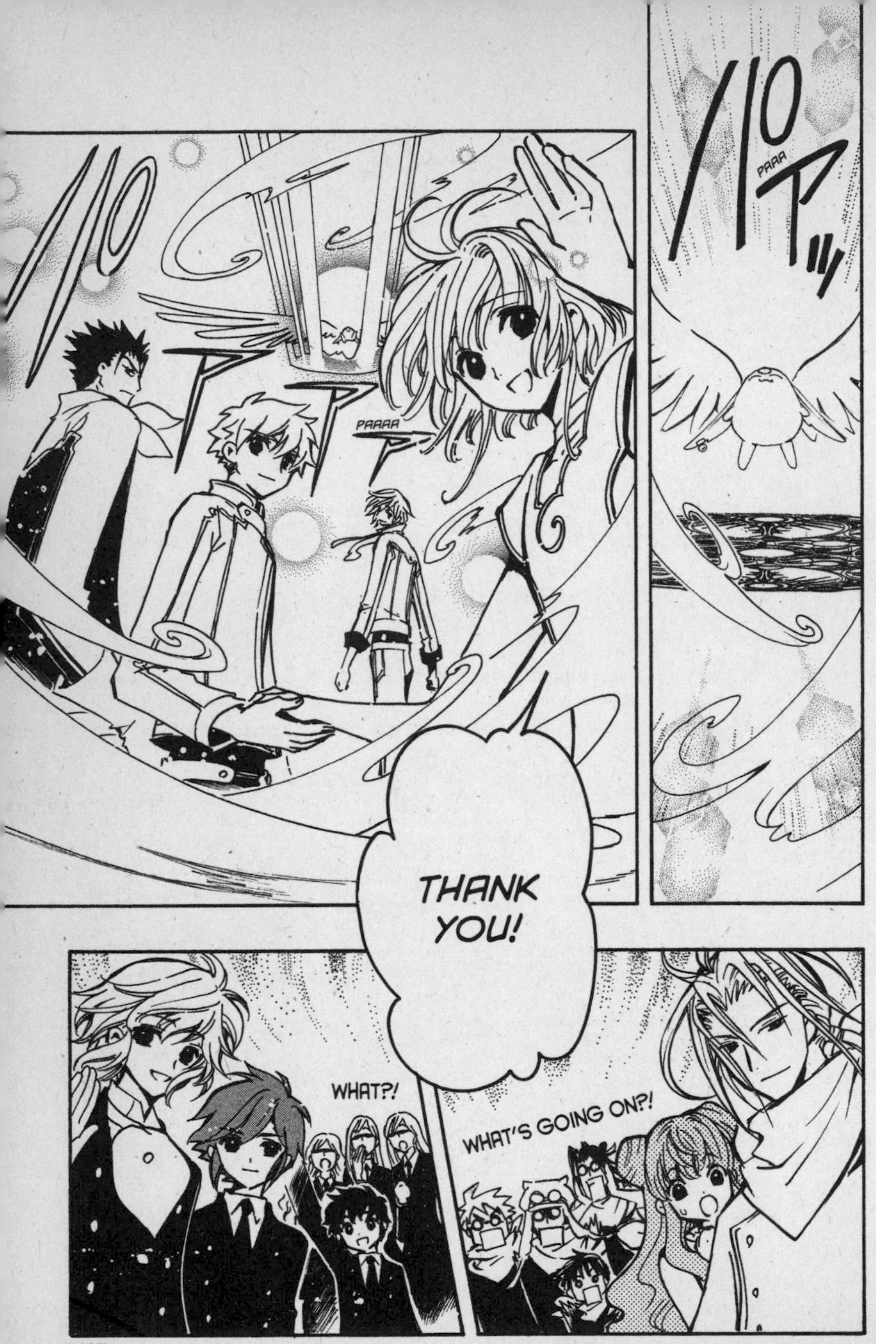
PAAA
PAAAA
THANK YOU!
WHAT'S GOING ON?!
WHAT?!

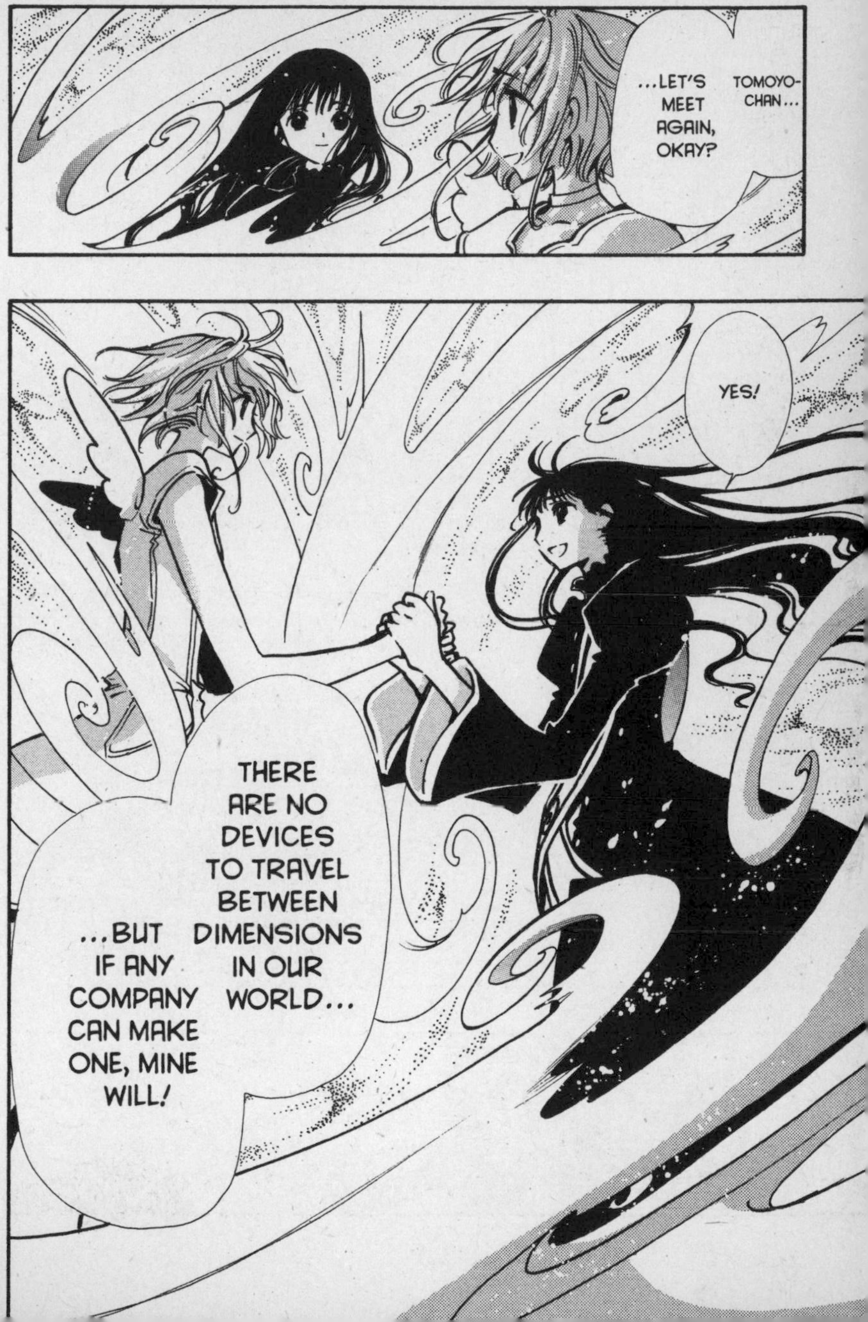

TOMOYO-CHAN...
...LET'S MEET AGAIN, OKAY?
YES!
THERE ARE NO DEVICES TO TRAVEL BETWEEN DIMENSIONS IN OUR WORLD...
...BUT IF ANY COMPANY CAN MAKE ONE, MINE WILL!

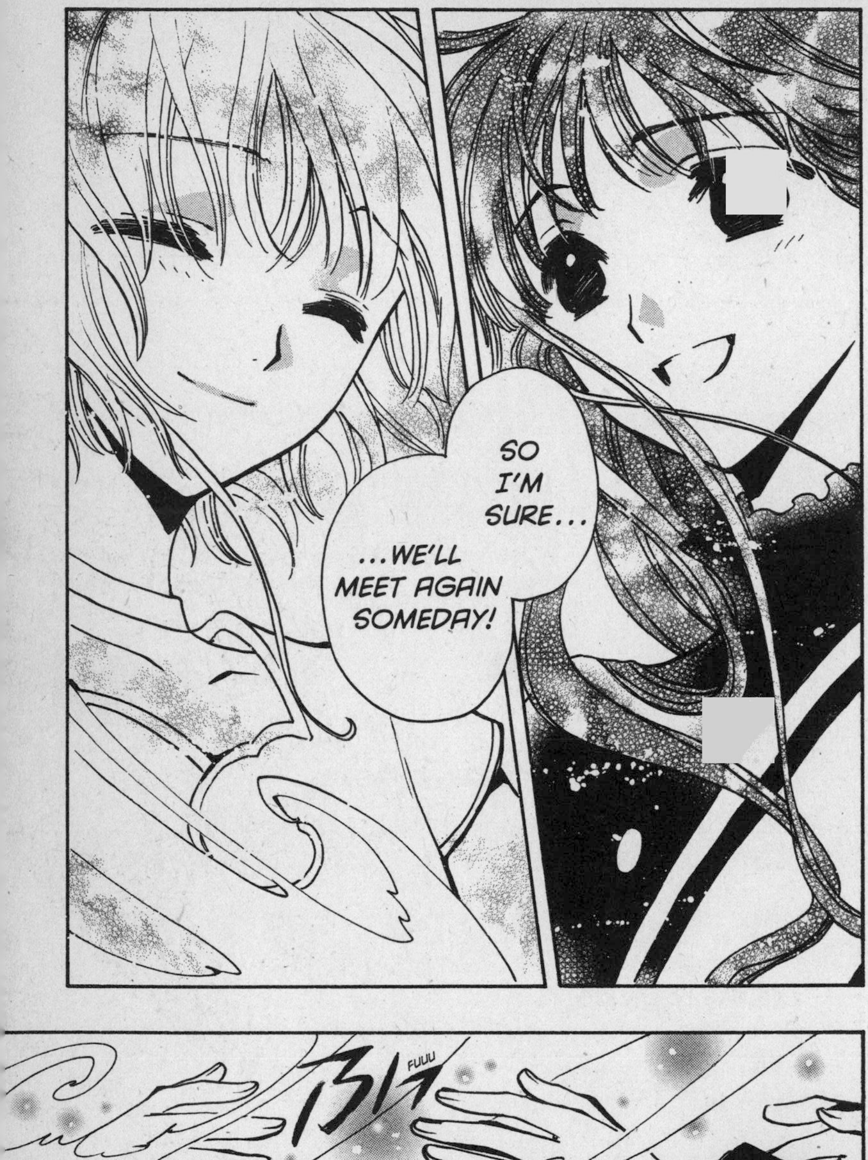
SO I'M SURE...
...WE'LL MEET AGAIN SOMEDAY!
FUUU

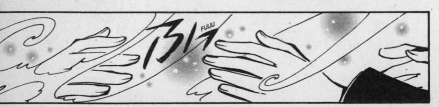

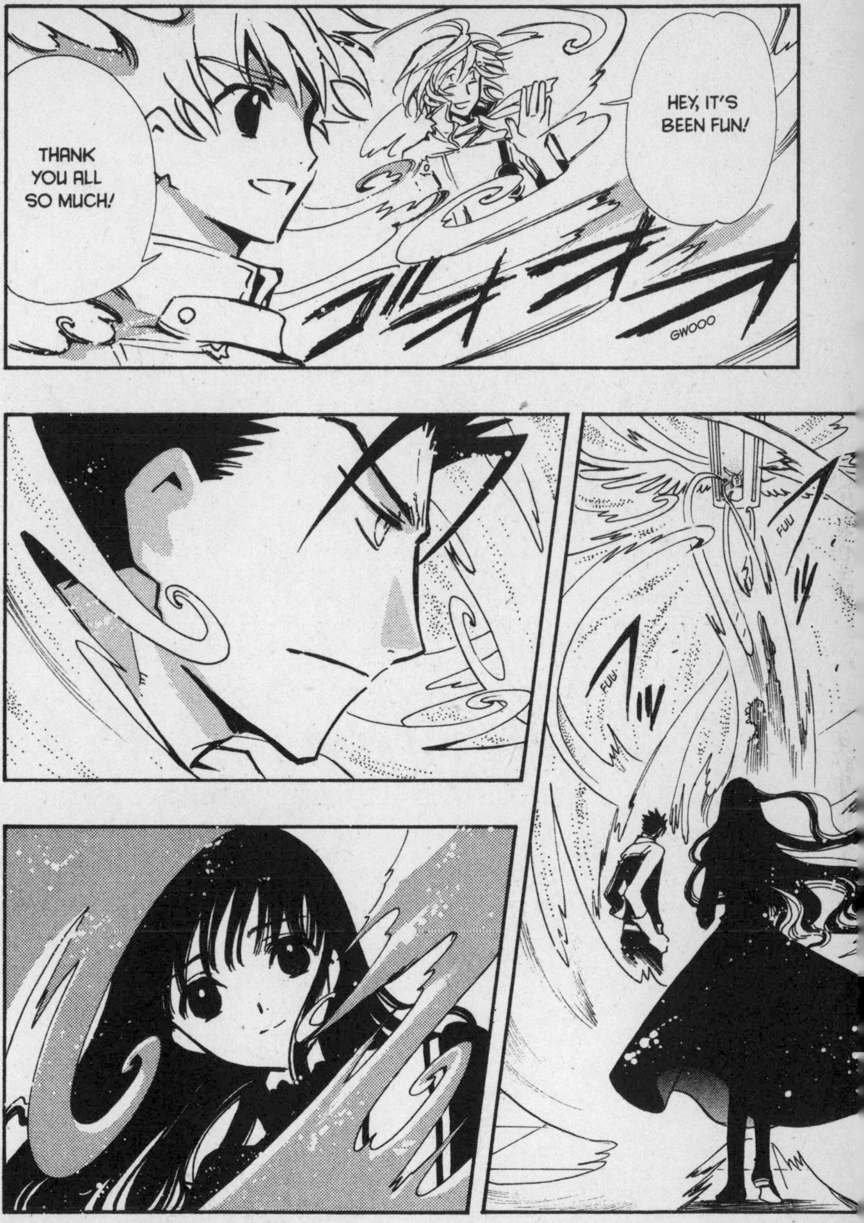
HEY, IT'S BEEN FUN!
THANK YOU ALL SO MUCH!
GWOOO
FUU
FUU

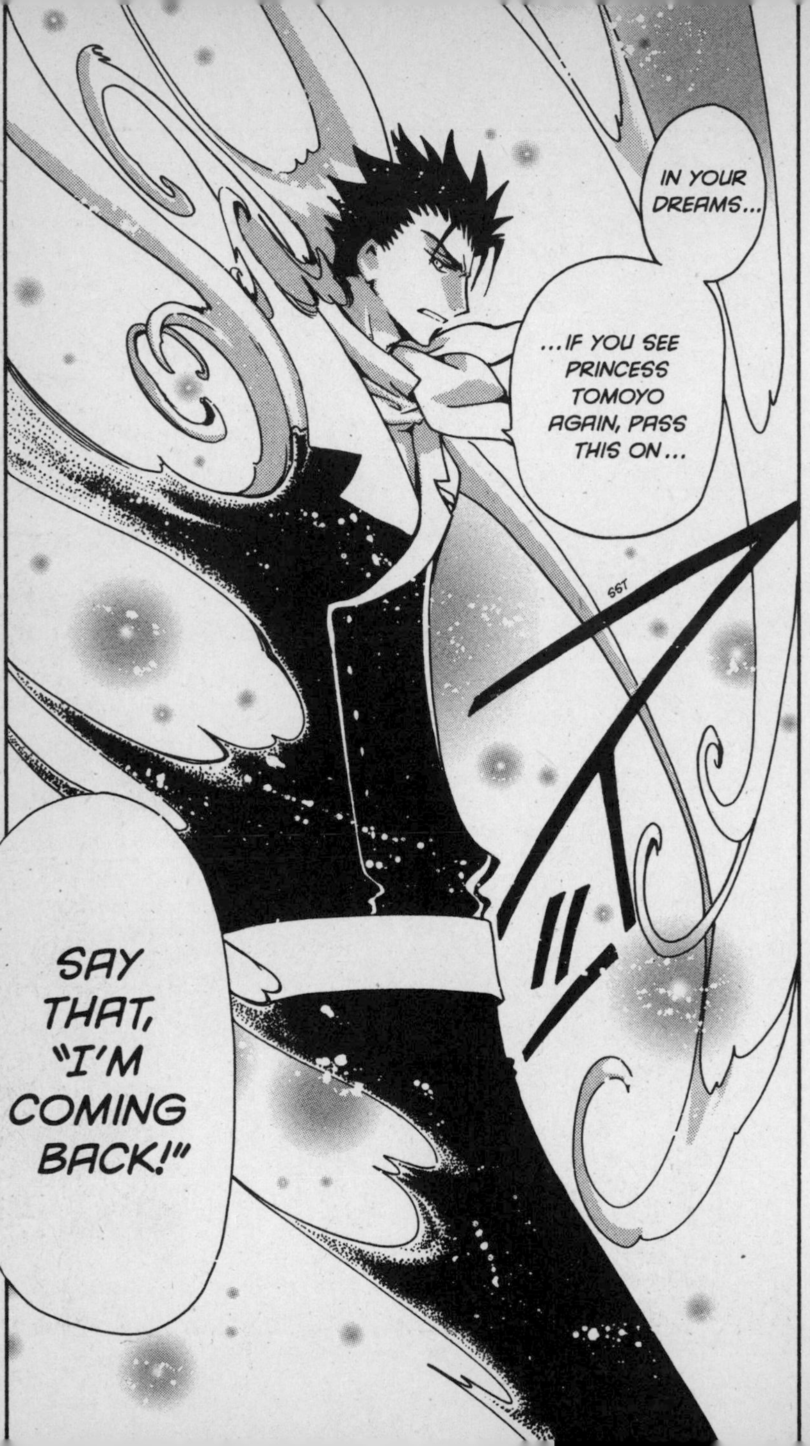
IN YOUR DREAMS...
...IF YOU SEE PRINCESS TOMOYO AGAIN, PASS THIS ON...
SST
SAY THAT, "I'M COMING BACK!"

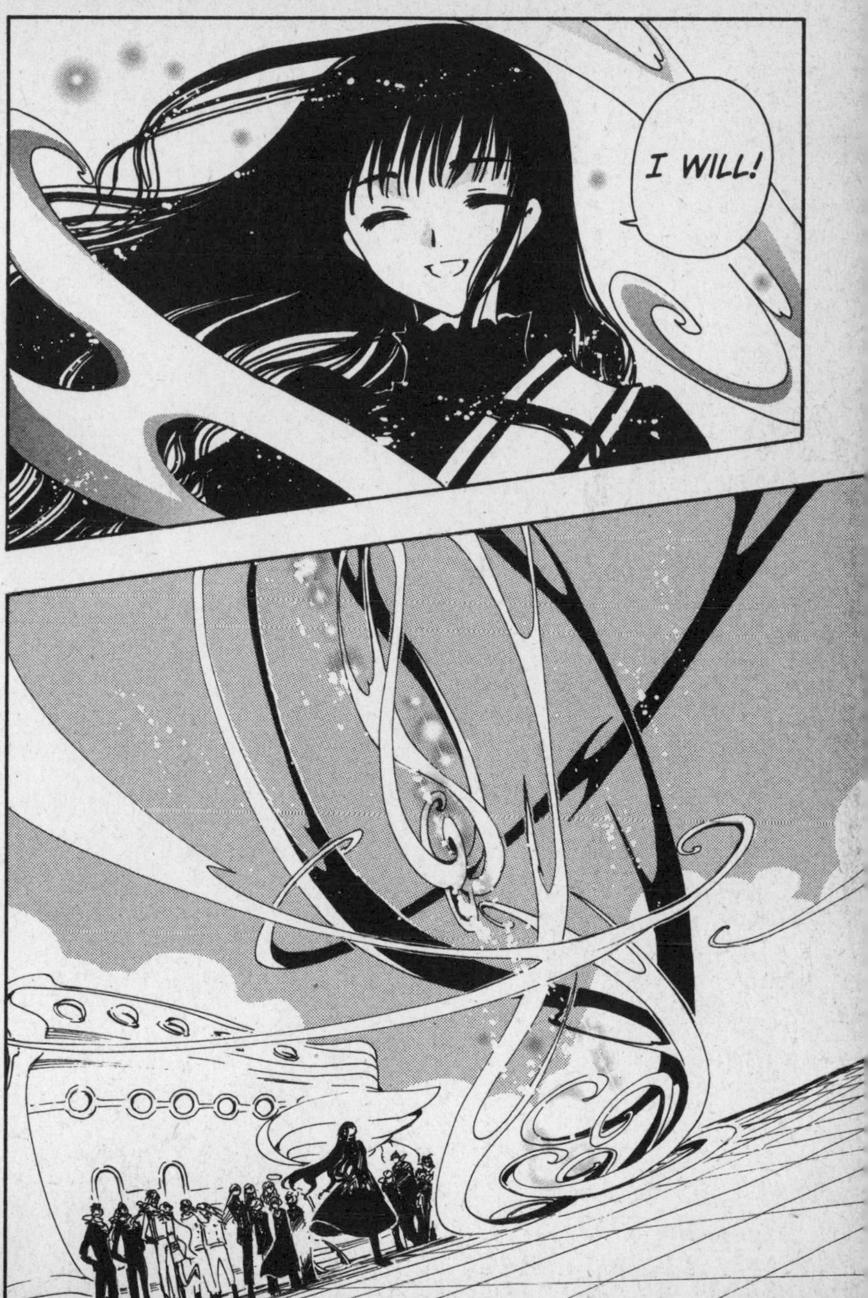
I WILL!

To Be Continued

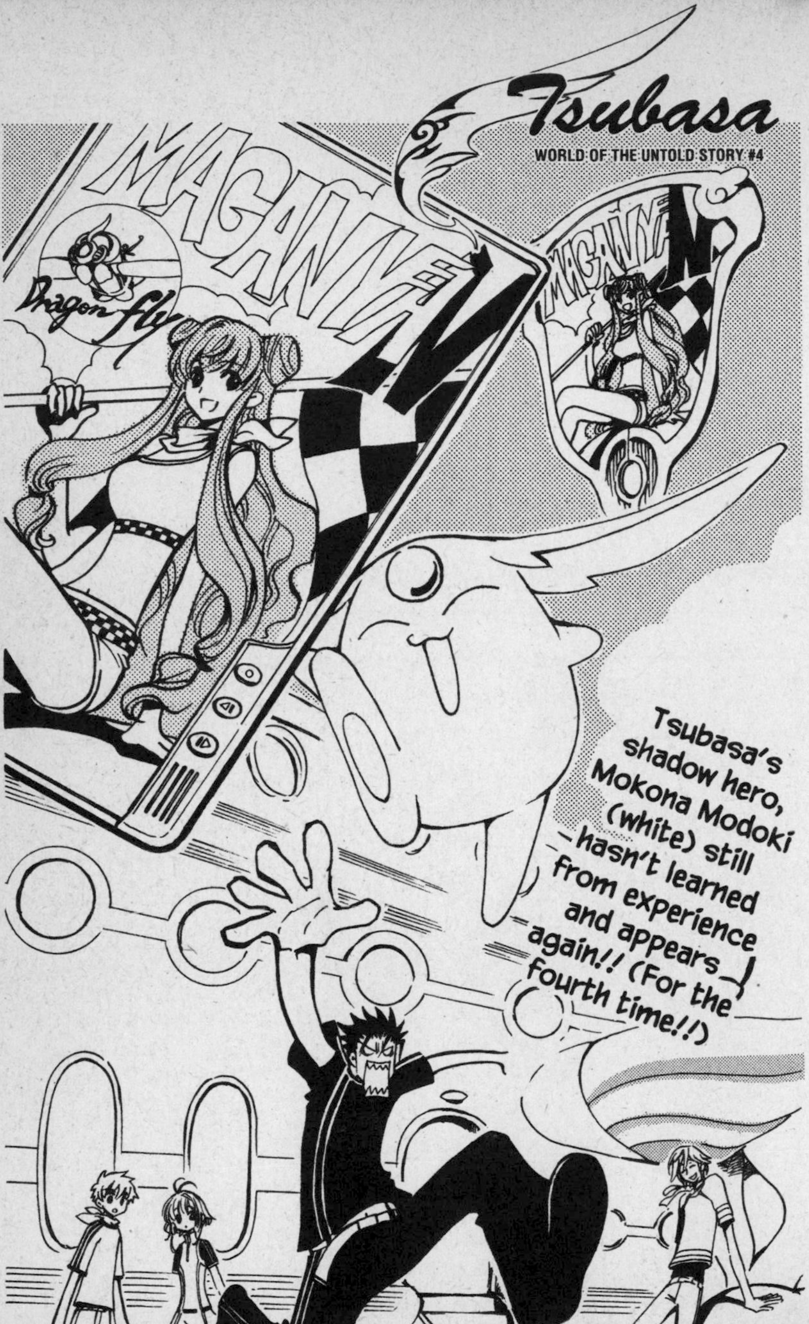
Tsubasa
WORLD OF THE UNTOLD STORY #4
Dragon fly
Tsubasa's shadow hero, Mokona Modoki (white) still hasn't learned from experience and appears again!! (For the fourth time!!)

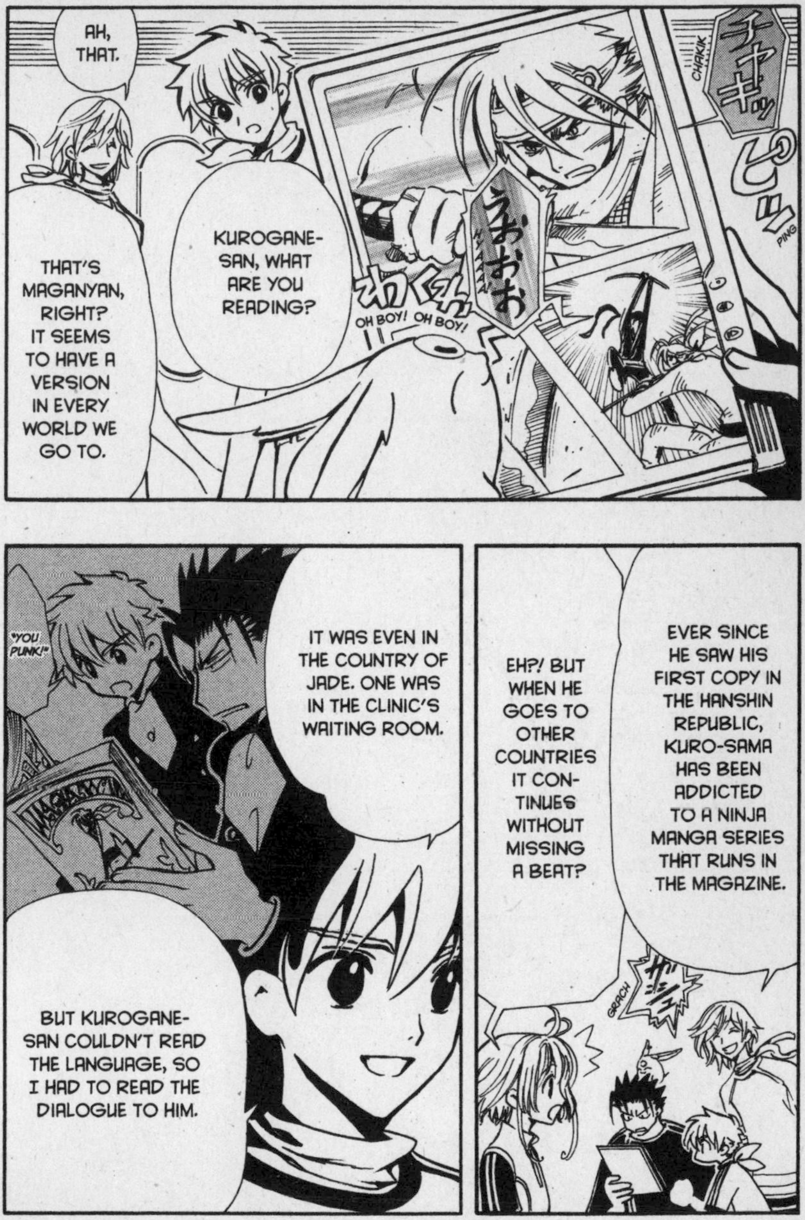
CHAKIK
PING
OH BOY! OH BOY!
KUROGANE-SAN, WHAT ARE YOU READING?
AH, THAT.
THAT'S MAGANYAN, RIGHT? IT SEEMS TO HAVE A VERSION IN EVERY WORLD WE GO TO.
EVER SINCE HE SAW HIS FIRST COPY IN THE HANSHIN REPUBLIC, KURO-SAMA HAS BEEN ADDICTED TO A NINJA MANGA SERIES THAT RUNS IN THE MAGAZINE.
EH?! BUT WHEN HE GOES TO OTHER COUNTRIES IT CON-TINUES WITHOUT MISSING A BEAT?
GRACH
IT WAS EVEN IN THE COUNTRY OF JADE. ONE WAS IN THE CLINIC'S WAITING ROOM.
"YOU PUNK!"
BUT KUROGANE-SAN COULDN'T READ THE LANGUAGE, SO I HAD TO READ THE DIALOGUE TO HIM.

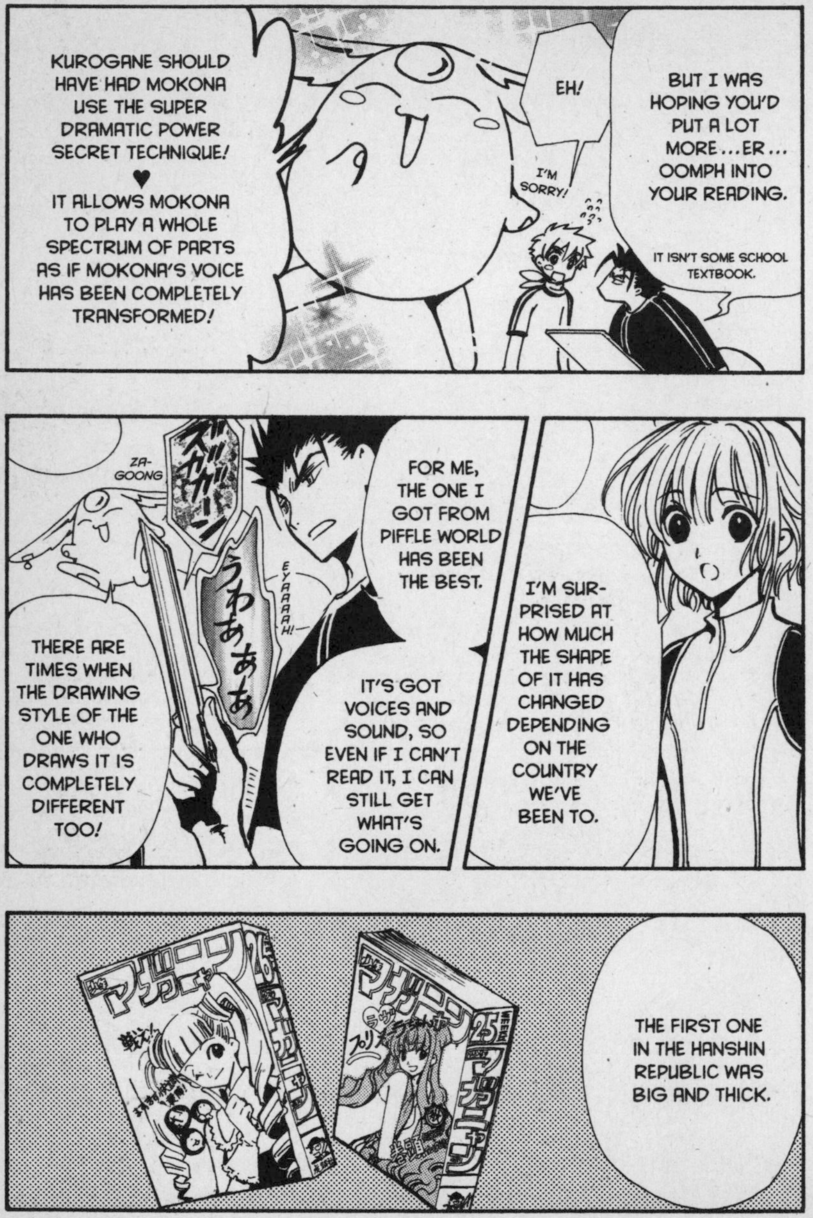
BUT I WAS HOPING YOU'D PUT A LOT MORE...ER... OOMPH INTO YOUR READING.
IT ISN'T SOME SCHOOL TEXTBOOK.
EH!
I'M SORRY!
KUROGANE SHOULD HAVE HAD MOKONA USE THE SUPER DRAMATIC POWER SECRET TECHNIQUE! ♥ IT ALLOWS MOKONA TO PLAY A WHOLE SPECTRUM OF PARTS AS IF MOKONA'S VOICE HAS BEEN COMPLETELY TRANSFORMED!
I'M SURPRISED AT HOW MUCH THE SHAPE OF IT HAS CHANGED DEPENDING ON THE COUNTRY WE'VE BEEN TO.
FOR ME, THE ONE I GOT FROM PIFFLE WORLD HAS BEEN THE BEST.
IT'S GOT VOICES AND SOUND, SO EVEN IF I CAN'T READ IT, I CAN STILL GET WHAT'S GOING ON.
ZA-GOONG
EYAAAAH!
THERE ARE TIMES WHEN THE DRAWING STYLE OF THE ONE WHO DRAWS IT IS COMPLETELY DIFFERENT TOO!
THE FIRST ONE IN THE HANSHIN REPUBLIC WAS BIG AND THICK.

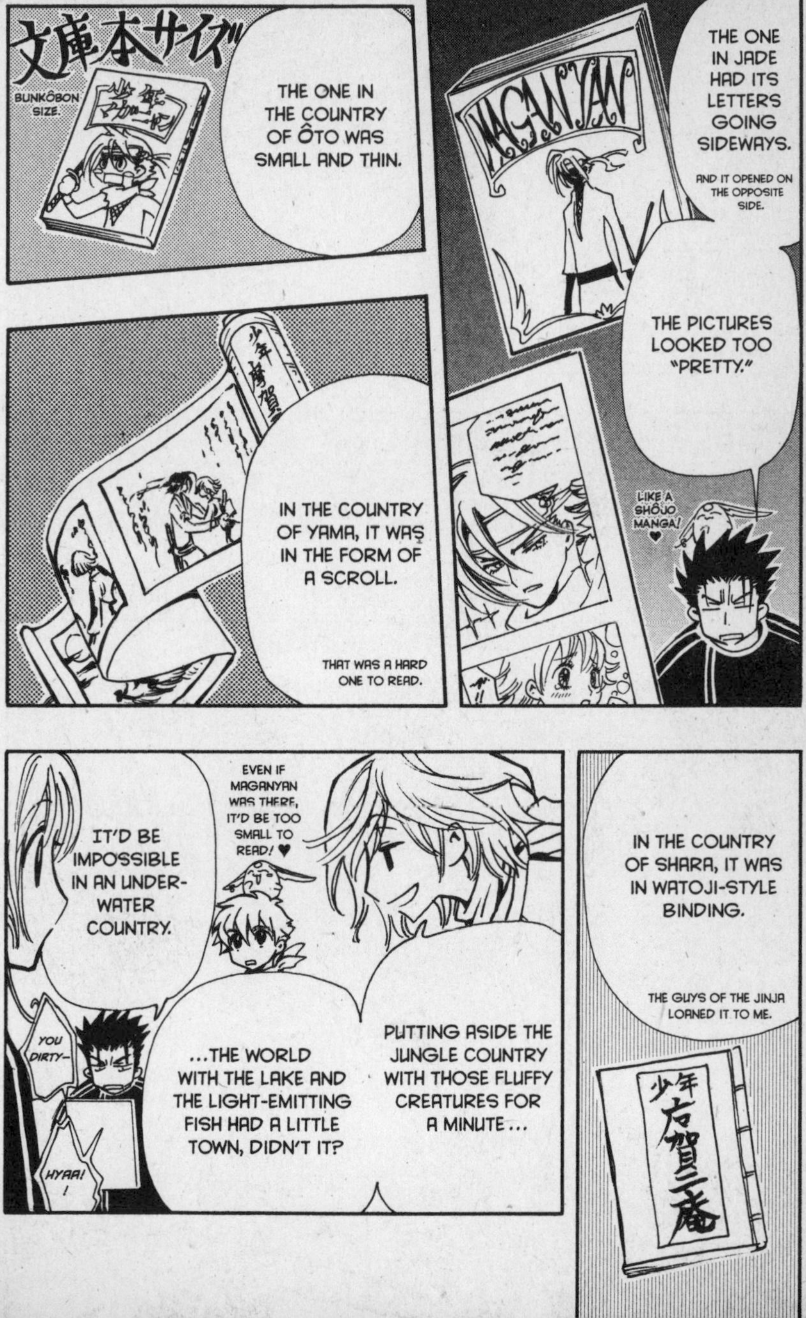

THE ONE IN JADE HAD ITS LETTERS GOING SIDEWAYS.
AND IT OPENED ON THE OPPOSITE SIDE.
MAGANYAN
THE PICTURES LOOKED TOO "PRETTY."
LIKE A SHÔJO MANGA! ♥
文庫本サイズ
BUNKÔBON SIZE.
THE ONE IN THE COUNTRY OF ÔTO WAS SMALL AND THIN.
IN THE COUNTRY OF YAMA, IT WAS IN THE FORM OF A SCROLL.
THAT WAS A HARD ONE TO READ.
IN THE COUNTRY OF SHARA, IT WAS IN WATOJI-STYLE BINDING.
THE GUYS OF THE JINJA LOANED IT TO ME.
PUTTING ASIDE THE JUNGLE COUNTRY WITH THOSE FLUFFY CREATURES FOR A MINUTE...
...THE WORLD WITH THE LAKE AND THE LIGHT-EMITTING FISH HAD A LITTLE TOWN, DIDN'T IT?
EVEN IF MAGANYAN WAS THERE, IT'D BE TOO SMALL TO READ! ♥
IT'D BE IMPOSSIBLE IN AN UNDER-WATER COUNTRY.
YOU DIRTY—
HYAA! !

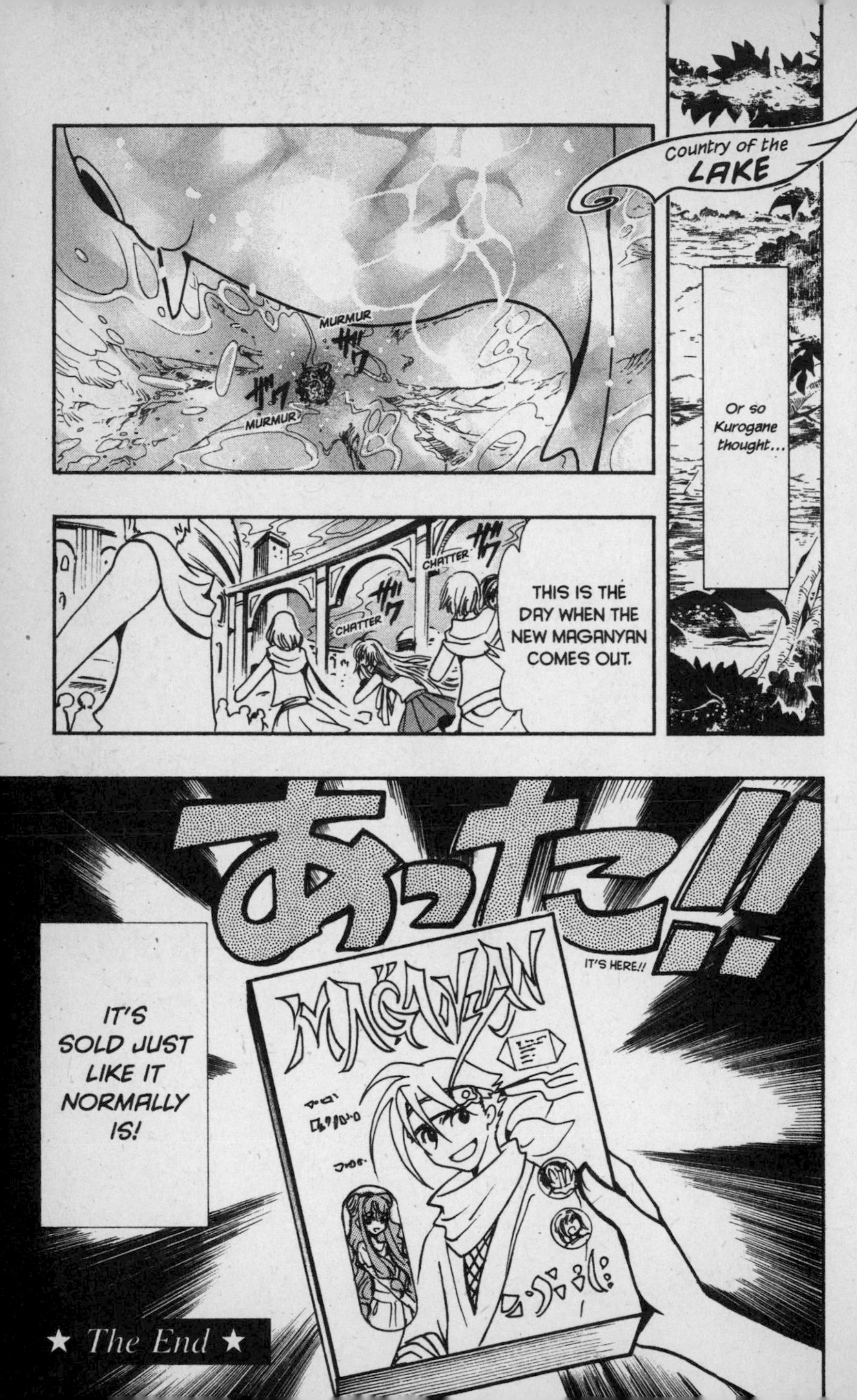

Country of the LAKE
Or so Kurogane thought...
ザワ MURMUR
ザワ MURMUR
ザワ CHATTER
ザワ CHATTER
THIS IS THE DAY WHEN THE NEW MAGANYAN COMES OUT.
あった!!
IT'S HERE!!
MAGANYAN
IT'S SOLD JUST LIKE IT NORMALLY IS!
★ The End ★

About the Creators

CLAMP is a group of four women who have become the most popular manga artists in America—Ageha Ohkawa, Mokona, Satsuki Igarashi, and Tsubaki Nekoi. They started out as *doujinshi* (fan comics) creators, but their skill and craft brought them to the attention of publishers very quickly. Their first work from a major publisher was *RG Veda*, but their first mass success was with *Magic Knight Rayearth*. From there, they went on to write many series, including Cardcaptor Sakura and Chobits, two of the most popular manga in the United States. Like many Japanese manga artists, they prefer to avoid the spotlight, and little is known about them personally.

CLAMP is currently publishing three series in Japan: Tsubasa and xxxHOLiC with Kodansha and Gohou Drug with Kadokawa.

Translation Notes

Japanese is a tricky language for most Westerners, and translation is often more art than science. For your edification and reading pleasure, here are notes on some of the places where we could have gone in a different direction in our translation of the work, or where a Japanese cultural reference is used.

Piffle World

If you're a CLAMP fan, then you've probably seen Piffle Princess products scattered throughout the various recent books by CLAMP. The most recent being the White Day gift that Kimihiro Watanuki gives to the Zashiki-Warashi in volume 5 of xxxHOLiC, but the heart and soul of Piffle Princess can be found in the CLAMP tournament manga, *Angelic Layer*. Piffle World looks like it's the ultimate evolution of the Piffle Princess store and line of products.

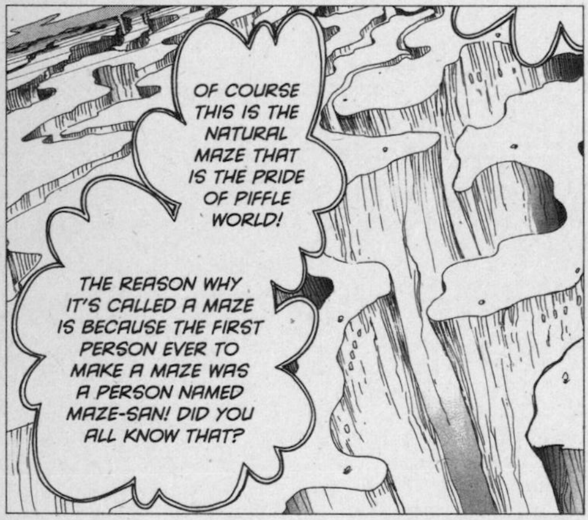
OF COURSE THIS IS THE NATURAL MAZE THAT IS THE PRIDE OF PIFFLE WORLD!
THE REASON WHY IT'S CALLED A MAZE IS BECAUSE THE FIRST PERSON EVER TO MAKE A MAZE WAS A PERSON NAMED MAZE-SAN! DID YOU ALL KNOW THAT?

Maze-san, page 5

Of course, the Japanese version used the word *meiro*, which are made up of the *kanji* pronounced *mei*, which means lost, and *ro*, which means road. Probably in Piffle World, the word that means "maze" was the name of the person who first made one, and Mokona translated it to "Meiro-san" in Japanese and "Maze-san" in English. Or the announcer might just be making up stories.

Renhi-go, page 26

The *kanji* for Renhi are the same *kanji* that are used for Ryonfi in the Country of Koryo. But *renhi* is the way the Japanese would pronounce those *kanji*. It's a fitting name for Chu'nyan's otherworldly double to give to her dragonfly.

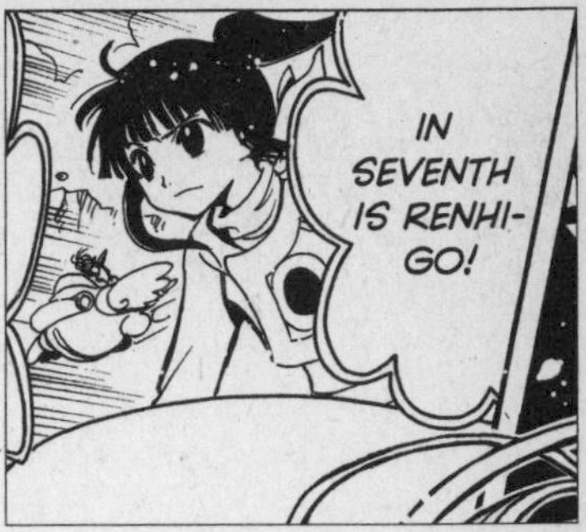
IN SEVENTH IS RENHI-GO!

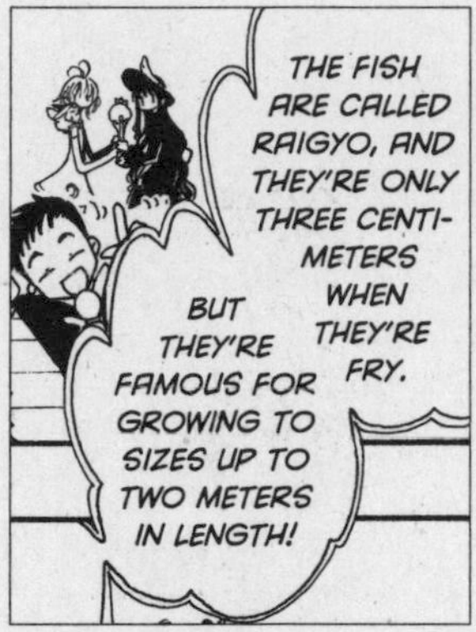
THE FISH ARE CALLED RAIGYO, AND THEY'RE ONLY THREE CENTI-METERS WHEN THEY'RE FRY.
BUT THEY'RE FAMOUS FOR GROWING TO SIZES UP TO TWO METERS IN LENGTH!

Raigyo, page 90

The name of the "electric eel" of Piffle World (which may or may not have been the inspiration for batteries) is taken from *rai* which means thunder or thunderbolt, and *gyo* which means fish.

"Pain" running joke, page 91

Kurogane keeps saying that things are a "pain." What he is saying in Japanese is *mendô-kusai*, a phrase meaning that it is too much trouble. In the Japanese as well, he said that the wound was only a little trouble. Unusually, the pun worked better in English with the wound causing only a little pain.

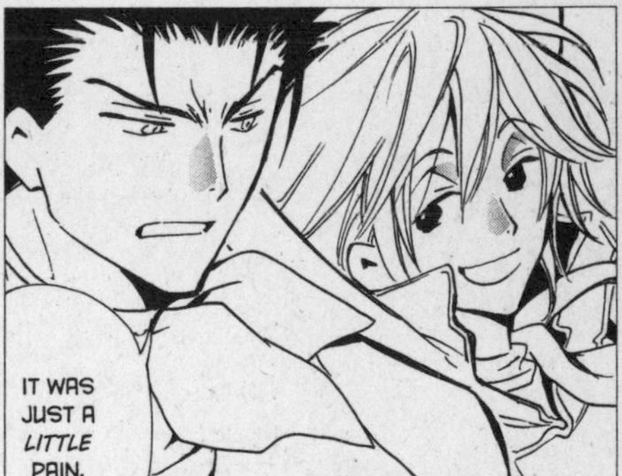
IT WAS JUST A LITTLE PAIN.

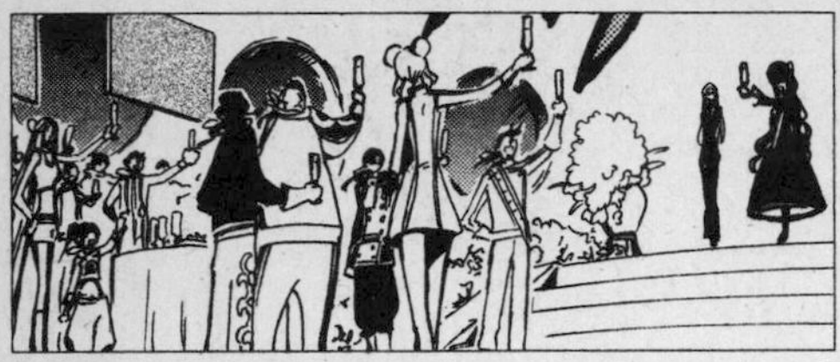

Kampai!, page 97

Every culture has its way of making a toast with a drink, and the standard word in Japanese is *kampai!* (alternatively spelled, *kanpai*) and pronounced "kahm-pie." *Kampai* is used in every situation that English speakers would use "Cheers," and means simply "empty glass."

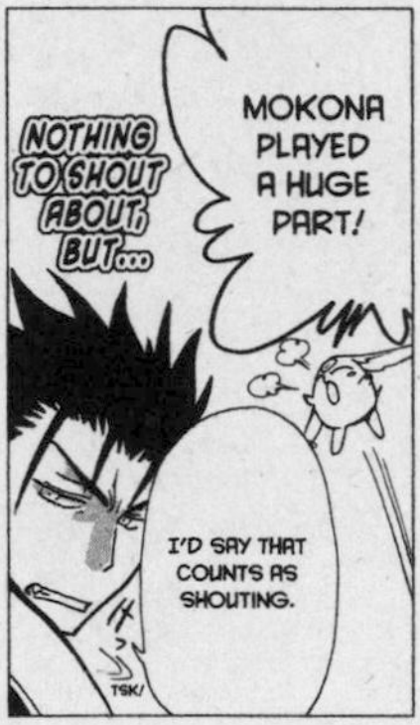
MOKONA PLAYED A HUGE PART!
NOTHING TO SHOUT ABOUT, BUT...
I'D SAY THAT COUNTS AS SHOUTING.
TSK!

Nothing to shout about, page 98

Here is one of those unusual phrases that translates perfectly to an English phrase. The Japanese means "I can't say it in a loud voice, but . . . ," which can convert over to the "nothing to shout about" phrase very well since they both indicate the same type of humility (false humility in Mokona's case).

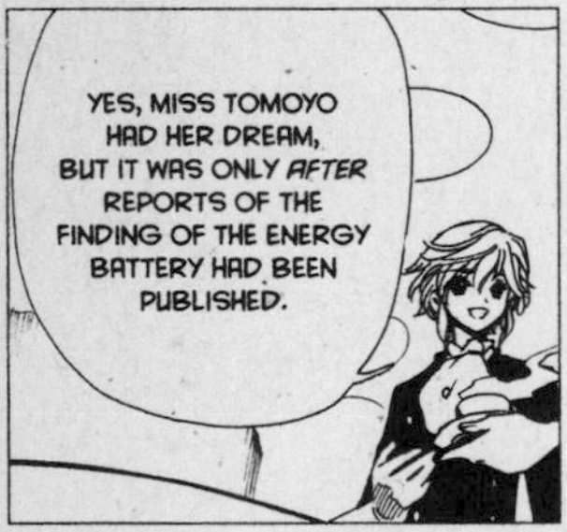
YES, MISS TOMOYO HAD HER DREAM, BUT IT WAS ONLY *AFTER* REPORTS OF THE FINDING OF THE ENERGY BATTERY HAD BEEN PUBLISHED.

Miss Tomoyo, page 132

Nokoru uses a slightly different method of referring to Tomoyo than he does for everyone else. He uses the *kanji* for *jô*, more commonly used in the phrase *ojôsan*, which is what one may call a young woman of high breeding. It isn't a commonly used honorific, and for Nokoru, who has breeding of his own, using the Jane Austen–like "Miss Tomoyo" is perfectly appropriate to his too-polite character.

Taking care of business, page 166

No, this isn't the 70s hit by Bachman-Turner Overdrive in the Japanese original, but it is a pretty direct translation of what Mokona says (Mokona's words were complete with musical note).

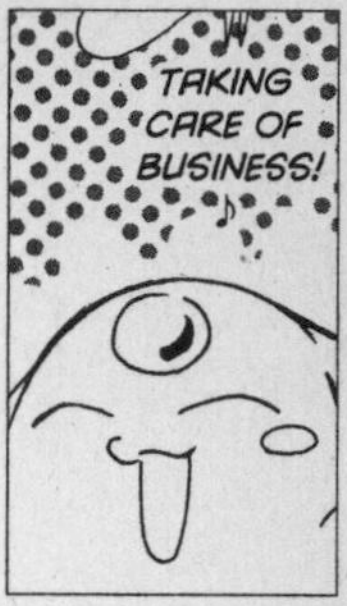
TAKING CARE OF BUSINESS! ♪

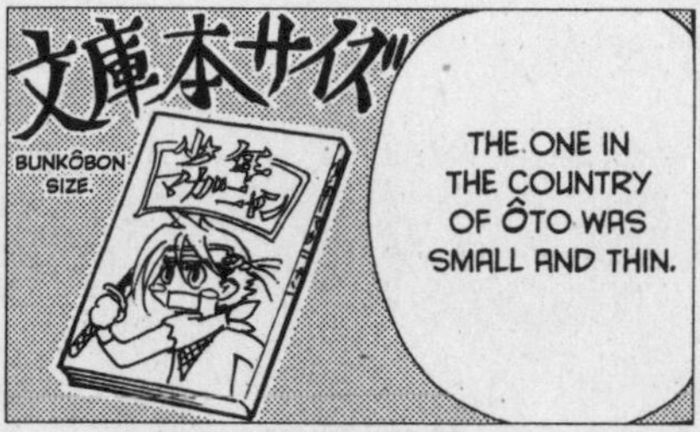
文庫本サイズ
BUNKÔBON SIZE.
THE ONE IN THE COUNTRY OF ÔTO WAS SMALL AND THIN.

***Bunkôbon* Size, page 178**

Bunkôbon are even smaller than the *tankôbon* size that Japanese manga usually come in. They are approximately 4 inches by 6 inches, which is a perfect small size for carrying and reading while one is commuting or waiting for an appointment. This is the normal size for most Japanese paperbacks, but it is also the final size for classic manga after they have gone through the original *tankôbon* size and the collector's-size *wide-ban* editions.

***Watoji*, page 178**

Watoji is the traditional Japanese style of book binding. It usually consists of two heavy covers (made of many different types of materials including wood and leather) and the pages all bound together with string. In Japan, book binding is considered an art in itself.

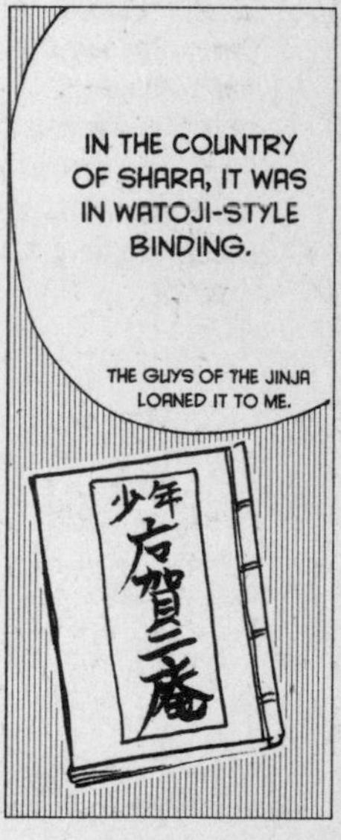
IN THE COUNTRY OF SHARA, IT WAS IN WATOJI-STYLE BINDING.
THE GUYS OF THE JINJA LOANED IT TO ME.

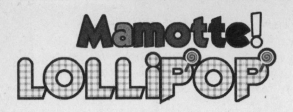

Mamotte! Lollipop

MICHIYO KIKUTA

BOY CRAZY

Junior high schooler Nina is ready to fall in love. She's looking for a boy who's cute and sweet—and strong enough to support her when the chips are down. But what happens when Nina's dream comes true . . . twice? One day, two cute boys literally fall from the sky. They're both wizards who've come to the Human World to take the Magic Exam. The boys' success on this test depends on protecting Nina from evil, so now Nina has a pair of cute magical boys chasing her everywhere! One of these wizards just might be the boy of her dreams . . . but which one?

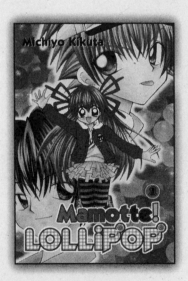

Special extras in each volume! Read them all!

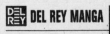

TOMARE!

[STOP!]

You're going the wrong way!

Manga is a completely different type of reading experience.

To start at the *beginning*, go to the *end*!

That's right! Authentic manga is read the traditional Japanese way—from right to left. Exactly the *opposite* of how American books are read. It's easy to follow: Just go to the other end of the book, and read each page—and each panel—from right side to left side, starting at the top right. Now you're experiencing manga as it was meant to be.